PLAIN & PRECIOUS

 AN

LDS DAYBOOK OF
RENEWAL AND JOY

BEPPIE HARRISON

DESERET BOOK COMPANY
SALT LAKE CITY, UTAH

Library of Congress Cataloging-in-Publication Data
Harrison, Beppie.
Plain and precious : an LDS daybook of renewal and joy / by Beppie Harrison.
p. cm.
Includes indexes.
ISBN 1-57345-317-X (hardbound)
1. Spiritual life—Mormon Church. 2. Mormon Church—Prayer-books and devotions—English. 3. Church of Jesus Christ of Latter-day Saints—Prayer-books and devotions—English. I. Title.
BX8656.H367 1997
248.4'893—dc21
97-29252
CIP

Printed in the United States of America

10 9 8 7 6 5 4 3 2 1

FOR MY SISTERS IN SPIRIT

For whatsoever things were written aforetime were written for our learning, that we through patience and comfort of the scriptures might have hope.

—ROMANS 15:4

CONTENTS

PREFACE

Search the scriptures; for in them ye think ye have eternal life: and they are they which testify of me.

—JOHN 5:39

I can't remember exactly where I encountered this verse when I suddenly paid attention; it certainly wasn't the first time it had ever been quoted at me. It must have been in a talk in sacrament meeting, or perhaps a Relief Society lesson. In any case, I was feeling a bit more unworthy than usual (there are those talks and lessons that make you feel that way), and for some reason this verse spoke to my heart as a challenge. Okay, I said to myself. Instead of feeling unworthy—and sulky—I'll do something about it. For one whole year, I promised myself, I would obey that verse. I would search the scriptures, day by day, week by week, month by month, and see what would happen. Instead of working my way stolidly and methodically through one book, I would pick a gospel principle to concentrate on each month and explore scriptures that fit in with that theme, wherever I found them. Then—and this was the important part—I would think about what exactly that scripture meant in my life.

Which is how this book you hold in your hands came to be.

As usual, when I actually set out to do what we have been commanded to do, I was astonished at how rewarding and fascinating it turned out to be. (Isn't it strange how some people seem to take a lot of convincing?) I discovered for myself the wisdom and beauty that was there all along. Sometimes I felt as if I were listening to one wise man talk. Sometimes it was like being surrounded by a congregation of voices, every one speaking with an individual point of view but all of them melding together into a magnificent affirmation of the divinity of our Heavenly Father and his Son, Jesus Christ.

The Topical Guide became my companion, leading me by the hand through the richness available to me. I would find myself being distracted sometimes, looking up Obedience and being sidetracked by Oblation. (What is an oblation anyhow, and why do we read about it in both Leviticus and the Doctrine and Covenants?) I started reading the Bible Dictionary. With its help, for the first time I got straight the historical sequence of the Old Testament.

To work out context, I read forward and backward from the scripture passages I started out with. I learned to remember that the original writers weren't thinking in chapters and verses, and sometimes those divisions were put in later in logical places that don't interrupt the thought, and sometimes they weren't. Most often, the context helped, but there were times when a single verse shone like a jewel on its own. I fell head over heels in love with Isaiah, with John the Beloved, with Peter, with Paul, with King Benjamin, with Moroni. Sometimes it was the clarity of their thought that charmed me; sometimes, the beauty of their words.

By the end of the year, I was enriched and humbled. I am certainly still unworthy, but I don't feel sulky about it now. Where I am is only the place from which I start, today and tomorrow and for all the tomorrows to come. My quadruple combination has become a wonder to me. I hold it in my hands, and I feel the strength of the men who sacrificed so much to write, and translate, and print this book. If I close my eyes, I can imagine all those men writing down their visions, and their wisdom, and their love for those who would read—and through it all I hear the voice of their God and my God, speaking to us all, down the ages.

And so now I give my book to you. Let it be your starting place. Find these verses in your own scriptures; see what comes before them, and what comes after. Explore the Bible Dictionary and the Topical Guide. Find verses that speak to your heart. Sometimes, I expect, they may be different from the ones that spoke to me. That's okay. There are enough for all of us. As sisters in spirit, we can reach out to each other and to our Lord.

Let the wonderful words of the One-Hundredth Psalm echo around us as we begin:

> Make a joyful noise unto the Lord, all ye lands.
> Serve the Lord with gladness: come before his presence with singing.
> Know ye that the Lord he is God: it is he that hath made us, and not we ourselves; we are his people, and the sheep of his pasture.
> Enter into his gates with thanksgiving, and into his courts with praise: be thankful unto him, and bless his name.
> For the Lord is good; his mercy is everlasting; and his truth endureth to all generations.

JANUARY

Thus saith the Lord, Set thine house in order.

—ISAIAH 38:1

JANUARY 1

When I consider thy heavens, the work of thy fingers, the moon and the stars, which thou hast ordained; what is man, that thou art mindful of him? and the son of man, that thou visitest him? For thou hast made him a little lower than the angels, and hast crowned him with glory and honour.

—PSALM 8:3–5

How perfect it is that this New Year's night the sky is clear and sharp, with the moon and the stars stirring the same wonder in me as David expressed when he wrote the psalm. Staring up at the sky at night (even when I have to be bundled up in a coat and scarf and my face still is cold) makes the reaches of eternity seem absolutely plausible. How far away are those stars, and how long do the astronomers say it has taken this twinkling light to reach me? How far away is heaven? Where do I fit into eternity?

It makes me remember a talk I heard once, with a never-to-be-forgotten quotation about how in the vastness of eternity, our life on this earth is like a single afternoon. "And surely," the speaker went on to say, "you can behave yourself for one afternoon."

Can I? I'm prepared to try. I'm not really sure I'm up to New Year's resolutions this year; they have such a depressing way of coming unglued sometime before February. But can I work at it a little harder during this year, this undefined segment of my earthly afternoon? Standing alone here in the backyard for a few minutes—the family sprawling around inside the house (nobody having noticed yet I'm out here), football droning away on TV—I have the lunatic impulse to reach out, pick one of those tiny sparkles of light, and tuck it in my coat pocket to keep as a reminder of my sense of wonder and promise brimming over the edge of the year ahead of me. Last night was the official celebration of a new year, but tonight, here on the back path, will be my private celebration. I have 364 days ahead of me to explore the possibilities and promise of this year of mortality.

I resolve—there I go again!—to make something of this gift, this year. I resolve to remember that the Lord *was* mindful of us mortals, *did* visit my brothers and sisters of another time and another place. I resolve to make that recognition, with all the awe and praise it inspires, the foundation of my year.

I can muse about eternity, but it's cold here and now. I'd better go in and find the extra bag of potato chips I said I was going out to the kitchen to get when I was distracted by the still night outside. The glittering starry sky hangs there above to inspire me, but mortality (potato chips and all) is where I live and where I have to start. I can remember the stars while I carry food in from the kitchen and gather up dirty dishes, blessed and encumbered by my family, who are still draped languidly around the untidy living room. I can yearn for holiness alone on the back path, but I have to find it in the middle of the most ordinary aspects of life.

Let the new year begin!

JANUARY 2

He that is slow to anger is better than the mighty; and he that ruleth his spirit than he that taketh a city.

—PROVERBS 16:32

Why is everybody always grumpy as the holidays wind down? Maybe it's the return to ordinary life, after all the excitement and anticipation is spent, and the surprises are all known. It's always more fun to put the Christmas tree up than it is to take it down again; when the children were little I could persuade them to help me happily by promising they could eat the candy canes that decorated the tree. Candy canes are still part of the decoration, but the children are less charmed by them than they were then, and the sweet peppermint taste now seems to them a wholly inadequate reward for spending a perfectly good couple of hours of their dwindling Christmas vacation time taking down ornaments, wrapping them and packing them carefully away in the box (because Mom yells at you if you just dump them in, that's why), and then getting stuck dragging the tree out of the house and carrying all those boxes with the decorations down to the basement. I do know how they feel; I'm not exactly crazy about the whole process, either. (Nevertheless, honesty compels me to admit I will definitely feel more satisfaction than they do in seeing the house returned to its accustomed order, with silk flowers and house plants taking over the spots where poinsettias and Santa music boxes have flourished.) Still, why do they have to be so crabby, and why is my automatic reaction to their lack of enthusiasm the edge even I can hear in my voice?

Maybe the hardest part about ruling one's spirit and being slow to anger isn't about coping with the big things. Maybe it has a lot more to do with letting the little things go. So the kids aren't bubbling with joy and delight. Well, it's probably unrealistic to expect that every household assignment is going to be accompanied by merry family togetherness. They are doing what they've been asked, aren't they? Maybe I can save my indignation for more important problems, and there's even the possibility that if I'm not grumpy, their mood will improve, too.

Or maybe not. But the tree will be down, and my semi-surly work crew can be released to freedom and whatever it was they wanted to do: video games, or telephone conversations, or curling up with a Christmas book with the delicious knowledge that the holidays might be almost over and school might be starting soon—but not yet. If I try, I can remember feeling like that, too.

Dear Heavenly Father, help me remember. Help me to keep a mountain and a molehill in proportion; above all, help me to be slow to anger about either one.

JANUARY 3

Set in order your houses; keep slothfulness and uncleanness far from you.

—DOCTRINE AND COVENANTS 90:18

Not a bad thought with which to begin the dailiness of the new year, although I must admit that slothfulness and uncleanness sound uncompromisingly unattractive, and I wouldn't like to think either of them has anything to do with me. I would prefer the more tactful "procrastination" and "untidiness" to describe what goes on at our house.

Some women may take positive pleasure in rolling up their sleeves and having a good, soul-satisfying clean, but I am not among them. I clean because houses are supposed to be clean and because it's easier to find things when the house is tidy. Is it embarrassing to admit that I have learned that from personal experience or that I am still trying to get that concept across to my children?

The beginning of the year gives me the feeling of a fresh start; I have several beginnings to my year in addition to this frozen January. Spring is coming (a blessing for those of us who endure northern winters that those who live in year-round temperate climates may not appreciate sufficiently), and then the beginning of the school year in late August or early September, when the sultry heat of summer is overtaken by the sharpness of autumn, the kids go back to school, and the feel of new starts is everywhere. I seem to need each of the beginnings to refresh my good intentions and put new enthusiasm into the daily jobs of straightening up and cleaning properly.

How nice to know these ordinary, routine jobs are fulfilling a commandment! Let me remember that today, as I scour out the corners and get the kitchen curtains washed. And please, Lord, just for once, today let none of the children come home, impressed by the order and tidiness, to ask expectantly if company is coming.

JANUARY 4

Behold, mine house is a house of order, saith the Lord God, and not a house of confusion.

—DOCTRINE AND COVENANTS 132:8

Order takes many forms, of course. Apart from the housewifely order, there is order in the relationships between people, and that may be part of what the Lord was addressing in the revelation about the new and everlasting covenant of marriage, which he gave more than 150 years ago. The idea that order and law should prevail in our most intimate relationships is perhaps even more relevant to us today.

What *is* order within marriage? As a married woman who has been working on that problem for many years, I suspect my answer now is different from what it might have been before I married. And I suspect my answer years from now, when—I hope—my husband and I have practiced for years longer on each other, will be different still. Before I married, I conceived of the patriarchal order as being a fairly clear-cut principle. Now, having some personal experience, I can see that the edges of who decides what are a lot blurrier than I thought they would be. Almost all our decisions are made jointly; the exceptions happen mainly when one or the other of us isn't available for one reason or another and whoever is there has to wing it. (And sometimes explain later if the winging wasn't precisely successful.)

In fact, when I think about it, if we're talking about unilateral decisions, I am usually the one who makes them. Do I really take his input into consideration as often as I should? Or do I tend to steam straight ahead and get around to telling him about it later?

Not that I think he really cares which detergent I buy, or whether I take the dog to the vet for her shots this week or next, but he might like to be informed, if not consulted, about whether the living room couch stays under the front window or is moved across the room before he walks absentmindedly into his own house and collides with the furniture because it isn't where it was when he left this morning. He might like to have his views considered (whether or not I would think it helpful) before I make the decision that that old sweater is ready for donating to charity. He might even like to express his opinion on the arrangement of our routine social life before I've told everybody we'll be somewhere.

Maybe today, as I ponder order in my life and my marriage, I can spend less time being idealistic about the principle of it and more time being honest about the practice of it. What's the Golden Rule? Do unto others as you would have them do unto you?

Let me resolve to do better. Let me make an honest effort to remember to counsel with (or, at a minimum, inform) him as he does me. Probably it would be a good idea to fish that sweater out of the donation bag (at least temporarily) and check with my beloved before I agree to dinner with the Hubbards this Saturday. Although I am strongly disinclined to move the furniture all back again, I could admit ungrudgingly and unprompted that I might have *mentioned* that I was considering how much better the room would look with the couch on the other side . . .

JANUARY 5

The steps of a good man are ordered by the Lord; and he delighteth in his way. Though he fall, he shall not be utterly cast down: for the Lord upholdeth him with his hand.

—PSALM 37:23–24

That could read "the steps of a good woman . . ." One of the great losses of this end of the century is that the feminists (who did have some genuine injustices to point out) have managed to strip from the English language the useful concept that *man*, used generically, has nothing to do with gender and is just a friendlier way of saying *human being*. Without that understanding, it's all too easy for women in our time to come to the morose conclusion that the scriptures are mainly relevant to the male sex.

But if we take it as David intended, this piece of a psalm can be a real comfort. One of the nicest parts of scriptures is that they do not depict some abstract, perfect life unlike anything we experience. When we read through the Bible, or the Book of Mormon, or the other scriptures, we encounter over and over again the faces of ordinary people like ourselves, who succeed sometimes and fail sometimes and get dispirited and discouraged often. Some of them are vain, deceitful, vengeful, or grouchy (think of Jonah, who had to be swallowed up and spat out before he went to do what the Lord had given him to do, and even then he groused because the people of Nineveh repented and so the Lord didn't destroy the city as Jonah had prophesied). In other words, the scriptures teach us about people who are guilty of all the petty and major forms of disobedience that we ourselves perpetrate.

That is why the promise in this psalm means so much. It doesn't promise us that we won't ever fall, because we have fallen, even when we were being good, and by all available evidence we will continue to fall. It does promise that when we fall, we will never fall "utterly." The Lord's hand will sustain us, if we have patterned our steps after the order of the Lord.

There is another promise, too: We can "delight" in ordering our steps as the Lord would have us do, finding joy in all the things that happen every day.

"Delight." What a wonderful, bright word for a cold wintry day. What a wonderful, bright promise!

JANUARY 6

Unchanging principles are so because they come from our unchanging Heavenly Father. Try as they might, no parliament or congress could ever repeal the law of earth's gravity or amend the Ten Commandments. Those laws are constant. All laws of nature and of God are part of the everlasting gospel.

—ELDER RUSSELL M. NELSON

This morning it is snowing heavily, and my world is blanketed with white. Cars move almost silently down the snowy street in front of the house. All the ordinary outdoor noises are muffled—and will be until the snowblowers start, but most people are waiting for the snow to stop before they begin clearing it away. It seems incredible, looking out at the all-encompassing white, to think that this is the same street that will gradually return to green life after the snows melt and spring begins, that during the hot summer the huge elms that line the street—now abstract sculptures of bare branches—will provide a cooling, shady canopy of leaves. Daffodils and tulips will bloom and be replaced in their turn by summertime impatiens and sharply white begonias flourishing under the trees, only to be covered, eventually, by the falling leaves as the year wheels around again, preparing for another winter. Change, constant change: The seasons steadily replace each other. My babies (and everybody else's) grow into children and then into adolescents and eventually adults; my face, as I contemplate it in the bathroom mirror while I brush my teeth each morning and night, is not the same as it was ten years ago, or even five.

No wonder some people who lack the strength and security of the gospel occasionally panic and do stupid things, trying to find a place to grab hold and hang on. Of course, there isn't any place to grab. Nothing stays put. The happiest day of anybody's life will come to a close and inexorably move into the past. There is no way to catch it and freeze it into forever, at least not here and now. (One compensation is that the really awful days slip away just as certainly.)

The comfort we find in the gospel is the knowledge that these kinds of changes belong only to this stage, to the kindergarten room of this world that we are inhabiting for the time being. We don't know—or more precisely, we can't remember—the details of what comes next. We just know that it is governed by the same unchanging principles and laws that govern our lives here. Our Heavenly Father is unchanging, and so is the power of the priesthood, the authority of divine or moral law, the inevitability of judgment assessing how we have used our time here on this earth, and the efficacy of truth. Those will never change.

When we are tossed about by the storms and tempests of our lives on this earth (those that devastate us on the outside and those that devastate us on the inside), we have those certainties to hang on to. Our Father in Heaven will always be there. The gospel will always be there. The eternal laws will always be there, not one set for this generation and maybe another set for another.

This snow will go, and another will come. Today let us find security in the absolute knowledge that the authority and principles that govern the order in our lives will stay with us, creating a beacon for now and a guide for eternity. We are blessed with solid ground beneath our feet, however the seasons may shift.

JANUARY 7

And see that all these things are done in wisdom and order; for it is not requisite that a man should run faster than he has strength. And again, it is expedient that he should be diligent, that thereby he might win the prize; therefore all things must be done in order.

—MOSIAH 4:27

Why, oh why, oh why, can't I master the use of the common word *no?* I teach school part-time, I run the house part-time, I have callings and responsibilities at church part-time, I have various bits and pieces of community involvement part-time, I am a wife and mother (and sometimes I think sourly that I'm doing *that* part-time, too), and because I am a spineless wimp (or feel like one on days like this), it never seems to occur to me until too late that all this part-time activity adds up to full-time-and-a-half or more, and all I've got is the same twenty-four hours per day that anybody else gets.

Now why do I go on saying yes? Not reluctantly, in most cases, but enthusiastically. Let me be honest: It isn't as if anybody is putting a gun to my head. Why do I do it?

Well, I guess partly because I usually like doing at least part of what I'm asked to do. I like spending time with people; I like being involved. So that's part of it. It's flattering to be asked to take responsibility for things. It's fun to be part of the group that's doing the activities. It's fun to know the administration and the teachers at school; it's handy to know who to go to for what. So that's part of it, too. And if I'm really going to be wholly honest, there is probably an appealing element of tightrope walking in the whole thing. "Wow, look at all the things she does!" Which is fine as long as I'm still walking; but what about when I'm hanging on by my fingernails or midway in a ragdoll drop to the ground? Do I really want to collect a crowd for that?

What is it about LDS women that makes us feel as if being Superwoman is the minimum requirement? We get running so fast and so hard that it's easy to discover that our priorities in practice are ordered on the principle of what absolutely has to get done today and what can wait until tomorrow, rather than on the principle of what is important and needs to be done today even if it would quite conceivably be physically possible to do it tomorrow. What about the people in my life—my husband, for example? Spending time with him is definitely postponable. I'm running too hard now, but presumably I can always spend some time with him tomorrow (it doesn't *have* to be done today). Even so, if I'm realistic, I have to know that tomorrow very likely will be filled up with things that always fill up today. It is possible that we might not spend time together until a month or so from next Friday—if then—if I don't get a grip on things. Is that doing things in order? This is my husband; this is my marriage. Logically, I would put him up among the top two or three priorities of my life, but would he ever figure that out from what actually happens?

Today let me sit down with Mosiah and read this scripture—out loud, if necessary—very slowly so I know I understand it. It is not requisite that I be Superwoman today or tomorrow or ever. Nowhere is it decreed that I have to perform for the admiration of spectators or even for my sisters in the gospel. It doesn't really matter if nobody but me ever knows what I'm doing, as long as I'm doing what I know needs to be done. (I do need to do that; I notice we are exhorted to be "diligent," which means that lolling on the couch doesn't count.)

I need to put my relationship with my Heavenly Father first, my relationship with my husband second, and my relationship with my children third, and then I need to behave as if those actually are my priorities. Everything else comes afterwards. If I can take care of those things and do extra stuff at church and do my job at work and volunteer in the schools and help with that community project . . .

Maybe I had better sit very quietly and practice saying no. No. No. No.

JANUARY 8

Hast thou not known? hast thou not heard, that the everlasting God, the Lord, the Creator of the ends of the earth, fainteth not, neither is weary? there is no searching of his understanding.

He giveth power to the faint; and to them that have no might he increaseth strength.

Even the youths shall faint and be weary, and the young men shall utterly fall:

But they that wait upon the Lord shall renew their strength; they shall mount up with wings as eagles; they shall run, and not be weary; and they shall walk, and not faint.

—ISAIAH 40:28–31

What a magnificent image! Just imagine that feeling of freedom, soaring over the mountains and plains with eagles' wings, glorying in the rush of renewed strength.

It does happen, you know. There are the down days—we all have them—but let's not forget the felicity of the good days. You remember them: the days when you wake up and you're ready to wake up, so you can lie there anticipating the day instead of burrowing back into the blankets, drowning in weariness. You swing your legs over the edge of the bed, and you're ready for whatever is going to come next, a whole delicious, fresh day out there waiting for you.

I think Isaiah is saying that if we are actively engaged in the Lord's work, the good days will be more frequent, and at times the good days will come for no good physical reason. We know that's true. There are those mornings after days when we have exhausted ourselves in the service of others. Maybe it was a general disaster like flood or earthquake; maybe it was a private disaster affecting only a family, but whatever it was, we let ourselves be an instrument in the hands of the Lord, and eventually when what had to be done was finished, we collapsed into bed fully expecting to feel like leftover garbage the next day. Instead, the next day was one of the good days, one of the days when we soared with the wings of the eagles, strength renewed and our deepest sense of the joy of life refreshed. Maybe it's just as well we can't choose to have those days. Maybe we would waste them, or take them for granted. Maybe it's better to have them just appear, a very special present from the Lord, the brush of eagles' wings—almost like the touch of his hand.

JANUARY 9

Whoso keepeth his mouth and his tongue keepeth his soul from troubles.

—PROVERBS 21:23

I do like the book of Proverbs. It has all these little nuggets of plain ordinary common sense, one after another.

Today I will consider this one and admire its practicality. How many times would I have been so much better off if I had had those dozen words flashing around my brain like the signs in Times Square and just kept my mouth shut? Oh, I don't necessarily mean betraying confidences (although I'm afraid I have probably done that in my time). I mean all the times I have opened my mouth and spoken without any perceptible prior thought and said things that were unkind or hurtful or just plain unnecessary. "Is something wrong? You look terrible today," is not precisely what somebody who is having problems needs to hear, and unless the person has already determined to confide in me, it's not the sort of encouraging remark that makes her more likely to do so. Nor do people need to be told that the color they're wearing brings out the yellow in their skin, factually accurate though that might be. Unrequested advice is another treasure that would be best kept to myself. Possibly the world *would* be better if it were left to me to organize, but I won't be harmed by keeping still about it.

Today, let me practice keeping my mouth closed and my ears open. What's that old adage? We have two ears and one mouth so we can hear twice as much as we speak.

I say no more.

JANUARY 10

All of us give our lives daily for what we believe is important. Those with whom we associate are silently assessing us, our values and character traits. Is there anything about our daily conduct that we would change if we knew someone was doing a written appraisal for publication?

—ELDER J. RICHARD CLARKE

Well, of course we do know that our conduct is indeed going to be subject to appraisal. Yet the Final Judgment is far enough off so that it is possible to think about other things for days at a time. (I'll bet the Puritans, who had hellfire and damnation preached at considerable length on a regular weekly basis, worried about it a lot more often than we do.) Besides, with the day of Judgment so far off, we think, repentance is always possible between now and then, a comforting if not entirely accurate thought for those of us who live in the world of fast-moving vehicles, sudden failures of body mechanisms, and even strikes of lightning.

But published in the local paper? Now that would give me immediate pause. Am I ready to be examined publicly as a proto-typical sample of a Latter-day Saint woman as I live my daily life? Does that life reflect what I think is important?

Maybe today I can spend some time thinking about that, notic-ing what I'm doing. Would my ordinary daily conduct be what I would choose for other people to notice? People all over the world are drawn to the gospel and the truths it contains because they have admired the way individual members of the Church behave. I cer-tainly wouldn't want to feel my primary reason for behaving well was so that other people would admire me, but how would I feel to discover that because I lost my temper or was less than entirely hon-est about some minor transaction somebody drew unfortunate con-clusions about Mormons in general and never opened his or her heart and mind to the fullness of the gospel?

It's so easy to speak quickly or act expediently and never con-sider any larger consequences, and the plain fact is that at times, nobody is watching. Yet it isn't just the outside world that is or is not observing our conduct: We have as many faithful recording devices as we have children at home, buzzing and whirring away, storing nuggets of behavioral information like squirrels storing nuts. My brother-in-law, in the course of a talk on honesty, once described explaining the function of a radar detector in his car to his then-ten-year-old daughter. He realized, once he began explaining, that he was specifically teaching dishonesty. He was teaching that it isn't speeding that matters; what matters is not getting caught at it.

And of course, even if nobody else on earth is observing me, I know what I'm doing, and so does the Lord. Does my daily life reflect accurately what I believe is important? Today maybe I'd better pay attention and find out.

JANUARY 11

And set in order the churches, and study and learn, and become acquainted with all good books, and with languages, tongues, and people.

—DOCTRINE AND COVENANTS 90:15

One of the things I love about the gospel is its open-mindedness. I love the fact that Joseph Smith felt that the admonition of Paul to seek after anything "virtuous, lovely, or of good report or praiseworthy" was so important that he used it to conclude his statement of the fundamental beliefs of Latter-day Saint people. I feel empowered by the idea that talents of great value are given to all people and that we are only enriched, not diminished, by recognizing praiseworthy work done in communities other than our own. I am intrigued by the memorable observation of the Jesuit theologian Teilhard du Chardin: "Everything that rises must converge."

There is so much beauty and goodness in this world. There's a lot wrong with it, too, and sometimes it is tempting to concentrate on the errors and the dangers and the haunting repetition of lost innocence and wickedness unpunished. But concentrating on the negative side alone closes out so much that is uplifting and healthy and promising.

The passage in Doctrine and Covenants 90:15 was given to the Prophet Joseph Smith originally, and though I would hesitate to say that he was given the time and opportunity to become acquainted with *all* good books, from the evidence I have found he was familiar with what was available to him. His life was cut short; yet his translation of the Book of Mormon exposed him to some languages, tongues, and peoples, and his work on the Bible and on the book of Abraham exposed him to others. Most of us living now in the world of instant communication have the chance to reach out beyond our narrower and wider communities, finding out what is good to learn and what will enrich us—at a minimum having the opportunity to look at our same old world from angles we might not have considered before.

It's cozy and familiar to stick with what we know. It's too easy to give up exploring and withdraw, when we're taken aback by something that we find puzzling or threatening.

Neither the apostle Paul nor the Prophet Joseph Smith admonished us to embrace whatever crossed our horizon. But if we won't look, we miss everything.

Today, I'll look for a book I've never read, an idea that is new to me, a different point of view. And I'll remember a quotation from President Gordon B. Hinckley, handed out at a Relief Society meeting ages ago and now a treasured bookmark in my scriptures: "What I am suggesting is that each of us . . . look for the remarkable good among those with whom we associate, that we speak of one another's virtues more than we speak of one another's faults, that optimism replace pessimism, that our faith exceed our fears" (*Ensign,* April 1986, 4).

There is magnificence out there in this world that the Lord has given us.

JANUARY 12

For we are saved by hope: but hope that is seen is not hope: for what a man seeth, why doth he yet hope for? But if we hope for that we see not, then do we with patience wait for it.

—ROMANS 8:24–25

Hope was an important concept to the apostle Paul—here he wrote about it to the small congregation of Saints in Rome and again to the Corinthians. Remember "and now abideth faith, hope, charity, these three"? (1 Corinthians 13:13).

What does the hope Paul is talking about mean to me? Hope to me is sort of like the mortar that keeps everything in order between the bricks of testimony. I know this, and I know that, and for the time being, holding this and that together is hope, the mortar that keeps the separate sections of my testimony from flying away into disarray.

I am getting older, and, thank goodness, with getting older comes experience. Some things that used to be mortar-like hope ten or fifteen years ago have settled into bricks of testimony. But there are other things (and some the same) that I still hope for. I don't *know* the things I hope; as Paul put it, if you can see it, what do you need hope for?

But Paul says we are saved by hope. For me that means that I am saved from falling into unbelief simply because I can't see the whole eternal picture spread out before me right this minute. Hope holds the bits I can see together, giving me faith to rely on as I work through prayer and study to fill out the picture.

Let me value that hope today. Let me take Paul's words as special reassurance to me: "But if we hope for that we see not, then do we with patience wait for it."

JANUARY 13

Organize yourselves; prepare every needful thing; and establish a house, even a house of prayer, a house of fasting, a house of faith, a house of learning, a house of glory, a house of order, a house of God.

—DOCTRINE AND COVENANTS 88:119

A wonderful and often-used scripture for today: As I read through this part of the revelation, the words are comfortably familiar from years of repetition from the pulpit and in Relief Society and Sunday School lessons. The splendid, rolling cadence in this particular verse charms the ear and captures the attention.

Does that make it easier to obey? Unfortunately not, at least for me—I would love to be able to report honestly, looking around my house this winter morning (or even looking around my ward house), that all those splendid phrases are reflected here. A house of prayer? Yes, I hope so. A house of fasting? Well, when required and sometimes when pressed by daunting circumstances. A house of faith? We try, some days more than others. A house of learning? Again, we try, but too often the press of those measly twenty-four hours gets too much, and the learning of the truths of the gospel gets postponed until tomorrow or the next available Sunday or until I have to teach a class or something. A house of glory? I wish! A house of order? Oh, *dear.*

Not good enough. Today, let me pick one of those and work on it, genuinely work on it. Let me not be hypnotized by the cadence of the words but focus on the meaning and see what I can do. Rome wasn't built in a day, and neither will perfection be, but they went on working on Rome, and I can go on working on perfection.

A house of glory, a house of order, a house of God: Wouldn't it be magnificent to be able to say yes!

JANUARY 14

Do not run faster or labor more than you have strength and means provided to enable you to translate; but be diligent unto the end.
—DOCTRINE AND COVENANTS 10:4

Those were the Lord's words to Joseph Smith after the episode of the pages lost by Martin Harris, but I believe what is said applies to us all. When we're trying to organize ourselves and make sense of our lives, we need to remember that it doesn't help anyone to try to run faster than is possible, whether that involves translation or anything else. On the other hand, we need to work diligently at what we are capable of doing until we finish whatever it is. The instructions are not contradictory. They're just difficult. It's difficult first because as women we seem to feel obliged to do anything we're asked to do or decide ought to be done. That makes it even more difficult because we are thus inclined to take on more than anyone can do and consequently get tired before we get finished. Then we feel guilty.

Unfortunately, few of our everyday choices—the choices which define our lives in practice—are between good and evil. I don't think many of us have to choose between doing our visiting teaching and selling drugs down on the corner. Most of the time what we do have to choose between is a whole selection of worthy alternatives. Are we going to do that visiting teaching or fix dinner for somebody who is in need? Or fix the dinner or help the missionaries? Or help the missionaries or clear out of the garden the weeds that are threatening to take over? Or—each of us has our own long list. It's tempting to avoid choosing by trying to do everything, which is impossible, none of us being blessed (as far as I can see) with time that stretches like elastic. So we don't get finished, and then we blame ourselves.

On the other hand, if we're disciplined enough to choose, it's too easy then to beat ourselves about the head and shoulders for not having tried to do the other jobs as well.

Maybe, if we really believe what we are told in the scriptures— and what's the point of reading them, if we don't?—we should do what they say and let go of our guilt. When we have two worthy choices, and we can't take on both and finish them, we have to take one and let the other one go. Isn't that what the Lord is telling Joseph Smith and, over his shoulder, telling us? "Do not run faster or labor more than you have strength."

Today, let me remember that. Let me make sure, when I'm making my choices, that I'm making sensible, prayerful ones. Let me be realistic about what is and what is not possible. I do have limited resources of time and energy. I can't do everything I wish I could, not all at once. Then let me let go of the things I didn't choose. I can't do them now.

Feeling guilty does not multiply my capabilities. Let me remember that today, too.

JANUARY 15

We tend to think only in terms of our endurance, but it is God's patient long-suffering which provides us with our chances to improve, affording us urgently needed developmental space or time. . . . Otherwise, if certain mortal experiences were cut short, it would be like pulling up a flower to see how the roots are doing.

—ELDER NEAL A. MAXWELL

Enduring to the end certainly sounds like an obvious idea. After all, if you endure only part of the way and then give up, what's the point of enduring at all? You wind up in the same mess you were in at the beginning. If you have to hang on to the rope to cross the river even though it's burning your hands painfully, letting go three-quarters of the way across would be foolish. You wouldn't have gotten where you needed to get, you're as wet as you would have been if you had fallen in the river at the start, and now your hands hurt as well. Therefore, just hang on as long as you have to (which sounds fine until you're having to do it).

That much I had figured out. The nugget that Elder Maxwell

has given me to chew over today is the idea that watching me try to endure might be difficult for Heavenly Father. Yet the Lord knows that if he heeded my desperate prayers (all the way across the river) to please, please get me out of this mess right this minute, I would never learn from the situation what I would otherwise have the opportunity of learning.

It's a familiar part of being a parent. Do you rush over and hold the baby through his first unsteady steps, or do you let him try it on his own, which inevitably means falling? As long as he lands on his well-padded rear, no harm is done, but I can't be the only one to have wound up with bruised and banged toddlers who fell frontwards, sidewards, and in directions I can't describe. Did they have to fall? Well, they have to gain their own balance, and I can't teach that. I can only make circumstances as safe as possible and let them teach themselves to walk.

Or make beds, or cook, or drive the car. Most people are unbelievably awkward the first time they try a new skill. Do we do our children any favors by rushing in and cutting short their period of struggle by doing the job ourselves? Well, only if we don't care if they ever learn to make a bed or cook or drive a car. There's no shortcut. You have to learn it yourself, and other people can only demonstrate. They can't learn it for you.

So what skills am I supposed to be learning from my trials? Sometimes I have to admit I don't have the faintest idea. I certainly hope the skills are going to be something really useful in the hereafter, because some of them cost me dearly in the learning process. I can see that some of them taught me patience, and understanding, and how complicated love is. Would I have learned those lessons as thoroughly if the Lord had stepped in, as I was beseeching him to do, to cut the lesson short?

I'll never know in the here and now. Maybe he *did* cut some of them short after all, figuring that I am a slow learner and need to have a second chance and we'll start up again from where we left off. Certainly there's a repetitious quality to some of my difficulties.

But let me learn from today that the Lord's wisdom and love are sometimes best shown by what Elder Maxwell calls his "patient long-suffering." After all, without that I could never have the deep inner satisfaction of knowing that I did it, that I endured to the end. And perhaps the richness of that knowledge is the greatest blessing of all.

JANUARY 16

Whom shall he teach knowledge? and whom shall he make to understand doctrine? them that are weaned from the milk, and drawn from the breasts. For precept must be upon precept, precept upon precept; line upon line, line upon line; here a little, and there a little.

—ISAIAH 28:9–10

Oh dear, oh dear, oh dear. Is my impatience really as obvious as that? Does the Lord really need to tell me that in order to learn anything I have to get past the baby stage, beating my spoon on the high chair tray imperiously when the food is not presented as rapidly as I want it?

Yes, it would be marvelous to understand the whole magnificent spread of the gospel and to understand it right now. Yes, I would love to read through the book of Isaiah from start to finish and understand precisely what that master of symbolism was telling us in each and every verse. Yes, I would love to see the Lord's plan of eternal order laid out plainly before me.

No, I don't think it's going to happen today. Line upon line—I just have to remember not to bang my spoon and instead bend my heart and mind to understand one scripture at a time, and to keep going at it and keep going, and maybe eventually . . .

Today I'll work on this one.

JANUARY 17

And now I desire that this inequality should be no more in this land, especially among this my people; but I desire that this land be a land of liberty, and every man may enjoy his rights and privileges alike, so long as the Lord sees fit that we may live and inherit the land, yea, even as long as any of our posterity remains upon the face of the land.

—MOSIAH 29:32

Today let me read over the wise words of King Mosiah, as he turned his nation's government over to judges rather than kings. Why? So that rather than having one mortal man, subject to weakness, presented with the temptation of absolute power, the responsibility—or "burden," as he called it—should be shared by all and administered by righteous judges, in the plural. There should be temporal order, then, as well as order in our spiritual lives and our family arrangements. A government should be an expression of the spirit of the people governed, representative and consistent with their wishes, because, as Mosiah also pointed out, "it is not common that the voice of the people desireth anything contrary to that which is right" (Mosiah 29:26).

It's interesting to note that he saw as the bedrock of a righteous system the principle that every man should be able to enjoy his rights and privileges alike, without inequalities. Order, he is telling us, can't exist where there is unjust inequality. There will always be unequal degrees of virtue and obedience to law—that's the whole point of why we are here on this earth, to learn, through a variety of means, to obey, and some of us do a better job than others—but as Mosiah taught, the threshold of opportunity has to be the same for all. What we do with that opportunity defines us; the existence of the opportunity defines our society.

It seems to me that when I was a child growing up here in the United States, almost every public prayer in the Church included the formula, "Bless the president of our church and the president of our country." It seems to me it's been a long time since I've heard that. Do the presidents of our country now stand in less need of blessings? I don't think so. Does whether we agree with a particular incumbent have anything to do with his need for divine help? I hope not. Will this be a greater and wiser nation if it is guided by the Lord's blessing? Definitely.

Let me remember that today. Let me get so enthusiastic that I pray not only for the president but for Congress and even the bureaucracy. Prayer can only help. After all, all but the most cynical would have to agree that the government is made up of a lot of people mainly trying to do the best they can in the middle of difficult circumstances. As are we all.

When I look at it like that, praying for them seems not only obvious but obligatory.

JANUARY 18

*There are wide areas of our society from which the spirit of prayer
and reverence and worship has vanished. Men and women in many
circles are clever, interesting, or brilliant, but they lack one crucial
element in a complete life. They do not look up.*

—ELDER HOWARD W. HUNTER

R ight, and a lot of them are on television.
We have cable television at our house, and that means we
have sixty-some stations available to us and a depressing percentage
of the time there is absolutely nothing to watch on any of them.
Even more depressing, here we are twenty years and more after
President Hunter (then an apostle) preached about the spiritual
emptiness of so much of our common culture, and the situation is
much worse. I'm not talking about the coarseness or the epidemic
promiscuity or investigation of sexual alternatives; that's obviously
unacceptable. I'm talking about the spiritual emptiness of so many
of the otherwise inoffensive dramas and programs, which seem to
assume that being reasonably responsible and reasonably thoughtful
of your fellowman is about as good as it gets. The idea that you
might actually be concerned about eternal consequences, or seek to
improve your character or conduct, or be conscious of religious
teachings—oh, my dear. Do you live in some dream world, or what?
The prevailing belief appears to be that I'm all right and you're all
right as long as you mean well. That's it. Nobody goes to church or
synagogue on TV; nobody seems to give a thought to religious practice of any kind.

Even many of the religious programs seem based, as far as I can
gather, on the premise that accepting Jesus and loving the Lord is
all that is required. The idea that those theoretical commitments
need to be backed up by action may be part of the package, for all I
know, but it certainly isn't mentioned very often. Not by TV evan-
gelists, anyway.

Today let me judge the flickering screen in my living room (and
kitchen and bedroom—believe me, I know about this stuff) by the
standards President Hunter was talking about. Maybe part of the
problem is me: Am I watching for programs that will offer me a spiritual uplift, helping me order my life? Am I rewarding the few artists
and entertainers who are trying to lift the tone of our common culture by giving them my business?

I don't honestly know. It's easier to condemn it all as a vast wasteland. It takes work to sift out the programs that have value. Today let me work. Let me decide what to watch and, if nothing is worth watching, let me have the integrity, the gumption, and the determination to turn the set off.

JANUARY 19

Our soul waiteth for the Lord; he is our help and our shield.

—Psalm 33:20

Forever true: That is what underlies the order of my life.

Curiously, that is what I discover I share with a surprising number of my students. I am constantly amazed at the openness with which my students at the business school talk about their faith and their trust in Jesus. Many of them are African-American, strong in their community's gospel traditions, and the straightforward, simple way they speak of their relationship with Jesus is a lesson to me, coming from a tradition that expresses the very same concept very differently.

Take LaKita, for example. LaKita and I were talking about another student's baby, born three months prematurely, weighing less than two pounds. Naturally, we were all concerned about the baby; his mother, who returned to classes only four days after the birth, was fine but getting visibly weary as she spent her afternoons and nights at the hospital and her mornings at school.

"I hope the baby's doing all right," I said one day when his mother didn't make it in.

"He's fine," LaKita told me. "I prayed on him. Jesus will take care of him."

I told her I was glad she did that, and we moved on to discuss the class assignment. As the class worked on their exercises, I sat at my desk and thought about LaKita and her plain and simple faith. She was right, of course. The baby will be fine, whatever happens. Jesus will take care of him. He is that baby's help and shield, as he is the baby's mother's, and mine.

When I went home, I prayed on the baby too.

JANUARY 20

I can do all things through Christ which strengtheneth me.

—PHILIPPIANS 4:13

What a wonderfully confident verse of scripture to hang onto! What I interpret it to mean is that if the Lord asks me to do something, he will make strength available for me to do it. That doesn't mean I won't get tired, or that I might not *worry* that I'm not strong enough to do it, or that I will necessarily have enough motivation to undertake everything the Lord would have me do in the order of my days. It does mean that if I ought to do it, I can do it.

Some of my ought-to-do's are easy; others challenge me more. Unfortunately, sometimes what starts out feeling like an easy one turns out halfway along to be something that demands more of me than it looked as if it would. I *can* get up in time on a Sunday to get the entire family to church before it starts. That's an easy one. (So how come we're so often late?) I *can* bite back the exasperated under-my-breath remarks before they become audible. Should be easy; isn't always. I *can* keep my patience with an adolescent flailing unreasonably against me even though I've been doing my best to be the Ideal Mother (whoever she might be). Depends how often that's happened in the last week, or the last half hour. I *can* forgive those who trespass against me, even if the trespassing was thoughtless and unfair. Medium level difficulty, depending on the trespass. I can always comfort myself by feeling noble. I can even forgive my husband, who took the doors off one of my kitchen cupboards (to fix the hinges) back last summer and can't seem to find a spare minute to replace them but can spend contented evenings perusing seed catalogs and planning next summer's garden.

Ah, now *there* we're into heavy-duty offenses!

So far I have led, mainly, a fairly comfortable life. I have known people, though, who have clung to this scripture through trials that tested them to the last strands of their endurance. Perhaps along with my gratitude for the strength it promises I should include gratitude that so far, I have not been so tested.

But when I am, I know that Christ's strength will be there.

JANUARY 21

*Ye are my witnesses, saith the Lord, and my servant whom I have
chosen: that ye may know and believe me, and understand that I
am he: before me there was no God formed, neither shall there be
after me.*

—ISAIAH 43:10

Isaiah again, this time quoting the Lord speaking to Israel, his chosen people. They let the Lord down over and over and were disobedient, generation after generation, and yet because of his promise to Abraham, and the unique mission his descendants were given, he lifted them up again and again. Israel is precious to the Lord; it always has been.

We share in that special mission, of course. We also are witnesses and servants of the Lord, testifying of his power and glory and unity. Sometimes we may forget that. There seem to be so many other things to think about: the restoration of the gospel, the wonderful gift of the Book of Mormon, and the renewed power of revelation in our own time, and those things testify of the message of this scripture.

The singularity of our Lord for our world—"before me there was no God formed, neither shall there be after me"—was a vital message back in the days of Isaiah, when multiple gods were worshipped on all sides. Is it not equally valid now, when sects and cults preaching strange gods and various forms of godlessness, are fighting for headline space in our papers? I remember in college having the opportunity to sing Ernest Bloch's *Sacred Service* in a synagogue in San Francisco as part of the University Chorus. I've long since forgotten the Hebrew words, but I remember the translation (Deuteronomy 6:4): "Hear, O Israel: The Lord our God is one Lord." We sang it as a triumphant declaration, and as I sang, the voices soaring around me, I felt that I, too, was a proud witness of my God's singularity and divinity to a disbelieving world. It felt magnificent. Remembering it, it still does.

Like the Jews, we have a mission to be witnesses of our God, of the order of his creation, and his primacy within it. "Before me there was no God formed, neither shall there be after me." Today let me remember that along with those long ago triumphant voices, and rejoice.

JANUARY 22

Labour not for the meat which perisheth, but for that meat which endureth unto everlasting life, which the Son of man shall give unto you: for him hath God the Father sealed.

—JOHN 6:27

Oh, priorities, priorities—what an important-sounding word to describe what lies behind the ordinary hour-by-hour choices of my life!

So how do I distinguish between the meat which perisheth and the meat which endureth eternally? Well, at least for a few minutes this morning, I guess I *have:* The scriptures are here, lying open in my lap, and the newspaper, with its tales of scandal, disaster, and human unkindness, is pushed over on the table. Can I take this for the start of my day and see how much further I can go with it? Can I concentrate on what uplifts my spirit—classical music on the car radio on the way to school—instead of leaving the tuner set on the oldies station that warbles continually of the frustrations of adolescent love? Can I devote my most single-minded attention today to the relationships that will last eternally (spend half an hour after school with my son, for example; I promised I'd teach him how to drive a stick shift) and let the more temporal concerns like getting the kitchen in order slide for another day? Can I call up my mother for a last-minute, spur-of-the-moment invitation to share dinner with the family (she's seen a messy kitchen before) and have some time with her, instead of letting the evening dribble out between my fingers in one little job or another or just in perching on the end of the couch meaning to get up in a minute but watching whatever anyone else has on?

Would that day match up more to what I say (and hope) my priorities really are? Would it feel natural? Perhaps I'd better try, and see.

JANUARY 23

Wherefore lay to with your might and call faithful laborers into my vineyard, that it may be pruned for the last time.

—DOCTRINE AND COVENANTS 39:17

I sn't it odd that with all the scriptures talking about last times and last days and the imminent onset of the chaos preceding the millennium, we still manage to potter along day after day behaving as if everything is going to last forever?

Of course, in some ways it's just as well if we do. After all, this instruction, with all its urgency, was given in 1831, and if the man to whom it was given had decided that this was the final word and, having finished his pruning, sat down with hands folded to await the Second Coming, he would have wasted his time. (As a matter of fact, it was given to James Covill, a Baptist minister who was enough persuaded by Joseph Smith's message to covenant with the Lord that he would follow his teachings. He was quickly persuaded by his former associates that the covenant was a terrible error, and so no "pruning," presumably, was in fact done by him.)

More than a century and a half later, the message remains, still urgent, still commanding—and we are all still here. So we are now, as he was then, required to continue to prepare, using each day we have been given to the fullest, and trying to live in such a way that if the Second Coming came on our watch, we'd be ready for it.

Am I? Not me. Not today, anyway. Maybe I'd better take today to reevaluate, to decide why not and what to do differently. Are we completing all *our* assignments?

Perhaps, James Covill having fallen down on the job, the pruning is up to us.

JANUARY 24

Let all things be done decently and in order.

—1 CORINTHIANS 14:40

H ow plainly and succinctly put!

Why do we have to be instructed over and over to keep our lives in order, to be organized, to obey the rules? I suppose because part of mortality seems to be a messy, disorganized business of emotions spilling over our activities and our intentions (good and bad) complicating our accomplishments. We have to be taught to think, to make judgments, to decide what has to be done first, and second, and then what comes after that.

We have to decide because we live in a world of ticking clocks and time that drifts away while we're busy doing something else. If we had all the time in the world, it wouldn't matter if we were messy and impulsive and disorganized. But we have only our own particular slice of it, and the older we get the more aware we are of being hurtled from childhood through adolescence to young womanhood to maturity to old age. We are drawn to and chuckle at the fresh spontaneity of our babies and young children, but we can't keep them stuck at that stage any more than we ourselves can stick at any other. All that bubbling energy and unguided experimentation has to be channeled and directed before it can be of any use. We can't do everything, as the baby wants to do; we don't have time. We have to choose, to decide, to take one path or another. There isn't time for all of them.

I don't always like the idea that I have to choose. I want to be young again, to try to do it all, to do cartwheels down the street. Well, in all honesty, I never *was* able to do cartwheels down the street or anywhere else, but I always wished I could. Still do. Maybe, if I am very, very good, that will be one of the treats I earn in heaven.

However, for the time being, I have to grow up. I have to face the fact that I am older, that there are jobs to be done and responsibilities to be shouldered. I had my time of being one of the children who was taught that everything had to be done decently and in order; now is my time to do the teaching.

Even so, I have my moments of staring out the kitchen window at the back yard and speculating. It's a good-sized back yard. Maybe this summer if no one is around, I could *practice* cartwheels . . .

JANUARY 25

Look thou upon me, and be merciful unto me, as thou usest to do unto those that love thy name.

Order my steps in thy word: and let not any iniquity have dominion over me.

Deliver me from the oppression of man: so will I keep thy precepts.

Make thy face to shine upon thy servant, and teach me thy statutes.

—PSALM 119:132–35

"O rder my steps in thy word"—what a lovely beginning to this day. Let me make this my prayer, as the psalmist did. What a gentle petition to hold in my heart this morning. Let me speak to the Lord with this simple directness; I think what catches my heart with this psalm is the sense of trust that overshoots the boundaries of faith. This is the child of man face to face with his Heavenly Father.

Whoever wrote this psalm isn't asking for the blessings needed to live comfortably on this earth. He isn't concerned with all the temporal things that so often preoccupy me. He isn't even fussing about his relationships with all the other people around him floundering through mortality, just as he is. For now, his eyes are fixed only on the Lord.

Yes, we are meant to live in the here and now, not closed off from the world. But before we go out into the world of our daily living, we need to turn away from all the gritty details of our lives here and reach up toward the life we had before and trust we will have again. I can't say I remember it—the veil separating eternity from mortality is too thick. But there is something familiar about the way this psalm makes me feel. I *did* know that Father once, and I still know that if I order my steps in his word I can find my way back to him.

Today, Lord, teach me thy statutes that will lead me back to thee. Look thou upon me and make thy face to shine upon me, thy servant, too. Today, with this psalm singing in my heart, I will wait quietly, trustfully, for the touch of thy guiding hand.

JANUARY 26

And I will also ease the burdens which are put upon your shoulders,
that even you cannot feel them upon your backs, even while you are
in bondage; and this will I do that ye may stand as witnesses for me
hereafter, and that ye may know of a surety that I, the Lord God,
do visit my people in their afflictions.

—MOSIAH 24:14

Bad news last night from a friend living far away; I went to bed distressed and slept fitfully, rousing and worrying, my mind going back and forth in the disorganized way it does in the middle of the night, trying to think of something useful I could do. Finally, it was morning and I got up, unrested and frustrated. With morning winter sunshine pouring unfeelingly through my bedroom window across the carpet, I have to be realistic and accept that even if I were there, I could do little about my friend's desolation. It's not that the succor of friends and family would be unappreciated. It's just that there are some trials that each of us has to endure alone.

Still, we are never truly alone, as this passage from Mosiah reminds us. Other people can help from time to time. I can write my friend, and telephone, and send flowers and my love. Our Heavenly Father will be there every hour of the day and night, lifting the burden even when the heart is so sore that the easing goes almost unnoticed at the time. It will only be later that we are able to look back and understand what made it endurable, and be grateful.

Be there today, O Lord. Let hearts be comforted and spirits soothed. Reach into the sore places where no one else can reach. Be with my friend, and with me, and with all the others who are burdened and grieving today in this beautiful, terrible web of mortality we all share.

Bless them; shelter them, dear Lord, that they too may stand as witnesses hereafter and forever.

JANUARY 27

Multitudes, multitudes in the valley of decision: for the day of the Lord is near in the valley of decision.

—JOEL 3:14

I t's always a temptation to believe that each of us exists as the center of our own private little solar system, and it's a slight shock to realize that there are lots of other solar systems out there, similar and dissimilar. Most of us deal with that by lapsing comfortably into feeling most at ease with people we know, the people we see going the places we usually go—usually, the people like us.

Those are the easy people—those we don't have to stretch to understand. But lots of others are out there, who, just like us and our kind, are inhabiting this world the Lord has given us. Lots of us are trying to be good people and do the right things. All of us have decisions to make daily, both important and trivial.

In fact, the valley of decision is a crowded spot.

Today, let me see if I can remember that and be a little more tolerant of my fellow inhabitants. I might have my problems to deal with today, but having problems is no excuse for being grumpy and snappish and quick to assume an attitude. Everybody else has problems, too. As people have pointed out for centuries now, it's not having problems that distinguishes us from each other; it's the way we choose to deal with them.

Today let me move out beyond my sense of myself as the center of it all. My sorrows are not universal sorrows and my frustrations are not the dictionary definition of frustration. There are lots of people with worse problems out here, just as there are undoubtedly others with less, and all of them, just like me, are mostly absorbed with their own decisions.

Today let me work on absorbing that and try to look outward more than inward. Let me spend a little less time in this valley mulling over my own decisions and expend a little more effort helping other people who are making their own, whether they are like me and mine or not. Haven't we been taught that the first step to spiritual progress is losing ourselves and finding our Heavenly Father by serving the rest of his children?

After all, this valley is certainly wide enough for all of us, and as we are reminded, none of us has unlimited time here. We'd better get on with it.

JANUARY 28

But speak thou the things which become sound doctrine: . . . that they may teach the young women to be sober, to love their husbands, to love their children, to be discreet, chaste, keepers at home, good, obedient to their own husbands, that the word of God be not blasphemed. . . . In all things shewing thyself a pattern of good works: in doctrine showing uncorruptness, gravity, sincerity.

—TITUS 2:1, 4–5, 7

P oor Titus! There's an assignment for you. Paul simply asks him to be a pattern of good works in all things. *All* things, mind you: not just every now and again, or even most of the time. That's asking for a demonstration of order in your house!

Compared to that, what the women are supposed to be doing doesn't seem quite as daunting. Even so, it's not the kind of list you undertake to complete before lunch. Are you sober, discreet, chaste, good, and obedient to your husband, and do you keep at home? I have a feeling that Paul would have taken a dim view of long days spent at the mall.

Love your husband and your children? Well, of course, with those as the foundation, all the rest of it comes a lot more easily. Maybe if the obedience and keeping at home part rub a little raw, we should get everything back in perspective and recognize that obedience woven together with love is not a problem and that the advice to stay at home is just the first-century version of what common sense and prophets in the twentieth century are continuing to tell us: that mothers and children, in general, do a much better job together than separately, and unless circumstances absolutely won't allow it, a mother should be at home with her young children, teaching them all the vital earliest lessons herself. None of this comes as news; the Lord's directions haven't changed much over the centuries.

So today let me have a stab at it.

Let me be sober, which here, I think, refers less to drunkenness than to taking my responsibilities seriously.

Let me be discreet. Just because I know something doesn't mean I have to talk about it.

Let me be chaste. Let me take a twenty-four-hour vacation from my society's obsession with sex and who's doing what with whom.

Let me not read those articles, and let me change the channel when necessary.

Let me be a keeper at home. Let me make sure I have finished what I need to do here before I start compiling lists of what needs to be done elsewhere. Of course millions of tasks need doing at the church and out in the world, but I am only one of the many people who could and should be working on them. Nobody else can carry my responsibilities here at home. (There is also the fact that my responsibilities here are in a sense time-limited: the children do grow up, whether I'm ready for it or not, and when they need me here less, I am more available for the needs outside my home.)

Let me be good. Well, at least today let me try. I know most of the places where I fall short: I can start on some of them.

Let me be supportive of my husband. Maybe for today I could try looking at things I'm doing with his sense of priorities instead of mine. He doesn't—he can't—understand all my daily responsibilities any more than I understand his, but maybe sometimes I have tunnel vision about them. Let me try looking at the situation from a fresh perspective—from his perspective, to be precise. Maybe, so enlightened, I will even find time to hunt for those pants he's been asking about.

Okay, Paul. Today I'll try it your way. And won't you have a moment of quiet amusement in heaven if it turns out to work better than mine?

JANUARY 29

Be ye therefore followers of God, as dear children: And walk in love, as Christ also hath loved us, and hath given himself for us an offering and a sacrifice to God for a sweetsmelling savour. . . . For ye were sometimes darkness, but now are ye light in the Lord; walk as children of light.

—EPHESIANS 5:1–2, 8

One of my absolutely favorite scriptures, a special treat for me today, my oldest child's birthday.

I always think of John as being the New Testament writer who overflows with love and compassion, but here it is Paul writing to the Ephesians with such tenderness. In a lot of other places Paul likens childhood to a stage to be grown out of, but here he calls us (to whom he is certainly speaking as much as to the Ephesians) to be children and followers of God, just as real children with shining faces and grubby hands and knees followed Christ during his time on this earth. "Ye were sometimes darkness," he tells us, "but now are ye light in the Lord: walk as children of light."

Light is easy; love is easy. Life is easy on the days when the light (even the winter light) pours through the windows and love is immediately accessible. How very much do I love that child sitting quietly at the counter eating breakfast, how endearing is the one who remembered to give me a casual hug before darting out the front door. How delicious it is that today I just happen to think about how nice the man I married really is.

Sometimes I get so caught up with the hard parts of the gospel, such as self-discipline and obedience, that I forget about the easy parts. But aren't the hard parts there to warn us away from the dangerous choices, the treacherous marshes, so that we can be free to reach the easy places, to move as children of light, completely at home in our Father in Heaven's presence? Maybe these random days, suffused with love, are sent to us to remind us of what it was like and will be again.

Moving here and there through the house, getting the day ready, I feel as if I am whirling and half-dancing in the light, the bright winter morning light. Let me hang on to this radiant feeling all day long; let me pour out the love I have known on everyone I meet today.

Let me walk, this whole day through, as a follower of God. Let me walk as a child of light.

JANUARY 30

Be thou diligent to know the state of thy flocks, and look well to thy herds. For riches are not for ever: and doth the crown endure to every generation?

—PROVERBS 27:23–24

Solid, hard-headed common sense, typical of the book of Proverbs. It has lasted through the centuries for good reason.

So what are my flocks and my herds? Well, it's coming down to the end of the month, and the pile of bills is not going anywhere unless I sit down with my checkbook. But I can't get started until I balance out with my bank statement.

Flocks and herds sound so much more romantic than bank statements and bills from the electric company and credit card establishments, although it probably would not if I were an actual herdsman out on the open hills and fields. I bet it got chilly and drafty out there and that sometimes hunting for that one elderly sheep seemed like a lot more trouble than it was worth (just like trying to work out why my bank balance remains stubbornly $1.23 off).

Today let me remember that proverbial counsel. Who knows when I might need that $1.23 or at least need to have developed better accounting skills so that it and all its bigger and littler brothers from other months don't keep accumulating? Today let me quit procrastinating and get down to it. Riches, after all, even our family's exceedingly modest riches, are *not* forever.

I don't do much worrying about the crown part.

JANUARY 31

Be still, and know that I am God.

—PSALM 46:10

A quiet thought with which to end the month. A quiet, peaceful mental picture.

So often I don't seem to have the *time* to be still. I am dashing from one place to another, making lists (and then forgetting to take the lists with me), picking people up from one place and delivering them to another, collecting possessions here and depositing them there, shopping for things I need and things I (and the family) want, working, and socializing. It all takes up so much time that some days I have the feeling I climb onto the assembly belt when my feet hit the floor in the morning, and I'm still buzzing with its vibration when I fall back into bed at night.

"Be still," my Lord tells me. "Be still, and know that I am God."

Today let me carve out time to obey. Let me sit quietly, let my heart and mind be still, and *know.*

Which would be the greater gift, as this first month of the year spins away from me into the past? The stillness or the knowledge?

FEBRUARY

Hear my prayer, O God; give ear to the words of my mouth.

—PSALM 54:2

FEBRUARY 1

After this manner therefore pray ye: Our Father which art in heaven, Hallowed be thy name.

Thy kingdom come. Thy will be done in earth, as it is in heaven.

Give us this day our daily bread.

And forgive us our debts, as we forgive our debtors.

And lead us not into temptation, but deliver us from evil: For thine is the kingdom, and the power, and the glory, for ever. Amen.

—MATTHEW 6:9–13

So this is the pattern. This is what Jesus Christ gave us to show us how to pray.

Of course, the problem is now that we may have heard—and read—it so often that we may no longer hear it as being fresh and new, the way the disciples first heard it. I have to admit I've heard it sung so magnificently that I can't read those last words without hearing the crescendo of voice and orchestra swelling from one phrase to the next. It's an uplifting experience.

What does the Lord's Prayer mean to us today? Well, as a start I would guess that we are supposed to learn that our prayers can be simple. The language sounds a little stilted to us now, but that's because we are reading Greek in translation by early seventeenth-century Englishmen, who spoke and wrote in the same English that William Shakespeare used. The point is that the disciples would have recognized his prayer as using plain and ordinary everyday words.

In Matthew's version, the Lord's Prayer is preceded by a discussion of how to pray, teaching in particular that you don't have to keep saying the same things over and over in order to make your prayer longer and more impressive. That's what the heathen do, Jesus said. Because our Father in Heaven already knows what we need, we need to beware of "vain repetitions" (Matthew 6:7).

In Luke's version, the Lord's Prayer is followed by a parable teaching that the Lord will no more ignore us when we pray than we would ignore a friend who came to our door in need.

So the prayer is to be simple, and it is taken for granted that we will be asking our Heavenly Father for blessings. Much of the time that's what praying is, after all. There are lots of other kinds of prayers, of course: There are prayers of desperation, and prayers of gratitude, and prayers of praise, just to begin with.

So our prayers are to be simple, and straightforward, and to the point. We are to praise our Lord, and above all we are to trust him—to believe that he does hear us, that he will answer. That is what we most need to know today and every other day.

FEBRUARY 2

Yea, and when you do not cry unto the Lord, let your hearts be full, drawn out in prayer unto him continually for your welfare, and also for the welfare of those who are around you.

—ALMA 34:27

Today, when I am at school, let me remember this. Since praying out loud continually is clearly impractical (I am, after all, supposed to be sticking to teaching Business English and Interpersonal Skills), let my heart be full of prayer instead, as Amulek recommends.

Heaven knows we have students here who need somebody to be mindful of their welfare. Take Trisha, for example. Trisha, like so many of our students, is a single mother, rearing her two little daughters with no support that I'm aware of. Trisha has a problem getting the bus fare together to get to school. If she doesn't get to school, she has another problem: We have firm attendance requirements, and when she misses more than five days, the grades she gets in her classes that term automatically drop. So far this term, she's missed four times.

We were discussing this the other day. I wish I could volunteer to pick her up, but apart from the fact that my route to school goes nowhere near her home, school policy discourages the faculty from socializing (or carpooling) with students on the sensible grounds that we could otherwise fall into providing a kind of disorganized taxi service for favored students. Loaning or giving money is equally forbidden, for obvious reasons. So discussing the problem with her (or trying to arrange a ride with another student) is the best I can do.

We had been tossing around various possibilities, none of which seemed immediately practical, when Trisha gathered up her books and said philosophically, "Well, I figure I do the best I can, and hope that's good enough."

I told her the best she could do in the classroom was definitely good enough. She's a very capable student.

"Well, then," she said, "it really doesn't matter what my grade is, does it? I mean, if I'm learning this stuff, I'll have it in my head anyhow. And you never know—maybe I can look after my sister's boy in the afternoon. She sometimes pays me if she has any money." She gave me a broad grin as she walked out of the classroom and added, over her shoulder, "There's always hope."

Dear Lord, look after Trisha today. Her requests are so modest. She isn't complaining because she doesn't have a car; all she's hoping for is some way to get here. Please, Lord, be mindful of this dauntless, determined daughter, and let me remember her in my heart as well. Tomorrow, let there be bus fare.

FEBRUARY 3

Do ye not remember the things which the Lord hath said?—If ye will not harden your hearts, and ask me in faith, believing that ye shall receive, with diligence in keeping my commandments, surely these things shall be made known unto you.

—1 NEPHI 15:11

Nephi is trying to get his stubborn brothers to understand their "visionary" father. They say they don't get it. He asks if they've prayed about it. They say they haven't, because they don't get any answers anyway.

It's easy to say that's just Laman and Lemuel, and they never did get it. What makes me a little nervous is the disturbing half-memory that at one time or another there have been questions I have felt peevishly I really ought to be getting answers to. Is it possible that I, just like Laman and Lemuel, am not getting it? Before I started feeling resentful because I wasn't getting instantaneous responses, did I check out my obedience level to the commandments? Or did I, just like Laman and Lemuel, expect to get answers when I hadn't gone to the trouble of actually asking for them?

The procedure is so simple, as Nephi explains it. First of all, we don't harden our hearts—which I interpret to mean, Don't start out with an attitude. Second, we ask in faith for what we need. If we don't have faith that the Lord answers prayers, why bother in the first place? Third, we make sure our behavior matches up with what we're asking for. After all, if we're estranging ourselves from the Lord by disobeying his commandments, how do we expect him to reach across the gulf we're building?

Three steps. Let's see if today I can remember them and put them into practice. I have a feeling the obedience thing is the one I need to think about.

FEBRUARY 4

I pray for them: I pray not for the world, but for them which thou hast given me; for they are thine.

And all mine are thine, and thine are mine; and I am glorified in them.

And now I am no more in the world, but these are in the world, and I come to thee. Holy Father, keep through thine own name those whom thou hast given me, that they may be one, as we are.

—JOHN 17:9–11

I suppose I must have been exposed to this scripture a good many times (usually focusing on the "that they may be one, as we are" part) before it suddenly came to me what really remarkable reporting it is. Here we are actually able to overhear Jesus Christ talking to our Father in Heaven because John, who was with him there at the time, heard him speak. We are able to see, in a flickering glimpse, the closeness between them and the tenderness with which he gives his disciples into his Father's keeping, now that he will be leaving them to manage on their own.

It is interesting to see that what he seems to be most concerned about is that they may be "one," that divisiveness and bickering not splinter them into disagreement. As long as they can stay together, then the things that each of them remembers that Jesus has taught them can be combined. The truths they learned will remain with the infant church they are establishing. That is exactly what happened, which is one of the reasons why we have the Four Gospels: four separate accounts of the life of Christ, each adding separate details so that we have the richness of the whole.

Can you imagine what it must have been like to be one of the disciples, which is what John calls them here? They were the closest ring of his associates who were now far more than followers. They had become what he called them that night, his friends. Can you imagine sharing that long evening after the feast of the Passover? First of all, there was Jesus' mysterious exchange with Judas Iscariot, which nobody else there understood until much later. Then Judas went out from the group, and the rest of them stayed in the upper room talking as the night wore on. Just think of what it must have been like to be in that quiet group, listening to his voice explaining so simply, so tenderly, the peace and love that suffuses his gospel. Imagine what it must have been like to be told that this magnificent, magnetic teacher that they loved so wholly, who had drawn each of them away from the life each man had had before, was going to be leaving them, but that in his place there would come a Comforter.

That last night, as he explained to them, he spoke to them plainly and without embellishment. And then, in their presence, he prayed to his Father in the same manner, leaving his disciples with the memory of our Lord Jesus Christ communing with his—and our—Father in Heaven simply, lovingly, and openly.

And after that, of course, he went out into the night, to the Garden of Gethsemane.

Today, let me remember that unforgettable night. Let me be grateful that the record of what Christ said that night has been preserved down through the centuries, so that I can read it now, from the pages of the book on my lap. Generations of men and women never knew this wonder at the immediacy of the whole experience, because they could not read or because the book was not available to them.

Dear Lord, let me never, never take it for granted. Today, let me treasure the reality of this worn little book that brings the riches of heaven into my ordinary hands on an otherwise ordinary morning. Today, fill my heart with the truths that were taught that night long ago in Jerusalem.

Today, Lord, I am blessed. Let me know that.

FEBRUARY 5

For my soul delighteth in the song of the heart; yea, the song of the righteous is a prayer unto me, and it shall be answered with a blessing upon their heads.

—DOCTRINE AND COVENANTS 25:12

My mother says my grandmother always used to sing hymns as she moved around the house, doing her ordinary daily routines. Sometimes she hummed them, but most of the time she sang the words, absentmindedly and out of comfortable habit.

I don't remember that. I knew her only when I was a small child, and I remember the things a small child remembers: the pattern of the linoleum on the kitchen floor, and the hiss of the gas fire in the dining room. I remember the good fried chicken she cooked on Sundays for me—every Sunday, when we were visiting—and the warm, familiar smell of her apron when I sat on her lap.

I wish I remembered the hymns. I wonder what my children will remember of me. I know I take some pride (probably a mistake) in knowing the words of many of the familiar hymns we sing at church. Why can't I let those hymns be part of the fabric of my life at home?

Grandma must have had one day, sometime, when she began singing the hymns Mother remembers. Why don't I let today be the day when I pull all those I-learned-them-by-heart words out of my sacrament meeting memory and begin singing at home, too?

FEBRUARY 6

If any of you lack wisdom, let him ask of God, that giveth to all men liberally, and upbraideth not; and it shall be given him. But let him ask in faith, nothing wavering. For he that wavereth is like a wave of the sea driven with the wind and tossed.

—JAMES 1:5–6

We're all familiar with the first verse; it is, after all, the scripture that inspired Joseph Smith to pray in the grove, where he was astonished by the First Vision. Even for purely historical reasons, that makes it memorable.

But I kind of like the second verse to go with it.

I don't know why I should half expect the scriptures to be pedestrian while "improving" to the mind, as opposed to being intrinsically interesting, but obviously at some level I do, because a vivid image like this one of the wave of the sea instantly catches my attention and enchants me. Isn't that just what indecision feels like, "driven with the wind and tossed"?

No wonder James tells us we must ask in unwavering faith. We need to be concentrated on what we are telling our Father in Heaven, and concentrated on listening for his answer. It isn't very often that the Lord shouts in our ears; far more often it is a very still, very small voice, and if we're not listening very, very intently we can miss it entirely and go off lamenting that we always knew nobody was paying attention anyway.

Faith smoothes out the wave of the sea. Faith makes the surface shine, so we can reflect the light we are given. Faith calms the wind of indecision and sets us free.

Today, let me remember that. When I am praying, let me remember that the wind-tossed wave of indecision ultimately crashes on the shore and disintegrates. Let me use faith to make prayer the strong, solid craft the Lord has given us. Let me seek the serenity of faith and in my prayers float tranquilly, gently in the sight of God, listening trustfully for direction.

And know by faith that it will come.

FEBRUARY 7

But will God indeed dwell on the earth? behold, the heaven and heaven of heavens cannot contain thee; how much less this house that I have builded? Yet have thou respect unto the prayer of thy ser-vant, and to his supplication, O Lord my God, to hearken unto the cry and to the prayer, which thy servant prayeth before thee to day.

—1 KINGS 8:27–28

Solomon uttered this prayer in his temple, just after the ark of the covenant had been installed in the most holy place, under the wings of the cherubim.

Why do we as mortal beings want so insistently to know where God is? Every society has had its own version of his whereabouts. For us, it's up there somewhere. I look up in the night sky, on a clear night, trying to guess where, beyond all those stars, heaven could be.

And yet, if we are to believe Solomon, heaven (wherever it is) could not contain the Lord anyway, not even the heaven of heavens. Maybe, when we speculate about the "where" of the Lord, we're coming to terms with his not-here-ness, the separation we agreed to when we came here in the first place.

For me, it gets a little clearer when I try to think about it logically. We talk about the presence of the Lord being with us in our temples, for instance. But does that mean that when I feel the sense of his closeness here, nobody else in the world (no matter how desperately they may be crying out for him) can feel the sense of his closeness there? Of course not; his Spirit can touch us all.

Solomon built the most beautiful temple he was capable of building, and it was one which the Israelites, and their descendants, the Jews, remember down through the centuries until today. In the most sacred heart of it was the Holy of Holies, with the ark containing the tablets of stone that Moses had brought from Horeb, and yet Solomon knew that the Lord his God was not always there in the earthly, ordinary sense of being one place rather than another. God does not indeed dwell permanently on the earth, although we understand from modern revelation that he has visited in person and continues to do so (see Doctrine and Covenants 110:7–8).

So what Solomon asked was realistic and appropriate. He asked only that his prayer in that temple be heard. Prayer transcends geography and the laws of physics. Prayers from anywhere can be heard and answered. It may seem easier to us to pray from our most sacred places, and we can feel our Lord's presence there, but so can our brothers and sisters worshipping all over the world at exactly the same time.

Today, let me remember that. Let me pray with faith, and gratitude, and humility. The Lord doesn't have to be anywhere in particular for me to pray. I don't have to be anywhere in particular for my personal prayers to be heard. I may be limited by time and space while I inhabit this earth, but the Lord is not. Solomon knew that. Let me know it, too.

FEBRUARY 8

Today, in a quiet grove at Valley Forge, there is an heroic-sized monument to Washington. He is depicted not astride a charging horse nor overlooking a battlefield of glory, but kneeling in humble prayer, calling upon the God of Heaven for divine help. To gaze upon the statue prompts the mind to remember the oft-heard expression, "A man never stands taller than when upon his knees."

Men and women of integrity, character, and purpose have ever recognized a power higher than themselves and have sought through prayer to be guided by that power. Such has it ever been. So shall it ever be.

—ELDER THOMAS S. MONSON

In my Interpersonal Skills class at school I teach about ethnocentrism, the skewed perception of members of all societies that leads them to conclude that the way they do things is the right and proper way and that anybody else's way of doing things is a departure from the norm and hence invalid.

Dear Lord, deliver me from the same kind of prejudice about prayer. I may believe that modern revelation has given me a clearer picture of the reality of eternity and God's plan for us, but how can I jump from that belief to a pious sense that somebody else's different prayers don't really count?

My mother says that understanding the gospel is like the three blind men describing the elephant. One is feeling the elephant's trunk; one, the elephant's tail; and the third, the elephant's side. Each man is convinced that the part he is touching expresses the essence of elephant, and each man, therefore, describes it entirely differently. Each description is accurate, but only in describing a part; no one description applies to the elephant as a whole.

We as Latter-day Saints believe that, unlike the blind men, we've been given the gift of revelation to see the whole creature. We may not understand it all, but we can see, in general, how the parts fit together.

But let us remember the most important fact: We are all attempting to describe the same elephant. In our different ways, coming from our different directions, we are drawn to the same Source of truth. Not all the good men or women have the gift of revelation, and some who do take little advantage of it.

Today, let me remember that. Let me appreciate the impulse for devotion. After all, Jesus taught us to love one another. He didn't say, "Love only those who pray the way you do."

FEBRUARY 9

Then were there brought unto him little children, that he should put his hands on them, and pray: and the disciples rebuked them.

But Jesus said, Suffer little children, and forbid them not, to come unto me: for of such is the kingdom of heaven.

And he laid his hands on them, and departed thence.

—MATTHEW 19:13–15

I know something about little children. I've had four of them, and when you have four, you inescapably learn about a lot of others because little children collect other little children and your house and backyard tend to be densely populated for a period of years. Little children are tremendously endearing. They are impishly spontaneous and love with absolute openheartedness. They can make you laugh and bring you to share their complete delight in life. Yet they also do what they feel like doing when they feel like doing it. They wriggle and they shriek and they poke each other and they make strange noises and they are very intolerant of any level of frustration: When frustrated they wail, loudly. More than one of us (particularly after a rough sacrament meeting) has come to the glum conclusion that small children and most kinds of adult religious observance are, for practical purposes, incompatible.

But that's not what Jesus said. He said, "of such is the kingdom of heaven."

Now what in the world could he have meant? We spend years and gain whole headfuls of gray hair teaching our little children to behave differently from how they are sometimes inclined to behave. We even have volumes of instruction (some of it from Church sources) on how this is to be done. We teach patience and self-control and reverence and unselfishness to our little children, who may not have arrived with those qualities.

Jesus knew about little children. He knew about their wholehearted ability to love and accept others. He knew that little children have the sovereign virtue of knowing they need to learn. A little child doesn't brush away attempts at instruction with an impatient, "Yeah, yeah, I know, I know, I know." Little children are like vacuum cleaners, relentlessly scooping up any information that crosses their path. (This unfortunately means, of course, that they retain the negative things that happen with the same tenacity as they retain all the lessons you want them to learn.)

Today let me check on my own teachability index. How often do I set aside something I should pick up (like the *Ensign* or a good book) and choose to leaf through the newspaper or turn on the tube to see what's on instead? How often am I open (really open) to an idea I haven't heard before? How humble am I when I am given a suggestion about different ways I might have handled a situation? Today, Lord, let me learn.

FEBRUARY 10

Wherefore, my beloved brethren, pray unto the Father with all the energy of heart, that ye may be filled with this love, which he hath bestowed upon all who are true followers of his Son, Jesus Christ; that ye may become the sons of God; that when he shall appear we shall be like him, for we shall see him as he is; that we may have this hope; that we may be purified even as he is pure. Amen.

—MORONI 7:48

These words of Mormon were copied down by his son, Moroni, in the bitter last days when Moroni seems to have been somewhat surprised each morning to find that he had not yet perished and so in his hiding place wrote a little more for the benefit of the Lamanites, "my brethren," even though he knew the Lamanites were relentlessly exterminating the Nephites from the face of the earth.

I like that phrase "pray unto the Father with all the energy of heart." To me, that means prayer should be an active process. That tells me that when my prayer is turning into a mumbling recitation that repeats (more or less) what I said last night and the night before that, I need to shake myself awake and start over. (An apology to the Lord for not having done any thinking before I got started would probably be appropriate.)

I like the part after the energy of heart even more: "that ye may be filled with this love, which he hath bestowed upon all who are true followers of his Son, Jesus Christ." To think that my energy of heart in prayer can be—will be—rewarded with the love that Jesus was talking about that night with the eleven apostles who remained, of whom the apostle John wrote in his gospel—what a golden promise!

That love. It's all around us; we just have to reach out to make it ours.

But we do have to reach.

FEBRUARY 11

For thou shalt be his witness unto all men of what thou hast seen and heard.

And now why tarriest thou? arise, and be baptized, and wash away thy sins, calling on the name of the Lord.

—ACTS 22:15–16

What a really amazing man Paul was, and what a fascinating story the book of the Acts of the Apostles has to tell, covering as it does the first thirty-five years of the Church of Jesus Christ. Apart from anything else, it's a wonderful adventure story.

At this point in the book, Paul has returned to Jerusalem (against the advice of many) and gone to the temple. There a crowd of irate Jews dragged him out of the inner court of the temple, open only to Jews, and were about to murder him as an infidel when the Roman soldiers stationed close to the temple were told that Jerusalem was in an uproar and went around to see what was happening. When the troops showed up, the crowd stopped beating Paul and waited to see what was going to happen next.

This scripture comes from the part where Paul is telling the crowd about his conversion on the road to Damascus and how his sight was restored by Ananias, who told him that he, Paul, had been chosen by "the God of our fathers" to be a special witness and then told him not just to hang around but to get started.

How often do I need to be given that advice! It happens over and over. I've been asked to do this, or that, or whatever, and I'll get to it: I just can't do it right now for this reason or that reason, or I have to finish this other thing first—and I comfort myself by saying these problems are the curse of a busy woman.

Today let me remember the words of Ananias to Paul. "And now why tarriest thou?" If I have too much to do to take on the job, let me say so (which might indicate it's time for a priority check); if I'm going to do it, let me get started and do it. Paul didn't dally; neither should I.

FEBRUARY 12

Pray always, and I will pour out my Spirit upon you, and great shall be your blessing—yea, even more than if you should obtain treasures of earth and corruptibleness to the extent thereof.

—DOCTRINE AND COVENANTS 19:38

The promise was given to Martin Harris originally, but like most scriptural counseling directed to one individual, it applies to the rest of us as well.

What would we want as a blessing? From the amount of time we spend talking about them and figuring out how to acquire them and comparing them, you could easily jump to the conclusion that material objects would come very high on the list. And yet it doesn't take an Einstein to figure out that many of the people who have every material object imaginable do not have particularly happy lives. Maybe they're just naturally petulant, but maybe it's more cheering to *believe* your life would be satisfactory if you just had a really nice car or brand-new living room furniture than it is to *get* the car and the furniture and discover you still have problems.

The Lord is not talking about cars or furniture here. The promise is made for the blessings of the spirit, incorruptible and eternal. Those are the blessings that will last and get better and better. The fancy new car of today will be the unreliable junker ten years from now; furniture styles, like everything else, change and look a bit out of date a few years down the road (and something always gets spilled on the upholstery anyway). The blessings of the Spirit—qualities such as wisdom, and testimony, and benevolence—grow deeper and more resonant as time goes by.

"Pray always, and I will pour out my Spirit upon you." How minimal the investment; how magnificent the return.

FEBRUARY 13

*And when ye stand praying, forgive, if ye have ought against any:
that your Father also which is in heaven may forgive you your trespasses. But if ye do not forgive, neither will your Father which is in
heaven forgive your trespasses.*

—MARK 11:25–26

J esus gave us more than the Lord's Prayer to teach us about
how to pray: He also was very clear about what wasn't appropriate. This one seems obvious. How can you possibly open your heart
to pray—especially to ask for forgiveness—if you are unforgiving
yourself?

Well (looking into my own heart), I guess it could happen
when we're not thinking about it being forgiveness, precisely.
Maybe we're thinking about it more in terms of "He's just a jerk."

Okay, why do you say he's a jerk?

Well, it still makes me mad the way he talked to my daughter
that time. I'm sure he thought he was justified, and I'm sure he was
doing what he thought was best, but . . .

Gotcha.

Have I always been tactful and kind and benevolent myself?

No, probably not.

Do I hope—no, *expect* is closer to it—to be forgiven when I
speak sharply?

I thought so.

So today should I get down on my knees and ask for help in letting go of my grudge before I start asking the Lord to persuade anybody else to let go of theirs?

Yes, I think so, too.

FEBRUARY 14

Ye have heard that it hath been said, Thou shalt love thy neighbour, and hate thine enemy. But I say unto you, Love your enemies, bless them that curse you, do good to them that hate you, and pray for them which despitefully use you, and persecute you; that ye may be the children of your Father which is in heaven: for he maketh his sun to rise on the evil and on the good, and sendeth rain on the just and on the unjust.

—MATTHEW 5:43–45

A Valentine's Day message, full of love.

This is one of the clearest statements in the New Testament of what we need to do to reach perfection. Here, it is defined. We are to follow the pattern set by the Lord, who loves all his children and treats them all impartially: His sun rises on us all and his rain falls with equal force, whoever we might be.

If we hope to reach the perfection that he embodies, we have to walk by the same path. We have to love all of our brothers and sisters in our Father's family, the people who are easy to love and the people from whom we almost involuntarily draw back. We not only have to love them, we have to pray for their welfare. We can't mutter disapprovingly and turn away, even if they may have done evil that directly affects us. This is where we decide whether to follow the law of Moses—an eye for an eye—or the fulfilled law of Christ—love one another.

Those other people may not obey the commandments. Whether they do or not is the concern of our Father in Heaven. The commandment for us is to love them, to bless them, to do good to them, and to pray for them regardless of what they do. The more we recoil, the more we need to recognize that by that action we are standing up and being counted—but on whose side?

I find my mind operates on two tracks here. I have been taught that this is the principle Heavenly Father wants us to follow. That's one track. But on the other, I hear counsel every day to watch out for strangers and to guard myself against associating with the wrong kinds of people. When somebody has violated my trust or been unkind to me, I'm bound to think of the old maxim "once bitten, twice shy," and I know that advice makes sense, too. It just isn't what Christ is saying here.

Jesus is preaching perfection. I can't believe that Jesus was advocating sending little children into danger, but I don't think the possibility of somebody like you or me exposing ourselves to hazards by following his teaching worried him as much as it worries us. For us, as hard as we try to think beyond it, the here-and-now is the significant dimension; for Christ, it is eternity. He gave his own life for us; most of his closest followers were martyred. As he died, he asked for forgiveness for his tormentors. I don't think his most important objective is that all of us lead long and pleasant, untroubled lives.

I think here he's thinking more about all mankind being part of the community of his Father's children; all of them loved. Some of them may seem unfamiliar to us, or strange, or dangerous, but the Lord knows them all. The closer we approach our Lord, the more we have to forget ourselves and reach out to all of his children. When we wall ourselves off from our brothers and sisters, we create a barrier between ourselves and him.

This Valentine's Day, let me try the path of reaching out in love. I may not have to start by fellowshipping down at the local jail (although that wouldn't necessarily be a bad idea), but I can certainly reach out past my familiar, comfortable orbit. Children I don't know are spending long hours in hospitals, and lonely old people are in rest homes. I can't save the world, but I can bake Valentine cookies. I can choose to give some of my carefully hoarded time.

The Lord loves us all; let us all begin to love each other as our way of becoming like him. Today, surrounded by red paper hearts and lace, we can take the baby steps. Today, we can start.

FEBRUARY 15

And it came to pass that so great were their afflictions that they began to cry mightily to God.

And Amulon commanded them that they should stop their cries; and he put guards over them to watch them, that whosoever should be found calling upon God should be put to death.

And Alma and his people did not raise their voices to the Lord their God, but did pour out their hearts to him; and he did know the thoughts of their hearts.

—MOSIAH 24:10–12

The Lord can reach us, wherever we are.

There are many occasions and places for prayers. I have certainly prayed in cars. I have prayed in the bathroom, often. I have prayed in airplanes, continuously. I am sure there have been prayers in far stranger locations.

I still think that, all other things being equal, praying humbly on my knees is best. Sometimes when I have been correcting papers late at night sitting up in bed, the temptation simply to murmur a token prayer right where I am and then roll under the covers is almost overwhelming. What usually stops me is the mental picture of me trying to explain to the Lord that this is really an important prayer and I do need the blessings I am about to ask for, but if it's all the same to him, I'll just stay here warm and comfortable in bed while I do the asking.

It doesn't sound convincing to me.

Sheer laziness is one thing. The desperate state of Alma and his men is something else entirely. If we ask, the Lord can be with us anywhere. He knows our needs; he knows our sufferings. His comfort can wrap around us wherever we might be. He doesn't need the words to understand us. The Lord can hear our hearts.

Today, let me tuck that away to reassure me. Let me know that when I need him, his presence will always be with me—but let me be humble enough tonight to kneel.

FEBRUARY 16

The Lord cannot always be known by the thunder of His voice, by the display of His glory or by the manifestation of His power; and those that are the most anxious to see these things, are the least prepared to meet them, and were the Lord to manifest His powers as He did to the children of Israel, such characters would be the first to say, "Let not the Lord speak any more, lest we His people die."

—JOSEPH SMITH

I remember one night years ago when for some reason I had been thinking long and hard about Joseph Smith as a boy and the heavenly visitations. Suddenly, lying in my bed, I thought, "What if I open my eyes and see an angel standing at the foot of my bed?"

What happened next was very instructive. I was absolutely terrified. I went cold all over, my heart pounded, and I didn't dare move. My first panicked reaction was to squeeze my eyes tightly shut and leave them that way, but eventually, my pulse crashing in my ears, I opened them a crack and peeked. Of course, nothing was there. But I will always remember the overwhelming sense of my unworthiness to be in the presence of any manifestation from heaven. For once I knew exactly what the "fear of God" meant for me.

When I read this statement from Joseph Smith, all I could say was "Oh, yes." How was he brave enough himself? He was so young, just a boy—so young to withstand the forces of evil that swept over him, so young to face the majesty of his heavenly vision. How could he bear it?

Well, of course, he was young and innocent, and full of faith, and he had found the scripture with its promise: "If any of you lack wisdom, let him ask of God." So with a child's directness, and a child's trust, he did.

No, I'm not waiting for my own experience of the glory of God or the thunder of his voice right here and now, thank you. I've got a good deal of preparation to put in before I would be worthy to receive one little heavenly squib, if there is such a thing. Let me therefore use my reluctance as a measure of my unworthiness, and set about correcting it.

Once that terrifying magnificence was home to me. Let me try today to live so that it will be again.

FEBRUARY 17

Remember that without faith you can do nothing; therefore ask in faith. Trifle not with these things; do not ask for that which you ought not.

—DOCTRINE AND COVENANTS 8:10

Here we are again, back pondering the interrelationship of faith and prayer. The two seem interlocked, wound around and through each other. Without the foundation of faith, prayer is simply words. Without prayer, we lose a primary way of expressing faith.

This revelation was addressed to Oliver Cowdery in 1829 when he was serving as a scribe for Joseph Smith during the translation of the Book of Mormon. At that time Oliver was a stalwart servant of the Lord, a good man, a man of faith. As time went on, it seems to me that he developed an unfortunate failing: He was not content to do only the assignments given by the Lord to Oliver Cowdery. He wanted to do the assignments given to Joseph Smith, too.

If so, he was not the first to hanker after what looked like greater glory, and he was certainly not the last. How many of us are privately convinced that we could run the wards and stakes of Zion (or at least corners of them) better than the people who are running them now? And there are always those who long for the prestige of a lofty position but never consider the weight of the responsibility.

Is that what the Lord foresaw in the part of this verse that says "do not ask for that which you ought not"? I suppose only the Lord and Oliver Cowdery (and possibly Joseph Smith) know. One instruction I take from this revelation is that we need to use all our powers of faith to understand what we should pray for. We should ask honestly and humbly and be prepared for the answers we are given rather than becoming discouraged or sulky when the answer we expect isn't forthcoming.

Let me remember always to ask in faith. Let me also remember the admonition "do not ask for that which you ought not." And while I'm at it, let me not worry about praying for extra responsibilities until I'm fulfilling those I have with evenness of temper and perfection of execution. That will keep me busy enough for the foreseeable future.

FEBRUARY 18

The Lord is far from the wicked: but he heareth the prayer of the righteous.

—PROVERBS 15:29

I t isn't so much that the Lord removes himself far from the wicked as that the wicked distance themselves from the Lord.

I don't think we really appreciate how much power we have over our own closeness to the Lord. When we feel alone and distant, it isn't usually because the Lord has gone anywhere: We have. We have become too busy to seek him out in prayer honestly and reverently. (What generally happens is that we fall back to "saying our prayers," in the sense of running through familiar words with a minimum of thought.) Or maybe we've let small disobediences add up in the way that small bricks add up to a wall. Or maybe it's a major disobedience. Whatever it is, it gets in the way.

Can't the Lord reach through the obstacle to us? Well, of course he can, and if it's necessary for a greater good, he will. We know he has. Think of Jonah being summoned back to fill his mission to Nineveh by a wholly unique method of transportation. Think of Zacharias, the father of John the Baptist, who had to be struck dumb before he would believe the angel's announcement of his son's impending birth. Think of Saul being intercepted on the road to Damascus. But for most of us, it would defeat the whole purpose of our earthly probation if the Lord were to routinely override our choices. If we choose to distance ourselves, distant we will be.

Lord, help me be aware of any wall that I'm building, and guide me in its demolition. Bless me with discernment. Bless me with the impulse of righteousness. Let me stay near to thee; let my prayer be heard.

FEBRUARY 19

With my soul have I desired thee in the night; yea, with my spirit within me will I seek thee early: for when thy judgments are in the earth, the inhabitants of the world will learn righteousness.

—ISAIAH 26:9

No wonder Handel built his magnificent *Messiah* with so many chunks of Isaiah! The vividness of his phrases leaps across the centuries to me.

"With my soul have I desired thee in the night." Yes; that's exactly what it feels like. For me, it happens most often when I am at a point of decision, or anguishing over a problem, and I am wakeful and wander through the quiet house in the middle of a winter night. Everyone else is asleep; I can hear the squeak of bedsprings, the rustle of bedclothes as they move, the evenness of their breathing.

In the stillness of the night, I am alone. It's then that I desire most for the Lord to be with me, to help me. What a wonderful blessing prayer is at times like that; what an enticing foretaste of coming home.

Let me remember that feeling in the full light of day, when my family and the rhythm of our common life are surging around me. "Yea, with my spirit within me will I seek thee early." Daytime prayers are different from those heartfelt prayers in the deep peace of the night. Still, there is a sturdy reality and practicality to prayers when the cold winter morning light has dawned again.

Today, let me remember I need both.

FEBRUARY 20

And when thou prayest, thou shalt not be as the hypocrites are: for they love to pray standing in the synagogues and in the corners of the streets, that they may be seen of men. Verily I say unto you, They have their reward.

But thou, when thou prayest, enter into thy closet, and when thou hast shut thy door, pray to thy Father which is in secret; and thy Father which seeth in secret shall reward thee openly.

—MATTHEW 6:5–6

It's really very fair: If we're parading our religious observances so that everybody can see what fine people we are, then we get what we want. Everybody does see what fine people we are. We have our reward, and a very appropriate one at that. Because our primary motivation for prayer had little to do with communication with our Father in Heaven, whether the prayer communicated anything doesn't matter.

On the other hand, if what we want to do in prayer is talk with our Father in Heaven and listen for his guidance, then whether anybody else knows we are praying is supremely unimportant. It has nothing to do with them. We can do as Jesus suggests here and retire into the innermost room of our house and shut the door and pray in absolute privacy, and nobody will know about it. We will be rewarded, too—rewarded by the Lord.

Which would you choose?

It sounds obvious, but I think it's easier to get caught here than it would seem. Having lived all my life on the geographic outskirts of the Church, I am always aware of being an example of what I believe, because some people's whole personal experience of The Church of Jesus Christ of Latter-day Saints might be simply what they have observed of my behavior. If I am faithful to my religion in public, am I like the hypocrites Jesus was talking about?

It all turns on the question of motivation. If I'm trying to be a good person and live as the gospel teaches me to live, and other people happen to observe me doing it and become interested in the gospel as a consequence, that's one thing. If, on the other hand, I'm trying to be a good person so that other people will see what a good person I am and thus become interested in the gospel, I'm on a very slippery slope. The honesty of my relationship with my Heavenly

Father has to be the primary element, way ahead of missionary labors.

After all, there's not much point in converting anybody to what would amount to an empty shell. My mother always said that the law of Moses as recorded in the Old Testament taught us to do the right things; in the New Testament, Jesus and his disciples teach us to do the right things for the right reasons.

Today let me remember my mother's words. Let me be very sure that my behavior (religious and otherwise) is not calculated with an eye on who's watching. I know the Lord is; let that be enough for me.

FEBRUARY 21

Watch ye therefore, and pray always, that ye may be accounted worthy to escape all these things that shall come to pass, and to stand before the Son of man.

—LUKE 21:36

Jesus was teaching in the temple, as the days of his mortal ministry drew to a close.

The chief priests and the scribes, whose livelihood depended on the order of things as they were, were already gathering privately to discuss what to do about this charismatic teacher who spoke so wisely and held the hearts of the people. And Jesus, knowing what was to come, tried to prepare his disciples. When they spoke of the beauty of the temple in which they sat, Jesus warned them that Jerusalem and the temple were to be destroyed: "There shall not be left one stone upon another, that shall not be thrown down." (As, in fact, happened in A.D. 70, well within the lifetime of many of those to whom he was speaking, when the Roman emperor Titus ordered that the city be destroyed.)

So this passage of scripture is in one sense very precisely directed to the people to whom he was speaking. Jesus warned them of something specific that was going to happen, and it did happen. That's over. But that isn't all Jesus told them. He also told them about the great disasters that would precede his second coming and that those events were not going to happen "by and by." At the time the King James Translation was being written, that English phrase meant "immediately," not "sometime in the indefinite future," as it does now.

So that prophecy concerns us, and so does this scripture.

We are warned over and over again, but here we are warned specifically to watch and be ready. Don't get careless, don't get so wrapped up in our ordinary affairs that we're not paying attention. Be prepared. Watch and be prayerful so that when the Son of Man returns in his glory, we are fit to be in his presence. (And from everything we've been told, nobody will have to tell us if we are unworthy: If we are, we'll know, and wild horses couldn't drag us near him. I personally suspect that's what they mean by hellfire and damnation—a burning sense of shame and fear and the hopelessness of escape.)

Today, let me pray and work on being ready. It seems unlikely that anything much (except maybe a snow shower) will happen on this gray, wintry day, but we have been warned that the Second Coming will be unexpected. Whenever it happens, let my hands be busy, my heart prayerful, and my daily life unfolding as he taught us then and his prophets teach us now.

That's plenty to go on.

FEBRUARY 22

Let us teach our children to pray for courage, for opportunity, for comfort, for peace, for understanding, and not for material gifts. Let us teach them to pray, "Thy will be done in earth, as it is in heaven." (Matt. 6:10) . . .

I can think of no greater teaching to our children than that of the power of prayer. We should do it by example, and take our children daily before the Lord and give them the peace and assurance that can come from knowing they are a child of our Father in Heaven.

—ELDER L. TOM PERRY

Little children, little children—they are so eager to learn! They come to us so ready to follow instructions, to copy what they see us doing, to try to please us. Some of them come to families that teach them to pray, to look for the presence of their Heavenly Father in their lives, to begin the lifelong task of building a testimony. Some of them come to families where those things are not considered important, and gradually the child's own impulse to seek after those things dwindles and dies away.

How well am I teaching my own children? I look around at them, all old enough now to be making many of their own decisions, and it's so hard to tell how they're doing. I can see what happens in the way of outward observance, but what goes on in their hearts? In our last testimony meeting, one of my dearest friends went up to the stand with her five-year-old daughter, Emma, so that Emma could bear her testimony. At first Emma kept leaning toward her mother for each phrase, but after about two or three, her mother whispered for a moment in her ear. Emma gave her mother a long dubious look and then turned back to the microphone. She took a very deep, very audible breath and then all by herself gave the kind of testimony that Elder Perry speaks of here: talking about the real blessings she has been given, not the things with which, as a middle-class child in the abundance of America, she is endowed.

Have I taught as well? I hope so. I wish I could just hand to each of them, like a present, the richness of the gospel that I have learned over the years. I wish I could let them feel the resonance and comfort it has provided for me in hard times and the guide and strength it is to me throughout every ordinary day. Unfortunately, that knowledge can't be distributed like apples in a basket or cookies on a plate. Each person has to develop a testimony in his or her own way, finding our own faith. The most we parents can do is offer our children the example of our lives and the reassurance of the reality of what we teach them.

Today, let me go on teaching. Dear Heavenly Father, bless me, too, with courage to persist when they are being adolescent and negative; bless me with opportunity. And bless me that I won't be too tired or too distracted to notice when I have one. Bless me with comfort, and with peace, and with understanding. Above all, bless me with the words to explain to them why these blessings are so important, and the strength to demonstrate them in my ordinary, everyday behavior that shouts more loudly to my children than words will ever do.

Dear Lord, help me to be good.

FEBRUARY 23

And this is not all. Do ye not suppose that I know of these things myself? Behold, I testify unto you that I do know that these things whereof I have spoken are true. And how do ye suppose that I know of their surety?

Behold, I say unto you they are made known unto me by the Holy Spirit of God. Behold, I have fasted and prayed many days that I might know these things of myself. And now I do know of myself that they are true; for the Lord God hath made them manifest unto me by his Holy Spirit; and this is the spirit of revelation which is in me.

—ALMA 5:45–46

The strong words of Alma ring down through the centuries to us as well as to the people of Zarahemla to whom he was speaking then.

Let us listen to his testimony about fasting and prayer. Why does fasting work? Maybe because it's a constant reminder, our mortal bodies being focused on food as much as they are. When our stomachs remind us that it's time to eat, we remember what we want our minds to be concentrating on. Maybe fasting works because it puts our daily routine to one side—all the fuss and labor involved in preparing meals—and lets us use that freedom to approach our Heavenly Father in prayer.

We know for sure that the combination of fasting and prayer does work. It is how prophets and ordinary people have been able to heighten their spiritual awareness over the centuries. It has been a spiritual exercise for those seeking the truth all over the world, all through recorded time.

Alma was a spiritual giant by any description. Let us who would have the strength of his testimony learn from the way that he gained it. Let us each be able to say as firmly and confidently as he did, "I do know that these things whereof I have spoken are true." The knowledge, after all, is available to all of us.

FEBRUARY 24

In thee, O Lord, do I put my trust; let me never be ashamed: deliver me in thy righteousness. Bow down thine ear to me; deliver me speedily: be thou my strong rock, for an house of defence to save me.

—PSALM 31:1–2

What a wonderful expression of the cry of the righteous facing trouble and iniquity! The whole psalm sings of the power of the Lord Jehovah and of the psalmist's simple and unswerving belief that the moral values of life will be upheld; that the wicked will be punished and the righteous rewarded.

I love the vivid pictures it creates so swiftly: "bow down thine ear to me," "be thou my strong rock, for an house of defence." The poetry of the Psalms makes me see, and the pictures embed the truths deeper into my heart.

Let me also approach the Lord with this trusting simplicity. It is so easy to make everything too complicated, to hedge with "generally" this and "in most cases" that. Today, let me see my relationship with the Lord clearly and plainly. Let me, too, see the Lord as my loving father, bending down to listen to me when I am troubled, wrapping his comfort around me like a house built of stones.

I have grown up. I can no longer be a child anywhere except here, when I approach the Lord humbly and ask for his protection. Today, let me be his child. Today, let me lean against the strength of the Lord.

FEBRUARY 25

And again, the Lord shall utter his voice out of heaven, saying: Hearken, O ye nations of the earth, and hear the words of that God who made you. O, ye nations of the earth, how often would I have gathered you together as a hen gathereth her chickens under her wings, but ye would not!

—DOCTRINE AND COVENANTS 43:23–24

If we sometimes yearn to be gathered up by our Father in Heaven, does he sometimes yearn to gather us? Certainly I understand the longing expressed in these verses. Aren't there times when I wish I could gather up my own children, when they are being stubborn and insistent on trying their own wings? It's worst when something has gone wrong, and they are torn between the temptation to return to home and comfort and the determination to handle things—whatever the things might be—on their own.

The big difference is that here, on this earth, my children must move out, free of their father and me, and take responsibility for their own lives. Maybe the same thing will eventually be true of us as the spiritual children of our Father in Heaven, but for the time being, true maturity for us consists of acknowledging our need for him and strengthening the relationship between us, instead of trying to move past it.

What a difficult concept that seems to be! All around us we can see men and women carefully constructing elaborate explanations that deny the existence of God altogether. Like children determined to prove they are not afraid, they shout bravely into the dark. The pity of it is that they are so busy shouting they can't see that the strength they are so eager to prove has its roots in the strength of the Lord and that only by recognizing those roots can they tap into the strength that will ultimately save them.

Today, let me make sure that I am not so busy trying to stand on my own two feet that I don't have any attention left to notice that the Lord is trying to draw me to him. Let me relax under his protection and feel the softness of his wing.

FEBRUARY 26

These things have I written unto you that believe on the name of the Son of God; that ye may know that ye have eternal life, and that ye may believe on the name of the Son of God. And this is the confidence that we have in him, that, if we ask any thing according to his will, he heareth us.

—1 JOHN 5:13–14

A letter from the apostle John. Like his gospel, this epistle is alive with the consciousness of God's love.

Here John is assuring his new Christian converts—and over the centuries, past them, assuring us—that those of us who believe in Christ can have faith in the greatest miracle of them all: that we, like Christ, can lay down our bodies in death with the certain knowledge that we will rise again and, if we are worthy, live with him.

We may get so used to that idea that we don't appreciate the wonder of it. Death, whether we choose to acknowledge it or not, is an inescapable part of life here on earth. From the moment we draw our first breath, each one of us is irretrievably committed to drawing a last breath.

We don't like thinking about that very much. Living as we do in a society incomparably endowed with medical skills and techniques, surrounded by sophisticated safety devices designed to protect us when we work and when we play, we sometimes have the feeling that death is an outrage, a mistake, an avoidable error that we must be able to blame on someone. Our brothers and sisters living in the long centuries before us recognized more easily than we seem to do that death is inevitable, whether it is unexpected or approaches with a slow and deliberate tread.

Christ freed us from the overwhelming finality of death. That was the great and triumphant message that the early Christians had to offer to the world. We will die, yes, but we will live again. And because of this eternal dimension to life, we have eternal access to Christ. He may no longer be on earth where we can see him, and listen to him, but he is not gone.

Imagine the power of that message to those early Christian colonies. Imagine the power for us, here and now.

Today, let me feel the wonder. Let me think, when I kneel to pray, that I can pray in the name of Christ because he lives, because he triumphed over death. He is still there.

And because he is, I can be, too.

FEBRUARY 27

In my distress I cried unto the Lord, and he heard me.

—PSALM 120:1

When we are scared, we all pray.

Well, maybe not all of us. I had a friend, years ago, who claimed he was a confirmed atheist. I have to say that in terms of ordinary behavior Paul was one of the nicest people I have ever met;

he certainly went out of his way to do things for others. But that, he said, was simply because life functioned better if people were considerate.

"Why should we have to believe some sugar daddy is going to reward us if we're socially responsible?" he asked.

I tried to explain that that wasn't exactly it, but Paul was one of those people who makes me feel tongue-tied and as if I don't quite get the point when I attempt to disagree. He seemed to have everything together; it seemed in a way presumptuous to tell him I thought he had a big empty place in the center.

We worked together well. We were not buddies, but we had a pleasant working relationship. When I was expecting my first daughter, Paul's reaction was interesting. He was pleased that I was pleased, but his own reaction was guarded.

One day Paul suddenly asked me, "Doesn't it ever worry you to think you're bringing a defenseless child into a frightening world?"

His question surprised me, and I guess I showed it. I sort of stammered for a moment, and then I found myself saying something to the effect that I had never really worried about that, because I felt all of us would be given the strength to meet whatever we had to meet and I didn't really feel the world was all that frightening, if you had faith.

Paul laughed. "Oh, yes," he said. "The sugar daddy."

Which sort of put an end to that conversation. After that, I didn't happen to work directly with Paul much, and then I left work to have the baby. After that I worked only on an occasional basis, and we didn't run into each other all that frequently.

The last time I saw Paul his head was badly bruised, and he had his left arm in a cast. I asked him what on earth had happened, and he said that he had been in an accident: A drunk driver had crossed over the white line. He said that he was really lucky—he could very easily have been killed. "And do you know what's really funny?" he asked me. "You'll appreciate this one. I could see the guy veer over, and there was nowhere for me to go—there were parked cars all along the side of the road—and as he came toward me, I was practically standing on the brake, and would you believe I was praying? I actually heard myself saying, 'Dear God, save me.'"

I looked back at him, straight in the eye, and said, "Oh, Paul, I'm so glad he did!"

He sort of laughed and shook his head a little and then moved on.

Maybe we all do pray, when we're scared.

FEBRUARY 28

Then shall ye call upon me, and ye shall go and pray unto me, and I will hearken unto you. And ye shall seek me, and find me, when ye shall search for me with all your heart.

—JEREMIAH 29:12–13

This passage is part of the letter sent to those Israelites that the Babylonian king Nebuchadnezzar had carried away from Jerusalem into captivity in Babylon. It was written by the prophet Jeremiah, who was still among those in Jerusalem. The remaining two tribes of the house of Israel (the ten others had been captured by the Assyrians about a hundred years before) had fallen into idol worship and immorality, and Jeremiah was called to warn them of the inescapable consequences of their actions. Because few of us then or now relish having our errors pointed out to us, Jeremiah led a hard and lonely life.

But his message here from the Lord to the captives is a tender one. Jeremiah conveys the Lord's promise to those carried away to Babylon that their captivity will last only seventy years. After that, they will be brought home, and "then shall ye call upon me, and ye shall go and pray unto me, and I will hearken unto you."

It is a glimmer of hope in a dark time. What the Lord is telling his children then is what he tells us all down through history. We may have to bear the consequences of our actions, but for those who turn to him "with all your heart," he is still there. He is always there.

Let me remember that when I feel distance starting to creep into my relationship with my Heavenly Father. I hope my problem isn't idolatry (unless idolatry is interpreted as getting too wrapped up in the importance of business and objects that surround me, in which case I guess from time to time it may be), but there are dozens of other little ways in which I distance myself. There are things I think I need to get on a Sunday, even though I know I should stay out of the stores. (How regularly can an ox be in the mire?) There are times when I say my prayers at night absentmindedly, because I'm still cross with one of the children and that's where my attention really is. I've knelt down irritably, and I'm still grumbling when I get up. There are certainly times when I am obedient to the letter of a law, but not precisely to the spirit, and I try to fool myself and the Lord by deciding it doesn't matter.

Let me catch myself. Let me remember the words of Jeremiah; let me search for my Father in Heaven with all my heart, knowing absolutely that then I will find him.

I have his promise.

FEBRUARY 29

And it came to pass, that, as he was praying in a certain place, when he ceased, one of his disciples said unto him, Lord, teach us to pray, as John also taught his disciples.

And he said unto them, When ye pray, say, Our Father which art in heaven, Hallowed be thy name. Thy kingdom come. Thy will be done, as in heaven, so in earth.

—LUKE 11:1–2

A bonus day to this short winter month, a bonus chance to finish as we began, with the Lord's Prayer.

I think what strikes me today when I look at the familiar words is the beginning: "Our Father." Not, you notice, "My Father," although he obviously is—and Jesus Christ of all people would be the most entitled to address him that way.

"Our Father." Each of us has a personal relationship with our Father, but we are also gathered together within the fellowship of the Church. That includes people of every conceivable shade of skin color; it includes the well-tailored gentlemen and their wives wrapped in fur as well as the families who arrive on the bus, whose children's clothes don't quite fit. It includes all of us from the time of Jesus himself forward: the early communities who had to come to terms with the issue of how Jewish Christianity was going to be; all the honest souls grappling through the darkness of apostasy who nevertheless managed to preserve the fragmented manuscripts of the scriptures for us, and some of whom were inspired to the magnificent eloquence of the King James translation; the frontier American Christians who met in the revival tents of the local and traveling ministers and spurred a young boy in upstate New York to pray for direction; and all the others in between. Whether we always think about it or not, we all belong together in one triumphant procession.

I am part of them, and they are part of me. If at times as brothers and sisters in the present-day Church we get on each other's nerves, we are just like a family. We can—and do—demonstrate the other things that happen in families: the love shown when somebody spontaneously offers to share an assignment, the support expressed in the familiar and comforting casserole brought to a family having difficulties or a new baby, and the understanding soul who puts an arm around our shoulder when we need it most.

Our Father, let me be grateful today, as this month slips away, for all the blessings I have. Let me be grateful for the warmth of community. Let me be grateful for prayer, for my knowledge of thy presence. Let me take my place in the Church family with thanksgiving and humility.

Thy will be done, O Father. As in heaven, so on earth.

MARCH

If ye love me, keep my commandments.

—John 14:15

MARCH 1

O, remember, my son, and learn wisdom in thy youth; yea, learn
in thy youth to keep the commandments of God.

—ALMA 37:35

Mable is a student at the business school where I teach. She is having a terrible time learning to type with any kind of speed. She does quite well in her other classes, but she finds keyboarding very frustrating. I had seen Mable around school but never in one of my own classes. When she was first assigned to me and we had a chance to talk, I was astonished to discover that one of the other students at school—a woman with whom I had become acquainted and who had adolescent children of her own—was her daughter.

I still can't quite believe it—Mable doesn't look anywhere near that old—but in light of that information, we've had a couple of discussions about how much harder it is to learn a physical skill when you're older than it is when you're young. It's like riding a bicycle; kids pick it up in no time, but I dread to think what it would be like if I had to start out to learn to ride a bike now.

Maybe the same thing is true of picking up some spiritual skills. It's not that you can't do it later on; it's just that it's a whole lot easier to do it when you're young and flexible and open to instruction. There are so many habits that we work hard to teach our children when they're small: practical hygiene such as tooth brushing and hand washing, basic safety rules such as looking both ways before crossing a street and being wary of strangers, elementary spiritual exercises such as going to church on Sunday and remembering to say your prayers. Isn't it also easier to learn to obey the other commandments of God at roughly the same time?

Obviously, when we're young and impressionable we might not understand all the ramifications, or appreciate the power and the promises, but how much less complicated life will be if we don't have to go through adolescence and early adulthood making daily choices about such principles as tithing and the Word of Wisdom. The pattern is there; the decisions are already made.

Perhaps that's the telling detail: "The decisions are made." I think it's fascinating how Alma phrases it as he speaks to his son, Helaman. As a young man, Helaman is responsible to learn wisdom in his youth, to learn at that time to keep the commandments of God. Nobody else can decide to do that for him. In other words, Alma, as the parent, is not compromising Helaman's agency in any way. He's just offering him heartfelt advice on how to use it.

We may not be in the first flush of youth, but each of us is younger today than we will be tomorrow. Might Alma's counsel apply to us as well? Will some principles and commandments be easier to learn and obey today than they will be tomorrow or in the chain of tomorrows stretching into the future? It may not be exactly like learning to type (or ride a bicycle), but perhaps some of the same principles apply.

Youth, after all, can be a relative concept. Think of Mable.

MARCH 2

Ye shall observe to do therefore as the Lord your God hath commanded you: ye shall not turn aside to the right hand or to the left. Ye shall walk in all the ways which the Lord your God hath commanded you, that ye may live, and that it may be well with you, and that ye may prolong your days in the land which ye shall possess.

—DEUTERONOMY 5:32–33

Snow again. It occurs to me, out here sweeping the path clear one more time (it's a light snow, a late snow) that Moses, speaking here to the children of Israel in the last days in the wilderness, knew a lot about many things but he probably didn't experience snow in March, when even people who like snow, like me, are beginning to get a bit fed up with it.

But I find myself thinking about some of what he had to say, as the broom swishes back and forth. There are ways in which sweeping the path is like obedience. It's a lot easier when you don't turn to the right hand or to the left. When I stay on the path, I just work on the path. When I get off to the side, not remembering to follow the bend in the middle or not noticing I'm going over the bump of accumulated snow along the edge, I find myself absentmindedly sweeping away at tufts of grass. It's harder and completely unproductive. Who needs the lawn clear?

The ease of obedience: I think that's the hardest part for me to really trust in, day after day. Life is so much easier when I am obedient to the commandments. I know that, in theory and from past experience. I have so much more freedom; so many more alternatives are available. So why should bending the commandments so often feel like the faster, more expeditious route?

Oh, Satan, you are a most persuasive fellow. You've had centuries of practice in twisting things so cleverly we might not even notice. As C. S. Lewis has his master tempter say in his wickedly funny *Screwtape Letters*, "Indeed, the safest road to Hell is the gradual one—the gentle slope, soft underfoot, without sudden turnings, without milestones, without signposts."

Get thee behind me, Satan. The path is done, neatly, properly, turning not to the right or to the left.

MARCH 3

Casting down imaginations, and every high thing that exalteth itself against the knowledge of God, and bringing into captivity every thought to the obedience of Christ.

—2 CORINTHIANS 10:5

A scrap—more of a scrap than most other scriptures, because this one isn't even a full sentence—but I find my mind playing around with the idea Paul is giving us. He was writing to the Corinthians, who were temporarily misled by some of the so-called Judaizers who believed that Christianity had to be channeled within the traditional observance of Jewish law. But I think what he is saying applies far more generally than that. I have a friend from many years back who has spent more time thinking about the gospel than practically anyone else I know, and who has now, apparently, chosen to follow her "imaginations" rather than obey the authorities of the Church. She is a good person—or at least she was, and I have no reason to believe she is not still. What has happened has grieved and troubled me; these words of Paul are the first to offer me an explanation of what may have gone wrong.

"The glory of God is intelligence" (D&C 93:36). But intelligence is not wisdom. Neither is it a strong, stolid thing like an ox, which once yoked does what it's told. Intelligence is a gossamer, will-o'-the-wisp inheritance that slips through your fingers as soon as you try to define it. Like fire, it can be applied to good or evil (or most of the way stations in between). The early Christian Saints, like Paul himself, were unquestionably brilliant men. There have been brilliant mass murderers, too. The intelligence itself, at least as we usually define that term, isn't in itself decisive.

What I think makes intelligence a glory to God is when it is firmly linked with obedience—Paul here calls it "bringing into captivity every thought to the obedience of Christ." Note that this does not mean obedience *to* Christ, but obedient *in the way* in which Christ was obedient. Think how many possibilities might have flitted through his imagination; think how wholly obedient he always was to his Father's will.

I'm sure those early Judaizers who preached to the Corinthians, like my friend with all her brilliance, never intended to stray from the truth. They started out well. They built structures of thought after splendid high thought, until what they built had an existence of its own, independent of the truth, and they gave their loyalty to it.

Today, let me remember the temptation of high things that exalt themselves and of imaginations untrammeled. Let me remember to check my logic against the purity of revelation, my enthusiasm against the counsel of authority.

Logic, after all, is a good servant. But it's a dangerous master.

MARCH 4

And God said, Let the earth bring forth grass, the herb yielding seed, and the fruit tree yielding fruit after his kind, whose seed is in itself, upon the earth: and it was so.

—GENESIS 1:11

Seed time again. My husband has his seed trays out and is bustling up and down the basement stairs, setting up his seed nursery in the bright artificial light he has rigged up down there. My husband comes from England; observing how many of the gardening books we acquire are of British origin, I am beginning to think that a passion for gardening is something that overtakes Englishmen of a certain age. Working with the potting soil, seed packets, and ingenious devices that will provide steady moisture, he is completely content.

I can see his pleasure in the neat seed trays, with the labels all standing at the right angle, but I like it best in a week or so, when the little green sprouts begin pushing through. I find myself getting sidetracked from doing what I have set out to do, standing there with my arms full of laundry, watching the tiny green shoots poking out of the soil.

How amazingly faithful nature is to its creation, when you think about it. Each little green shoot knows exactly what kind of leaves to unfurl, how tall to grow, what shape of flower (or vegetable!) it should sprout. All it needs is the light and the moisture, and a place to begin.

Dear Heavenly Father, thank you for seeds, and their annual renewal. On this bleak and windy March day, thank you for reminding me of the promise of warm gardening days to come.

MARCH 5

Yea, and they did obey and observe to perform every word of command with exactness; yea, and even according to their faith it was done unto them; and I did remember the words which they said unto me that their mothers had taught them.

—ALMA 57:21

Helaman talks about his Ammonite stripling warriors: How proud their mothers must have been to know that they had brought up sons who were both courageous and obedient.

Of course, mothers are famous for being proud of their children, and the sentiment is often independent of the state of virtue or attractiveness of their offspring. I will always remember our doctor looking thoughtfully at my oldest daughter when she was in the full glory of chicken pox and remarking, "A face only a mother could love." Too true.

I am always touched by the enormous pride the students at my business school take in their children. A lot of them, probably the majority, are mothers; most of them are raising their children on their own, or close to it. Most often the children are babies or toddlers, but occasionally we see somebody older. One day Julie, who is one of my students, brought in her daughter, Tiffany. Tiffany is about six, hair pulled back in eyebrow-tightening braids, face scrubbed, dressed in an absolutely spotless parochial school uniform.

Julie, who has worn alternately the same two faded shirts ever since she has been in my class, was beaming with pride.

"Say hello to Mrs. Harrison," she ordered.

Tiffany ducked her head and murmured, "Mrs. Harrison."

"Tiffie's going to go to school just like you, Mrs. Harrison," her mother told me firmly. "She's not going to stop, like me. Tiffie's going to go on."

Tiffany watched her mother's face eagerly.

Julie went on. "I've told Tiffie that she's gotta learn now what it's taken me all this time to learn. I had to try breaking rules before I found what happens. Life'll get you if you don't follow the rules." She pulled her daughter to her side with a firm, enfolding arm. "Tiffie's not going to get got."

I hope Tiffany makes it. Her mother is certainly determined—whatever the cost to herself—to make sure that Tiffany has all the chances. But how much wisdom can you pass on? How much will we accept? I think of all the things I had to learn the hard way that I could have learned secondhand, if I had only listened. I hope Tiffany—I hope my children—will be less stubborn than I've sometimes been.

Whatever happens, Julie's right about one thing: You gotta follow the rules. If you don't, you'll get got.

MARCH 6

And now I beseech thee, lady, not as though I wrote a new commandment unto thee, but that which we had from the beginning, that we love one another. And this is love, that we walk after his commandments. This is the commandment, That, as ye have heard from the beginning, ye should walk in it.

—2 JOHN 1:5–6

The identity of the "elect lady" to whom John wrote these words is lost in history; perhaps just as well, because this way we can take his letter to apply to us personally. Perhaps it's just because I find myself so attracted to the warmth of John's words, the immediacy of his experience as being the disciple "whom Jesus loved"—that I love to imagine I might have been the one to read this letter first, to put it away carefully, and treasure it forever.

As he says, what he is telling her (or me!) is nothing new. He is reminding us again that loving the Lord and loving each other are vital. Those are the first and basic commandments. But we express our love by following his word. Just sitting with our hands folded having good thoughts isn't love. The expression of love is obedience.

This reminds me of an article I saw years ago in the *Ensign*. In the margin was a phrase, in large type, lifted from the article. It was about a child of busy parents. They were good parents, doing good things, but they were always busy doing them, and the child said, poignantly (and these were the words in the margin), "Don't love me. Spend some time with me."

Please, Lord, let me never make thee say those words to me. Let me learn from John, thy beloved, that love lives only when I take the time, and bend my efforts, to be obedient to thy word.

Let me love thee in deed as well as word.

MARCH 7

Yielding one's heart to God signals the last stage in our spiritual development. Only then are we beginning to be fully useful to God! How can we sincerely pray to be an instrument in His hands if the instrument seeks to do the instructing?

—ELDER NEAL A. MAXWELL

We get used to being in control of things, organizing things. Many women, single and married, do a lot of this in the course of running their homes, or their homes and families. Who would arrange the food at priesthood and ward events, if not us? Who would do three-quarters of the telephoning that goes on around the ward, knitting us together and clarifying who is doing what where? (Oh, okay, so some socializing goes on, too; who wants to get a bare naked directive to do something?)

Maybe that's why we find it so easy to carry on and try organizing our obedience, which is exactly what I think Elder Maxwell is talking about. It's fatally easy to find ourselves being very obedient about commandments that fall into Category A (which would probably be the biggies), reasonably obedient about those in Category B (that gets more individual; some of us have no problem with tithing but are inconsistent about observing Sundays reverently or whatever, or maybe it's vice versa), and, to the extent we think about it at all, think that Category C isn't talking about us. Category C would probably include such things as obeying all the laws—driving within the speed limit and coming to a full stop at stop signs, for example. Maybe it includes being honest, which would take in such details as including all cash income on your income tax return or returning excess change given by mistake, even if you're already out in the parking lot when you figure out what happened.

But as long as our obedience is selective, we aren't yielding our hearts to God. Yielding our hearts is pretty basic. It means that instead of deciding for ourselves what's important, we submit to the will of our Father. Instead of us telling him, we open ourselves wholly to his direction. Then he can use us for his work; then we can be the instrument in his hands.

That's hard. That's really hard, and the more I try to do it, the more I appreciate its difficulty.

Bless me today, Lord. Bless me with the honest desire to be obedient. Bless me that I may learn to yield my heart, that I may submit my will to thee. I still have far to go.

MARCH 8

And he took the book of the covenant, and read in the audience of the people: and they said, All that the Lord hath said will we do, and be obedient.

—EXODUS 24:7

The "he" here is Moses. He had come down from Mount Sinai with the Ten Commandments, and then he went back into "the thick darkness" (Exodus 20:21) to speak with the Lord to receive further directions, which included those now thought of as the basic Mosaic laws: an "eye for eye, tooth for tooth, hand for hand, foot for foot" (Exodus 21:24). When he returned, he first told the people the laws, and then he wrote them down and read them to the people. And they promised to be obedient.

Oh, the children of Israel! They promised, and they tried, and they failed, and they were punished, and they were given another chance, and they promised, and they tried, and they failed, and they were punished, and they were given another chance: The story goes on and on, and we call it the Old Testament. Sometimes they were brilliantly successful, and those are the heroes. Generally the heroes, such as Daniel, developed their strength in times when the children of Israel as a whole were being punished for earlier disobedience.

It's easy for us to be smug about the people of the Old Testament. Their faults are so obvious; they are so clearly human, say, and the Old Testament doesn't mince words. We, on the other hand—yeah, right. How are we doing, say, on the law of consecration? How close are we to holding all things in common and taking only what we need and sharing the rest with those whose need is greater? What's the current divorce rate churchwide? What about the disturbing propensity of Church members to get involved in confidence schemes of one kind or another?

Obedience doesn't come naturally. If it did, the Lord might have to mention it only once. Open the Bible, open the Book of Mormon, open the Doctrine and Covenants. Take any page you please, and there will be something on that page about obedience. It is the leitmotif of the gospel. We clearly need to hear it again and again and again—and praise our Savior for the promise of repentance. Second chances saved the children of Israel time after time.

Repentance can help to save us, too.

MARCH 9

And it came to pass that I, Nephi, said unto my father: I will go and do the things which the Lord hath commanded, for I know that the Lord giveth no commandments unto the children of men, save he shall prepare a way for them that they may accomplish the thing which he commandeth them.

—1 Nephi 3:7

Faith isn't easy either, and the thing that will sustain us when we honestly, from the fullness of our hearts, try to obey, is simply faith. Faith and obedience are like one of those Chinese boxes that has to be opened here, and there, and over on the other side all at once, simultaneously.

It's always easier to talk about following the commandments, of course, than it is to actually get on with the business of doing it. They say talk is cheap; they ought to also mention that it's comfortable. Action, on the other hand . . .

All right. Now say, just for instance, that you are on a very tight budget. There's nothing for extras, and just barely enough—if all goes well—for essentials. As we all know, all never goes well; something always comes up.

The relevant commandment, say, is tithing. Now, if you can barely manage essentials on 100 percent, how are you going to survive on 90 percent?

That's where faith comes in.

How does it work out? Nobody can really tell you. Sometimes you pay your tithing and some extra money appears from somewhere: a refund you'd forgotten about, an extra job you can fit in, even an anonymous gift. Sometimes you pay your tithing and for some unexplained reason your expenses are reduced. Something you thought would cost fifty dollars costs only twenty-five dollars; it turns out you inadvertently paid the telephone bill twice last month (how could that have happened?). Sometimes you pay your tithing and there's no extra money. You have the same old expenses, but you just discover something you can do without, and somehow you've made it through to the end of the month—maybe eating noodles the last couple of days. But you did it, and you find you have the blessing. You may not be able to put your finger precisely on what the blessing is, but you have it and you know you have it. Faith held you together to get it.

When I was living in a branch in England, I spoke with one of the members who was having a very hard time. She was on welfare, and she told me forlornly that the branch president had told her she needn't pay tithing on her welfare stipend, which the Lord knew was small enough. I don't know if she or the branch president was mistaken, but she was very distressed about the instruction.

"I need the blessing," she told me. "That's a commandment. I can't be too poor for that blessing."

Now that is faith. May I be blessed with even a mustard seed of such faith.

MARCH 10

The law of the Lord is perfect, converting the soul: the testimony of the Lord is sure, making wise the simple. The statutes of the Lord are right, rejoicing the heart: the commandment of the Lord is pure, enlightening the eyes.

—PSALM 19:7–8

Oh, spring, beautiful spring! It can't last—this is just a sneak preview—but how wonderful to have a warm, sunny day when the sky is bright blue and I can see the buds fattening on the bare branches. Spring will come. The world will be green again, the lush summertime green will come.

On such a morning everything seems joyful. Getting along with people is easy. How could I ever have thought that my son's thundering down the stairs could be irritating? He's just not used to his size yet. My daughter will eventually get herself together to leave the house; why should I waste this glorious morning crabbing at her because she's going to be late?

Being good—being obedient—seems automatic when everything is going smoothly. Was this what it was like before we came here? Is this what it will be again? It's odd to visualize life without opposition. Will it be like that for everybody, or only for those in the celestial kingdom?

Time to worry about that tomorrow. Time now to leave for school. Take the dark glasses; I'll be driving into the sun. Happy day! God's in his heaven, all's well with the world, and the song of the psalmist sings triumphantly in my heart.

MARCH 11

*And under this head ye are made free, and there is no other head
whereby ye can be made free. There is no other name given
whereby salvation cometh; therefore, I would that ye should take
upon you the name of Christ, all you that have entered into the
covenant with God that ye should be obedient unto the end of your
lives.*

—MOSIAH 5:8

B ack to the connection of freedom with obedience: "Obedience
is the first law of heaven" (Bruce R. McConkie, *Mormon Doctrine*, 539).

I envision it as the hub of the gospel wheel, with love and faith
and freedom the spokes radiating out from it.

We cannot be free without obedience. The widespread belief
that obedience to the commandments is restrictive is one of Satan's
greatest triumphs. Anyone who needs convincing should just take a
look around. Are liars free? They have to remember everything
they've said, keep track of the lies that camouflaged lies, maintain
two scenarios in their brains: the one that did happen and the one
that didn't. Are adulterers free? They have all the problems of liars
and in our wonderfully emancipated times, the further thought that,
in terms of disease transmission, they are sleeping with everyone
anyone they sleep with has slept with—and then becoming disease
transmitters themselves. Thieves? Well, if you can dismiss from your
mind the possibility of detection and can figure out some way to
enjoy whatever it is you took without creating suspicion about how
you acquired it . . . not likely.

Obedience means you are free of all that. Obedience means
that you have the comfort of a clear conscience; that you never
need to look nervously over your shoulder. Some people try to find
something like that freedom in pills or capsules, or by investigating
mystical formulas, but as King Benjamin told his people, "There is
no other head whereby ye can be made free." When we place our
lives in accord with the commandments of our Father in Heaven,
then and only then are we able to be our best, our freest selves.

Help me to remember that, dear Lord, and give me the faith to
hold on should my memory grow weak. Today, help me to remain
close to the truths I have been taught. Help me now to become and
remain obedient to the end of my life.

MARCH 12

Though he were a Son, yet learned he obedience by the things which he suffered.

—HEBREWS 5:8

We have never been promised that obedience would be easy. Joseph Fielding built a house on twenty acres of land that he had purchased wild, for one hundred sixty dollars. His house was a frame house, filled in with bricks, with a pretty garden and apple and peach trees that bore delicious fruit. Then Joseph Smith and his brother Hyrum were murdered, and Brigham Young and the other apostles came to the conclusion that the only possible way the Church could survive was to go west. The order went out to sell, pack up, and leave.

Joseph Fielding anguished over his decision to follow. He had worked so hard; after traipsing from pillar to post, he had thought that this place was going to be home. For the weary wanderers of those early days in the Church—first Kirtland, Ohio; then Missouri; then Nauvoo—"home" had a ring that is hard for us to appreciate.

He anguished, but he did as he was instructed. It was a buyer's market, of course: Not only did he have to give up his home, but he had to give it up for a pittance. In theory, he sold it for two hundred dollars in trade (forty dollars profit for all the slogging labor of clearing the land, fencing it, building the house, establishing the garden and fields, planting the trees), but of course what he got was worth far less. He got two horses, one of which was useless, a wagon, a cloth coat, and four dollars and fifty cents in cash. Was his obedience easy?

Jesus, knowing precisely what suffering lay ahead of him, literally sweat blood as he prayed on our behalf and as he asked if it were possible to be spared the ordeal. But, he said, let it happen according to his Father's will, not his own. Was his obedience easy?

Sometimes obedience is easy and natural, and we can do what's right cheerfully and automatically. Still, we have no promise that it will always be that way. Sometimes ease lies down one path and obedience down another, and we must choose. As Paul suggests in his letter to the Hebrews, if the choice involves suffering, we can learn obedience by means of that suffering.

Dear Lord, when I have to choose, bless me with courage and fortitude. Help me to use the easy days, like today, to build my resources for when the hard days come. Bless me with the will to be obedient; bless me with the strength to find the way.

MARCH 13

Then Peter and the other apostles answered and said, We ought to obey God rather than men.

—ACTS 5:29

One of the most magnificent things about the New Testament is the absolutely honest way it shows men growing and maturing in the gospel. We see it happen around us, but it seems incredible to us that it could happen to the people who are spiritual giants—the great men such as Peter, James, John, and Paul. Weren't they always giants among men? Not as the books of the New Testament report, clearly and matter-of-factly.

Peter was filled with fear when Jesus was taken prisoner. All four gospels tell the story. As Jesus was led away, Peter followed, but "afar off," and although he waited around the palace anxiously, he was apparently terrified that anyone might associate him with the captive and was quick to deny he had anything to do with him. As Jesus had predicted, Peter was just assuring the third person that he knew nothing about this man called Jesus when the cock crowed.

As Luke tells it, at that moment the Lord turned, and looked at Peter. And Peter remembered what Christ had said and went out and wept bitter tears.

After that look, and those tears, Peter grew up into majesty. After he received the Holy Ghost, no one could do anything to frighten him. By the time the Sadducees imprisoned Peter and John the second time, Peter was immovable. He simply walked out of the prison with John, having been released by an angel according to the book of Acts, and went back to where they had been, teaching in the porch of the temple. When the Sadducees went and got them again (but this time without violence, for fear of the people) and charged that they were doing what they had been ordered not to do, their answer was simple and unyielding. It wasn't men they were concerned about obeying. It was God.

Let me remember the early weakness of Peter so that I can more fully appreciate his strength. He did not begin as a spiritual giant. He started out with ordinary weaknesses and only the potential for greatness. How many of us start out with weaknesses, as he did? How few of us manage to get anywhere near where he came to be!

MARCH 14

We have been reminded frequently of the commandments of the Lord. We have had set forth before us the counsel of his prophets. All of the counsel will have been in vain if those of us who have heard it do not have added resolution in our hearts to go forth now with a fortified spirit of obedience to the will of the Lord.

I know that frequently it is not easy to face up to that which is expected of us. Many think they cannot do it. We need a little more faith. We should know that the Lord will not give us commandments beyond our power to observe. He will not ask us to do things for which we lack the capacity. Our problem lies in our fears and in our appetites.

—PRESIDENT GORDON B. HINCKLEY

What an odd sensation: to be going through an old *Ensign* to get some material for a Relief Society lesson and suddenly finding the words of the prophet, from a conference of years ago, addressed very precisely to me.

Obedience: We can go around and around and around it. It should be such a simple matter, and maybe that's the way it seemed to be, back in the premortal existence when we were deciding whether we wanted to try the great experiment of testing our own strength. Then we got here and discovered it isn't simple. We discovered that however much we might wish to be obedient in theory, the unfortunate fact is that too often we just plain don't want what we ought to want. As President Hinckley puts it so baldly, the problem is our fears (of being different? of being laughed at? of hardship or sacrifice?) and our appetites (but it feels good! but I want to!).

Dear Lord, help me deal with my own stubborn, unyielding self. Bless me that I may see—that I may *want* to see—where my wishes and thy will for me diverge. Lord, help me to be good; more than that, help me *want* to be good.

MARCH 15

If ye will fear the Lord, and serve him, and obey his voice, and not rebel against the commandment of the Lord, then shall both ye and also the king that reigneth over you continue following the Lord your God: but if ye will not obey the voice of the Lord, but rebel against the commandment of the Lord, then shall the hand of the Lord be against you, as it was against your fathers.

—1 SAMUEL 12:14–15

As a society, we seem to have a problem with authority. We need it, since few of us are inclined to believe that anarchy would really work, but we've spent so much time laughing at the excesses of authority, mocking it, and even (to be honest) sneering at it, that the idea of automatic obedience feels uncomfortable.

Until you go to court.

I spent several years transcribing tape recordings of court proceedings—primarily trials—and found it truly an eye-opening experience. There is still one place in our society where you sit up and do as you are told. There is an absolute authority, and it wears a black gown, and it sits high up in a chair we call a bench. We do not interrupt it, or contradict it, or speak out of turn. We call it "your Honor," or, in the transcripts, "The Court." More commonly, we refer to it (it can be male or female, but in the black robe, it is genderless) as the Judge. And, believe me, we don't trifle with the Judge.

I found it curiously refreshing. Having from time to time been told peevishly, "It's a free country," by grumpy adolescents when some curb of their freedom of action was announced, I found it reassuring that there are, in fact, limits to that freedom. It's not that you can't be impudent to the Judge—you are obviously big enough and strong enough—but the consequences are swift and unforgettable. I can't imagine many who would try it once; I don't know any who would try it twice. I have seen prestigious attorneys and drug lords and arrogant street gang commanders being rebuked like naughty children, and they stand there and take it. As I say, it's reassuring.

Now, if the consequences of the displeasure of an ordinary mortal dressed in a black gown (symbol of the authority our society gives that man or that woman) are so memorable, what must it be like to rebel against the authority of the Lord our God? If majesty in the courtroom is so impressive, what must the majesty of the Lord be like?

Today, let me take this scripture and think about it a little. Should you happen to flip through the channels on Sunday morning, it's easy to visualize Jesus as being sort of soft and squashy, loving us all in a benevolent, uncritical way. Isn't there something bracing and refreshing about being reminded that something is required of us as well? That there are rewards if we obey, but penalties if we rebel? That, spiritually speaking, there are times to sit up straight instead of slouching?

Today, I will do as I am told.

MARCH 16

Blessed is the man that walketh not in the counsel of the ungodly, nor standeth in the way of sinners, nor sitteth in the seat of the scornful. But his delight is in the law of the Lord; and in his law doth he meditate day and night. And he shall be like a tree planted by the rivers of water, that bringeth forth his fruit in his season; his leaf also shall not wither; and whatsoever he doeth shall prosper.

—PSALM 1:1–3

Another harbinger of spring: This morning it is raining, a hard, steady rain. I called my mother and told her very firmly not to go out; there are "rivers of water," all right, but they are rivers running over the top of the already existing rivers of ice, and the footing is hazardous.

Still, it's good to hear the steady beat of the rain after long weeks of snow. Snow is so silent, wrapping the world in a white blanket that absorbs sounds almost before they are made. Rain rattles the glass in the windows and thrums on the roof. (It also insistently draws attention to any deficiencies in either windows or roof, but we won't worry about that right now.) The dog, who bounces out happily in the snow, rushes to the door and then backs up abruptly, almost like a cartoon dog, when she realizes it is wet out there. It takes a firm hand on her collar to convince her that wet or not, out she is going to go.

So what does the rain have to do with the law of the Lord? I suppose what I am meditating upon this rainy morning is the comfort of knowing that the world is indeed held to the Lord's law, as we are: Spring does follow winter, year after year, and we are held accountable for our faithfulness to the commandments, season after season as well. I choose to try to follow those commandments. I won't claim total success, obviously, but most of the time I do not walk in the counsel of the ungodly (by which I probably mean all those people who think God is a fine idea just as long as it doesn't get in the way of doing what they want to do) or stand in the way of sinners (by which I mean exactly what you think I mean) or sit in the seat of the scornful (by which I mean all the people who snicker on the grounds that obedience is ludicrous).

And if I try, what a lovely reward I am promised. How odd that it should be a cold, rainy morning when I experience a taste of delight in the law.

MARCH 17

Therefore to him that knoweth to do good, and doeth it not, to him it is sin.

—JAMES 4:17

Eric came to school drunk again yesterday. What are we going to do with him?

If he were less likable when he is sober, or less manageable when "under the influence," as one of the other teachers primly describes it, the solution would be obvious. He would be out on his ear. But Eric is one of those people who appears to have the resilience of a cheerful rubber ball. First of all, he is lucky enough to pick the right days to come wandering unsteadily to school: Each time, it has been a day when the director happened to be away on business somewhere else or (once) home with the flu. Because none of us who are ordinary teachers really carry her responsibility, and because Eric doesn't do anything objectionable (unless you count his alcoholic breath, which radiates around him about three feet in all directions), so far we have all chosen to pretend it isn't happening and, as long as he behaves himself, studiously look the other way.

The problem is that Eric doesn't really possess that rubber-ball resilience. If he did, he wouldn't be retreating into the temporary oblivion of drink. Nor would he tell the tall tales that we all really know are fictional even while we're enjoying the telling. Dear old, courtly old Eric, leaping to hold open a door—"Let me get that for you, ma'am." What must it be like to live inside his head? Where does he go during the hours he spends away from school?

Would he listen to me if I tried to talk to him about it? I have the sinking feeling that all of us, his teachers, are failing him if we go on pretending, like those three supposedly wise monkeys, that we see nothing, hear nothing, and therefore speak nothing. This scripture from the book of James just makes the sinking feeling more pronounced. To see good that needs to be done, and not do it, is sin. You'd have a job to interpret that any other way.

Oh, dear. Why can't somebody who has more experience dealing with drinking than I do rise up from somewhere and take the responsibility? I feel strongly inclined to fall back on my Mormon background and explain that I'm not experienced at this kind of thing. I don't know about this stuff.

Only that doesn't wash.

Dear Lord, today help me find the right words. Bless me that I may be caring, not accusing. Let me find a way to help, truly and legitimately help. Maybe I can be an instrument in thy hands to reach Eric, thy funny, engaging son.

Above all, let me keep things in proportion. Eric has his faults and failings. But it seems to me that to know to do good and fail to do it is a sin far graver than drinking too much. Let me never fool myself about that.

MARCH 18

Obedient application of truth is the surest way of making it eternally yours. The wise use of knowledge will permeate your life with its precious fruit.

—ELDER RICHARD G. SCOTT

In other words, just reading the scriptures isn't enough. If you can't put them into practice, you haven't gained a lot. If you read the words of the Lord, murmur, "Oh, my," in an interested way, and then go back on your own merry way, you might as well have saved your time. As the psychologists who specialize in learning theory might put it, the traces of neural connections made with the initial reading are so faint that unless they are reinforced with repetition and input from closely related experiences involving other senses, they quickly fade. It's not really that you forgot whatever it was; you never had it well enough in the first place.

If you go on doing what you've always done, you'll end up where you've always been. If I want to improve myself—and I do—then I need to make changes, and that means doing something more than just thinking about them. (A pity, that: It's always much easier to make lists than to do what's on them.) If I want to learn to be more patient—and I do—it's not enough to gain knowledge about being patient. I have to practice doing it. There's no shortcut.

Today, let me practice by refraining from getting cross about my daughter leaving laundry all over the basement floor until (or unless) she actually does leave it there. Just because that's what she always does doesn't mean she necessarily will today. When I see her emerge from her bedroom with her arms full, let me practice patience by holding my tongue. Maybe she will actually put it in the machine this time, instead of waiting until she has leisure in some undefined future. Let me consider the possibility that nagging in advance just might contribute to her decision that because Mom is going on about it anyway, she might as well do what's most convenient . . .

Peace in the morning would be precious fruit indeed. Whether it keeps the basement any tidier remains to be seen. Still, it's a start.

MARCH 19

I, the Lord, am bound when ye do what I say; but when ye do not what I say, ye have no promise.

—DOCTRINE AND COVENANTS 82:10

Another of those seemingly simple little scriptures, almost as terse as one of the Proverbs.

Blessings are predicated on laws. When the law is obeyed, the blessing follows. If we do not obey the law, the Lord cannot supply the blessing. Does this mean that when a specific blessing is promised in connection with a law, no one except those who obey the law receive it? Obviously not: Take the Word of Wisdom as an example. We are promised health in our navels and marrow to our bones if we are faithful to the commandments (see D&C 89:18). Does this mean that no one except those who obey the Word of

Wisdom faithfully is healthy? Well, if that's true, what about all those vigorous centenarians who happily attribute their long lives to the regular use of whiskey and strong cigars?

We don't know all the rules. We just know that if we are faithful, we will be blessed in ways in which we would not have been blessed had we disregarded the law. We know that we take our chances with all the ordinary causative factors such as heredity and environment and, for all I know, rampant carcinogens and other behavior-specific triggers for disease. If we drink like a fish, our chances of developing cirrhosis of the liver are excellent. Maybe that's why we have the law, but we don't know if that's the only, or even the primary, reason. We can only speculate.

What we do know is as simple and terse as the scripture: Obedience is to our benefit. Every time.

MARCH 20

Wherefore, I, Lehi, have obtained a promise, that inasmuch as those whom the Lord God shall bring out of the land of Jerusalem shall keep his commandments, they shall prosper upon the face of this land; and they shall be kept from all other nations, that they may possess this land unto themselves. And if it so be that they shall keep his commandments they shall be blessed upon the face of this land, and there shall be none to molest them, nor to take away the land of their inheritance; and they shall dwell safely forever.

—2 NEPHI 1:9

Winter is in retreat: This morning yesterday's gray skies are brilliantly blue, and the breath of spring is in the air. I can't define it, but when I went out to get the paper, I could feel it.

We are creatures of this world. I'm sure there has to be some physiological reason for it, but the fact is that the world seems a much more satisfactory place when the sun shines. Or did, until I opened the paper and read the melancholy stories of whole groups of people doing their best to annihilate other groups of people for no other reason than their membership in those particular groups. The details reported turned my stomach, and I'm sure those details were carefully selected and censored to make them endurable for the reading public over breakfast.

How could those people deserve their fate? Forlorn, frightened children stare blankly at me from the pictures on the front page. What did they or their parents do, besides be born to those whom somebody considers the wrong people? How do I conceivably deserve my safety, spooning up raisin bran and milk in a comfortable kitchen on a quiet, peaceful street?

Lehi and his descendants were given this promise. They lost it, when they were disobedient over centuries, but we have inherited it. And how are we doing? Check the rest of the paper.

Time to go. Rinse out the bowl, put it and the spoon in the dishwasher, and get on my way. But today, let me think about the promise. Think hard.

MARCH 21

And Moses went up unto God, and the Lord called unto him out of the mountain, saying, Thus shalt thou say to the house of Jacob, and tell the children of Israel; ye have seen what I did unto the Egyptians, and how I bare you on eagles' wings, and brought you unto myself. Now therefore, if ye will obey my voice indeed, and keep my covenant, then ye shall be a peculiar treasure unto me above all people: for all the earth is mine.

—EXODUS 19:3–5

The children of Israel have just come into the wilderness of Sinai, after journeying for two months and traveling no great distance—moving such an enormous, straggling encampment was a major accomplishment.

To this barren place the Lord had brought his chosen people, "on eagles' wings," as he tells them. Tradition says that the parent eagle flies beneath the eaglets as they learn to fly, to catch and carry them on strong wings should they falter. On eagles' wings, the Lord had carried his people out of Egyptian captivity into this strange new freedom, where they had to learn all over again who they were and how they were to conduct themselves as free men. As he would do again thousands of years later, the Lord selected territory far from the places where anybody else lived to shape and discipline his people. There, in the middle of nowhere, he could teach them and establish his law, and so he called Moses to come to the mountain to receive that law. By obeying his voice and keeping the covenant which they were to make, the children of Israel would be established as a "peculiar treasure" above all other people: the people chosen to be a witness to God and his dealings with man for the rest of mankind.

We have been called peculiar, too—of course, what the translators of the King James Version of the Bible meant by that word was "special," or "treasure," or "one's very own." It didn't mean eccentric or odd to them, although undoubtedly it does to many of the people who have called us that (and if you measure us against the standards of the world, we probably are).

The children of Israel got into difficulty when they began to assume that because they had been told they were the treasure of the Lord brought out of the hands of the Egyptians on eagles' wings, they always would remain so. They weren't listening to—or they forgot they had heard—the part about "if you will obey my voice indeed, and keep my covenant." They presumed upon their possession of God's favor as his chosen people, assuming the possession was unconditional. This is exactly the belief from which the later prophets—Jeremiah and all the others—were trying to dissuade them during the dreary years when the Israelites moved from one captivity to another, disorganized, disobedient, and incredulous that this could be happening to the chosen people.

Can we learn from their example? Can we listen to all of what our Father in Heaven is telling us, instead of choosing to rely on a self-edited version? How good are we at humbling ourselves and accepting his guidance as given to us by the prophets, ancient and modern?

I can't do much about anybody else's decisions. Today, let me be more aware of my own. Let me be upheld on eagles' wings, but let me remember the conditions that sustain me there. Let me be faithful. Let me, above all, be obedient.

MARCH 22

And Noah and his sons hearkened unto the Lord, and gave heed,
and they were called the sons of God.

—Moses 8:13

I t's a funny thing about Noah. He was a great prophet. He had three righteous sons who followed in his footsteps. He was obedient to the Lord's commands and thereby saved himself, his family, and the creatures of the earth from calamity.

So how is he remembered today? Not usually as a giant among men, which he clearly was. No, we very often remember Noah as a whimsical figure, part of a child's toy. Who hasn't had a Noah's ark playset at one time or another? Our babies practice their finger skills in their quiet books on Sundays during sacrament meeting, tucking flannel animals into flannel arks. At home our children play with wooden arks with wooden animals and wooden Noahs. I even have a ceramic Noah canister set in my kitchen: The ark is divided into three separate compartments, with animals on the side, an extra elephant and a lamb on top, and a dove as a central handle. Noah: a man of such integrity and nobility turned into a decorative theme!

And yet—and yet. There is a lot to learn from Noah, and those odd single animals on the top of my canisters make me think. If there is anything famous about the Noah story, it's the pairing up, male and female. But what is important to remember is that Noah and his sons (and presumably their wives) were living righteous lives before the rains came. They had had the individual boldness to obey what they knew was the will of God, even before the strange commandment to build a boat when there was no apparent reason to build one. Each one of them acted singly when they decided to do that. Being obedient is always an individual decision. You can go to a class or a meeting and come away full of inspiration and good intentions, but you have to make the decisions to carry out those intentions by yourself. Minute by minute and hour by hour we have to decide all on our own to make the best choices rather than easier, second-best ones.

Today, let me use my Noah kitchen canisters, with the single animals on top, and this scripture to remind me that as universal as pairing up sometimes seems to be, when I think—really think—about Noah, he stands alone, as we all must, in his choice to serve his God. As Moses wrote, "And thus Noah found grace in the eyes of the Lord; for Noah was a just man, and perfect in his generation; and he walked with God, as did also his three sons, Shem, Ham, and Japheth" (Moses 8:27).

I can't make the choices that lead to walking with God in a group—not even in a pair. Those choices have to be made in the individual privacy of my heart.

Today let me make those choices.

MARCH 23

Wherefore gird up the loins of your mind, be sober, and hope to the end for the grace that is to be brought unto you at the revelation of Jesus Christ; as obedient children, not fashioning yourselves according to the former lusts in your ignorance: but as he which hath called you is holy, so be ye holy in all manner of conversation.

—1 Peter 1:13–15

In our sisterhood (take an ordinary homemaking meeting of Relief Society, for example), what is holy conversation?

We all can tell when it happens. Those are the meetings when you come home with a light heart, feeling good about yourself and what you're doing. Not that it's all being done perfectly; after all, much of the point of going to Relief Society is to learn how to improve. Still, in the good meetings, with the good chatter as people dawdle about collecting their possessions, there is the atmosphere of support. You go home not only knowing you need to improve but believing you can do it. After all, if Cheryl's daughter came home from your Primary class talking about the story you told, you must be doing *something right* . . .

Unfortunately, it isn't always that way. Does that come, do you suppose, at least in part from fashioning ourselves according to "former lusts in our ignorance"? Do we talk about the things we've acquired or things we're trying to get rather than ideas or activities? Do we include the sister who has been there two or three times but clearly still feels a little bit like a stranger? We're usually pretty good about paying attention to visitors the first time, but what about when the newcomer has been there before, but is still hesitant, standing on the edge? Are we still remembering to update her on what we're talking about, or is it easier to talk to the old friends who already know? Do we pay attention to the sister who seems quieter than usual, or do we just carry on talking about ourselves and what our kids are up to?

Being a woman at the end of the twentieth century is hard. Young, old, married, single, at home with children, out there working (or any combination of those conditions), all of life has to be figured out on a practical, daily basis against a backdrop of constantly changing social expectations. And as if that isn't enough, we have a whole other set of standards as daughters of God, subtly threaded through the social expectations. To top it off, we expect ourselves to do all of it well. Cheerfully, stylishly, and well.

We're never going to cope with all those expectations at once (nor, necessarily, should we), but at least we can enjoy our companionship while we work on them. And when we get together, at Relief Society or anywhere else, we can love each other. Most often we really do care about each other already; maybe all we need to do is make sure we don't assume that others know we care and let it go at that. Don't we all have days when we need to know unambiguously that what happens to us matters to somebody else?

Any conversation that demonstrates our caring is holy, even when what we think we're talking about is how to get stains out of white T-shirts.

I think Peter would agree.

MARCH 24

So shall I keep thy law continually for ever and ever. And I will walk at liberty; for I seek thy precepts.

—PSALM 119:44–45

There are times when promising to keep the law of the Lord for ever and ever is very hard.

Have you ever wanted something very, very much, and almost without being aware of it, made a deal with God in your head? "I'll be very good, and do everything I ought to do if you will only let me have this one thing." Sometimes the one thing is a perfectly good thing to want: to have a baby, for example. Everybody else seems to be able to have a baby, even people who are not particularly virtuous at all. If you can be worthy enough, surely the Lord could bless you with one, too. Please, Lord. I'll be *so* good.

And the months slip by, one by one (breaking your heart each time), and there is no baby. So what about the deal then?

That, of course, is the problem. Nowhere, at any time, did our Heavenly Father agree to a deal. His plans for us are far too magnificent for bargains in the light of here and now. We operate in three dimensions; we cannot even conceive of the dimension of eternity that our Father commands. Like the psalmist, we have to seek his precepts and wait patiently in his love. When it is time, and we are worthy, we will have the blessings that will truly bless us, not necessarily those we think will do the job. Sometimes that means the baby will come eventually, one way or another; sometimes not. Maybe the Lord has some other blessing in mind.

What I have to remember is that the Lord's benevolence is not like a vending machine into which I stick obedience and then what I desire comes out. Let me remember that today, when I have a whole list of what seems to me to be worthy desires. Let me seek the precepts of the Lord instead, and be content.

MARCH 25

It is obvious we either discipline our lives here, or pay the price for the undisciplined life in the world to come.

—ELDER DELBERT L. STAPLEY

We keep coming back to it. Obedience to the commandments of God opens all the other possibilities to us, which is why we came here to earth in the first place: to discover if we are capable of being obedient when memory of why it is essential has been taken from us.

Why do we try to be obedient? Because unless we purge ourselves of all the selfishness, greed, envy, impatience, and other unpleasant characteristics that are part of human nature—the parts that Satan is so clever at exploiting—we will never be comfortable in our Heavenly Father's presence. We will not be able to tolerate his glory; he cannot tolerate our impurity. Obedience to God's laws is necessary because it is through the daily, small choices we make to comply with eternal law that we become the sort of beings who will be able to come home.

With his usual gift for the felicitous phrase, C. S. Lewis expressed the same idea: "I would much rather say that every time you make a choice you are turning the central part of you, the part of you that chooses, into something a little different from what it was before. And taking your life as a whole, with all your innumerable choices, all your life long you are slowly turning this central thing either into a heavenly creature or into a hellish creature" (*Mere Christianity*, rev. ed. [New York: Collier Books, 1952], 72).

Our choices, then, in the fullest sense define us. Most of our choices seem little and inconsequential. We speak sharply to an irritating stranger; we fudge some figures on an expense account. Some feel that nothing is wrong with such behavior and may even congratulate themselves for getting away with it. But by those choices they are determining who they are, just as the man who tells the truth even if it makes him look like an idiot at the time is refining his innermost core.

Dear Lord, let me remember that today. Let me make the choices today that will bring me comfort in thy presence. Let me remember who I was; let me remain steadfast to thy vision of who I am to be.

MARCH 26

But he said, Yea rather, blessed are they that hear the word of God, and keep it.

—Luke 11:28

One of my responsibilities at the business school has been to review the resumes of the students as they approach graduation, to make sure they're clear of any typographical errors and that they look crisp and businesslike. Sometimes the students and I have different opinions about what is crisp and businesslike (I always win on the typographical errors), and I have let some go by that look very peculiar to me.

Ruth's resume wasn't one of them. Ruth was very conscientious, and her resume was neatly and carefully worked out. She didn't have much work experience, and most of what she did have was working behind a fast food counter. But she had put it down with a list of her responsibilities, which looked fine to me. I gave it back to her and told her to go ahead and get it duplicated. It looked great.

The next day she brought the package of resumes to me to be forwarded to our placement director. She'd had it done on heavy resume paper, and it looked very impressive. Ruth, like many of our students, watches her pennies carefully, and I knew it represented an investment to her, an investment in her future success.

I was therefore somewhat surprised when she showed up the next day to ask for the resume back, clearly distressed but very resolute.

I asked her why. She took a deep breath, looked me straight in the eye, and said, "I messed up. I said I closed up at night, and I never did. Not by myself. I was there a lot of times, but I just helped."

Considering the amount of fudging that goes on in the preparation of resumes, I thought we could probably live with that, and I told Ruth so. She knew the process of closing up, which was what an employer would be interested in.

She shook her head. "No, ma'am. It wouldn't be true. I messed up. I gotta get it back."

So we went up to the front office and retrieved it from the intercompany mail (fortunately, it was still there), and Ruth clutched it gratefully to her chest. "I'll get you a new one on Friday," she said. This was Tuesday. "I get my money on Friday."

I warned her it would mean nearly a week's delay in getting her file to the placement service, and she tightened her lips and hesitated, but then she nodded and said that would be okay. She couldn't send this one. When she handed me the new resume package that Friday, she said very deliberately, "This one is okay. This one says it right."

Ruth had earlier asked me if I would be a reference for her, and I had agreed, as I routinely do. It must have been a couple of weeks later that a prospective employer called me to ask about her. I told him she was a good worker, learned quickly, had had excellent attendance, and—oh yes, she was honest. Without question, she was honest.

"Great," he said. "Thanks."

I was tempted to tell him the whole story, but he wasn't the chatty type and sounded rushed. "You can hire her without a moment's hesitation," I said, and Ruth's name showed up a week or so later on the weekly employment report, so I guess he did. Would he have hired her on the basis of the first resume? I'm sure he would have. Did he even read the part about her responsibilities at the fast food place? Quite possibly not. So for whose benefit was this whole episode? His? Ruth's? Mine?

Dear Lord, when I am tempted to bend the truth even a little, let me remember Ruth. Let me always remember Ruth.

MARCH 27

Seek ye earnestly the best gifts, always remembering for what they are given: for verily I say unto you, they are given for the benefit of those who love me and keep all my commandments, and him that seeketh so to do; that all may be benefited that seek or that ask of me, that ask and not for a sign that they may consume it upon their lusts.

—DOCTRINE AND COVENANTS 46:8–9

And him that seeketh so to do": Oh, Heavenly Father, you do know about me! I do try. Most of the time I try very hard, and the fact that some of the time I don't is part of what I'm trying so hard to overcome. I sit here, and I think, and I talk, and I wonder to what extent what I say is hypocrisy and to what extent it simply reflects my aspirations—oh, dear Lord, how I wish I were better than I am at keeping the commandments!

Is that true of everybody, or is it just me? To an extent, I guess I know the answer to that—I mean, no one that I know of has been translated straight to heaven—but sometimes it seems so hard, when I'm going through a struggling patch, to go to church and see all my good sisters and brothers who are bustling around, doing the Lord's work, and seem to have it all together. I sit there in a back row quietly, off to the side, and watch them and wonder how they manage to do everything all the time and how they have such space in their hearts and lives for others. I seem to be running around in little tight circles and hardly have time to spend with my own family, let alone extending myself to everybody else's.

"And him that seeketh so to do." There is room for those of us who are trying. This scripture is like a balm to my troubled spirit today. Help me, dear Lord, to get past this rough patch. Help me remember the paradox of love, that by turning myself outward, there will be more to strengthen me inside. Help me turn myself, Lord.

And bless me with thy Spirit while I try.

MARCH 28

Beware that thou forget not the Lord thy God, in not keeping his commandments, and his judgments, and his statutes, which I command thee this day: Lest when thou hast eaten and art full, and hast built goodly houses, and dwelt therein; and when thy herds and thy flocks multiply, and thy silver and thy gold is multiplied, and all that thou hast is multiplied; then thine heart be lifted up, and thou forget the Lord thy God, which brought thee forth out of the land of Egypt, from the house of bondage. . . . And thou say in thine heart, My power and the might of mine hand hath gotten me this wealth.

—DEUTERONOMY 8:11–14, 17

You know, there are times when you would think the Lord would get discouraged. What ungrateful children we can be!

What is it about acquiring earthly goods that makes us convinced we are somehow in possession of wisdom and virtue as well, that we deserve everything we're getting, and that God's part in it is clearly limited, if present at all? Whatever it is, it is a universal impulse. It is recorded over and over again in the Old Testament; it happens just as repeatedly in the Book of Mormon. We mortals know to turn to the Lord in adversity; give us prosperity, and roll out those golden calves. We're at it again.

Here the Israelites are being given the word by Moses, being reminded of their very recent history, told what they should not do, and what happened? They went into the promised land and did exactly what Moses warned them against.

Today, let me think about that. Bill-paying time is rolling around again, and rampant prosperity (at the moment) is not among my afflictions, but the principle still holds. Can I be grateful that I have enough? Can I be an obedient daughter of the Lord my God when everything is going well, or do I have to have my nose rubbed in trouble in order to get me to pay attention? Bless me that I may swim upstream against my human nature. Bless me to remember my Lord in good times as in bad.

Bless me to ever acknowledge the hand of the Lord. Bless me that I will remember that all my blessings are of thy doing and not of my own cleverness. Above all, Lord, bless me to keep remembering thee. Today, tomorrow, and forever, let me remember.

MARCH 29

If ye keep my commandments, ye shall abide in my love; even as I have kept my Father's commandments, and abide in his love. These things have I spoken unto you, that my joy might remain in you, and that your joy might be full.

—JOHN 15:10–11

Words, again, that Jesus spoke to his disciples during the last evening that he was with them all, alone, as a mortal being.

It seems to me that Jesus was yearning over them that night, knowing that he was going to leave them on their own. Until then they had been sustained daily by his presence. From that point forward, they would have to rely on their faith. He knew he was going to undergo a fierce ordeal; he knew that they would as well, in their time. He knew their weaknesses. He knew their strengths, and he knew that those strengths would have to be deepened and intensified if they were going to be able to hold on through the trials to come.

He knew about Peter. Peter had already told him, proudly, that he would lay down his own life for Jesus' sake.

Really? The Lord asked, lovingly. By the time the cock crows, you will have denied me three times. John doesn't record what Peter said or did then, but we can imagine his indignant disbelief.

Jesus knew that Peter was going to panic. He also knew of Peter's incomparable integrity and sturdiness and his capacity to grow past his fear. Peter had a tremendous assignment to fulfill; had Jesus not believed in him, Peter never would have been given that authority. But that night, in the upper room, did the Lord watch Peter anxiously, knowing exactly what was going to be asked of this faithful disciple?

Jesus wanted to leave the disciples with the best protection and preparation that he could, and it's exactly the protection he offers to us. He told them over and over that evening, in many different ways, the same thing. If they kept his commandments, they could be kept in his protective love, and his love would hold them safe through any trial the mind of man or even the adversary could devise.

We have the same promise. Nobody can predict exactly what will be asked of us as individuals. So far, I've led a fairly ordinary life. Looking back on my trials, I can see that they have been nothing out of the ordinary, either, so far. But through those ordinary trials, through whatever may be asked of me in the days of my life to come, I know I have felt and will feel Christ's love as my shield and support, as long as I do not distance myself from him by disobedience. He will always be there. It's up to me if I will be.

MARCH 30

Not every one that saith unto me, Lord, Lord, shall enter into the kingdom of heaven; but he that doeth the will of my Father which is in heaven.

—MATTHEW 7:21

Or as we might put it, talk is cheap.

I have a good friend who is a Catholic. She and her husband tried long and hard to have a baby and eventually adopted a baby girl. Two years later she gave birth to a son. You would have thought everything was perfect then, but something went wrong, and the marriage crumbled. I don't know what happened; she says only that there was fault on both sides and in hindsight she can see things she could have, should have done differently—but that's in hindsight. In bitterness and anger, they divorced.

What concerns me now is what has happened since.

They have been divorced now for fifteen years or more. He has remarried; she has not. They still live in the same town, still unfriends, and the children move back and forth uneasily between them. For my friend, her faith is central. It has sustained her and continues to hold her life together when the middle of it has collapsed.

Her former husband has joined his new wife's church. It is a new sect that blossomed in the seventies and eighties: It preaches that love is all that is important, and as long as you love people around you, you're just fine. There are virtually no responsibilities. It strikes me as an adolescent worldview; certainly it is tremendously attractive to adolescents. A charismatic minister, no nerdy rules, pop music during the short services. It is hardly surprising that my friend's children find it much more appealing than the rigors of Catholicism, which, like our church, demands a great deal of its members. Neither of the children chose to be confirmed as Catholics.

My friend doesn't know what to do. All she can hope for is that eventually life will teach her children that they need more than froth and that obedience opens the way to understanding. All any of us can do is love her, reassure her that she did the best she could, and hope with her.

Not everybody that calls "Lord, Lord," will be saved. Dear Lord, I thank thee for the strength of thy laws, leading me, guiding me. When I sometimes chafe at rules, let me remember my friend and her children. Bless her; bless them. Help us find the way to draw them closer to thee.

MARCH 31

Let us hear the conclusion of the whole matter: Fear God, and keep his commandments: for this is the whole duty of man.
—ECCLESIASTES 12:13

What a neat, succinct statement to wrap up the month, as March slides away softly into the emerging spring!

Fear God. Yes, because the price of disobedience is high. It's not arbitrary, or set up by whim: It's just the way eternal reality functions. If we do not keep his commandments, we cannot come where he is, and where he is will be the only place where we can find joy, and peace, and the freedom to grow into our possibilities. Where he is not, there is darkness and despair.

Keep his commandments. Yes, because only by making those daily choices, one piled upon another, can we become the kind of beings who can bear his presence. From all we have been told, even if it were possible to slip under some heavenly fence or slide through some heavenly gate, if we have not been obedient, heaven would not be heaven for us. It would be a place of inexpressible torment, made even more so by the full knowledge of the opportunities we had squandered.

Today, the sun is shining. The grass is turning green. This beautiful world that God has created is unfolding, according to law, into its annual renewal. Today let me live contentedly, happily, within that law. Today, the yoke is easy, and the burden is light.

I thank thee, Lord, for today.

APRIL

For as in Adam all die, even so in Christ shall all be made alive.

—1 CORINTHIANS 15:22

APRIL 1

We believe in God, the Eternal Father, and in His Son, Jesus Christ, and in the Holy Ghost.
We believe that through the Atonement of Christ, all mankind may be saved, by obedience to laws and ordinances of the Gospel.
—ARTICLES OF FAITH 1 AND 3

During the years we lived in England, I encountered a grumpy old gentleman who had apparently grown up with the firm belief that the strange young men called Mormons (this was before so many young sisters were going on missions) who periodically knocked on doors in his neighborhood belonged to some peculiar sect most likely akin to what he called the Mooslems (well, they do both start with "M"), or even possibly the Hare Krishnas, who at that time were often walking in parks and through the airports chanting, wearing a British interpretation of eastern robes.

I tried to enlighten him, but he was exceedingly dubious about what I had to say. He could understand *church,* he said (which in English usage generally means the established Church of England, closest to the Episcopal Church in the United States), or *chapel* (which is used to refer to any of the nonconformist Protestant faiths—usually, in the part of England where my husband's family lives, the Methodists). He even knew about the papists, by which he meant the Roman Catholics. But Mormons were beyond him.

I said that nonetheless, we were Christians as well.

He lifted his eyebrows dubiously. "Well, not proper ones," he said, and that, as far as he was concerned, was that.

I suppose in his terms I am, as a member of The Church of Jesus Christ of Latter-day Saints, an improper sort of Christian. So what sort does that make me? Perhaps I can start this new month, which marks what we believe is the anniversary of the Savior's actual mortal birth and also most often includes the celebration of Easter, with trying to figure out what sort of Christian I am.

Am I Christian, in Christ's own terms? If I didn't happen to say I was, could someone tell it from the way I live?

Today, let me mull over that challenge.

APRIL 2

I shall see him, but not now: I shall behold him, but not nigh: there shall come a Star out of Jacob, and a Sceptre shall rise out of Israel, and shall smite the corners of Moab, and destroy all the children of Sheth.

—NUMBERS 24:17

This is the wonderful prophecy of the magician Balaam, who spoke the words God told him to say to Balak, the king of Moab. This was not precisely what Balak thought he would say; Balak had originally summoned Balaam to come curse the Israelites, because there were such a lot of them (by this time they were within sight of the promised land), and they were getting a good deal too close for Balak's comfort. Balaam, after a certain amount of strong-armed persuasion by the Lord, which included an angel with a drawn sword, reported instead what the Lord gave him to see. The unhappy Balak complained, "What hast thou done unto me? I took thee to curse mine enemies, and, behold, thou hast blessed them altogether."

From very early times, the Jewish commentators interpreted this prophecy as speaking about the coming of the Messiah. Taking that as a given, scholars argue about whether the star here refers to the star of Bethlehem or to Christ himself. Either way, it is a wonderful image to contemplate. "I shall see him, but not now; I shall behold him, but not nigh": The words have a splendid mystique to them.

Today let me remember that Christ's coming was part of the pattern from before the world began. The plan was in place; whenever the veil was lifted, even for a instant, it was all there, even for poor old Balaam, who, had he feared the Lord less, would have loved to receive the gold and silver that Balak offered for the cursing. Balaam might not have been a great man, but he knew better than to trifle with God. When he saw the vision of the Almighty, he reported faithfully, and what he reported is wonderfully familiar to us who know the rest of the story: "There shall come a Star out of Jacob."

APRIL 3

I will declare the decree: the Lord hath said unto me, Thou art my Son; this day have I begotten thee. Ask of me, and I shall give thee the heathen for thine inheritance, and the uttermost parts of the earth for thy possession.

—PSALM 2:7–8

Over and over throughout the Old Testament the prophecies look forward to the reign of the messianic king, who would overwhelm all Israel's adversaries, and rule the world in triumph.

Thinking about those prophecies might help us understand why the Jews weren't quite prepared for a carpenter's son, with no authority, majestic or otherwise, that they could figure out. When they asked him about the taxes that were a symbol of Rome's iron grip on their country, he asked them to show him a coin. (Not much of a ringing call to independence there, they must have thought.) He asked whose image was on the coin. Well, Caesar's, of course. Jesus then said mildly, "Render to Caesar the things that are Caesar's."

It's easy for us now to be patronizing and scornful about the Jews' failure to comprehend that they were in the presence of the true Messiah, the Son of God. We are the beneficiaries of nearly two thousand years of western Christianity and, comparatively recently, further confirmation of Christ's mission by means of the Book of Mormon. If we had been in those dusty villages, faithful followers of the traditions of our fathers, and somebody told us that someone was walking around saying he was the Messiah, and he didn't dress any better than any of the rest of us, what would we have done?

I hope I would have been in the crowd following our Lord Jesus Christ. I hope I would have recognized my Savior, however his greatness was disguised. But before I start pointing fingers of derision at the people who didn't, perhaps I ought to consider myself fortunate at never having been put to the test.

Maybe for me the test, knowing he is the Christ, is whether I can be faithful to his commandments. Do I truly love my fellowmen, including those who are not very nice? Do I serve gladly all the time, and not just when it's convenient? Do I forgive every offense seventy times seven, rather than hold even one tiny grudge?

Today maybe I'd better work on those. When I'm perfect, then maybe I can get around to considering how obtuse the Jews of Jesus' time seem to have been.

I'm not holding my breath.

APRIL 4

So all the generations from Abraham to David are fourteen gener-ations; and from David until the carrying away into Babylon are fourteen generations; and from the carrying away into Babylon unto Christ are fourteen generations.

—MATTHEW 1:17

Two genealogies of Jesus are recorded in the New Testament (the other is Luke 3:23–38). There are a couple of interesting things about them: The first is that both of them trace the geneal-ogy through Joseph (which, as Luke points out, was Jesus' father "as was supposed"). The second is that a lot of the names are different. Luke gives twenty-one names between David and Zerubbabel and seventeen between Zerubbabel and Joseph; Matthew gives fifteen and nine, respectively. So which, if either, is correct? And because we are all agreed that Jesus had no blood relationship to Joseph, what difference does it make anyway?

Bible scholars point out that no one at that period would have thought of tracing a woman's ancestry, but that it is probable that Mary was also of the house of David. Certainly "the son of David" was a standing title of the Messiah among the rabbis of Jesus' time and before, and the descent of Jesus' family from David was never questioned in his lifetime, even by his enemies.

The scholars also note that the differences between the line of descent in Matthew and the line in Luke are largely explained by their different purposes. Matthew, who was writing primarily for the Jews, was concerned to show Joseph's claim to being a rightful heir to the throne of Israel and therefore included several adoptions by childless monarchs. He began with Abraham, to show that Jesus was the Messiah of the Jews as promised to Father Abraham. Luke, who was writing more for the gentile world, gave Jesus' lineage through actual parentage, going all the way back to Adam.

What difference does it make? Part of it obviously shows the fulfillment of the ancient prophecies, but few of us, I would guess, hinge our testimony of the divinity of Jesus Christ on the identity of his triple great-grandfather. Most of us (like those ancient rabbis) accept that Jesus descended from David, and back from David to Abraham and Adam, and through which individuals in between isn't all that important. (Presumably, if the line could be traced through Mary, the names would be different from those in either Matthew or Luke in the later generations anyway.)

I suppose what it means to me—what I'll think about today, when I think about Jesus and his ancestry, accurate or not—is that Joseph came from a good family, and showed himself to be a good man. He and Mary were "espoused," or betrothed, which at that time was a contract, almost equivalent to marriage, that could not be broken without legal action. When he found Mary was with child, Joseph felt obliged to take such action, but he was kind enough to want to have it taken care of privately, without specifying the true cause. The legal penalty for Mary's presumed sin was stoning.

But Joseph was more than kind and merciful. When the full situation was explained to him by an angel in a dream, according to Matthew, he woke and obediently, without questioning, did as he was bidden to do. From that time forward he was Mary's stalwart support and a father on earth to the young Jesus.

Today let me remember Joseph. Let me remember how he obeyed, without asking a lot of questions or demanding that somebody come explain to him why it had to be his wife. Let me admire his calm acceptance, and model myself on it. Let me, like Joseph, trust the Lord implicitly. Let me, like Joseph, do as I am bidden.

APRIL 5

Lift up your head and be of good cheer; for behold, the time is at hand, and on this night shall the sign be given, and on the morrow come I into the world, to show unto the world that I will fulfil all that which I have caused to be spoken by the mouth of my holy prophets.

—3 NEPHI 1:13

Even on the eve of all the momentous events—the beginning of his earthly sojourn—Jesus remembered his "other sheep" and came to reassure Nephi, the son of Nephi and grandson of Helaman, that the time had come for his long-promised mission to bring salvation. Perhaps because his people in the New World were to see so much less of him than the people in the Old would see, the prophecies of his coming had always been much more explicit and unveiled. Now, certainly, unequivocally, Nephi was told that the day was here, and, indeed, the promised events came to pass: There was no darkness for a full day and a night, and then there was the star.

We are used to thinking of the birth of Christ as a wintertime event, inseparably linked to the time of year when we celebrate it, but there is something fitting about Jesus coming to earth in the spring, the season of renewal (although in the place where he spent his life the seasons may not be nearly as marked as they are for those of us who live in more northerly latitudes). But it was spring, and I like the idea of his star in a springtime sky being visible on this side of the world as well.

Today, let me celebrate the eve of Christ's birth, cut free from the holly and ivy and mistletoe and the rush of Christmas preparation. Let me celebrate the sense of wonder, clean and clear and by itself. A baby was born, and because of what that baby was and became, we will be born ourselves through death to eternal life.

It's a miracle. It was, and it is, and it always will be—the most public of miracles, because it came to all of us, and the most private of miracles, because of what it means to me as a singular daughter of God. Tonight, let me open this window and lean out into this fresh springtime night, wishing that by another miracle I, too, could see the star.

Still, seen or not, I know it was there.

APRIL 6

For unto us a child is born, unto us a son is given: and the government shall be upon his shoulder: and his name shall be called Wonderful, Counsellor, The mighty God, The everlasting Father, The Prince of Peace.

—Isaiah 9:6

Oh, wonderful Handel! Once having heard *Messiah*, who can read these words without hearing the triumphant voices tumbling over each other in rejoicing at the birth of our Lord?

I remember (again with the University Chorus) singing *Messiah* with the San Francisco Symphony Orchestra, and feeling the floor of the opera house tremble under our feet with the volume of sound we produced. I remember the voices chiming in and around each other, proclaiming and repeating the wonder of it all. It was a wonderful, never-to-be-forgotten experience.

I also remember my father coming to collect me and some friends after one of the performances, wearing for some absurd reason a safety helmet painted gold: he looked exactly like a walnut decorated for Christmas.

Oh, dear Heavenly Father, thank you for this world and all the sublime and ridiculous experiences I have had here. Thank you for the magnificence of music and the lovableness of a father who was perfectly happy to look like a walnut if it made a daughter laugh.

How rich my life has been, and is. How fortunate I am that, thanks to this Child, I have the promise of living with him (and with my father who looked like a walnut) through the boundless expanses of eternity to come.

APRIL 7

And Jesus increased in wisdom and stature, and in favour with God and man.

—LUKE 2:52

Years ago, I was involved in editing a book about the Dutch and Flemish masters who illuminated manuscripts in the Middle Ages. I remember one of the illustrations in particular. Even that early, Dutch artists chose to show life as they knew it, in its most practical aspects. This one little picture (tiny enough to fit within an initial capital letter) showed Joseph in his carpentry shop, and in the middle of the shop, navigating in a sturdy walker, was the toddler Jesus.

I loved it; it was so real. Jesus, like all the rest of us, had to learn to walk. In fact, that is one of the elements that makes Jesus so accessible to us. He knows about our life. He was here, a person, as we are.

He lived most of his life in relative obscurity. According to Luke, Jesus didn't begin teaching until he was about thirty and his ministry lasted for only three years. Most of his life is unrecorded. Presumably he was in Nazareth, the village where Luke says he was brought up, passing his days much like the other people in the village. Joseph, his father in the eyes of the world, was a carpenter, and Jesus learned to be a carpenter as well. I don't suppose that makes carpentry a more holy occupation than any other; what that means to me is that ordinary work is meant to be part of our life here on earth. We were not sent here to waste our time on trivial pleasures: We came to learn to use our hands, our minds, and above all our free agency, and one of the best uses of free agency is to choose to be good at whatever you do. If you are a housewife, you do well to choose to be a good housewife. If you are a carpenter, there is virtue in being a good carpenter. I am sure he was.

Today, let me remember that and take pride in my ordinary occupations. Let me air the bedding, straighten the kitchen, dig in the garden—the baby lettuces are ready to set out—and take pleasure in the good, honest work. Let me take the time to do it well, rather than being tempted to slide through the jobs on the theory that it doesn't matter, really; today let me imagine how Jesus would have done the ordinary jobs in his life.

I thank thee, Lord, for the artists who let us look at our own lives from a different point of view. Let me remember the Dutch master lovingly painting the details of the Baby Jesus' gown in his walker; let me remember Joseph at work. The gown had to be washed every day. Whatever Joseph did as a carpenter, it must have involved repeating the same operations over and over. That is the way, I'm sure, that the young Jesus learned to work at Joseph's side.

My jobs are repetitive, too. If Jesus was not too grand to do his, I am certainly not too grand to do mine. I will not moan. If the beds have to be made and the kitchen floor has to be scrubbed again tomorrow, help me to remember not to complain. Let me do the jobs again tomorrow, too, and let me be content.

APRIL 8

Now when all the people were baptized, it came to pass, that Jesus also being baptized, and praying, the heaven was opened. And the Holy Ghost descended in a bodily shape like a dove upon him, and a voice came from heaven, which said, Thou art my beloved Son; in thee I am well pleased.

—LUKE 3:21–22

Sunday morning, and it's the usual disorganized rush trying to get people in and out of the bathroom, into Sunday clothes, and out to the car. My husband hates being late. Because of the family with which he has equipped himself, he too often is, and today looks as if it's falling into the familiar pattern. He is therefore stalking around the kitchen threatening to get in the car and drive away this minute. The children, having heard this before, are coming—or so they say. I am running up and down the stairs trying to find things.

It's at moments like this that I think wistfully of all the people who claim that church attendance and religious ritual are nothing but unnecessary fuss. They, so they claim, can feel close to God anywhere. You don't need to go through all this Sunday bustle.

Today let me remember that Jesus, the perfect God made man, faithfully observed religious ritual. He did not sit under a tree and think beautiful thoughts; he went to John the Baptist to be baptized. He did not habitually retire into the desert to feel close to God; as Luke reports, he went to the synagogue "as his custom was."

If Jesus had lived in our house, Jesus would have gone to church on Sunday morning, too. (He would, however, have been on time.) Perhaps what I need to do is pay more attention to my real problem—which is the need for better organization on Saturday—and less attention to the reasoning of people who don't value church attendance and religious ritual.

Maybe Sundays are a test of character. Maybe next week I'll pass.

APRIL 9

But charity is the pure love of Christ, and it endureth forever; and whoso is found possessed of it at the last day, it shall be well with him.

—MORONI 7:47

If the gospel were a piece of music, love would be the leitmotif that threads through it, repeated in different voices and different modes but forever the same in shape and pattern.

Why is love so important? Today let me think about that, as I move through my day doing all the things that need to be done. Why should love be so fundamental to the gospel of Christ? Why should love be an integral part of the first two commandments, as Christ taught them?

What does love feel like? When I put it like that (pausing in the middle of putting breakfast dishes in the dishwasher to look out the window at my daughter helping my son pick up the books he just dropped all over the driveway), something snaps into focus. When you love, you are filled with peace and contentment. When you truly love, you are spilling yourself outward. There's no way for irritation or anger or jealousy or insecurity to worm their way against that flow into your heart. There's no room for Satan. There is only warmth and, rising from it, the serenity of harmony.

No wonder love is of Christ. No wonder Satan fears it. Today, let me open myself to love. Today, let that serenity of harmony be mine.

APRIL 10

Again the next day after John stood, and two of his disciples; and looking upon Jesus as he walked, he saith, Behold the Lamb of God! And the two disciples heard him speak, and they followed Jesus. Then Jesus turned, and saw them following, and saith unto them, What seek ye? They said unto him, Rabbi, (which is to say, being interpreted, Master,) where dwellest thou? He saith unto them, Come and see. They came and saw where he dwelt, and abode with him that day: for it was about the tenth hour.

—JOHN 1:35–39

One of those disciples, John goes on to say, was Andrew, Simon Peter's brother. The other, whom he does not name, was himself.

It was no part of John's purpose in writing his gospel to magnify his own importance. What he wants to share with the rest of the world is his own transcendent faith in Jesus as the Messiah and the Son of God. He was one of the disciples closest to our Lord; he is described as the disciple "whom Jesus loved." It was into John's care that Jesus gave his own mother, as he hung dying on the cross; John ran with Peter to the tomb when they received word of the Resurrection. It was John, at the sea of Tiberias, who recognized the resurrected Christ when the other disciples did not; based on his word that it was the Lord, Simon Peter flung himself into the water to get to the shore where Jesus was.

It is, of course, our good fortune that John was not only in a position to be able to give an intensely personal view of Jesus' ministry but that he was also an incomparably gifted writer. His words are so beautiful that even people who choose to disbelieve its message are captivated by his book as literature.

Do I show that I love the Gospel of John? Today, let me be grateful for this wonderful book. Let me delight in the near-poetry of its expression and be moved—again, and forever—by the story it tells.

How wonderful it would have been to be there. How blessed we are that John lets us come so close to sharing it.

APRIL 11

And we talk of Christ, we rejoice in Christ, we preach of Christ, we prophesy of Christ, and we write according to our prophecies, that our children may know to what source they may look for a remission of their sins.

—2 Nephi 25:26

The message is triumphant and single-minded. Why should it be so difficult to keep our lives centered upon Christ?

Satan's way would have been easier. But we chose the path of centrifugal forces, to come to an earth where we would be distracted by thousands of alternatives. We have the freedom to choose and only the opportunity to choose wisely. No one will compel us to do so.

What does Christ's mission mean to me? It means that there is a being who knows all about me. He knows about my failures as well as my successes; he knows about the gap between my intentions and my performance. He knows when my motives are mean and selfish. Knowing all that, he chose to take responsibility for my sins and shortcomings and, by accepting the punishment himself, he freed me from the irreversible consequences of error. He made repentance possible.

I could not have done that for myself. No one else could have, either. What more important message can I teach to my children? What more important message can I treasure, this bright spring day?

APRIL 12

The Lord works from the inside out. The world works from the outside in. The world would take people out of the slums. Christ takes the slums out of people, and then they take themselves out of the slums. The world would mold men by changing their environment. Christ changes men, who then change their environment. The world would shape human behavior, but Christ can change human nature.

—PRESIDENT EZRA TAFT BENSON

Sometimes it's hard to step back and trust—really trust—that the Lord will take care of our problems. It's not that we doubt he will, exactly, it's just that we want to keep offering advice on how it should be done and make suggestions about the timing and arrangements.

Say, for instance, you have a family disagreement on your hands. Nothing really serious—I mean, nobody's talking about suing anybody or anything—but there is a distinct coolness on all sides. Your family is primarily made up of good members of the Church, so it only makes sense to suggest that everybody pray about the problem—or at least make that suggestion to the members of the family with whom you're feeling friendly enough to make suggestions.

Fair enough. So what do you pray for? Well, it seems perfectly clear that somebody needs to have a softening of the heart so that you can get the problem dealt with, but because it isn't *your* heart that's being the problem (you, after all, have been amazingly mature and long-suffering through the entire affair; you're absolutely certain of that), you have a few ideas about what the Lord needs to do about the other parties in the dispute.

You get the idea.

Today let me practice putting problems in the hands of the Lord and then waiting quietly for guidance—not suggesting, not getting started on what I'm sure the Lord will tell me to do, and above all not framing the problem in such terms (even in my own head) that I am the Perfect Princess and everybody else is unfortunately falling short. Simon Peter walked on water; let me not start with such virtuoso exercises but instead be content to listen for guidance without interrupting.

As President Benson pointed out, Christ has the power. I am the one who needs the faith.

APRIL 13

They say unto him, Master, this woman was taken in adultery, in the very act.

Now Moses in the law commanded us, that such should be stoned: but what sayest thou?

This they said, tempting him, that they might have to accuse him. But Jesus stooped down, and with his finger wrote on the ground, as though he heard them not.

So when they continued asking him, he lifted up himself, and said unto them, He that is without sin among you, let him first cast a stone at her.

And again he stooped down, and wrote on the ground.

And they which heard it, being convicted by their own conscience, went out one by one, beginning at the eldest, even unto the last: and Jesus was left alone, and the woman standing in the midst.

When Jesus had lifted up himself, and saw none but the woman, he said unto her, Woman, where are those thine accusers? hath no man condemned thee?

She said, No man, Lord. And Jesus said unto her, Neither do I condemn thee: go, and sin no more.

—JOHN 8:4–11

A long scripture for today, but no reasonable way to cut it short. What a lovely vignette! The details are there; you can read it and see the whole scene played out before your eyes. There was the crowd, huffing and puffing (as I imagine it) with belligerence and the auxiliary hope of catching this peculiarly authoritative teacher in some breach of the law. There was Jesus, paying little attention to them, stooping down to write in the dust with his finger. There was the woman, shamed, humiliated—caught in the very act, mind you. (Where, I wonder, was the man?)

Jesus answered the challenge of the accusing scribes and Pharisees with the simple suggestion that whoever was without sin should start the stoning. Then he went back to writing, stooping back down to the ground.

Whatever it was that he wrote, the crowd searched their own

hearts and slunk away. At the end, Jesus looked up and only the woman was left there, standing alone. Gently, warning her to sin no more, he sent her on her way.

Let me remember today from this story that it is not my job to judge anybody but myself. Nor is it my responsibility even to discuss anybody else's faults and failings. Strengthen me against the temptation of gossip, Lord. It's so easy to start, and so hard to stop.

Above all, let me master perfection for myself before I get started working on anybody else's. I'm short of time as it is.

APRIL 14

But straightway Jesus spake unto them, saying, Be of good cheer; it is I; be not afraid.

And Peter answered him and said, Lord, if it be thou, bid me come unto thee on the water.

And he said, Come. And when Peter was come down out of the ship, he walked on the water, to go to Jesus.

But when he saw the wind boisterous, he was afraid; and beginning to sink, he cried, saying, Lord, save me.

And immediately Jesus stretched forth his hand, and caught him, and said unto him, O thou of little faith, wherefore didst thou doubt?

—MATTHEW 14:27–31

Remember that Primary song, "Tell Me the Stories of Jesus"? This is one of my favorites, about what happened when the disciples looked out of their boat to see Christ walking on the sea towards them in the middle of a storm.

Dear, faithful Peter. It was Peter who went out to meet Jesus. Notice that even when Peter felt himself sinking (because fear had overcome his faith in what he was doing), he still trusted implicitly in Jesus' ability to save him. How must it have felt to have that strong hand catch you, even as the beloved voice so lovingly reproached you?

Peter was a plain and honest man. His personality shines, plainly and honestly, through the gospel accounts.

When he had a question, he asked it. When he was afraid, he called for help. He seems incapable of deception: The one time he tried, when he denied Christ three times during the long night after

Christ's capture, he was unnerved instantly when Jesus turned and looked at him. Peter left the place and wept the hard tears of a strong man who had the courage to look at his failure squarely. As far as we can tell from the New Testament, he never failed again.

I doubt I have enough faith to walk across water, but, when I look back at it, I realize I have felt the strong grip of the Lord many times, rescuing me from my stupidities and reminding me of my faith when I seem to be woolgathering. Please Lord, help me make myself worthy of what I so much want to possess: that sense of closeness to thee.

Let me, like Peter, grow under thy care and keeping. Let me be working on it today.

APRIL 15

Then cried Jesus in the temple as he taught, saying, Ye both know me, and ye know whence I am: and I am not come of myself, but he that sent me is true, whom ye know not. But I know him: for I am from him, and he hath sent me.

—JOHN 7:28–29

When I teach the Interpersonal Skills class at the business school, I have the students keep a journal for the six weeks that the class lasts. I do that for several reasons. One is that most of them can use the practice in expressing themselves in writing; also, as adults having decided to take a new direction in life, they can use some introspection on how it's going. It makes interesting reading. Obviously, the students all know I am going to read the journals, but sometimes they are amazingly candid in spite of that.

I remember one in particular that was kept by a young woman who was just a couple of years out of high school. She never did a thing, according to her journal, without consulting Jesus about it, and she consulted on everything. She consulted Jesus prayerfully about which route to drive to school, whether to have lunch before she went home, whether to bring her mother french fries from the fast-food store, whether to go to a movie. And for each successful consultation (which they all were), she praised Jesus at length.

Now of course this may have been simply a way to use up space and thus produce a nice full journal for her teacher, but, having known the student, I don't think so. I think much of my response to her journal writing is simply that she had grown up in a different style than is familiar to me. And what I need to remember, particularly as the Church becomes more and more global, is that there is a difference between doctrine and style. Doctrine doesn't change from place to place, even continent to continent, and century to century. Style does, and there's nothing wrong with that.

Here, in this scripture, Jesus laid down the bottom line. What we must know is that Jesus came from our Heavenly Father and was sent by him to redeem us. As long as we know that, how we express it is less important.

I was brought up with the idea that the glory of God is intelligence and it is a slothful servant who needs to be commanded in all things, but maybe my student wasn't looking for commandment, just guidance. In any case, what difference does it make? She was seeking to have a genuinely close relationship with her Savior Jesus Christ. So am I. Does it matter what the style of that relationship might be?

Today, dear Lord, help me to be less arrogant and self-righteous. Today, let me recognize faith when I see it, instead of presuming it has to come in the shape I recognize and be exhibited by people like me.

Today, let me concentrate on my own relationship with Jesus, and leave other people's alone.

APRIL 16

How can ye believe, which receive honour one of another, and seek not the honour that cometh from God only? Do not think that I will accuse you to the Father: there is one that accuseth you, even Moses, in whom ye trust. For had ye believed Moses, ye would have believed me: for he wrote of me. But if ye believe not his writings, how shall ye believe my words?

—JOHN 5:44–47

This followed Christ's healing of the man at the pool of Bethesda on the Sabbath. The Jews, who were already unhappy about the amount of attention Jesus was attracting, were made even more angry by the fact that he was now, in their terms, disregarding the sanctity of the Sabbath and on top of that, saying that God was his father, "making himself equal with God."

Jesus answered them reasonably, citing several witnesses to his claim: he named the witness of John the Baptist, the testimony of the Father himself (which, as he points out, they don't believe anyway), the witness of the character of the works he has done, which show that they are of the Father, and here in this scripture, he explains that he is fulfilling the words of Moses himself which prophesied of his coming.

He didn't expect the angry Jews to be convinced, and they were not.

It's odd, isn't it, that intellectual polemic never does work in convincing people of the truthfulness of the gospel. We can marshal all the logical reasons (and there are many) why the gospel has to be true, but unless the person to whom we are talking is listening with the Spirit, he will remain unconvinced. Only when a person is prepared to take the leap of faith will the whole picture make sense. Faith is not only useful; it's essential. The Jews who argued with Jesus were not prepared to rely on the faith they unquestionably had in other things—in Moses, as Jesus points out here, for example— and so they would not and could not believe. They never did.

Today let me think about that faith which is so important to my testimony. It is the foundation upon which everything else rests. Let me remember the certainty that faith offers; let me trust in my faith to trust in the Lord.

Today, let me know that I know.

APRIL 17

Peace I leave with you, my peace I give unto you: not as the world giveth, give I unto you. Let not your heart be troubled, neither let it be afraid.

—JOHN 14:27

A spring storm. The lightning is blazing across the sky almost simultaneously with the crack of thunder that you can feel as much as hear. The storm is on top of us now; one cat jumps under the bed and the other curls up as close to me as she can manage. The dog wanders around the room unhappily, now sitting by the side of the bed anxiously watching me, now peering out of the bedroom into the hall. She doesn't like it.

Neither do I.

Still, this is only a spring storm. It will pass, and so will the rain. Jesus was promising his peace to his disciples who had a far more threatening storm ahead of them. He himself was going to die, as he had to. They would have to watch him die, only half understanding what his promise to them meant: They were not to be afraid, because this death would have a transcendent meaning. By means of this death would come eternal life.

Today, while the storm cracks and flashes overhead, let me remember and trust in his peace. Let not my heart be troubled, nor afraid. Because Jesus Christ sacrificed himself for us, all mortality exists in the frame of eternity. We cannot be trapped by what happens here. Christ brought us eternal life, and if we live up to his gift of repentance, we will live with him again in the life to come.

Christ spoke the simple truth: His peace is not the peace of the world. It is a deeper peace than the world can offer. Let me look past the lightning and the rain and all the other perils of this life to the reaches of eternity that can be open to me. Let me trust, today, in that peace which Christ brings to all of his disciples, even—in the midst of this storm—to me. Let me be worthy to have that peace enfold me.

APRIL 18

He is despised and rejected of men; a man of sorrows, and acquainted with grief: and we hid as it were our faces from him; he was despised, and we esteemed him not.

Surely he hath borne our griefs, and carried our sorrows: yet we did esteem him stricken, smitten of God, and afflicted.

But he was wounded for our transgressions, he was bruised for our iniquities: the chastisement of our peace was upon him; and with his stripes we are healed.

—ISAIAH 53:3–5

How wonderful it is that a man who died seven hundred years before Jesus Christ was born wrote one of the most vivid accounts of his sufferings! Read his words: They all came true.

In this month that so often includes our Easter observance, let me remember the price that was paid for my eternal life. Let me not get so absorbed with colored eggs and jelly beans and chocolate rabbits that I forget the core of it all.

Did Jesus know from the beginning what he would need to do? If Isaiah knew seven hundred years before, certainly Jesus knew. Did he dread it? Did he hope, right up to the end, that some other way might be found? Perhaps; remember his prayers in the Garden of Gethsemane. But he overcame his human reluctance to obey his Father's will. That's what our Easter celebration is all about.

Rightly, I believe, our church chooses to concentrate more on the glory of his life than on the agony of his death. The life is what is everlasting; the death was only a door enabling him, and all of us, to move from one life to another. Still, let me remember the prophetic words of Isaiah and never forget the sacrifice that gained us such a magnificent reward.

Isaiah saw it all. "With his stripes we are healed," he wrote. Those were literally stripes from the beatings Jesus endured. Let me also remember that the healing is literal, too. Let me live to be worthy of it. Let me live to be healed.

APRIL 19

Therefore doth my Father love me, because I lay down my life, that I might take it again. No man taketh it from me, but I lay it down of myself. I have power to lay it down, and I have power to take it again. This commandment have I received of my Father.

—JOHN 10:17–18

Right here is the nub of the mystery. We may never be able to understand precisely how the Atonement worked, but here Christ explains, clearly and matter-of-factly, the central equation. Only he, as the literal son of God the Father, had the capacity to voluntarily give up his mortal life and then pass through the miracle of resurrection to take it up again. Only he, as both God and man, could make that sacrifice on behalf of all the rest of us. If any of us (unavoidably sin-stained from our time on this earth) had tried to do such a thing, it would have been in part self-interested.

We would have needed absolution for ourselves as well as for the rest of humankind. Jesus needed no forgiveness. He had done nothing wrong, literally, and because of that, his sacrifice was wholly altruistic. He suffered and died because we, for whom he died, are careless, and greedy, and capable of evil. Yet he gave up his life so that we may live again.

This Easter, let me look past the cute fluffy chicks and the chocolate eggs. Let me concentrate on the awe I feel when I think—really think—about the Atonement. This Easter season, let me choose to express my gratitude. This Easter season, let me reach out for his love.

APRIL 20

My God, my God, why hast thou forsaken me? why art thou so far from helping me, and from the words of my roaring?

—PSALM 22:1

We know this psalm best, of course, as the words Jesus Christ cried out in his death agony as he hung on the cross.

It reminds me, therefore, of two things. First of all, it reminds me that Jesus had used his childhood and youth and his early years as an adult to learn a lot of things, including this psalm. We are told that he "increased in wisdom," so we know he learned.

He knew the scriptures. He knew the law. He was perfectly capable of arguing the fine points of rabbinical theory with the scribes and the Pharisees, and on occasion he did; more often, he told them it was a waste of time.

Jesus, then, knew the scriptures so well that in the moments of his greatest suffering he automatically used them to express the anguish of his heart. Could David have imagined when he wrote these words the situation in which they would be so poignantly used?

The second thing I think about when I consider the beginning of this psalm is what the words mean.

When Jesus came to this earth, he embraced the whole spectrum of human experience. He had to learn to hold his head up and to walk, just as we do—maybe not in the little wooden walker imagined by the Dutch manuscript illuminator, but it is nice to think he did. Anyway, he was a baby, and he had to learn. He grew up, and he got hungry, and he ate; he got tired, and he slept. There is the recorded instance of him getting angry: Remember when he threw the money-changers out of the temple? He knew love, and tenderness, and pity.

And here, hanging on the cross surrounded by the crowd jeering and laughing at him (and this psalm goes on to quote precisely what some of the priests were saying to him: "He trusted on the Lord that he would deliver him: let him deliver him, seeing he delighted in him"), Jesus felt what most of us, maybe all of us, feel at one time or another. He felt totally alone and abandoned. Even the presence of his Father was withdrawn from him. He had to do it alone. Nothing about this sacrifice was made easy.

Let me remember that, next time I am wallowing in self-pity. Feeling this way is part of the job. Was Jesus alone on the cross, even though it felt that way? Of course not. His Father and the legions of angels in heaven were waiting to welcome him home. His disciples wept at the foot of his cross. Down the centuries the people proud to carry his name have worshipped and adored him for what he was doing that day.

Am I then so alone, either, when I feel forsaken? Not really. Even if no other human being cares (which is unlikely, if I'm being realistic), there is always Christ. He shared that experience, and he understands. More than any other, he understands, and he is always there.

APRIL 21

And Jesus cried with a loud voice, and gave up the ghost. And the veil of the temple was rent in twain from the top to the bottom.

—MARK 15:37–38

I t was over. He had done what he came to do.

The veil of the temple tearing (two huge veils hung before the Holy of Holies, a little less than two feet apart; both tore) was only one of the physical signs of disturbance. For three hours the sky had been darkened; at the moment of his death not only did the veil tear, but there was a sharp earthquake, strong enough so that

Matthew reports "the rocks rent" (Matthew 27:51). There have, of course, been all sorts of ingenious explanations as to what actually happened. That there was a quake, that it did in fact get dark, that the veils were torn seems indisputable: The earliest authorities are all unanimous on those points.

Does it matter to me what the physical explanation might be? Not really. My testimony certainly wouldn't depend on it. I suppose what it mainly reminds me of is that as mortals we are part of the materials of the earth. Just as we feel cheerful on sunny days and are inclined to be depressed when it's gray and gloomy, so are we earth's creatures, and when Christ, who at least in part was one of us, voluntarily tore himself out of life, the earth itself shuddered.

What must it have been like for his disciples, standing at the cross, listening to the mocking voices, aiding in the hasty burial so that all would be in order for the Sabbath? Jesus had told them that this would happen, but how hard would it be to believe that this ignominious ending was not the end? After all, dead is dead. Jesus had said that he would rise again, but how many of them could have truly known what he meant? Resurrection had never happened before.

But it was to happen.

Let me remember that when I mutter over elements of the gospel that seem difficult to believe in mortal terms or by relying on mortal wisdom. What did Paul tell us? "For now we see through a glass, darkly" (1 Corinthians 13:12).

Let me remember the glass. Let me remember there is vastly more to be seen than I can imagine. Let me grow in faith.

APRIL 22

And it came to pass that when the thunderings, and the lightnings, and the storm, and the tempest, and the quakings of the earth did cease—for behold, they did last for about the space of three hours; and it was said by some that the time was greater; nevertheless, all these great and terrible things were done in about the space of three hours— and then behold, there was darkness upon the face of the land.

—3 NEPHI 8:19

I t was not only in Jerusalem that the earth shuddered.

We get so used to the earth behaving in orderly and predictable ways. Scientists explain to us how various phenomena come to be, and theorists put together evidence to account for the cataclysms of our natural history. None of their work acknowledges the existence of miracles. Still, miracles there have been.

The death of Christ unleashed extraordinary natural events. What was it like for the Nephites caught up in that great and terrible storm or swept away by the whirlwinds or swallowed by earthquakes? When the earth itself heaves under your feet, where is there to hide?

Similar great and terrible upheavals will announce the second coming of our Lord, and only our faithfulness to his commandments will give us safety. But how can an earthquake, tempest, or flood differentiate between the disobedient and the faithful? Maybe that will be part of a miracle. More often, I suspect, safety is important only because of our foreshortened perspective. If we look at our existence with eternity in mind, the distinction between being swept away by a flood next week and being hit by a bus fifty years from now fades a bit.

In any case, it's not our job to work out such problems. For centuries, mankind has fussed with theological conundrums, whether it's angels on a pin or whether the earth will tremble more in Missouri or in Utah, when the real problem at hand is considerably more pedestrian—making peace with the aggrieved lady next door, for example, when your dog has been chasing her cat. That may not be as *interesting*, but it is an everyday problem, and everyday problems are what we have been sent here to solve.

We have important things—everyday, nonmiraculous things— to accomplish here on this earth, and we have little enough time as it is. Our job is to learn to do as we have been commanded, which generally means leaving explanations of the miraculous to the Lord.

Please, Lord, today help me to do better at my job.

APRIL 23

*And he said unto them: Marvel not that I said unto you that old
things had passed away, and that all things had become new.*

*Behold, I say unto you that the law is fulfilled that was given
unto Moses. Behold, I am he that gave the law, and I am he who
covenanted with my people Israel; therefore, the law in me is fulfilled, for I have come to fulfil the law; therefore it hath an end.*

—3 Nephi 15:3–5

Every now and then, on a slow news day, the papers will run a
story on some of the antique laws that are still on the books. It's
meant to give us a smile, take a glimpse back at a vanished society,
make us grateful that we live now (although some of the laws on
Sunday observance weren't half bad, and we have clearly demonstrated that without them greed and/or sharp business practice will
have us running commerce full-bore what my daughter calls 24–7,
which is to say all of the time).

We always say that the eternal laws don't change, and they
don't. Yet the laws of man that regulate our behavior here on earth
clearly have, and in this scripture Jesus, during his ministry on the
American continent, is explaining precisely that. He had given the
law in the first place, and he had fulfilled it. All those detailed rules
in what the scholars call the Pentateuch, the first five books of the
Old Testament compiled and written by Moses (presumably among
the records which Lehi and his family took with them into the
wilderness), were now of historical interest only. What the Lord
told the Nephites applies to them, to the Jews, to the Gentiles of
that time, and to all of us who have lived since then.

Times change; circumstances change. Although such a major
upheaval as the replacement of Mosaic law by the law of the Savior
happens only once, other changes do affect what is required of us.
The pioneer companies crossing the plains, for example, had a code
of behavior no longer required now that most of us live in settled
circumstances, spread across the countries of the world. This is
exactly why we need, why we must have, continued revelation. Are
we to believe that our Lord has told us everything we need to know
for all time? Are we so much better than our predecessors that we
can rely solely on our own judgment? Looking around at the corruption and mayhem we manage to create, faithfully chronicled in
those same newspapers, I don't think so.

Today, while I'm rushing around doing all my end-of-the-twentieth-century jobs, let me be particularly grateful for the end-of-the-twentieth-century counsel. General conference was not long ago; the *Ensign*, with the permanent record of what was said, will come in the mail soon now. I don't know if I will ever be fortunate enough to hear the words of my Lord in person while I live on the earth, as those Nephites did, but I do know I can listen to the words of his prophet, seer, and revelator for my time.

All mankind is blessed by that prophet's presence. Let me be grateful that I am one of those who knows it.

APRIL 24

But we must . . . follow the doctrine of Christ, which is to believe in Jesus, rely on him, repent of our sins, take his name upon us by being baptized in his Church, receive the gift of the Holy Ghost, and faithfully follow Christ all of our lives.

He knows we need much help to do this, so he provides that the ordinance of the sacrament be repeated often.

This invitation of the Savior to come unto him is issued regularly and is universal. Everyone is included—men, women, and children. Old and young alike participate. None are barred except by themselves.

—ELDER JOHN H. GROBERG

Sunday morning and the babies are wiggly.

How many miles did my babies march over me (hard little heels digging into my thigh bones and up my front) during sacrament services? There's a different quality to the silence during the sacrament. I'm afraid Latter-day Saint meetings (except funerals) are rarely entirely silent—I am always impressed by the reverence when I visit another denomination—but during the sacrament usually the only sounds you hear are the deacons' feet shuffling (because twelve- and thirteen-year-old boys shuffle) and the squeaks and protests of the babies. Those protests always sound a lot louder to their mothers during the sacrament, and there are times when the squeaks are entirely joyful. What do you do then? How do you shush a happy baby?

It is very difficult to focus your thoughts on Christ and the

Atonement when you are being walked over. It's hard to do much of a spiritual summing-up of the past week when your two-year-old is trying to fish something out of the bottom of the diaper bag and is flinging rattles, empty bottles, and other miscellany noisily to all sides. Only very, very seldom do the dumplings choose to collapse in sleep that early in the service—it's too quiet, is my theory.

My kids don't walk on me anymore. Now my problems are more along the line of making sure they are not dozing off (Saturday nights must be hard on them) or nudging each other inappropriately. Most of the time, I do have the opportunity to concentrate.

But conditions are never perfect. Now my problem is to keep from being distracted by all the memories: watching Jane climb over her mother, I remember the hard little heels digging into my stomach . . .

It's a good thing we have the sacrament repeated frequently. Dear Lord, I thank thee for these memories, whether they should be entangled with the sacrament or not. But let me never forget thy sacrifice and the promise of eternity it brought. Let me remember that, too.

APRIL 25

Jesus saith unto her, Woman, why weepest thou? whom seekest thou? She, supposing him to be the gardener, saith unto him, Sir, if thou have borne him hence, tell me where thou hast laid him, and I will take him away.

Jesus saith unto her, Mary. She turned herself, and saith unto him, Rabboni; which is to say, Master.

Jesus saith unto her, Touch me not; for I am not yet ascended to my Father: but go to my brethren, and say unto them, I ascend unto my Father, and your Father; and to my God, and your God.

Mary Magdalene came and told the disciples that she had seen the Lord, and that he had spoken these things unto her.

—JOHN 20:15–18

According to Mark and Luke (who got his information from Peter), the disciples couldn't believe her. According to John, it was that night, when the disciples had slipped away from the Jews and were gathered in a locked room, that Jesus appeared in the room in the midst of them. Then they knew him, could see the wounds in his hands and side; then they were able to put aside their grief and fear and were "glad." What a small word for such a tremendous emotion!

If his disciples had such trouble believing it, do we truly believe? Well, I suppose in some ways it's a lot easier for us: We benefit from the centuries-long tradition that it happened. When we're little we start out with Easter eggs and bunnies and flannel-board stories in Primary; the fact as a fact kind of seeps into our consciousness. In the Christian world at large, a lot of theological argument has gone on, particularly recently, about whether the Resurrection really happened, or if it is meant to be an allegory from which we can be expected to glean the following universal truths . . . etc., etc., etc. I've never been quite clear about what we were expected to glean.

As Latter-day Saints, we escape most of that revisionist nonsense. But one thing that occurs to me to wonder is whether the fact that it's easier for us to believe in the Resurrection makes us less sensitive to the wonder and marvel of it. Jesus had told his disciples what was to happen. They saw him die as he had told them he was going to, but they still could not fully believe that he was indeed going to rise again, that the body they had seen tortured and tormented into death—and there is no question that Jesus was dead—was going to be reinhabited by his spirit, that they were going to be able to see that body moving, and talking, and know their beloved Savior was alive again.

Unless we understand why it was a struggle to accept the evidence of Mary Magdalene, and even of their own eyes, we can't understand the wonder: Jesus was dead on Friday and alive again on Sunday. Because of his death and resurrection, exactly the same thing will happen to all of us. If we don't understand how that might seem incredible, we don't understand the miracle.

Lord, help me understand.

APRIL 26

*And when he had spoken these things, while they beheld, he was
taken up; and a cloud received him out of their sight. And while
they looked stedfastly toward heaven as he went up, behold, two
men stood by them in white apparel; which also said, ye men of
Galilee, why stand ye gazing up into heaven? this same Jesus, which
is taken up from you into heaven, shall so come in like manner as
ye have seen him go into heaven.*

—ACTS 1:9–11

And so they were on their own. For forty days, the resurrected
Christ had appeared intermittently to his disciples, demon-
strating that he indeed inhabited a real body, that he could eat and
drink, that he had risen. He no longer lived among them, as he had
done before: He appeared abruptly, no longer subject to the earth's
physical laws, and presumably disappeared the same way. But he was
there, and I would think that the apostles might have been getting
used to an idea that he was going to continue to be.

This departure was different. When the apostles still stood
there, staring up at where he had vanished (probably somewhat
confused by what was going on), the two angels made it clear. Jesus
had returned to heaven, and it was time for them to stop gazing up
at the sky. They needed to get started on their own duties here on
earth.

We may need the same counsel. It is wonderful to immerse
myself in the stories of Christ on this earth. The stories are familiar
and yet new, when I think about them in new ways. It's a temptation to go on thinking. It's harder to do the doing.

The admonitions are all there, chiming in my head like the
overlapping clamor of bells. "Judge not, that ye be not judged." "No
man can serve two masters. . . . Ye cannot serve God and mammon."
"Seek ye first the kingdom of God, and his righteousness; and all
these things shall be added unto you." "Inasmuch as ye did it not to
one of the least of these, ye did it not to me." "Why call ye me, Lord,
Lord, and do not the things which I say?" "No man, having put his
hand to the plough, and looking back, is fit for the kingdom of
God." "I am the way, the truth, and the life: no man cometh unto
the Father, but by me."

How many of those are part of my most ordinary, daily life?

Having put my hand to the plough, the time is for doing, and the time for doing is now.

Today, let me remember to do.

APRIL 27

Jesus Christ never did reveal to any man the precise time that He would come. Go and read the Scriptures, and you cannot find anything that specifies the exact hour He would come; and all that say so are false teachers.

—Joseph Smith

There have been false teachers throughout history—before Jesus Christ ascended into heaven—and those teachers have had followers. A good many congregations climbed up on rooftops or took refuge in caves against Armageddon at one time or another, and they eventually had to climb down (or climb up) sheepishly because nothing much happened.

But what's wrong with waiting for Armageddon? We know it will come.

The main thing that's wrong with waiting (by which I mean making waiting my main business) is that some teachers' prophecies giving time and date are not true, and following falsity never helped anybody. The second problem is that it would prevent me from facing non-millennial problems and giving non-millennial service. (It occurs to me that cowering in a cave might be difficult, but sometimes getting dinner together for a sister who's just had a baby and getting it to her house hot and on time might be harder.)

Joseph Smith made it clear. Nobody knows when the Messiah will make his triumphant second coming. Nobody knows, because we're supposed to be using our time here on this earth usefully, and hanging around waiting is not a useful use of time. If Jesus Christ were to return tomorrow (and he might), would I be doing anything differently today? And if so, why?

Today, let me concentrate less on the prophecies and more on perfection, starting with mine. Let me be a dutiful daughter. As long as I'm a dutiful daughter, it doesn't matter when my Lord comes. I will be ready.

APRIL 28

Therefore, I would that ye should be steadfast and immovable,
always abounding in good works, that Christ, the Lord God
Omnipotent, may seal you his, that you may be brought to heaven,
that ye may have everlasting salvation and eternal life, through the
wisdom, and power, and justice, and mercy of him who created all
things, in heaven and in earth, who is God above all. Amen.

—MOSIAH 5:15

I've known some good women who were abounding in good
works. I've also known one or two who undoubtedly did good
things from time to time but who I would never think of as
"abounding." Suspecting nervously that I might be in the latter category, I ask myself, What makes the difference?

When I think about the first kind, I think about Sharon. (That
isn't her real name; if I used her real name, it would embarrass her,
which is one of the nicest things about her. She turns bright pink
and changes the subject if you remark on her virtues.) Sharon
knows everything about everybody. Not in the sense of knowing
who's up to what or whose activities are a little suspect—although
she may know all that; she's just never said—but in the sense of
knowing who's having a hard time and who's just moved into the
ward and who could use a phone call or an offer of a ride or a loaf of
bread. She has had callings in which this was part of the job, but
when the calling moved on to someone else, Sharon went on doing
the good stuff informally. She no longer has to arrange compassionate service, but when the sister who does starts making her calls, she
usually finds that Sharon is already over there, taking care of things
until the Relief Society gets organized.

I have no idea how many showers she has given over the years.
I've been to a bunch of them; sometimes I've even had the presence
of mind to call her ahead of time and ask if I can bring something
to help. When I have, Sharon always tells me to bring whatever I'd
like to bring. It doesn't have to fit in with her color scheme or whatever; she's just plainly delighted that you want to help and be part
of it. It makes her a very comfortable person to be around.

She's not a saint, except in the Latter-day sense. I'm sure she's
got her faults and failings; I just can't think of any of them at the
moment. I know her daughter got irritated with her on occasion,
because I saw Sharon work on controlling her temper and try to

smile, and she did not burst into loud lament to anyone who would listen, as I am wont to do. I know that her daughter, who is a mother herself now, hangs on her advice and visits whenever she can.

I see less of her these days. Our children are past the small and demanding stage, and both of us have outside jobs. (Besides, she also visits her grandchild.) Still, my life is richer for knowing her. Because of Sharon, I know that it is possible to live a good life in an ordinary way. It is possible for us, here and now, to be the kind of people King Benjamin was asking his people to be, all those many centuries ago.

Would Jesus Christ recognize Sharon and seal her his, in King Benjamin's terms? I think perhaps he already does.

APRIL 29

Angels speak by the power of the Holy Ghost; wherefore, they speak the words of Christ. Wherefore, I said unto you, feast upon the words of Christ; for behold, the words of Christ will tell you all things what ye should do.

—2 NEPHI 32:3

The words of Christ—what a wonderful month this has been, reading and savoring the words of Christ!

My quadruple combination is getting battered on the edges, and tucked in it are various small pieces of paper with thoughts to remember and an angel that my niece made for a special Relief Society program a couple of years ago; ever since, the angel has marked my way through whichever standard work we're studying in Sunday School.

I don't think much about the book as a priceless possession most of the time. It's probably good for me to pause and look at it and recognize what a miracle it is that I can hold it and read it freely. How many men were prepared to risk everything (some did, and lost) to translate and print it so that those who followed them could have this book? How can I take it for granted? It lies now by the side of my bed, now down on the kitchen counter, now somewhere in the living room, even, temporarily, goes missing (as I, on the way to church, frantically ask, "Has anybody seen my scriptures?").

I'm very attached to this book. The idea of losing it appalls me. It takes rational thought to reassure me. What makes this book precious? It's not the book itself, not the binding, not the pieces of paper or even the angel. What makes this book precious is the words. Dear Lord, let me remember the words. Let me always remember the words.

APRIL 30

And the seventh angel sounded; and there were great voices in heaven, saying, The kingdoms of this world are become the kingdoms of our Lord, and of his Christ; and he shall reign for ever and ever.
—REVELATION 11:15

Handel again: the final triumphant chorus of *Messiah*, and a good day for it. Spring has finally come. The grass is green; the trees are coming into leaf: fresh, delicate, yellow-green leaves. The crocuses are out, and so are the daffodils. Even the early tulips are starting to color, reminding me which flowers we planted where.

The spring sky is a bright blue vault over my head, seen through tree branches. And heaven? Where is heaven? On a day like today it feels as if you could reach up and touch it.

On a day like today it would be wonderful to be one of those privileged to see our Lord Jesus Christ returning in triumph, when the kingdoms of this world would truly have become the kingdoms of our Lord, and of his Christ. Imagine all of creation feeling the sense of triumph and harmony that rushes through me if I turn up the music loud enough to hear when I walk out on this beautiful day.

Even so, I won't hold my breath for the Second Coming, for the King to claim his kingdom, for me to see my Lord. It may never happen for me until I make the unknown crossing to the other side. On a day like today, that crossing doesn't seem to be anything to worry about, just a step as natural as the breeze ruffling my hair, and the sun shining down on me.

A voice from the house. I can't wander around in a mystical ecstasy forever, unfortunately. I've got rooms to straighten and dishes to do. The laundry isn't going to take care of itself, and my daughter can't find something. I can't hear exactly what her problem is; guess I'd better turn down the music.

The kingdoms of this world—another day, perhaps. For today let me be content with the joy of now.

MAY

Give unto the Lord the glory due unto his name; worship the Lord in the beauty of holiness.

—Psalm 29:2

MAY 1

The heavens declare the glory of God; and the firmament sheweth his handywork.

—PSALM 19:1

A cold spring night, the way they still tend to be, with stars shining through the lacy tree branches. The new leaves are just unfurling; they are dark shapes against the sky now, but in the daylight they are almost fluorescent yellow-green. There's a whole sky full of stars tonight, even though we're in a metropolitan area. If I were out in the country, the display would really be awe-inspiring.

Even as it is, I know exactly what David was talking about. Think how bright the stars must have been for him, standing in Jerusalem at night, maybe on the roof of his palace, where the only competing lights from the city would have been flickering candles and lamps—nothing compared to all the blazing lights around me, lighting such important civic monuments as the supermarket and its strip mall, the restaurants up and down the main drag, and, oh yes, the local cineplex. All important, mind you (and if I'm honest, all of them part of the reason we live in town instead of out in the boonies), but they do cut into star-gazing.

Not tonight, though. Tonight I feel like David, looking at the stars against a black velvet heaven. How can you not believe in God, when you look at the majesty of the night sky? How absolutely beautiful this world he created is, with such a spectacular backdrop.

I don't think about that often enough. I get so wrapped up in my busy little life (running around just like the ants—which are emerging from wherever they spend the winter, by the way—scurrying back and forth endlessly) that I don't take time to think about the magnificence of creation. That's one excellent reason to read the Psalms: Over and over, they remind me of God's greatness. Over and over, they remind me to praise.

Glory be to the Lord. How glorious is his world—how beautiful his firmament.

MAY 2

*Rejoice, O my heart, and cry unto the Lord, and say: O Lord, I
will praise thee forever; yea, my soul will rejoice in thee, my God,
and the rock of my salvation.*

—2 NEPHI 4:30

Many years ago (when I was very young), I went to hear Martin
Luther King Jr. preach at the University of California at
Berkeley. Well, I guess it wasn't really straight preaching—or at least
not advertised as such—but I remember being fascinated, if a
little taken aback, at the cadences of his voice. Of course, I was
young and pretty inexperienced with any religious idiom other
than Latter-day Saint. As a society, we had not yet been exposed
to such wonderful flights of oratory as his "I have a dream" speech
on the steps of the Lincoln Memorial. But I remember the
almost sing-song quality of his voice and his passionate praise of his
Lord.

This scripture makes me remember that and think of the
Reverend King. (Not that I can quite imagine he ever expressed
himself in the words of Nephi. How strange and satisfactory that
would have been!) The gospel tradition of southern churches, gain-
ing sonorous richness from African roots grafted onto Christian
stock, has a magnificence of praise that those of us who come from
the less exuberant north would probably feel a little awkward trying
to emulate.

It's not our style.

Which makes me chuckle when I think about the threat of a
good sister who used to live in our ward. She was just recovering
from a stint as Young Women's president, which happened simultaneously with major house renovations and the production of a
fourth child (her oldest being about seven at the time). At that
point she and her husband were moved to another city. She
promised grimly that when they first attended the new ward, she
would stand up and shout, "Praise the Lord!" at the end of every
prayer and whenever possible in the middle of each talk: She figured
that way nobody would dare give her a major calling, or possibly any
at all, until they figured out what to do about her. I don't know if
she ever tried it, but if she did, it didn't work. When last heard from,
she was Primary president.

Maybe a little bit of praising the Lord would do us all good. It's one thing to hang back because it's an unfamiliar style; it's another not to bother because it doesn't occur to us to praise in our own style or anybody else's. Praise and thankfulness, after all, are very subtly different. Praise and worship go together, hand in hand. When we are grateful, we are counting our blessings. When we praise and when we worship, we are expressing reverence and devotion, pure and simple.

Today, let me remember to praise. I may not have the soul-stirring cadence, but I have Nephi's beautiful words. Let me worship with them.

MAY 3

Our Father who art in heaven, even the God of our fathers, who keepeth covenants and showeth mercy; thou Almighty Elohim who liveth and reigneth, from everlasting to everlasting; thou Man of Holiness and Man of Counsel who hast created us in thine own image and likeness and commanded us to worship thee in spirit and in truth; thou who knoweth all things and hast all power, all might, and all dominion—hallowed be thy great and holy name!

—PRESIDENT JOSEPH FIELDING SMITH

On the other hand, when we find the right occasion, I guess we can praise and worship along with the best of them! What magnificent words to remember, these from President Smith.

Much of the time we worship in deed, and that's not a bad thing to do. When we look after each other, when we take care of those who are in need, when we reach out to ease a tormented heart, we have been told, we are in fact worshipping our Lord Jesus Christ. That's good. In fact, if you had to choose excess on one side or the other, that's probably not a bad side to choose.

But a major occasion like the dedication of a temple gives us an opportunity to stop and think, to consider the grandeur and majesty of our Lord. (The 109th section of the Doctrine and Covenants, another grand statement, is the prayer offered at the dedication of the first temple of the restored Church at Kirtland, Ohio.) How wonderful is our God! His people have been nourished by his strength down through the centuries, ever since the Old Testament days when, as far as any outsider could judge, our God was only one god among the competing claims of diverse other gods, worshipped

here and worshipped there. Now we are more likely to be surrounded by people who believe in no particular god, or even disbelieve in the possibility of the existence of any god at all.

To whomever and however, it is our sacred obligation to bear
testimony to the reality and eternal glory of the Lord our God. It
sometimes seems to me it might have been easier back then, being
considered an outsider because I worshipped the God of Israel in
preference to a golden calf, as compared to now, being considered
an outsider because I insist on our Lord's actual existence when
people either shrug their shoulders as if God is irrelevant or take the
view that if I want to believe in a personal God, that's all very well,
but they are more sophisticated than that. Of course, I wasn't there
when golden calves were the big thing; it's hard to know.

In any case, what the prophet Joseph Fielding Smith describes
is what the Lord forever was and forever will be. Let me remember
that splendor and come gladly, wholeheartedly, to worship. Let
praise be woven through my life.

MAY 4

*O Lord God of Israel, there is no God like thee in the heaven, nor
in the earth; which keepest covenant, and shewest mercy unto thy
servants, that walk before thee with all their hearts.*

—2 CHRONICLES 6:14

This, the opening of Solomon's dedicatory prayer for his temple,
has its own kind of eloquence.

It's easy for us to take monotheism for granted. At our time in
history, the major religions with the greatest number of adherents
worldwide (Christianity, Judaism, and Islam) are all strictly
monotheistic. The concept that there is one God and one God
alone to worship is no longer wonderfully novel. We've moved on
to disagree about the nature of the one God and the methods by
which we worship.

But when Solomon was praying, this was nowhere near a settled
issue, and the children of Israel were certainly not above worshipping the odd idol here or there, or participating in most peculiar rituals on occasion. Why do you suppose the Ten Commandments are
so adamant about not making, not possessing, not having any
graven images, or even any likeness of anything in heaven, earth, or

in the water beneath the earth? Because given an inch, the Israelites would have been dancing worshipful circles around the images, just like all their neighbors. As it was, it kept happening anyway. As Jeremiah pointed out at some length (obviously offending large numbers of his countrymen), this was exactly why the Lord their God allowed the Babylonians to sweep over their land and carry them off into captivity.

Our God is one God. Today, let me remember the importance of that simple statement. Our God is without equal, and he has covenanted with us just as with Abraham. As long as we are worthy, we are his people. Today and forever, let me be counted among them.

MAY 5

Man goeth forth unto his work and to his labour until the evening.
O Lord, how manifold are thy works! in wisdom hast thou made
them all: the earth is full of thy riches.

—PSALM 104:23–24

All very true, but unfortunately the man with whom I am most closely associated is currently laboring into the evening out in God's earth, and what he is doing is happily tearing up more of the lawn to make another sunny bed for his roses. This, I regret to say, is unilateral garden design: I think it's a dumb idea, and I thought it was still in the discussion stage. Apparently I was wrong, because rather large chunks of grass are at this very moment being loaded into the wheelbarrow to be deposited on the compost heap. At this rate we are going to wind up with a lawn the size of a pocket handkerchief with flower borders fifteen feet deep, all of which have to be *weeded!*

O Lord, how manifold are thy works! And because it started with Adam and Eve, I guess marriage should be counted among those works. What a firm but elastic structure marriage really is: There's room for being as cross as I am right this minute (I mean, who do you think is going to wind up doing the lion's share of the weeding? What's wrong with lawn, anyway?), knowing all the time that we're going to navigate this rough patch and be friends again on the other side (which at the moment makes me almost as cross as I am about the lawn; feelings will get back to normal, but the stupid flowerbed will still be there). I can tell from the angle of his head that he's not happy that I'm not happy. If he were the explosive type, we probably would have yelled and screamed some; because he's English and reserved, we just glare at each other.

"In wisdom hast thou made them all"—I guess that means that marriage is meant to refine and purify us. The delicious parts are stuck in there to keep us motivated, it would seem: How else but in this long-term intimacy could we learn to flex and give around another human being? Marriage—real marriage—goes way past politeness. It progresses deep into the territory of love, which includes dealing with the realities of irritation and exasperation and genuine disagreement and sacrifice.

Sacrifice—in this case, lawn. Okay. I will admit to myself I intend to go on loving him, regardless. We will be friends again. I may even be so great-hearted as to sympathize when he complains about the crick he's bound to have in his back after all this digging and stooping.

But he'd better be planning on doing some of the weeding, come hot and sultry August.

MAY 6

That the trial of your faith, being much more precious than of gold that perisheth, though it be tried with fire, might be found unto praise and honour and glory at the appearing of Jesus Christ: whom having not seen, ye love; in whom, though now ye see him not, yet believing, ye rejoice with joy unspeakable and full of glory: receiving the end of your faith, even the salvation of your souls.

—1 PETER 1:7–9

Here Peter is writing to the new Christian converts who came to their belief after Jesus had ascended into heaven, and so, over their shoulders, to us, who also have not seen but have believed.

We too can look forward to having our faith found with praise and honour and glory at the coming of our Christ. Those new Christians might well have expected his coming to be a lot sooner than it has turned out to be; one of our problems then and now, I expect, is that we're running on an earthly timetable neatly divided into days and years, and our Lord functions within the expansive boundaries of eternity.

Even if we aren't here to welcome him back to his earthly kingdom, we have what Peter talks about here: the joy unspeakable of believing. When I think—really think—about the gospel and the wonderful promise it offers us, I find myself with an almost physical sensation in my chest: an airy, bouncy, buoyant delight. Wherever he is, whether in heaven or here on earth, Jesus is my Savior and he knows and cares about me, enough to have sacrificed everything for my benefit. What more could I possibly ask? What greater possibilities could he possibly give me?

Joy unspeakable? Absolutely. And in my turn, whether I ever see him with my earthly eyes or not, let me remember to give "praise and honour and glory," day after day after day of my life.

MAY 7

Behold, my soul delighteth in the things of the Lord; and my heart pondereth continually upon the things which I have seen and heard.

—2 NEPHI 4:16

Gina brought her baby in today. He's less than two days old; it was just a couple of days ago that Gina was lumbering around, coming to her classes looking like a ship in full sail. But there she was today, with her baby fast asleep in his baby carrier, fair, fair newborn skin with a mass of dark hair, perfect miniature features, and tiny curled fingers.

I'm not sure he is one of the "things of the Lord" that Nephi had in mind, but that's exactly what he made me think of. What a marvelous example of the divine plan he is, lying there so peacefully in this new life he has just begun. It was Wordsworth who wrote about the newborn, "trailing clouds of glory . . . from God, who is our home" (*Ode: Intimations of Immortality from Recollections of Early Childhood*). You can see that glory, looking at this little morsel in his blue stretch suit. Two days ago, he was there!

Poor little mite, he is going to have a rougher row to hoe than many in this world: His father, according to his mother, is a real jerk who is no longer predictably part of her life. She wasn't really thrilled about this pregnancy, but she mellowed as it went on, and today her face was soft with love. She means to do well by him, and she probably will, most of the time, which is about as much as any of us can promise. Now she has somebody to protect and look out for; the casual selfishness of her former life is cut off as sharply as by any guillotine.

I think she came to see us on her way home from the hospital; she was still wearing the plastic identification bracelet. She must have been dying to show him off, and I don't know if she has anyone at home to admire him. Here at school she got all the fuss her heart could have longed for. Her classmates and teacher happily abandoned their work and circled them, mother and child, cooing and murmuring like so many maternal doves.

Welcome to the world, little new one. You are indeed one of the great things of the Lord, and I hope your mother finds the wisdom to teach you so. Let me praise the Lord my God for the magnificence of life itself and for all the potential of all the world's babies. Let me remember this one and his mother in my prayers, and call blessings down on their heads. Their adventure is just beginning.

MAY 8

Daniel answered and said, Blessed be the name of God for ever and ever: for wisdom and might are his: and he changeth the times and the seasons: he removeth kings, and setteth up kings: he giveth wisdom unto the wise, and knowledge to them that know understanding: he revealeth the deep and secret things: he knoweth what is in the darkness, and the light dwelleth with him.

—DANIEL 2:20–22

The prayer of praise of Daniel, when the interpretation of the king's dream had been revealed to him by the Lord.

Apart from the beauty of the poetry, one of the things that always strikes me most about this scripture is in the last verse: "he knoweth what is in the darkness." It is like a human voice reaching across the centuries. Haven't we all wondered (and feared, from time to time) what might be in the dark? I used to teach a night class, and coming home very late, when the house was still, walking down the path from the garage to the house in the darkness was an odd experience. I wasn't frightened, not really—after all, this is a quiet neighborhood and it's my own back yard, for heaven's sake—but I can't say I dawdled around getting into the house. Think how often men and women in Daniel's time, when illumination was less a science than an art of candle and lamp, must have walked through the uncertain dark. How reasonable that one of the attributes of God that would be most remarkable to them is that he "knoweth what is in the darkness"!

If darkness is the place of subtle (or unsubtle) threat, then light is the natural characteristic of virtue and godliness. "The light dwelleth with him." Remember how Paul urged us to "walk as children of light"?

Like Daniel, I reverence our Lord, who "knoweth what is in the darkness." Like Daniel, I lift my eyes to our Heavenly Father, who dwells in the light. Let me feel the presence of the Lord with me in the darkness; let me move ever more strongly into the light.

MAY 9

Remember, our real calling to be a compassionate Christian came when we stepped out of the waters of baptism. The gift of the Holy Ghost is ours by right of confirmation. We don't need to check it out of the meetinghouse library. We don't need a bishop's assignment to be kind. We don't need to sign up to be thoughtful. We don't need to be sustained by our wards to be sensitive. Rejoice in the power you have within you from Christ to be a nucleus of love, forgiveness, and compassion.

—SISTER CHIEKO N. OKAZAKI

How blessed we are to have such articulate women in the Church as Chieko Okazaki! Somehow she has the gift of speaking straight to the heart, moving past the ordinary obstacles of age and race and experience. Sister Okazaki speaks to all of us about the experiences that are common to all of us, in plain everyday English.

Her love of Christ, her rejoicing in the gospel, spill over me, splashing radiance on all sides. It's good to be reminded that we all have the opportunity and the obligation to be accessible, to step out of our own circle of concern to be aware (as a first step) of the people around us and what they might need, and then (as the natural second step), to move to meet those needs. You can't help with what you haven't noticed.

Blessed be the name of the Lord, that he has filled this world with people to reach out to and serve other people! None of us is perfect, and sometimes the help is imperfect, too, but the more we do it, the better we get at it. The more often we reach out, the more often we see the need that longs for someone to respond. The best sensitivity training comes when we turn away from contemplating our own sensitivities and pay attention to somebody else's.

I thank thee, and praise thee, Lord, for the opportunities that surround me today. Help me to see them; help me to find the generosity of spirit to meet them. Blessed, O blessed, be the name of the Lord.

MAY 10

Behold, they will crucify him; and after he is laid in a sepulchre for the space of three days he shall rise from the dead, with healing in his wings; and all those who shall believe on his name shall be saved in the kingdom of God. Wherefore, my soul delighteth to prophesy concerning him, for I have seen his day, and my heart doth magnify his holy name.

—2 NEPHI 25:13

I sit with the book in my hands and think how fascinating it is that here we are, I in the chair and Nephi's words on the page, each of us contemplating the same events. For Nephi, it was a glorious promise for the future, revealed to him in a vision and treasured as a guide for him and his descendants to use to order their lives.

For me, on the other hand, it is a brilliantly lighted episode in the past. I can turn from Nephi's writings in the Book of Mormon to the New Testament and read other words of praise and reverence written by men who were actually there, who knew Jesus as a man, and by the early believers, such as Paul and Luke, who worked tirelessly to spread the fledgling gospel across their world.

Nephi, looking forward; I, looking back. Time feels jumbled—past, present, and future mix together. Is this what it will be like in eternity? How splendid the day when Nephi and our Lord Jesus Christ and the prophets of our day can be gathered together to rejoice in the salvation of men!

Let that day come.

MAY 11

For I know that this shall turn to my salvation through your prayer, and the supply of the Spirit of Jesus Christ, according to my earnest expectation and my hope, that in nothing I shall be ashamed, but that with all boldness, as always, so now also Christ shall be magnified in my body, whether it be by life, or by death.

—PHILIPPIANS 1:19-20

Whatever Paul did, he did it with his whole heart. When he was a Pharisee, brought up by a good family strong in the law, he saw Christianity as heresy and did his best to stamp it out. When enlightenment crashed upon him like a bolt of lightning—first on the road to Damascus and then in Damascus itself as he came to understand what had happened to him—he was teachable enough to admit his error and turn his life inside out to follow the truth he recognized. He became the most dynamic of Christians. The Lord needed Paul for his work; it is almost impossible to imagine what the early Christian Church would have been without his energy and determination.

In this letter to the Church members at Philippi, one of the groups closest to his heart, Paul speaks freely and lovingly. He was a prisoner in Rome at the time of this letter. He was under close guard but apparently had considerable personal freedom; his friends and supporters were able to visit with him. In this letter he points out that his imprisonment in Rome has had some benefits for the Christian cause, attracting attention and curiosity, which inevitably led to conversions. This was his first Roman imprisonment, which later ended in acquittal. (It wasn't until three, or possibly six, years later that he was again arrested and, according to tradition, beheaded just outside Rome.)

When he was writing this letter, he apparently had not foreseen any of that, and so here he is contemplating the possibility of his imminent death (which, as he points out later in the letter, would let him be with Christ immediately) versus the possibility of regaining his full freedom, which would enable him to continue his work for Christ here on earth. Either way, as he says here, "Christ shall be magnified in my body."

Could I say the same thing with such justified confidence? Is Christ magnified in my body for as long as I live on this earth?

(And, my conscience whispers again, uncomfortably, If not, why not?)

Dear Lord, help me to find the way to live up to my possibilities. Bless me, too, that like Paul, I may not be ashamed but assert my faith in all boldness. I may not match up to his greatness, but I can learn from his example. Help me today to learn.

MAY 12

I will love thee, O Lord, my strength. The Lord is my rock, and my fortress, and my deliverer; my God, my strength, in whom I will trust, my buckler, and the horn of my salvation, and my high tower.

—PSALM 18:1–2

A hard day. Why do these days come swirling out of a succession of what seemed like happy, peaceful days? One of my children is caught up in largely self-created difficulties. Now I realize that I've been troubled by some vague foreboding, a presentiment of trouble. Unfortunately, I was right. Would it be better to have faced it before? At the time, I guess I was telling myself not to borrow trouble. "Sufficient unto the day is the evil thereof," and so forth (Matthew 6:34). Was I right then, or was I hiding? The questions swirl round and round as I try to concentrate on what can be done to make the situation better now. The choice of whether to deal with the difficulty no longer exists. Like a child, I want to wail to the Lord, "Take it away! Make it so it never happened!" But he doesn't, and it did.

The headnote says that this scripture was the song of David when the Lord delivered him out of the hands of Saul and his enemies. Had his heart ached like mine? It must have, for he came up with words that perfectly express the way I feel today. At this point all those I would normally turn to are angry, or defensive, or drawn away into their own unhappiness. Only the Lord is there, my rock and my fortress. He will always be there. Let me rest in thy strength, Lord.

We will get through. We will learn from this, all of us, and after all, why else are we on this earth, except to learn?

But, O Lord, grant my prayer: Let other lessons be easier.

MAY 13

*Why art thou cast down, O my soul? and why art thou disquieted
in me? hope thou in God: for I shall yet praise him for the help of
his countenance. . . . Yet the Lord will command his lovingkindness
in the daytime, and in the night his song shall be with me, and my
prayer unto the God of my life.*

—PSALM 42:5, 8

How resilient is the human spirit! We take it for granted, and yet
there it is, astonishing and reliable. Each day, whatever it has
held, draws down to a close, and then in the morning there is a new,
fresh day, and the morning after that there will be another.

It is night, and everyone else is in bed. I am on the way to bed
myself, but the stillness has captivated and calmed me. "In the night
his song shall be with me." It is, and my soul is rediscovering a space
or two of peace. The night is warm enough so that I can throw open
a window and look out across the still lawns and see dark houses
sleeping under a quiet sky. The moon swims high above them,
scraps of cloud drifting across its face.

The song of the Lord in the night: I can't begin to explain how
it is I hear it, but it eases the sore spots. How many other people
before me, and even on this very night, have taken these words and
found comfort in them? One of the many elements of richness in
the scriptures is the knowledge that these words have been read and
treasured by generations of men and women before me, and that
other hands—far from me in distance, but close in spirit—may be
holding these same books at the same moment that I am, seeking for
the same comfort I am trying to find. The words are particular
enough to apply to me in my trouble; general enough to have
reached the hearts of other seekers across space and time. I feel part
of the great community of my brothers and sisters who have reached
out for the Lord their God when they knew no other direction in
which to turn. Let me join my voice with theirs and praise the Lord,
who is always there.

Oh, my Lord, how grateful I am for the calm that comes after
the storm. I may be sore and aching, but I will heal; others before
me have been much more afflicted, and they were strengthened by
thy hand as well. Let the shadow of that strength sustain me.

The curtains stir gently in the night air. Time to pull the window shut and go on to bed; tomorrow will be here soon enough. As

the psalmist sings, the Lord will command his lovingkindness in the daytime. I can sleep, comforted by that promise.

MAY 14

Do you read the Scriptures, my brethren and sisters, as though you were writing them a thousand, two thousand, or five thousand years ago? Do you read them as though you stood in the place of the men who wrote them? If you do not feel thus, it is your privilege to do so, that you may be as familiar with the spirit and meaning of the written word of God as you are with your daily walk and conversation.

—PRESIDENT BRIGHAM YOUNG

It seems to me there are several different ways to read the scriptures. One way (which is probably the way I read them through seminary and other classes, for years) is simply to read the words, memorizing when necessary. Each bunch of words came with a citation, which was memorized right along with it. The whole thing was a formula to be produced when required.

Another way (which I find is an insidious temptation) is to scrub through the scriptures in search of a verse that can be interpreted to say what I want to hear, even if it means cutting it loose from its context. When I think of all the different points of view that have been argued over the centuries, using the scriptures for authority, it occurs to me that I am not the only person so tempted.

There are, of course, many other ways to read the scriptures, many of them much worthier, but I find myself charmed today by the idea Brigham Young proposes here. What would it feel like to be David, writing those marvelous psalms? How must it have been to be Nephi, yearning after his rebellious brothers, seeking over and over again to fire them, however unwilling they seemed, to a knowledge of the truth? Or to walk in the steps of Luke, the physician, using his personal experience and his carefully gathered research to provide us with the adventure story that is the Acts of the Apostles? What would it have been like to stand near them as they wrote, to ask all the questions that come tumbling out as soon as I begin to imagine the possibility of answers? Or even more wonderful, as Brigham Young suggests, imagine writing those words myself, possessing their grasp of the realities of eternity and their testimony of our Father in Heaven and his gospel, having their spiritual experiences to relate.

Today will I be Isaiah? or Jeremiah? or Helaman, or Mosiah? Or even, perhaps, John? Praises be to thee, O Lord! Let me never take their words, or this tattered book, completely for granted. Let there always be the sudden rush of wonder and awe that I can hold all this magnificence in my hands. Today I hold it.

MAY 15

And again, he that trembleth under my power shall be made strong, and shall bring forth fruits of praise and wisdom, according to the revelations and truths which I have given you.

—DOCTRINE AND COVENANTS 52:17

This to the elders of the Church at Kirtland, Ohio, shortly after the conference held there in 1831.

What it makes me think of is my father, who joined the Church when I was in my twenties (he eventually was called as a bishop, thus proving that when he did join, he was prepared to serve). To say that he was unenthusiastic about public speaking is putting it mildly, and I often wondered (but never actually asked him) if dread of being summoned to stand up before the congregation was one of the factors that delayed his decision to join the Church. He never did take to public speaking, and, to his dying day, his heart sank at the prospect of giving a talk, although he found conducting a meeting no problem at all. Aren't people delightfully illogical?

I suspect he was not alone, and to me one of the wonders of the restored Church is the surprisingly high quality of the talks given at our meetinghouses, when you consider that most of the speakers are not formally trained and many of them are afflicted with trembling knees and shaking hands. Or perhaps it isn't surprising at all, when you consider the promise the Lord gave us all: We shall be made strong and shall bring forth fruits of praise and wisdom. And if it happens to be my knees that are doing the trembling, I can hang on to this promise as well. It belongs as much to me as to anyone.

Let's go to sacrament meeting next Sunday, and see.

MAY 16

Trust in the Lord with all thine heart; and lean not unto thine own understanding.

—PROVERBS 3:5

W hen, oh, when will I learn to leave well enough alone? My poor unfortunate child: Circumstances were doing a perfectly adequate job of teaching the eternal law of consequences, and I knew it perfectly well. I had asked prayerfully for guidance. So what did I do? Haunted by the conviction (erroneous, as it happens) that there was a slight chance that a similar error was possibly about to happen—it was just about that tenuous—I started lecturing with greater and greater fervor, warming to my subject, while my child passes from meek bewilderment to irritation to complete exasperation. Now, by the time I have finally run down, we are at war.

My husband says there are times when a muzzle would be nice.

Oh, dear Lord, I don't even know what to pray for. Maybe a giant cone, like a heavenly candle-snuffer, descending from the heavens to firmly, definitively, muffle me, would be good. Why do we—why do I—go on talking when we ought not to? Why do I lean with my full weight on my own understanding when I know perfectly well I was told not to—centuries ago? Why can't I do what I was told and just trust in the Lord?

Maybe I can find a crumb of comfort in knowing that that particular proverb has probably applied to somebody other than me somewhere along the line. Maybe I can remember, and apply, the principle of repentance. This, after all, is the kind of thing it's for.

Maybe I can start by finding my outraged child and offering a heartfelt apology. We can go on from there.

MAY 17

O Lord our Lord, how excellent is thy name in all the earth! who has set thy glory above the heavens.

—PSALM 8:1

The first hot day. We will have summer! The trees are in full leaf, offering a shady avenue down our street. We used to have elms lining both sides, but in spite of vigorous community effort, Dutch elm disease conquers a couple each year. Fortunately, as they come down, the city plants new trees. Some of the oldest of the new-comers are now reaching respectable size, although they are still dwarfed by the remaining elms that meet across the road, forming a cool green canopy.

In the winter you seldom see anyone outside their houses. Come spring, we gradually begin to emerge, like so many bears coming out of hibernation, but today, the first really beautiful summery day, practically everybody is out. Lawnmowers are roaring and some people are down on their knees getting muddy, sticking in summer annual bedding plants (we're not supposed to be frost-free until the end of May, but there's always hope and most years you do fine planting a little earlier). Neighbors gather in little clumps to chat and then drift back to their separate projects.

What catches my eye is the little boy across the street, from one house down. He must be about five or six, and he's got the training wheels off his bicycle. (I remember him riding with them up and down the sidewalk in the fall.) He is clearly absolutely determined to learn to ride his two-wheeler today. I've watched him tumble over a dozen times, and each time he scrambles back up, glances around to check if anybody saw it happen, and then picks up his bike and flings his leg back over to try again. Little by little, he's managing it. He gets a little farther almost every time before he topples over again. I wonder if his mother is watching as closely from their house as I am watching from ours; I hope she's getting the chance to appreciate the battle her son is waging.

What a glorious day for a small boy to take on a personal challenge! And how am I doing on mine, I wonder? There's this to be said about learning to ride a bike: Success and failure are easily measured. Either you clonk off on one side or the other or you wobble successfully forward, and there's the wonderful moment when you're no longer wobbling and the bike seems to have wings, and you're flying down the pavement alight with triumph.

Unfortunately, my personal challenges are less straightforward to evaluate. Am I getting to be a better person, for example, by which I suppose I mean am I becoming kinder, and more grateful for my blessings, and less grumpy when I'm having a bad day, and more aware of the goodness of the Lord? It's harder to tell. I may think my grumpiness level has dropped dramatically, but would my daughters say so? At what point do I get to fly down the pavement?

At least this gorgeous day makes one thing easier: My heart spontaneously fills with praise for the Lord. "How excellent is thy name in all the earth!" This is why people go on living in the places where the four seasons are distinct and marked—who could possibly appreciate a day like today if they had not endured the bleakness of March?

O Lord our Lord, blessed be thy name. Creator of this wonderful world and of small boys learning to ride bicycles, I will praise thee with my whole heart, today and forever.

MAY 18

Jesus was careful to place the petition "Hallowed be thy name" at the very forefront of his prayer. Unless that reverent, prayerful, honorable attitude toward God is uppermost in our hearts, we are not fully prepared to pray. If our first thought is of ourselves and not of God, we are not praying as Jesus taught. It was his supreme hope that our Father's name and station would be kept beautiful and holy. Living always with an eye single to the glory of God, he urged men everywhere to so speak, and act, and live, that others seeing their good works might glorify their Father in heaven.

—ELDER HOWARD W. HUNTER

So my job is to keep my eye single to the glory of God and, with that glory ever before me, to live and speak and act in everything I do so that those who encounter me will be aware of the magnificence of our Lord shining through me and glorify him in their turn.

Wow. So must it be somebody heroic to act in the ways that could conceivably glorify our Father in Heaven?

Well, there was Mr. Cercone. In the eyes of the world, Mr.

Cercone wasn't particularly important. He was the social studies teacher at the middle school my children attended. In the summers, he taught drivers' training. He had the gift of dealing well with early adolescents. Some of them caught fire in his classes and suddenly saw the possibilities of education—not all of them, of course, but enough. He got along well with parents, too. He was a good guy.

One Friday afternoon they were going to take Mr. Cercone's picture for the school yearbook (just a paperback booklet, really), but he didn't have his tie on. He said to come back Monday, and he'd be ready then. That Saturday, he went up a ladder at his parents' house to knock down a squirrels' nest and touched a live wire with a metal pole. He died instantly.

About three thousand people attended Mr. Cercone's funeral, far too many to fit in the church. The crowd poured out into the forecourt and out onto the street in front of the church. Lots of parents were there, and lots of kids—his present students, high schoolers who had been in his classes, kids who came home from college to be there, and even young businessmen in their suits and young mothers with their babies in their arms. Mr. Cercone would have known them all. His family was there: his wife and his five children. I hope it made them all proud.

I don't know what Mr. Cercone would have made of it. (The local newspaper said there were almost eight hundred cars in the cortege going to the cemetery.) I'm sure he would have been astonished. But he was a good man, and we all knew it. He was not a wealthy man and he was never very important—in the world's way of measuring. He just taught twelve- and thirteen-year-olds at the middle school. He was a good teacher, and from what the priest said at his funeral, a good Catholic. The priest had tears in his eyes and had to fight for control; apparently Mr. Cercone did a lot of extra jobs at his church, just as he did at school.

Did he glorify the Lord by his good works? I believe he did. We all recognized Mr. Cercone as a good man while he lived; we came away from his funeral with a fuller knowledge of how he had served his God by serving us. I hope my children learned from his example that greatness comes in a multitude of sizes and shapes, and that they were lucky enough to bump into it in a middle school classroom.

They planted a tree in his memory at the school. It's a small tree now, but it will grow. Like the effects of his good works, it will grow.

MAY 19

And they of the circumcision which believed were astonished, as many as came with Peter, because that on the Gentiles also was poured out the gift of the Holy Ghost. For they heard them speak with tongues, and magnify God. Then answered Peter, Can any man forbid water, that these should not be baptized, which have received the Holy Ghost as well as we?

—Acts 10:45–47

In the early days after Christ's ascension, it was very much a question in the minds of his apostles whether it was necessary for a Christian to be a Jew first—which, we can see now, would have relegated Christianity into being a sect of Judaism. But Christianity was never meant to be an appendage of Judaism; Christ came to supersede the old law.

The issue was settled in Peter's mind when he was shown a vision directing him to eat creatures which he had been taught to consider unclean. When he said so, the voice in the vision told him, "What God hath cleansed, that call not thou common" (Acts 10:15). Immediately following this vision he was visited by three Gentiles who had also been given a vision telling them where to find Peter. Understanding then what he was being instructed to do, Peter, who had never associated with Gentiles before, taught them about Christ, and as he taught, the Holy Ghost fell upon them all.

What impresses me about this whole sequence of events is the humility and teachability of Peter. He was ready to accept what he was told, and when these Gentiles began to magnify the Lord, Peter argued eloquently on their behalf. It was against everything he had ever been taught or believed before; it was completely foreign to his tradition. But Peter was shown, and Peter believed.

Dear Lord, help me to be as open to instruction. Bless me that I may be prepared to listen to what I am taught. Bless me that I may magnify thee in my obedience to thy word, whether it is what I expect or not. Help me to learn from Peter; bless me with his trust in thy word.

MAY 20

So I say unto you, my brethren, that if you should render all the
thanks and praise which your whole soul has power to possess, to
that God who has created you, and has kept and preserved you, and
has caused that ye should rejoice, and has granted that ye should live
in peace one with another—. . . I say, if you should serve him with
all your whole souls yet ye would be unprofitable servants. And
behold, all that he requires of you is to keep his commandments.

—MOSIAH 2:20–22

From the wonderful speech of King Benjamin to his people—
there's lots more. I must read it all.

"All the thanks and praise which your whole soul has power to
possess"—how much would that be? How bursting with joy was I
when my babies were first handed to me? How much did I praise the
Lord the time I was on a wind-tossed and stormy flight (I don't like
even smooth flights much) and landed safely and felt the good old
firm earth under my feet, even if my knees were still wobbly? How
grateful was I when one of my daughters was stuck in a storm late at
night, and I went out to find her, driving through frighteningly deep
water across the roads, and then I saw her, illuminated by a flash of
lightning, but safe? If I could somehow summon up all that, combined and magnified by all the other times when my heart has been
full, and pour it into praise, I would still, if strict justice were to be
invoked, be an unprofitable servant.

No, the Lord lavishes on us much more than justice would ever
require. And, as King Benjamin reminds us, all he asks in return is
that we keep his commandments; in return for that, still more blessings will be poured out upon us.

How much do I love my children? Probably far more than they
are worthy of on any particular day. And here I am just an ordinary
mortal, with all the shortcomings and failings mortals have in such
abundance. If I, with all my limitations, can love my children so
much, how much more does the Lord, in his perfection, love me as
his child? Love all of us? How much does he want us to reach back
to him as he reaches out to us?

Oh, Lord, my rock and my stay. Let me always feel thy presence
close to me. Let me praise thee and obey thee; let me be thy daughter now and forever.

MAY 21

For you shall live by every word that proceedeth forth from the mouth of God. For the word of the Lord is truth, and whatsoever is truth is light, and whatsoever is light is Spirit, even the Spirit of Jesus Christ.

—DOCTRINE AND COVENANTS 84:44–45

L ight sometimes comes from the oddest places.
  I was out in the back yard weeding. I didn't feel like weeding, but it had to be done, and this is a good time to do it: The weeds are still small and the earth is still damp enough so that they come out easily, and it's not too cold or too hot to be outdoors.

I had just pulled up a dandelion, long skinny root intact, and rocked back on my heels to feel pleased with myself—there are few deeper satisfactions when weeding than getting the whole dandelion—when I suddenly realized that right then, out there in the yard with the sun and shadow moving over me, I was totally at peace. I could almost reach out and feel the light of truth flowing through me, firm and strong, like a rushing stream. I've been having sort of a struggle the last few days: nothing major, just feeling unsettled and praying in an unhappy sort of way that I could somehow be given a soul-easing patch of tranquillity. And then suddenly I had it! I had gone out to do a job and found a blessing instead.

I don't think I had to be out in the garden to get it. I think I probably could have found the same calm if I had been scrubbing the floor or folding laundry or washing down woodwork—anything plain and simple and routine enough so that my mind could be set free from scrabbling around demanding peace. I guess I had been so busy specifying where and how and in what way I needed to be blessed that I didn't notice whether it was already happening. All I needed was to stop grabbing and open my hands to see if they were already full.

Today, let me open my hands. Let me remember the words of the Lord—"ask, and ye shall receive"—and believe them. I always will receive, but in the Lord's way, not necessarily mine. The amazing part (and this is why I must have faith) is that the Lord's way will always turn out to be better than what I could have imagined. When I really have faith in that, the spirit of truth and light will flow through me, just as it does right now.

Let me praise the Lord this glorious day—even if I don't get all of the next dandelion root!

MAY 22

Sing unto the Lord a new song, and his praise from the end of the earth, ye that go down to the sea, and all that is therein; the isles, and the inhabitants thereof.

—ISAIAH 42:10

H is praise from the end of the earth"—when Isaiah wrote these words, the end of the earth for him and his countrymen was the unimaginable distances beyond the sea—what we know as the Mediterranean Sea—stretching out to the horizon in the west. The isles rising out of that sea would have been heard of but seen only by mariners.

We are children of a different time. Our horizons stretch far beyond the oceans of our world. We know exactly where the ends of the earth are, and that our planet hangs like a brightly colored jewel, blue and green and brown and white, in the blackness of space. You can see the oceans and the land in the photographs from space, but of course you have to imagine the people who scurry around on the face of that vivid spot of life in the universe.

"Sing unto the Lord a new song." Just imagine if we all did. Do you remember that old Coca-Cola song about teaching the world to sing? Even though it was an advertisement, there was something moving about that long line of people, all different races and colors and sizes, holding hands and singing. That's what it will be like, one day. That's what the prophets have promised us will happen. All the people who lived then, and live now, and will ever live, will be joined together in one vast hymn of praise.

We'll be there, too. Perhaps today we can begin with just a little foretaste of it by starting the hymn of praise in our own hearts. As the psalmists sang centuries ago, sing praises to God, sing praises. There's no reason why we can't start working on that song now.

MAY 23

Thou shalt be diligent in preserving what thou hast, that thou mayest be a wise steward; for it is the free gift of the Lord thy God, and thou art his steward. If thou art merry, praise the Lord with singing, with music, with dancing, and with a prayer of praise and thanksgiving.

—DOCTRINE AND COVENANTS 136:27–28

This is the only revelation (or "Word and Will of the Lord," as it is captioned) given to Brigham Young that is included within the Doctrine and Covenants. It deals with practical arrangements, exactly the kind of thing for which Brigham Young, a genius of practicality, was eminently suited to carry out. The Lord chooses his prophets carefully. Joseph Smith had one kind of mission; Brigham Young had another.

What charms me about this revelation is, first of all, the common sense in reminding Brigham Young, and through him, the Saints (at that point a beleaguered and tattered jumble of men, women, and children swarming across the Missouri River into the refuge of what was then being called Winter Quarters), that they had better take care of what possessions they had been able to carry off with them. Second (and this is the really amazing part if you think about it), that instruction, "if thou art merry," to express that merriment with praise to the Lord. In the middle of everything they were going through, there was to be singing and music and dancing!

If they had time and reason for music and praise, then certainly so do I. Here I am, in my nice comfortable house (maybe not as grand as I might wish, and the furniture has a rather more lived-in look than furniture in magazine pictures does), with nobody trying to drive me and my family out of town, and instead of being grateful for all of it, I can, and definitely do, go through periods of feeling sorry for myself.

Dear Lord, let me get my act together. Let me praise thee for the good life which thou hast given me. First of all, for the gift of life itself. Yes, I get frustrated, and yes, there are parts of it which I think are hard, but I wouldn't have missed the whole experience for the world. I'm glad I decided the way I did in the premortal existence, and I'm most of all glad I had the opportunity to decide.

Let me praise the Lord for the magnificent gift of my body. It may not be exactly as I'd like it, and a few more athletic genes would have been nice, but when I think about all the marvelous things it does quite routinely, I am overwhelmed with wonder and appreciation. It doesn't dance and sing well, but if that's the way to express praise, I will happily dance and sing.

Let me praise thee for the gift of my family. They are sometimes enough to drive me nuts, but I am grateful notwithstanding. Let me praise thee for my children. They are funny and adorable and irritating and rewarding. Let me praise thee for my husband. He is all of the above and more, and I love him dearly. Let me praise thee for my parents and my sisters and the warm ring of family that has encircled me over the years.

Most of all, Lord, let me praise thee for the gift of thy presence. I can't see thee with the eyes of this body, and I can't hear thee with my ears, but by the gift of the Holy Ghost, I always know that thou art with me, anytime I reach out with an honest heart and true intent.

Those Saints in Winter Quarters knew that, too. It sustained them through great trials; it sustains me through my lesser ones. Let me sing and dance and praise with the memory of their song and dance: Blessed be the name of the Lord. O Lord my God, let me praise thee.

MAY 24

Wherefore, let no man glory in man, but rather let him glory in God, who shall subdue all enemies under his feet.
—DOCTRINE AND COVENANTS 76:61

Who, us? We don't glory in man, do we?

Well, that sort of depends. How many column inches in the newspapers, how many minutes of TV time, are devoted to the antics of the rich and famous? How many to the majesty of God?

I rest my case.

It's perfectly true that we can learn a lot from observing the behavior of our fellow men, but I don't think education is really what we have on our minds when we fall into our national enthusiasm for gossip. I think we just want to know everything about the stars. Look at how many magazines are devoted to nothing more than tracking those who are in the public eye, primarily those who can loosely be classified as entertainers. And if we're discussing glorying in men, just contemplate what goes on in the average pop concert, with the yearning fans stretching their arms toward the stage, faces uplifted and shining. Put a golden idol up there, and it would look quite a lot like an Old Testament illustration of what the prophets were preaching against.

Of course, many of the human idols we have turn out not only to have feet of clay but heads apparently made out of a similar substance—at least nothing similar to thinking seems to be taking place as too many of them drink and drug themselves to death. They shine and sparkle and plunge themselves into oblivion.

Dear Lord, let me direct my attention instead to such wonderful experiences as the vision of the three degrees of glory that Joseph Smith and Sidney Rigdon shared, which is recorded in Doctrine and Covenants 76. That is the kind of magnificence that endures; the glories which they saw go on from everlasting to everlasting. The really astounding part is this: I will never be anything but an audience at the glitzy entertainments of this world, but if I am worthy, I can absolutely take part in the splendor of the resurrection.

Lord, help me fix my gaze on what is real. Help me to learn to know thee, the Lord my God.

MAY 25

And Miriam the prophetess, the sister of Aaron, took a timbrel in her hand; and all the women went out after her with timbrels and with dances. And Miriam answered them, Sing ye to the Lord, for he hath triumphed gloriously; the horse and his rider hath he thrown into the sea.

—EXODUS 15:20–21

That scripture makes a wonderful picture in my head. I think I must have seen illustrations of it somewhere (probably among those we keep in the library for Primary), but I can't remember anything specific. Even the picture in my head is irritatingly foggy on details. Would they have been dressed in bright colors as they sang and shook the timbrels with a sharp metallic rattle? Probably not: They had so recently been slaves, and bright dyes back in those days were precious and expensive. I doubt that Miriam's resources, whatever they might have been, would have run to that. But their eyes would have been sparkling bright, and it doesn't cost money to dance, especially when your captors and masters, hot in pursuit, have just been swallowed up by the waters that miraculously parted for you. The Egyptians were gone, and the children of Israel, praising God and singing, were free!

How long has it been since I praised God for my freedom? I probably spend a lot more time lamenting about how tied down I am. Poor me. I have a husband, three children at home, too many pets, and they all need feeding. I have a house that I can't get to clean itself. I have a job. I have church responsibilities. I have *too much* to do to allow me to sit around as much as I'd like or watch television whenever I'd like or chat with my friends as often as I'd like. (They're all too busy, too.) I get *tired*. Woe is me. Of course, I've never had anybody enforce my labors with a bull whip.

Today, for a change, instead of bemoaning my difficulties, let me celebrate my liberty. Let me remember Miriam with her timbrels and song and her glorying in the Lord's strength. Let me look around at all the Lord has given me—that family, those pets, that house, that job, and above all the rest, the restored Church—and glory with her. A few centuries between us don't make all that much difference. We are both daughters of the Lord, and we know it.

Together (give or take a few thousand years) we can magnify and praise him.

MAY 26

This is the Almighty of whom I stand in awe and reverence. It is He to whom I look in fear and trembling. It is He whom I worship and unto whom I give honor and praise and glory. He is my Heavenly Father, who has invited me to come unto Him in prayer, to speak with Him, with the promised assurance that He will hear and respond.

—PRESIDENT GORDON B. HINCKLEY

I think I need to be reminded of that sometimes. I think we have a natural inclination to concentrate on the ways in which our Lord is close to us. We like the pictures of Jesus with the little children. I am comforted and inspired by the warmth Jesus showed with his disciples.

But that's not all there is to the gospel. If I am tempted to believe that it is, I'm afraid I'll wind up with the milk-soppy sort of vision of Deity smiling with permanent benevolence on mankind, rather like an overindulgent mama dismissing her destructive little brat's misbehavior as unimportant. If being selfish or cruel or greedy is unimportant, where is the virtue in keeping the commandments?

No, I need President Hinckley's reminder of God's majesty. I need to recognize that there is an ultimate authority, and that actions have consequences. If I am to teach my children, I need to be taught. I need to remember that humility is not just a form of politeness but a heart-and-soul recognition of the infinite gap between the Lord's understanding and capabilities and mine as a mortal being. What does eternal progression mean, if we sort of see God as almost like us?

Help me to keep President Hinckley's words as a talisman to protect me from falling into the world's eagerness to demystify Christ and our Heavenly Father. Let me always remember the kingdom, and the power, and the glory.

In honest humility, Lord, let me worship thee.

MAY 27

The Lord is my strength and song, and he is become my salvation: he is my God, and I will prepare him an habitation; my father's God, and I will exalt him.

—Exodus 15:2

First and foremost, we praise the Lord because he is the Lord, and our recognition of his power and goodness and mercy is the bedrock of the gospel. Our relationship with our Father in Heaven is what the first three of the Ten Commandments of Moses are concerned with; when Jesus was asked which was the great commandment in the law, he answered that it was the commandment to love the Lord our God with all our heart and soul and mind (Matthew 22:37–38). We bless the name of the Lord because without our faith in him, faith itself becomes meaningless.

But it seems to me there is another hidden blessing in praising the Lord. The more I turn myself outward to concentrate on my relationship with him, the more I am healed inwardly. It's as if by devoting myself to the Lord, I forget about myself for a while, and when I remember, the me I then find has improved somehow during my absence. Is that maybe part of what Jesus meant when he said that the man or the woman who loseth life for His sake shall find it?

O Lord, let me worship thee. Let me praise thy goodness. Let me remember thy mercy. Help me to be worthy to be in thy presence.

MAY 28

Rejoice ye with Jerusalem, and be glad with her, all ye that love her: rejoice for joy with her, all ye that mourn for her.

—ISAIAH 66:10

The last chapter of Isaiah, looking forward to the Second Coming, when the nation of Israel shall be born in a day. That prophecy we have already seen come to pass; Jerusalem once again is, at least mainly, the city of the Jews.

Through the centuries there have been special cities. Jerusalem has been the foremost. With its special significance for the children of Israel—the city of Solomon's temple—and then for us as Christians, being the city where Jesus was crucified and then resurrected, Jerusalem has sparkled as a special jewel, a place where we can feel especially close to our Lord.

But we have had our own cities on this continent. First there was Nauvoo, the beautiful city built from nothing on the banks of the Mississippi River. The Spirit of the Lord was there, too. Then, after Nauvoo had to be abandoned when the Saints moved west, there was Salt Lake City. As a child growing up in the mission field, I knew that Salt Lake City was very special. When I visited there, I made the pilgrimage from the "This Is the Place" monument down to Temple Square, and I remember what were to me the very high walls and the almost palpable sense of tranquillity once you were within them. I remember thinking that the temple was a beautiful house for the Lord to live in. In a child's direct way, I assumed that the Salt Lake Temple was the Lord's main house. I accepted that he visited the others (and this was back in the days when we memorized the locations of the temples along with the Articles of Faith). I don't remember ever asking anybody about the matter; I certainly don't remember ever being specifically told anything like that. That was just my conclusion, which I assumed everybody else shared.

Now, years after I've grown up, and particularly right now when we've shaken off winter and spring is settling into the warmth of summer here in the Midwest, the whole question of place seems less important to me. As the Church expands and becomes worldwide, the exact location of Zion seems, for me right now, to have a lot more to do with what is going on in my heart than with geography, at least as a practical matter. Can I worship the Lord just as well here in the lush green as in the arid mountain west? I certainly expect so. Would my prayers of praise be heard better if they were a couple of thousand miles to the west? It seems unlikely to me.

What a beautiful world we have—all of it. There may well be some places that have special significance, but at the moment I am not called to live in any of them. This is my home now, and its own particular beauties make it especially precious to me.

Dear Lord, today I thank thee for all of the world: the part I live in and all the parts I have never seen. Bless me to always remember to notice what a wonderful place it is. I thank thee for Jerusalem, and Nauvoo, and Salt Lake City, and right here. Today, I am particularly grateful for right here.

As Isaiah wrote, rejoice for joy. I do.

MAY 29

And when the day of Pentecost was fully come, they were all with one accord in one place. And suddenly there came a sound from heaven as of a rushing mighty wind, and it filled all the house where they were sitting. . . . But Peter, standing up with the eleven, lifted up his voice, and said unto them, Ye men of Judæa, and all ye that dwell at Jerusalem, be this known unto you, and hearken to my words: . . . This Jesus hath God raised up, whereof we all are witnesses. Therefore being by the right hand of God exalted, and having received of the Father the promise of the Holy Ghost, he hath shed forth this, which ye now see and hear.

—ACTS 2:1–2, 14, 32–33

Wouldn't it have been marvelous to be there?

Pentecost was a Jewish religious feast, coming fifty days after the beginning of the Passover, and it had come to be a harvest celebration. People gathered together—the feast lasted just one day—and the offering was two loaves of leavened bread made from the freshly harvested wheat. The apostles were celebrating Pentecost when the Comforter that Jesus had promised them descended upon them like tongues of flame, and they were filled with the Holy Ghost and began to speak in other languages.

Luke gives a long list of languages which were heard, but the really remarkable thing is that in all the languages they were speaking of the wonderful works of God. It must have been in a way as if a videotape of the Tower of Babel was put in reverse: Suddenly, instead of all the languages being confounded, they were all, through the Spirit, brought together again. Everyone could understand the same message, and that message was of the glory of God.

Remember the prophecy that every knee will bend and every tongue confess? (Mosiah 27:31). I have no idea in what language the tongues will confess, but I must say I like the mental images of all the languages rising and intertwining as everybody together glorifies our Lord and Maker. What a colorful explosion of sound and praise that will be!

In the meantime, I'll stick to English and the words of the inspired scholars who worked under King James to assemble our Bible: "Glory to God in the highest, and on earth peace, good will toward men" (Luke 2:14).

MAY 30

O give thanks unto the Lord, for he is good: for his mercy endureth for ever. Let the redeemed of the Lord say so, whom he hath redeemed from the hand of the enemy; and gathered them out of the lands, from the east, and from the west, from the north, and from the south.

—PSALM 107:1–3

A thought for Memorial Day (whenever we might happen to celebrate it this year).

I think the first time the real pointlessness of war struck me was during the time I was working for an English publisher. The designer of the books we were working on happened to be German. At one point I flew over to his home in Germany with my assistant, who was English. After we had worked all day, we had a pleasant dinner together at the designer's house and sat around the fire talking. In the course of the conversation, we got talking about the war and discovered that the designer had fought in North Africa under Rommel, the German general. My assistant's father had also fought there—under Montgomery, the British general. Whether they had ever actually fired a shot at each other is impossible to know, of course, particularly since Peter, my assistant, was understandably vague about exactly where his father had been when.

But as we all sat there, looking at the fire and musing, it struck me how arbitrary and illogical war is. Somebody decides it's time for war, so the German book designer Guenther goes to the desert and tries to kill the British; Peter's father, who had been working in a bank, goes out to the desert and tries to kill Germans. Later somebody decides it's time for peace, and so years later the same men (well, technically, one of them and the son of the other) sit around a fire together and tell stories. Has Guenther changed? Has Peter (or Peter's father)? No. They were decent men then, obeying orders, and they are decent men still. They never hated each other; they both did what they had to do.

War is the anomaly.

Does that mean I think World War II was fought in error? No. There was a real question of evil there. Having come to know many Germans in the long years since the war, I think it was a problem of evil leadership, but whatever it was, it had to be stopped. All that being true, the price that ordinary decent people paid to stop it was a horrendously high one, and it was paid on both sides of the line. It is that price, I believe, that we honor on Memorial Day.

We are no longer as innocent as the world was at the beginning of the First World War, when men went off to war singing. If the improved communications of the twentieth century have taught us anything, it is that war is a long, nasty, brutish business and neither victor nor vanquished escapes unharmed. The sacrifice is real. Some men died, and some men survived with their lives irretrievably broken, and some men returned home with their memories. It was not easy for any of them, in either of those great wars or in all the other wars and "police actions" of the subsequent years.

Today, let me remember them. Let me honor them and praise the Lord that so many did return. Let me glorify God for our victories, like the psalmist, but let me never, never glorify war. Let me always remember too much about it.

MAY 31

And I saw another angel fly in the midst of heaven, having the ever-lasting gospel to preach unto them that dwell on the earth, and to every nation, and kindred, and tongue, and people, saying with a loud voice, Fear God, and give glory to him; for the hour of his judgment is come: and worship him that made heaven, and earth, and the sea, and the fountains of water.

—REVELATION 14:6–7

The last day of the month—May is sliding gently into the summer of June. I am bundling up the winter clothes to take to the cleaners and put away for the fall; when I do the laundry, the white loads are mushrooming with piles of T-shirts and light-colored shorts, and the dark loads, no longer full of sweatshirts and jeans, are shrinking until I have to go find some towels or something to make it worth running the machine.

In the middle of the dailiness of life, let me remember eternity and its meaning. Now that summer is coming, busy with activities to supervise and errands to run and time outdoors to enjoy, let me remember to worship. Let me watch the silent starry skies at night and think of my Creator, and feel the breeze stirring the leaves during the day, and remember the Lord my God.

Let me praise him, now and forever.

JUNE

Home should be a haven of love. . . . Where love is, there God will be also.

—Thomas S. Monson

JUNE 1

I, Nephi, having been born of goodly parents . . .

—1 Nephi 1:1

Of course, when Nephi wrote that, he was an adult and a parent himself. You sort of have to be, to know about goodly parenting. Until you've been an adult for a while and/or have children of your own, you probably don't understand fully what the expression "goodly parents" really means.

When you're a child you can claim you have the best parents in the world. You can growl (particularly if you're adolescent and fighting a war about curfews or something) that you have the worst. But until you have walked a distance in their footsteps you would never use the measured wisdom of "goodly" to describe them. You have to be mature to think in terms of goodly.

Goodly isn't perfect. Goodly is real: I would guess myself that the best practical definition of "goodly parents" is parents who are doing their best the great majority of the time.

Not all the time, you notice. We all have those moments when maybe we've been jerked out of sleep in the middle of the night, or when we are beset by a thousand unrelated exasperations and our child's behavior becomes the final straw, or when out of sheer irresponsible carelessness some precious object is smashed and all our veneer of perfect parenthood is ripped away and the natural man boils out in unadulterated outrage. These things happen. Do we pound on our children then? No. We can normally hold it together enough to stay on the far side of that. Are we therefore continuously maintaining our ongoing noble efforts to do our absolute best at parenting? I don't think so. Not right then. (Five minutes later, maybe.) For the time being we are breathing fire and just trying to keep the wheels on the track.

It seems to me that keeping that kind of control is in no way a shabby effort. We're supposed to be working on perfection, not beating ourselves up for not being there yet. And after all, most of the time parenting is tremendously rewarding. The closer you get to your own children's independence, the more you treasure the rewarding parts—all of them, from the times when they are round and firm and solid in your arms, to when they first learn to put their arms around your neck, to when they take their first steps away from you and then turn and flash you that million-dollar grin of accomplishment, through all the years when they have that warm grubby-child smell every time they've been out playing. You always remember how endearing they are when they're sprawled asleep and how trustful they are when they're awake. Then they gradually grow to your size and even bigger, and the son who sat on your lap becomes the son you can lean your head against, only your head just barely reaches his shoulder.

And over all the same years you're racking up your own successes and your own failures, and getting to understand more and more clearly what your own parents were all about. Maybe you won't make the same mistakes they did, but at least you'll have a clearer appreciation of how the mistakes came to be made, and it's guaranteed you'll make your own. Some you'll make out of love, and some out of exasperation and irritation, and some out of the kind of stupidity that afflicts us all at one time or another.

And in the end, if you do it all as nearly right as you can, your children may—if you're very, very fortunate—look at you with love and complete understanding and pride, and say, like Nephi, that they came of goodly parents.

I sure hope I eventually measure up to "goodly."

JUNE 2

And I, God, created man in mine own image, in the image of mine Only Begotten created I him; male and female created I them.
—MOSES 2:27

M en and women are different. They always have been. Men, for example, don't like to ask for directions. They prefer to drive in circles waiting for their sense of location or inspiration to take over, whichever happens first. Women like to talk to each other and organize things, preferably both at the same time. (A man may do one or the other, but separately.)

But for some time the idea seemed to flourish that the only significant difference between infant girls and boys (except for the obvious one) was that their mothers dressed them in either pink or blue. This was the first way in which seemingly neutral entities were socialized into producing what our society chooses to consider male or female behavior. My husband and I had three daughters, spaced out, before we had our son, and I was therefore able to accept this point of view as possibly plausible a lot longer than most of my contemporaries who had children of both sexes earlier or had more common sense to start out with.

My son was a revelation to me. Someone had clearly given him the Book of Boy Behavior to read before he was born, because he arrived knowing what to do. Almost as soon as he could make any meaningful noises at all, he started making car noises. (Back in the days when we were cave dwellers, did little cave boys make car noises?) He and his boy cousin of the same age did not play sedately next to each other as my daughters and their girl cousins had done; they grabbed at each other and pummeled each other and rolled over each other, all in great good humor. Our son methodically went through the toy trunk he shared with his sisters and extracted the most masculine toys available there. In short, he was definitely a boy and thus assisted me in coming to the conclusion that the so-called authorities didn't have any idea what they were talking about.

Now I am reading with considerable interest that the same people (or their direct intellectual descendants) are arguing forcefully that a great deal of medical research needs to be redone because so much of it was based on the unexpressed assumption that male and female bodies react in the same way both to disease and to treatment designed to ameliorate disease and it is becoming increasingly obvious that they don't.

My, my, my. Today let me contemplate what a circuitous path the human race is taking to come up with the same conclusions that are reported in both the book of Moses and the book of Genesis. "Male and female created I them."

Yes, indeed.

JUNE 3

A brother offended is harder to be won than a strong city: and their contentions are like the bars of a castle.

—PROVERBS 18:19

Like much of Proverbs, this is just plain common sense. Who hasn't noticed that family fights are more bitter than any other kind? We know too much about each other: Our ability to hurt each other is the dark underside of our ability to comfort and console each other. Not only that, but all our antennae are super-sensitive when it comes to family. Transgressions that would be mildly irritating or even on occasion endearing if anybody else committed them can drive you nuts if it's your sister.

The situation isn't helped by the fact that "company manners" got their name precisely because they are the manners reserved for outsiders. The accompanying assumption is that you can be your own unlovely ungracious self around family, and your long-suffering relatives will put up with it because you belong.

Dear Lord, today help me to repent. Bless me first with objectivity, so I can see when I am being a sore trial, and then bless me with tolerance, so I can overlook the exasperation caused by those near and dear to me who might be sore trials, too.

None of us is perfect yet. Bless us with gentleness, that we might love each other no matter what.

JUNE 4

The health of any society, the happiness of its people, their prosperity, and their peace all find their roots in the teaching of children by fathers and mothers.

—PRESIDENT GORDON B. HINCKLEY

In the journal that I have my students keep in Interpersonal Skills for the duration of the class, Darcelle was mulling over a problem. Her husband's sister and two children have taken refuge in her apartment from the sister's boyfriend, who has been beating her. The sister is asking Darcelle's husband to lend her five hundred dollars so she can set herself up in a new place, and he is willing (and marginally able) to do so.

Darcelle knows, however, that her sister-in-law has been sneaking out to meet the boyfriend. (She also knows that because she and her husband have three children of their own, three extra people are causing a population problem in the apartment.) Darcelle strongly suspects that if she says nothing, the sister-in-law will take the five hundred dollars, set up housekeeping again with the boyfriend, and the cycle of abuse will begin again. She also fears if that happens, her husband (who is 6' 5" and weighs 335 pounds, she tells me) will go after the boyfriend. On the other hand, if he finds out his sister is sneaking out now, he might go after his sister. Darcelle doesn't know quite what to do. And, as she points out, what about the little kids?

Darcelle herself is quiet and neatly dressed, good at her class work, and has amazingly good attendance, if you consider what's going on at home. You'd never suspect all this, just to look at her.

I think this kind of thing is exactly what President Hinckley is talking about—maybe a bit more raw in detail than what most of us are accustomed to, but our school is on the edge of the inner city, and many of our students don't have the safety nets and financial security that enable the rest of us to soften the details, if not the central realities. As long as we live in a society in which the happiness of the individual is considered primary (as in, it's better for the children that we split up so I can follow my new attraction rather than having us argue here at home since, unless I have what I want, I'm not happy), we're going to have people like Darcelle's sister-in-law who take this concept to the logical extreme: He's my boyfriend, and if it's distressing for the children to have him beat me up, it's still better that I be with him because I love him and I need to have what I want.

Darcelle didn't ask me for my advice on what to do. She did say that she was counseling with the Lord, and I wrote a note in her journal telling her I thought that was the wisest thing she could do and that I admired the strength of family feeling they were all showing.

Dear Lord, help Darcelle. Help her misguided sister-in-law, and help those children. Bless her husband who is, after all, trying to maintain order in the way he has been taught men should behave.

And bless me when I am tempted to put my near-sighted interests ahead of correct choices. Bless me that I will always remember what comes first and have the self-discipline to act accordingly.

JUNE 5

Behold, thou art fair, my love; behold, thou art fair; thou hast doves' eyes. Behold, thou art fair, my beloved, yea, pleasant: also our bed is green.

—SONG OF SOLOMON 1:15–16

For centuries rabbinical and Christian scholars have tried to find ways to argue that the Song of Solomon wasn't really a love song at all, that it is really about the relationship of Jehovah and his people, or Christ and his Church (St. Bernard wrote eighty-six sermons on the first two chapters alone). This has never persuaded a lot of people, and the Joseph Smith translation manuscript contains a note that the Song of Solomon is not inspired scripture, which would seem to settle the matter. Some passages, however, are plainly beautiful poetry.

Why has it not been extracted from our scriptures? I'm not enough of a biblical historian to know, but I'm glad it's there. On a wonderfully warm early summer day, it's delightful to be reminded that the love between a man and a woman is a good thing. Men and women have loved each other through the centuries, and they are meant to do so. Love is wonderful. There have been so many poems, and love letters, and sappy songs that it's hard to find something new to say, and yet when it happens, it's new for each of us. The freshness and vitality of love is one of the most magnificent parts of human creation.

Today, let me remember how I love my husband. Not how I admire him, or enjoy him, or like him—let me have a day to just plain love him. It's not the same as it was when we first met, of course—you can't have that newness when you've been hanging around together for decades—but the intimacy is a lot better, and every now and again, the intensity still catches us.

It'll do. Oh, yes. It'll do.

JUNE 6

I believe in indulging children, in a reasonable way. If the little girls want dolls, shall they have them? Yes. But must they be taken to the dressmaker's to be dressed? No. Let the girls learn to cut and sew the clothing for their dolls, and in a few years they will know how to make a dress for themselves and others. Let the little boys have tools, and let them make their sleds, little wagons, etc., and when they grow up, they are acquainted with the use of tools and can build a carriage, a house, or anything else.

—PRESIDENT BRIGHAM YOUNG

I was wandering through the trendy toy store in our town the other day and was interested to see that the trendy (and expensive) toys were either old-fashioned toys made fresh and eye-catching or new educational toys cleverly planned to encourage a child to decide what to do with them rather than coming equipped with flash and glitz and batteries and only one possible method of operation. I wondered what Brigham Young would have made of them.

Now I have to admit that those trendy but old-fashioned toys are not exactly what he had in mind. I think he was visualizing a length of remnant cloth for the girls and real tools for the boys. Still, I suspect he was innovative enough to be charmed by some of the ingenious toys now available. Wandering around the toy store from brightly colored display to display and wishing I had a bottomless checkbook, I saw a lot of tempting toys and games that clearly would introduce a child to skills he or she will need in our vastly more technologically sophisticated world.

So do we now, over a hundred years after Brigham Young gave his counsel, follow it word for word? Probably not. But the principle still rings true as a bell: Don't give children toys that waste their time. Oh, I doubt that the odd mechanized spaceship or battery-driven doll is going to do any permanent harm, but the toy that does only one thing gets discarded quickly. It's not really meant to be played with; it's to entertain, and once you've seen what it can do a couple of dozen times, what's the point?

Still, maybe there's one thing about that toy store that is a decided improvement over toy stores of the past. Most toys there are designed to appeal to both genders. Little girls are not restricted to dolls these days, and little boys are not discouraged from playing with them—or if not dolls as such, certainly toys that come very, very close.

It seems to me that makes sense for a lot of reasons unrelated to feminism. Life is uncertain and always has been. Pioneer women built and repaired houses, fixed fences, and worked with the whole range of tools when they had to, as their descendants do today, some of whom are raising families on their own. Learning how to handle a hammer and a screwdriver and a saw (not to mention a calculator and a computer) before the necessity arises is not an unwomanly accomplishment.

Nor is practicing looking after kids unmanly. Maybe a man who dimly remembers the boy doll or stuffed toys he cared for and took to bed with him is a little better prepared for sharing routine daily care of his own children and discovering, as his wife does, that doing ordinary things with little children and spending ordinary time together is what builds bonds of mutual knowledge and love that outlast the dependency of childhood. We forgot that for a few generations, but we seem to be remembering it again. That closeness, after all, has always been our long-term goal.

I'll bet it even has a lot to do with what Brigham Young was talking about in the first place.

JUNE 7

For verily, verily I say unto you, he that hath the spirit of contention is not of me, but is of the devil, who is the father of contention, and he stirreth up the hearts of men to contend with anger, one with another.

—3 Nephi 11:29

Or the hearts of sisters.

Why, oh, why do they have to fight so much? Today the battle was about a sweater, borrowed or not borrowed, returned in good condition or not—and this is June! What on earth are they doing with sweaters at this time of year anyway?

I try to be reasonable, but neither one of them is buying reason right at the moment. I try strong parental authority: That gets a measure of compliance, but now they're glaring at me as well as at each other. I'm not sure this is progress.

What I am sure of is that the father of lies has something to do with the whole business, and the spirit in the house at the moment is malevolent. When in these straits, the only logical course of action is prayer. I find even compulsory prayer helps somewhat—compulsory prayer, and enforced separation.

Let me pray for peace, but let me also pray for understanding. (Now why should a random memory flash into my head of standing in the hall one night, when I was about sixteen, white with fury that my sister had gone to bed with my curlers in her hair?) Growing up, after all, is a long process of discovering what works with human relationships and what doesn't. Help me make it clear that anger doesn't work, but help me also remember that trying it out is not unprecedented.

And because I don't remember learning many lessons overnight, help me remember to teach it tomorrow again, and probably the day after that. Maybe even next week, or next month, or next year.

Oh dear. Amen.

JUNE 8

And he stretched forth his hand toward his disciples, and said, Behold my mother and my brethren! For whosoever shall do the will of my Father which is in heaven, the same is my brother, and sister, and mother.

—MATTHEW 12:49–50

The real Jesus is so much more interesting than the sweetly simple, all-forgiving, all-loving version that seems to be popular now, when we are so sensitive to any form of criticism. Still, here is Jesus, being anything but soft and cuddly. We talk about eternal families, about the bonds that hold us together, and here is Jesus, being told that his mother and his brothers are waiting outside to see him. He answered that the people who were his disciples were his mother and his brethren, and they are already in. Unfortunately the story stops there.

Now, if Jesus really had been sickly sweet, he might have embraced everybody simultaneously and had a general lovefest. The real Jesus had work to do, and if there were possibly times to be interrupted, this seems not to have been one of them. Given his nature, I can't imagine that he left anybody standing out in the street, but neither did he stop what he was doing.

Part of what he was doing is what I want to remember today. He was telling us that if we do his will, we will have the closest possible relationship with him. Because he is God-made-man, he can be to each of us as mother, and brothers, and sisters. As a believer and an obedient disciple, each one of us can have a place in his Church and, even more, in his heart.

Let me remember that today. Let me remember that I have my family, and they are dear to me. But beyond my family, I am a part of the great congregation of Christian believers, and I belong in that congregation just as I belong in my family, so long as I am obedient to the will of our Father in Heaven. By baptism I was gathered in, and only by my disobedience can I ever be excluded.

What a magnificent heritage; what a comforting promise!

JUNE 9

Honour thy father and thy mother: that thy days may be long upon the land which the Lord thy God giveth thee.

—EXODUS 20:12

The words of the Lord which we know as the Ten Commandments, given to Moses on the top of the mount—this one is the fifth.

It comes after the commandments forbidding the worship of any other god, the making of graven images, taking the Lord's name in vain, and the commandment to honor the Sabbath day. It comes before the commandments forbidding murder, stealing, bearing false witness, and coveting that which belongs to other people. If the commandments are listed in order of importance, its position is an interesting one.

So why do we have to be commanded to honor our parents?

I suppose partly because being a parent is hard work, and not all of us do it well 100 percent of the time. Most of us, if we're being really honest, can remember parental flaws (although that's not the sort of thing we tend to mention in testimony meeting). Some of us have a hard time remembering past the flaws.

It's my theory that that is why we have the commandment.

Parenting is hard, and parents deserve to be honored for staying the course. If we were only to be honored when we were doing it well, there'd be a lot of thin patches. There are many rewarding aspects of parenting, but we need to remember that a lot of parenting consists of doing things you don't want to do when you don't want to do them. Few of our mistakes are made deliberately. We make mistakes because we're imperfect ourselves, because we get tired, because we're inexperienced. One of the real ironies of life is that when you finally have figured it out (having learned by trial and error), the kids are all grown up and don't need what you've finally figured out how to do.

And then it's another generation's turn, anyway.

Honor thy father and mother. Forgive them for their stumbles, as we hope our offspring will forgive us. Most of the stumbles don't add up to all that much, when you look back at the years of devotion and service. They did, as we are doing in our turn, the best they could.

Today, let us remember with love.

JUNE 10

Thou shalt love thy wife with all thy heart, and shalt cleave unto her and none else.

—DOCTRINE AND COVENANTS 42:22

The commandments of the Lord given through Joseph Smith to the elders of the Church in 1831 have definite similarities to the Ten Commandments, which shows that not all that much changes, give or take a millennium or two (or four or five). Moses had to tell his people not to commit adultery because some of the children of Israel were inclined to sleep with each other's wives, or husbands. Joseph Smith had to reiterate the message because people in this dispensation have similar temptations. I don't know if fidelity is a universal problem because infidelity is more "natural" (the natural man, we have been told, is an enemy to God) or if infidelity is just so effective for Satan that it gets used with great frequency.

You can ask why adultery is such a big deal only if you have never experienced it or seen the pain in the eyes of those who have. The commandments of the Lord are commandments because he said so and because they make a great deal of common sense on their own.

Adultery hurts because it is a betrayal. The strength of marriage is its permanence. Two imperfect people agree to share a life together and work toward perfection together.

That's why marriage ceremonies mention things like "richer or poorer" or "in sickness or in health." Marriage is constructed for getting through problems. You can deal with difficulties today because you have tomorrow to enjoy the rewards.

Adultery—with the reality of divorce and human estrangement—casts a dark shadow across tomorrow. All of a sudden everything has to be good now (and how can it be?), because you can't count on anything past today. Adultery is a betrayal of the innocent party in the most personal way possible, and it is a betrayal of the marriage relationship itself. Adultery, whatever you see on the silver screen (big or little) or read in romance novels or hear about on the gossip programs, is a big deal. It matters.

Unfortunately, few who get there start out in that direction intentionally, and some of those who do are not all that different from me. Dear Lord, please bless me that I never become complacent about fidelity. I've seen too many who have found themselves in deeper waters than they ever meant to swim. Bless me with radar for the pitfalls. Let me feel the warning twinges. Let me keep my attention fixed where it belongs, on my own endearing, faulty, funny spouse. (And let all of us always remember to let our spouses know how much we love them, lest their attention wander, either!)

Today, let me count all the ways my husband is my blessing. That should keep me busy.

JUNE 11

But what about you? Have you prayed about your own ancestors'
work? Set aside those things that don't really matter in your life.
Decide to do something that will have eternal consequences.
Perhaps you have been prompted to look for ancestors but feel that
you are not a genealogist. Can you see that you don't have to be
anymore? It all begins with love and a sincere desire to help those
who can't help themselves.
                                                    —ELDER RICHARD G. SCOTT

A conference address in which Elder Scott was enumerating the
ways in which modern technology has made the work of
genealogy more straightforward—ways which have only multiplied
in the years since he spoke.

Most families have one or two individuals who sort of get nomi-
nated or are self-selected for the task. Still, as we keep being reminded
from the pulpit and in Relief Society, we each come furnished with
a whole galaxy of ancestors: Expecting a couple of individuals to
keep track of all that for all of us is expecting rather a lot.

It makes me think of my father. He had a major heart attack,
which should have killed him; once it was apparent that he was
going to survive, the doctors warned us that it would most likely be
for a very short time indeed. He defied their predictions by living
four more years, during which time he traveled to Europe, to
Hawaii, to Australia, and spent a lot of good time with his family
and doing genealogy. He discovered he liked genealogy. He liked
poking around in the past, and he liked what I think of as horizontal genealogy: locating cousins he had never heard of, spread all
over the world. The letters he got back were fascinating.

His primary work, however, was gathering names for the
temple. Altogether, we figure he gathered about eight thousand,
give or take a few. Eight thousand of his—of our—kindred, who
would get the chance to choose. Eight thousand is a lot.

My father's closest friend was president of the Chicago Temple
at the time. When my mother called him, he had been about to call
my father to tell him that that day they had finished the work on the
last name he had submitted. Time for him to get busy on some more.

Mother was calling to tell him Daddy had just died.

Today, let me find some time to get started where my father left
off. Eight thousand is a lot, true. But it's not all. It's nowhere near all.

JUNE 12

Reproving betimes with sharpness, when moved upon by the Holy Ghost; and then showing forth afterwards an increase of love toward him whom thou hast reproved, lest he esteem thee to be his enemy.

—DOCTRINE AND COVENANTS 121:43

G ood advice. Given, as it happens, from Liberty Jail to the priesthood bearers, but it will do for women in Zion as well.

If only we never had to scold the dear little things! That's one of the many nice things about little babies. They sit there and smile and love you and there's absolutely nothing they can do wrong yet.

Unfortunately, this changes. For one thing, they gain mobility, and suddenly there are all kinds of dangers you have to stop them from getting into. There are electrical sockets, and bathtubs, and flights of stairs, and older siblings who don't take well to homework crumpled in chubby fists and drooled on, and dogs or cats who feel much the same way about having their fur clutched and twisted or their ears pulled (although I did have one young cousin who took her first steps following the retreating pompom tail of the poodle we owned at the time).

Things only get worse from there. For one thing, the child advances from inadvertent hazard to deliberate mischief—agency rearing its head—and defiance and rebellion and all the rest. Through it all we are continually handicapped because we love them so much. What we have to remember is that it isn't really love to let them go their own way. The lessons we are meant to teach them the world will teach them if we do not, but the world is not a gentle teacher.

Which is where this counsel from the Doctrine and Covenants comes in. We can teach gently if we remember what the Lord teaches us here. Sometimes it takes sharpness to get somebody's attention, but it can't be sharpness born of anger. When we speak out of anger, we are concentrating more on how the behavior outraged us than we are on helping the offender. It takes a while to get over being angry; showing "an increase of love" is almost impossible if you're gritting your teeth at the same time.

Today let me remember all that. If sharpness is needed and is prompted by the Holy Ghost, let me think of a surgeon's purposeful scalpel rather than a meat axe. And above all, let me remember the love. Always let me remember the love.

JUNE 13

And the king was much moved, and went up to the chamber over the gate, and wept: and as he went, thus he said, O my son Absalom, my son, my son Absalom! would God I had died for thee, O Absalom, my son, my son!

—2 SAMUEL 18:33

Absalom rebelled against his father, David; Absalom conspired and won the support of the northern kingdom of Israel; Absalom usurped the throne; and even so, David thought his heart would break when Absalom, his son, was killed.

David was his father. Being a parent is like that.

What is this bond between us and our children? They can disappoint us, they can anger us, they can make us so sick at heart that we can feel the physical pain in our chests, and still we are connected to them with a steel cable of love.

Of course, not all our children put us to those kinds of tests. There are the easy children, those who seem to have no difficulty following the right path. We hear a lot about such children, because their parents (quite justifiably) like to tell everybody else about them.

It's the black sheep who teach us about the reach of love. Those are the children whose parents lie awake in the night, listening to the small hours chime away on the clock, wondering if things would have been different had they done x, or y, or z. Those are the parents who say little in public, whose anguish is private and hidden. Over and over they wonder, Is it our fault?

David believed that Absalom's death was in part retribution for his own sin: The son he fathered illicitly with Bathsheba died, and his son Absalom was first estranged from him and then killed to cut short his rebellion. David, the proud king, considered these events a punishment to humble him.

That was David and Absalom. What about the parents now, who know David's grief but have no such clear-cut cause and effect to point to?

We don't know. We don't have all the answers—in fact, we have few of the answers—now. Perhaps the only comfort is to remember how short-sighted our perspective is. The prodigal returned; maybe the black sheep will as well—if not now, later. In the meantime, we have love. We cannot lose if we love. We lose only if we let our love turn to bitterness, or self-pity, or obsessive reliving of the past.

There is, after all, eternity. There's lots of time in eternity. Maybe the answers come then.

JUNE 14

And ye will not suffer your children that they go hungry, or naked; neither will ye suffer that they transgress the laws of God, and fight and quarrel one with another.

—MOSIAH 4:14

Oh, you mean this quarreling business comes up in more than one time and place? You mean somebody else's children sometimes had a rough time getting along with each other?

My mother, who grew up an only child, said she was immensely relieved when our dog had puppies. To my mother's fascination, the puppies yipped and snapped at each other, growled over toys, and shoved each other out of the way. (They also slept piled on top of each other in a contented pack.) "They're just like the children," my mother marveled at the time.

As this scripture points out, however, we're not trying to raise children the way we raise litters of puppies. We are required to teach our children to behave somewhat better. The comfort comes from realizing we're starting from approximately the same point.

For a long time there have been two contradictory theories about the nature of children. One is that children are pure and innocent. The other is that children will behave in totally self-centered and destructive ways unless they are taught otherwise. Interestingly, both theories contain much truth.

We do believe that children arrive here fresh and sinless. Adam's transgression—the consequences of which are inherited by all the generations of his progeny, which is to say the human race—brought evil into the world, and our fresh, sinless children can choose evil as well as anybody else. We don't believe, though, that they're responsible for what they choose until they're old enough to be accountable for knowing the difference between good and evil—which is why we baptize eight-year-olds instead of infants—but we believe we have to teach them to know that difference.

Which brings me back to the yah-yah-yah-yah-yah going on in my kitchen on this gorgeous summer morning. I'm standing at the sink briefly contemplating what would happen if I emptied this pitcher over their heads. Reluctantly I discard the idea: It would get me right down to their level and leave a huge mess on the floor. (In all honesty, I have to say I'm more deterred by the thought of the mess on the floor.)

Dear Lord, help me find the patience to teach, not to mention the wisdom. Help me to find the right words, and help me to restrain myself from the overwhelming wish to crack heads together. Help me to think more about what I'm teaching and less about how sick and tired I am of teaching it.

Next time, I think I'll try puppies.

JUNE 15

If ye endure chastening, God dealeth with you as with sons; for what son is he whom the father chasteneth not? But if ye be without chastisement, whereof all are partakers, then are ye bastards, and not sons. Furthermore we have had fathers of our flesh which corrected us, and we gave them reverence: shall we not much rather be in subjection unto the Father of spirits, and live?

—HEBREWS 12:7–9

Isn't this exactly what we say? You remember: One of your children is protesting about a criticism you've made, and you say, "If I didn't love you I wouldn't care what you do. I'm scolding you only because I care about you."

Does this make the chastisement any easier to bear? Unfortunately, not really. (No child to whom I have explained the above ever immediately brightened and said, "Oh, yes, Mother, now I understand exactly what you're saying and appreciate your point.")

None of us likes being scolded. We don't like being scolded directly, and we don't like having things go wrong because we went at them the wrong way, which is usually the indirect method that the Lord uses to teach us that it was the wrong way. What usually happens is we get grumpy and surly and resentful, just like the children.

Lord, today help me to grow up. Bless me with humility and open-mindedness. Help me realize that chastening for something

I've done may not necessarily be pig-headed and inaccurate. Help me over the difficult hump of pride. Help me to become grateful for the correction.

Let me be thy daughter. Then help me be thine obedient daughter.

JUNE 16

Behold, their husbands love their wives, and their wives love their husbands; and their husbands and their wives love their children; and their unbelief and their hatred towards you is because of the iniquity of their fathers; wherefore, how much better are you than they, in the sight of your great Creator?

—JACOB 3:7

Jacob, speaking to the Nephites during one of their periods of ungodliness and disobedience, contrasts their sorry state with that of the Lamanites, who at that point were doing a lot better.

Isn't it amazing how long it takes us to figure out some very elementary premises? One of them is that life in general goes much better when we are all doing what we ought to be doing. When husbands love wives, and tell them they do, and wives love their husbands back, and act as if they do, it is so much easier for both of them to be loving to their children on a comfortable, daily basis. Moods are catching: When you're in a good mood, the people around you tend to catch it and be in a good mood, too. Unfortunately the reverse is what we usually notice. You wake up in a bad mood, and it spreads faster than pinkeye; by the time you get downstairs, everybody is snarling at everybody else.

It's back to the old riddle. Is it a commandment to love one another because God said so, or is it a commandment because love is an eternal principle that governs our universe? At our stage, it seems to me that's one of the things we don't have to worry about. It's like explaining an arithmetic problem two different ways: Either way, you come out with the same answer. The answer here is that we are to love each other. The good stuff is what happens when we do.

When you have a family, you have a whole bunch of people with agency. When agency is flying off at a dozen different angles, everybody is pushing and shoving in different directions, cutting across each other and getting in the way. When the agency is flowing in the same direction, you have peace and serenity and love.

Can you remember a breakfast—or maybe it was a dinner—when everybody was talking and laughing and getting along and the only interruptions were giggly ones, and the whole family was circled around the table in mutual pleasure and enjoyment because you all wanted to get along, and because you knew each other so well and had loved each other for so long? And the food was good, too?

The Lamanites back in the time of Jacob seem to have had something like that. We can try for it today.

JUNE 17

And now, my son, I have told you this that ye may learn wisdom, that ye may learn of me that there is no other way or means whereby man can be saved, only in and through Christ. Behold, he is the life and the light of the world. Behold, he is the word of truth and righteousness.

—Alma 38:9

This is a testimony of Alma to his son Shiblon. The Nephites were sinking into iniquity (again), and Alma wanted to counsel his sons about the critical importance of understanding the principles of the gospel and obeying the commandments of the Lord.

What I like is Alma's plea "that ye may learn of me." How many lessons would we love to have our children learn of us, instead of through hard experience? How few of us figure out that telling the truth is easier in the long run without telling a few lies by way of experiment? How many of us learn why there is a commandment forbidding covetousness without learning the hard way that envy simply corrodes your own soul and does nothing to make up for anything you might lack? How many of us learn (without trying it both ways) that a soft answer works better when you're dealing with an angry person than shouting back at him or her?

Thank goodness, only a tiny minority has to try out murder to find that it simply gets you in a bigger mess than you started out with (not to mention having eternal consequences to deal with), but I think all of us at one time or another, usually as children, have taken something that didn't belong to us and discovered one of these consequences:

(a) the theft was promptly discovered, and we were forced to return the item publicly with considerable humiliation, or

(b) nobody found out about it, but our guilt rendered the object undisplayable and hence unusable and even undesirable in our own eyes.

If we could just figure out how to give our children a transfusion of our own wisdom in the same way that we inoculate them against measles, we would do so in a flash. And yet, are we so much better at learning lessons as adults from what we are told as opposed to working from what we discover is ineffective?

Unselfishness. Tolerance. Integrity. Sobriety. Chastity. Humility. Diligence. Patience. Obedience. Kindness. Charity. Faith.

We don't have to learn about them from our own lives: The scriptures are full of instructions and cautionary examples to show us how they should work. And how many of us follow those instructions and learn from those examples instead of trying it our own way first?

Please, Lord, let me start today learning better from what I have been told. Maybe if I get the hang of it, I can show my children how it's done.

JUNE 18

Now there stood by the cross of Jesus his mother, and his mother's sister, Mary the wife of Cleophas, and Mary Magdalene. When Jesus therefore saw his mother, and the disciple standing by, whom he loved, he saith unto his mother, Woman, behold thy son! Then saith he to the disciple, Behold thy mother! And from that hour that disciple took her unto his own home.

—JOHN 19:25–27

Here, in the last minutes before he died, in agony on the cross, Jesus made provision for his mother with the disciple that he himself had loved. If earlier he was emphasizing the larger family of membership within his Church—that his mother and brothers and sisters were the disciples who believed him and spread the gospel of his work—now he was concerned with his own earthly family and the mother who had cared for him. His last mortal task was to care for her.

What a valiant soul Mary must have been. She didn't ask for the mission she was given (how could she have? how could any woman have ever imagined such a thing?) but she accepted it gracefully. She asked only one question, which surely any woman would ask: How can I, a virgin, conceive a child? Having had that explained, she went forward not only with obedience but with rejoicing and praise.

It could not have been easy. She reared a child who must have puzzled her at times, as well as pleased her; she saw him reviled and executed in the cruelest possible way, and she was faithful. She was there, at the cross, sustaining him to the end.

Today, let me learn from Mary. Let me appreciate the strength and magnificence of this woman who believed and endured. We have only scraps of information about her life, but her graceful integrity shines through, like the star at his birth. Let me learn from her. Let me follow her star.

JUNE 19

And the angel of the Lord called unto Abraham out of heaven the second time, and said, By myself have I sworn, saith the Lord, for because thou hast done this thing, and has not withheld thy son, thine only son: that in blessing I will bless thee, and in multiplying I will multiply thy seed as the stars of the heaven, and as the sand which is upon the sea shore; and thy seed shall possess the gate of his enemies; and in thy seed shall all the nations of the earth be blessed.

—GENESIS 22:15–18

The blessing of the Lord and the renewal of the covenant came when Abraham demonstrated his obedience to the word of the Lord, even when he was commanded to sacrifice his only son. Abraham (as we know from latter-day revelation) was one of the most valiant spirits in the premortal life, which earned him his opportunities here on the earth, but it was his faithfulness here that earned him the eternal blessings.

Abraham is known as the "father of the faithful" (D&C 148:41), and his offspring, as the Lord promised, became the Lord's covenant people, chosen to bear testimony to the nature of God and his relationship with mortal men. It has not always been an easy mission, nor has it always been carried out with honor: The Old Testament is the record of the struggles and failures of Abraham's descendants in what we now call Israel and the surrounding territory. The Book of Mormon records the history of Lehi, one of Abraham's descendants, and his children and their struggles and failures on the American continent.

We are all children of Abraham, by birth or through the ordinances of the gospel, and have access to his blessings. That doesn't mean they are ours automatically, any more than they came automatically to Abraham's descendants who lived before us. Through him we are entitled to the opportunities of the blessings of the gospel, but like him, we have to earn those blessings through our obedience.

Dear Lord, I have never been required to sacrifice one of my children; let me not be reluctant to obey thee in easier ways. Help me today to remember thy promises to Abraham, the father of us all. Bless me that I may make myself worthy of them.

JUNE 20

And Ruth said, Intreat me not to leave thee, or to return from following after thee: for whither thou goest, I will go; and where thou lodgest, I will lodge: thy people shall be my people, and thy God my God: where thou diest, will I die, and there will I be buried: the Lord do so to me, and more also, if ought but death part thee and me.

—RUTH 1:16–17

This is one of the loveliest passages in the Bible, I think: The rhythm sings in my soul. The words have a wonderful lyrical sweep, and the meaning is particularly significant to me.

Ruth was not an Israelite woman. She was born and raised in the land of Moab, across the Dead Sea from Judæa. Had there not been a famine, she would never have had a place in our Bible. But when Elimelech and his wife, Naomi, sought refuge in Moab, bringing their two sons, Ruth's life and Naomi's crossed. Ruth married one of Naomi's sons, and the direction of her life was forever changed.

My husband and I have two adopted daughters, one from Asia and one from South America. Like Naomi and Ruth, our lives and those of our daughters have crossed and been knotted together. Like Ruth, they have chosen to forsake the gods of their ancestors and become children of Israel. Like Ruth (to use Keats's immortal phrase), they are making their lives "amid the alien corn" (*Ode to a Nightingale*). The direction of their lives, too, has forever changed, and who knows where those lives will lead?

The seed of Abraham has indeed spread far and wide, but adoption is an ancient and honored tradition as well. After all, Ruth chose her adoption and has a high and noble place in our history because of it—and because of her loyalty and faith.

Ruth ultimately had a son. His name was Obed. Obed had a son, and his name was Jesse. And Jesse had a son, and his name was David: David the great King of Israel, whose line ran directly down to Jesus Christ, our Lord.

Blessed be Ruth, who was faithful. Blessed be the name of the Lord.

JUNE 21

The proverbs of Solomon. A wise son maketh a glad father: but a foolish son is the heaviness of his mother.

—PROVERBS 10:1

Now wait a minute. Is that fair? As long as they behave themselves, they're their father's? When they go rocketing off the rails, it's my problem? I don't like the sound of that at all.

Of course, I have to admit it's not an entirely unprecedented thought. Have we ever greeted our husbands returning from work with the ominous announcement, "Do you know what your son (or daughter) has been up to?" Maybe we'd better admit that if we—mothers and fathers alike—intend to preen when the kids prove they used their heads, we both have to stand up and be counted on the occasions when we might wonder wildly what's holding their ears apart.

But one thing we do have to keep straight is that whereas Proverbs could not be more accurate in describing the way it *feels* when your child acts foolishly, we have to keep clear in our own minds that our children are not an extension of us. Do we take pride in them? Of course. Do they embarrass us? Well, of course. They all do, at one time or another. But are they separate from us? You'd better believe they are.

Children are not possessions. They belong to themselves and to our Heavenly Father. They're lent to us, placed in our custody for the time being, but sooner or later, we go back to being comrades and equals. For now, my job is to teach and their job is to learn, but who knows what our assignments will be in the eternities to come? (As far as that goes, I find myself doing a lot of learning from my children right here and now.)

We get into trouble when we start thinking "my son" or "my daughter" in the same way we think "my bathrobe" or "my pair of shoes." Life doesn't work like that—and you know, when you think about it, it's just as well. At least my bathrobe stays where it's put.

Today let me enjoy my son and my daughters, whatever they're doing—and even while I'm beaming or cringing, help me keep in mind that they belong to themselves. Good or bad, they never belong to me.

Or to their father, either. So there, Solomon.

JUNE 22

Therefore shall a man leave his father and his mother, and shall cleave unto his wife, and they shall be one flesh.

—ABRAHAM 5:18

Which should take care of the in-law problem, shouldn't it? But one of the opportunities and challenges of life here on earth is that we generally go through the same situations more than one time, going at it each time from a different perspective. I read a book once in which the process was described as a spiral: We go around once as children, then the spiral carries us on to being parents of children, and finally we spiral into being parents of parents. What's happening is the same, but we're in a different position in relation to it.

As we mount higher and higher in the spiral, we see things differently. When we're little, there's Grandma, and that's good news. Then we're the mom, and Grandma (particularly if it's the grandma from the other side) may not be quite such good news. For one thing, she probably doesn't do things exactly the way we did them in our house, which is by definition the right and proper way to do them. This can be a problem, and sometimes is—sometimes a big problem. Even so, one way and another time passes, and then we get to be Grandma. Are we good news? We're not the ones to decide.

It sometimes feels as if it would be a lot easier to turn the spiral upside down and have the benefit of everything we learn right from the beginning. Unfortunately, life isn't like that. Learning is part of the program. So when we go by the second time, we suddenly understand a lot of what baffled us about our mothers the first time, and when we go by the third, we suddenly understand our mother-in-law's perspective—or, if all went well before, we can try to live up to her example, which may be harder than we expected.

Today, let me take it on faith that most people act on motives that are honest and sensible to them. Let me trust in that and figure that maybe I'll understand the motives better later. Let me enjoy the swings on the spiral, neither reaching forward nor trying to hang back. Let me let this good life slide through my fingers and savor it as it comes—in-laws and all.

The spiral is going to keep moving, and so must I.

JUNE 23

Bring up your children in the love and fear of the Lord; study their dispositions and their temperaments, and deal with them accordingly, never allowing yourself to correct them in the heat of passion; teach them to love you rather than to fear you.

—PRESIDENT BRIGHAM YOUNG

Who better than Brigham Young to understand that children come in different packages, with different dispositions and temperaments? I think if there is any one thing I have learned as a mother, that is it. Before you have children (note the plural) of your own, you can be very stupid about it. Take me: Exhibit A.

My first child was an easy one. She and I harmonized readily; she liked to do what I wanted her to do (with a couple of interesting exceptions), and because I am naturally modest, I assumed it was because my management procedures were superior to those of people who were having problems.

Then I had my second child and learned some humility. My third taught me more, and by the time my fourth came along, I was just grateful if anything worked. By that time I recognized that there was no magic formula, no one-size-fits-all method, and that what Brigham Young could have taught me in the first place—to study the disposition and the temperament of the individual child—is the only rule you can rely on. Moreover, his counsel offers as well the charm of getting to know a wholly unique individual: your own child.

I am getting to know these four separate people, and because I love them most when I think about them most, and I think about them most when they're challenging me the most, I love them for entirely individual and somewhat peculiar reasons. I love one of them because she is endowed with truly remarkable common sense and gets herself into hair-raising predicaments because she never completely believes that everybody else doesn't think the way she does. I love one of them because he always has an answer for everything, but because he doesn't always pay sufficient attention to the question the answers are sometimes unnervingly irrelevant. I love one of them because she is always unsure of herself and she has such a good time when she discovers she can do what I've been telling her all along she can do. I love one of them because she will always take the most complicated route to find the simplest solutions, and we all go careering along on the journey.

That's just four. When I think about the troop that Brigham Young had to keep track of, I wonder how he did it!

Today let me enjoy my individuals. Let me enjoy them, and go on studying. The Lord knows I need to.

JUNE 24

And again, inasmuch as parents have children in Zion, or in any of
her stakes which are organized, that teach them not to understand
the doctrine of repentance, faith in Christ the Son of the living God,
and of baptism and the gift of the Holy Ghost by the laying on of
the hands, when eight years old, the sin be upon the heads of the
parents. . . . And their children shall be baptized for the remission
of their sins when eight years old, and receive the laying on of the
hands. And they shall also teach their children to pray, and to walk
uprightly before the Lord.

—DOCTRINE AND COVENANTS 68:25, 27–28

H ow can our children learn these things if we don't undertake
the responsibility of teaching them?

There are all kinds of reasons for postponing such teaching. We
get so busy. Right now isn't the right time. I'll do it in a minute.
Can't manage it today; it should be better tomorrow. Maybe next
week we'll get a chance to spend some time together.

The Lord is telling us here that some things can't wait.

Children learn lots of things in Primary. They learn about
Daniel in the lions' den and about Nephi and his brothers. They
learn about the pioneers crossing the plains. They learn about
Jonah, who was swallowed by the whale. All of them are important
things and are used to teach the principles on the Lord's list.

But the things on that list are so important that they can't be
taught just in Primary. The central concepts have to be learned at
home. Our children need their parents to teach them because they
already know that we teach them what we think is important. They
need us to teach them because these lessons need to be taught over
and over again until they are second nature. They need to learn
about prayer in theory, and they need to pray beside us, night after
night after night. They need to learn about repentance, and they
need to see us practice it, because we are the people most important
to them. They need to be part of the preparations for baptism, if
they have older brothers and sisters, and they need to have us tell
them about it so they can look forward to it, if they have not.

Those are lessons for us to teach, and we will be held responsible if we don't. But that might not be the most important reason
for us to teach. Maybe we need to teach because we need to be
reminded about these principles ourselves. How many of us have

learned all there is to learn about repentance? How many of us know it all about prayer?

Bless me to remember that, so that it's a priority to be working on today—today, tomorrow, and the day after that. As long as they need to know—or I do—let me teach.

JUNE 25

And why take ye thought for raiment? Consider the lilies of the field, how they grow; they toil not, neither do they spin: and yet I say unto you, That even Solomon in all his glory was not arrayed like one of these.

—MATTHEW 6:28–29

A hard summer's day gardening: finished off with sitting on the swing with a cold glass of orange juice, looking around at everything that still needs doing and, in spite of that, taking time to admire the overwhelming beauty of the roses, tumbling over the props that hold up the huge antique bushes, filling the air with their unmistakable fragrance. I don't have lilies yet (maybe next year?), but how nice to think that Jesus, too, thought flowers were so lovely that he used them as an example of the felicity of the natural world.

What kind of gardens did Jesus sit in during the years before he started his ministry, when he might have had time to admire the wonderful shape and scent of the lilies? Sitting here in my own back yard, it suddenly makes real the fact that some of his pleasures must have been the same mortal blessings that pleasure me.

Dear Lord, I thank thee for this garden. I thank thee for this world, and for thy Son, who loved it, too.

JUNE 26

For I rejoiced greatly, when the brethren came and testified of the
truth that is in thee, even as thou walkest in the truth. I have no
greater joy than to hear that my children walk in truth.

—3 JOHN 1:3–4

This letter of John's is addressed to Gaius, and that's all we know about him, except that John wrote to him as one of his children—one of his converts, perhaps? The letter was written very early, probably in the last quarter of the first century, when Christianity was new and fresh and the scattered little congregations knew of each other only through letters and the reports of the missionaries who were passing through.

Apostasy was a constant problem; in fact, later in this letter John, who was of course an apostle, mentions another member of the Church, Diotrephes, who apparently held some position of authority. Diotrephes not only had refused to receive John's messengers, but he threatened to excommunicate anyone of his congregation who did. Gaius, by contrast, had treated John's brethren and other travelers well and, given the problems, we can understand John's rejoicing to hear that Gaius remains faithful.

How many other missionaries, returning to visit the branches where they have labored, rejoice with John when their "children"— the good souls they introduced to the gospel—are still walking in the truth! For the time they are out in the mission field, those new members become the missionaries' family, and how comforting it is to find that the family is still faithful, that the promises they made are still being kept, that the rewards will still be theirs.

And those of us at home—are we still faithful? Do we still walk in the truth? I doubt any of us now would turn away a messenger from an apostle, but do we always listen to—and obey—their messages? Today let me think that over and watch where I'm walking.

JUNE 27

Every spirit of man was innocent in the beginning; and God having redeemed man from the fall, men became again, in their infant state, innocent before God. And that wicked one cometh and taketh away light and truth, through disobedience, from the children of men, and because of the tradition of their fathers. But I have commanded you to bring up your children in light and truth.

—DOCTRINE AND COVENANTS 93:38–40

So we start out fine. We're just not very good at staying that way. This is not hard to believe, particularly if you happen to have given a birthday party recently. Maybe there are birthday parties at which all the invited guests (not to mention the honoree) behave beautifully for the entire time, but I haven't been present at any of them. Which is not to say that children are universally little horrors. It's just that there tends to be pushing and shoving at children's parties, and not all the rules of the games are universally obeyed, and at least one person usually feels she (or he) should have had the prize that somebody else got. In my experience, birthday parties are generally splendid evidence that we learn things gradually over time, and sharing and unselfishness are lessons that take longer than average.

Do grownups share willingly, and are grownups universally unselfish? I don't think so; however, most of us have learned to be a little more subtle about it. But managing subtly is not an alternative to learning the lesson itself. The idea is that we start out learning to be polite, and we end up learning to be good—the goodness enveloping the politeness, making the form into the substance.

We need to bring up our children in light and truth. Of course we do. But we also need to stand in the light and truth ourselves. Today, let me consider how far along the path from politeness to goodness I've come. (I might start by considering whether I invariably manage even politeness.) Today might be a good day to measure how far I have to go.

JUNE 28

God setteth the solitary in families: he bringeth out those which are
bound with chains: but the rebellious dwell in a dry land.

—PSALM 68:6

We must not be rebellious today; it's anything but dry. The rain is pouring outside, a wonderful steady summer rain. Goodness knows we need it; each morning I hear the hiss of the neighbor's sprinkler system and debate whether I have to get out and start watering, or whether the rain is going to come.

But it has come, and we're all inside staying dry. School is out; one of my daughters offered to make a french toast breakfast for everyone, so we are sticky and full and content. So far nobody has volunteered to do the dishes (so I don't need to worry about the family becoming so virtuous that they are all translated straight to heaven without me), but at least the dishes got stacked ready in the sink, and I can take care of them later. For now, I can be glad that families were invented and that God setteth the solitary into them. Where else is the kind of contentment that we can have at home?

It's raining, it's pouring; one of the girls is dozing over a book, curled up in a chair, and I can hear voices chattering away happily upstairs. It's raining, it's pouring; God's rain is falling on the lawn and the flowers, and God's peace is in the house.

JUNE 29

In the enriching of marriage the big things are the little things. It is
a constant appreciation for each other and a thoughtful demonstra-
tion of gratitude. It is the encouraging and the helping of each other
to grow. Marriage is a joint quest for the good, the beautiful, and
the divine.

—ELDER JAMES E. FAUST

We know so little about marriage when we get started on it. We may have had years of being around our parents' marriage, but few of us paid much attention to how it worked, particularly if it worked well. It was just there, like the wallpaper on the walls or the jelly on the peanut butter sandwiches. We were probably considerably more attentive to the images of marriage on the screen, in the books we read, and in our own imagination. That's where marriage was exciting. That's where marriage was romantic. That's how we wanted it to be.

And so it is. Sometimes. I suppose it shows I've been married a long time when I say that though our children may not be able to see it, a lot of the romance of marriage lies in how ordinary it ·is. Anyone can find you attractive when you are beautifully dressed and smell wonderful and have your hair straight. It takes a husband to scoop you up when you have encountered a bitter disappointment and your face is wet and your nose is runny (that's what happens when you cry a lot), and he can hold you and rock you like a baby because that's what you need right then. It takes a wife to see from the expression in his eyes that you need to get through that crowd right this minute and rescue him from his Aunt Ruth before he blows his cool and says something we will all regret. Your kids aren't much good at seeing where the romance lies in either of those situations, but believe me, it's there. A comforting cuddle or a rescue when it's needed come out way ahead of a bathtub full of long-stemmed roses.

Not that the roses wouldn't be nice.

Marriages when they're working are private, which is why people talk about them in generalities. There's no way to explain how my husband makes my marriage good for me, nor would it do anybody else any good to try to copy it. When my marriage hits a bump (and like most marriages, I suspect, it does from time to time), nobody can tell me exactly how to fix it. All anybody can give me are principles.

It probably involves a lot of attention to the little things. (Which little things? I can't tell you; you have to figure it out.) I would do well to show gratitude and appreciation. (For what? How? Pay attention; it's probably obvious.) The closer we come to our Heavenly Father, the closer we come to each other. (How do you know? How can you tell? Open your soul and trust. You'll know.)

Marriage is a gift, but it's one that takes earning. Some days are easier than others, but all days are worth it. Your children may not understand that, but you will. When you put the whole thing together, you will.

JUNE 30

*Train up a child in the way he should go: and when he is old, he will
not depart from it.*

—PROVERBS 22:6

Or so they say. Is it really true? Does it mean that if I go on harping about brushing your hair and cleaning your room and picking up stuff instead of creating trails around the house, they will grow up to be well-groomed, tidy adults? If I insist that they speak kindly to each other and arbitrate serious disagreements and praise them like crazy when they're nice to each other, will they grow up to be friends as well as siblings? If I remind them on a nightly basis—"Have you said your prayers?"—will they grow up to be prayerful and endowed with strong testimonies?

Is this a promise? In Proverbs, it sounds solid; I guess I would say (looking around at families I know) that it's probably more likely than not. There's one hitch, though: Your children have agency. You can't make their choices for them. You can emphasize what you know is important now, and you can pray for them then, but if it were possible to make all the decisions for them ahead of time, we'd be living in the universe Satan envisioned, not the one we chose. That's what Satan wanted: All of us would be good, all of us would return to the presence of our Father in Heaven, and not one of us would have learned a thing.

So in this world we chose we do our best. We teach, and we cross our fingers, and we pray. We love a lot. We try to do the right thing, and we try to fix it up when it turns out we didn't. We encourage them and help when it's possible, and they learn a lot and so, by golly, do we.

Just for today, Lord—it's the last day in the month—let me do everything right. Let me be wise and benevolent, and let them believe that I love them as much as I do. Let me keep my temper and not yell (not once) and—just for today—not get distracted by things that are really less important. Just for today, Lord, let me do it right. Let me train them up in the way they should go.

And bless them—bless me—that when they are old, they will not depart from it.

JULY

Now faith is the substance of things hoped for, the evidence of things not seen.

—HEBREWS 11:1

JULY 1

And now as I said concerning faith—faith is not to have a perfect knowledge of things; therefore if ye have faith ye hope for things which are not seen, which are true.

—ALMA 32:21

Faith, then, lies somewhere in that misty territory between I-don't-know and the certainty of having seen it with my own eyes. If I have to say I'm not sure but I *think* so, that's not faith. On the other hand, if I can verify it from my own experience, that's not faith either. Faith is somewhere in between.

The funny thing is that faith sometimes feels so much like knowledge. Do I *know* that I came from our Heavenly Father's presence to live here on this earth and prove how I can manage on my own? Of course not. I can't remember; none of us can. A part of the condition set was that we would be rendered amnesiac. But it sounds so right. I may not be able to remember anything precisely, but I have to say I've had fleeting moments of knowing that once there was something to remember. So is that still faith? It must be, but my certainty shapes the way I look at my life.

Do I *know* that Jesus Christ once lived and by his choice to give up his own life made it possible for me to overcome the fact of mortal death? No. I never had the privilege of knowing him in mortality nor of witnessing the miracle of his resurrection with my mortal eyes. But when I read the Gospels and feel the sense of recognition in my heart—which is, after all, the evidence of the Comforter which he promised—it feels as if I know. Like my "knowledge" of the premortal existence, it feels right.

When I was a child, I thought I knew. When I grew older, I went through a period of questioning, and I doubted. I wondered if faith was maybe just another word for hope that we fool ourselves with. Now I would say I know again. Did I change my mind because I saw something? No. Can I prove what I now believe? I don't think I'm meant to.

But when I come to the end of my life, I expect that I will step back into a world that is familiar to me. If I've made sufficient use of my opportunities, I will be home. The veil will be gone, and I can fold up my faith, like an outgrown sweater, and put it away.

Then the truth will be there to be seen; there will be no need to prove it. We will all know.

JULY 2

Look unto me in every thought; doubt not, fear not.
—DOCTRINE AND COVENANTS 6:36

It's been hot, the first really hot weather of the summer, now coming to a sharp conclusion with a violent summer storm. The sky turned a sulfurous yellow, and then came the rumble of thunder—like giants roller-skating—and flashes of lightning. Find the children; find the animals. Get everyone inside, including the timid gray cat who has to be persuaded to run through the rain to the back door. (No, you foolish animal, sheltering under a rose bush isn't going to make it. Leaves don't work as well as roof tiles.)

So now the storm is raging, a vigorous crashing storm. There's this to be said for the Midwest: We do storms thoroughly. I remember once having visitors from the West Coast here when we had one of these storms. They absolutely loved it. Went out on the front porch to savor the experience, just like a sound and light show. I can't say it affects me that way. While they were out on the porch, I was inside hoping it would stop soon, preferably without us (or the house) getting struck by lightning.

"Look unto me in every thought." Yes. Help me not to be silly about things—even about storms—in front of the children. "Doubt not, fear not"—that's where the faith comes in. I doubt that the Lord was referring to a summer storm when he gave this revelation to Joseph Smith and Oliver Cowdery, but I believe what he said applies, regardless.

Today, bless me with faith. Bless me with faith in thy watchful care, summer storms or not. After all, after the storm comes the calm and the cooler weather. I'll place my trust in that.

JULY 3

And because of the knowledge of this man he could not be kept from beholding within the veil; and he saw the finger of Jesus, which, when he saw, he fell with fear; for he knew that it was the finger of the Lord; and he had faith no longer, for he knew, nothing doubting.

—ETHER 3:19

Moroni, writing about the brother of Jared, that man of faith. What must it be like to have faith like that? How must it feel to believe so completely that you *see* and, seeing, know what is in front of you, and so fall down to the ground with fear, because you are looking at the finger of the Lord? Is it great simplicity of mind, or great sophistication, or maybe just a matter-of-fact acceptance of the absolute reality of our Lord's presence?

There are so many exceptional people whose stories are in this book I hold here on my lap, but I think the brother of Jared must be one of the most remarkable. I suppose part of the reason he fascinates me is that the scriptures don't even give his name. Nevertheless, putting that aside, I keep coming back to the strength of his faith—faith which went so far that it became absolute knowledge. As it says in the scripture, the brother of Jared "had faith no longer, for he knew, nothing doubting."

What did that feel like? I can't imagine.

Today, let me flex the muscles of my own faith. Let me use the example of the brother of Jared to help them grow: knowledge like his is possible. It has happened. I can believe it because I have had moments of almost feeling the veil between me and eternity brushing against my face—when my father died was one such moment. Let me allow those moments to enrich my faith. Let me dare to know; let my spirit reach toward home.

JULY 4

And ye shall know the truth, and the truth shall make you free.
—JOHN 8:32

Banners and bunting and picnics—the smell of barbecue shall be known in the land! Potato salad in the refrigerator, potato chips and lemonade all over the place, and fireworks to look forward to tonight.

Our ward has had the tradition of an early-morning flag-raising ceremony on the Fourth of July, with the faithful few (many of us think the Fourth can start a little later, thank you) gathering around the flagpost, listening to a short talk, singing the national anthem, and slapping at mosquitoes that zing and zap us from the dewy grass. We finish up with doughnuts and orange juice, feeling virtuous and patriotic, a nearly unbeatable combination. It's a splendid start to the Fourth.

I don't think I understood patriotism until I lived in England for so many years. England is a wonderful place; it was where I lived the early part of my marriage and had our first two children. I came to understand how my English friends—and my English husband!—could love their country as they do. I could even imagine being one of the Englishmen or women who circled the globe in the glory days of the British Empire, always keeping the memory of that green and pleasant land warm in their hearts. I came to love England myself.

But on the Fourth of July we would always troop over to the acre of land on the hill overlooking Runnymede meadow where the Magna Carta was signed. The people of Britain gave that acre to the people of the United States after Kennedy's assassination. There, on our American acre, we would have an American picnic: I, my English husband, my half-English children, and whatever English friends were willing to come wave American flags and be respectful for a day. No jokes about Yanks on that day or they didn't get any fried chicken. One year we flew kites: red, white, and blue kites climbing high up in the wind over Runnymede.

Yes, I came to love England, but during those years I learned I was American to the bone. This is my land, blessed by God and established on the American continent, the land of the brave and the free. Now we're home again—well, at least, home to me, and the children are now more aware that they're half American—and tonight we will go over to the golf course and sing "The

Star-Spangled Banner" (again), and watch the fireworks hiss and splatter up in the night sky, and slap at the mosquitoes.

Today, let me remember my heritage—and maybe those kites, sailing free over an American acre, through an English sky.

JULY 5

When Jesus heard it, he marvelled, and said to them that followed, Verily I say unto you, I have not found so great faith, no, not in Israel.

And I say unto you, That many shall come from the east and west, and shall sit down with Abraham, and Isaac, and Jacob, in the kingdom of heaven.

—MATTHEW 8:10-11

This was when the Roman centurion asked Jesus to heal his servant. Since the centurion knew that Jewish tradition considered it defiling for a Jew to enter the house of a Gentile like himself, he did not ask Jesus to come there. He simply asked Jesus to "speak the word only, and my servant shall be healed" (Matthew 8:8). He explained that he was a man who understood authority. He could give a command and it would be obeyed; so, he said, it was with Jesus also.

It is this centurion's faith that Jesus is talking about.

What is interesting is the prophecy Jesus goes on to make. Matthew reports it fully, although as a Jew himself, writing primarily for an audience of Jewish Christians, he almost seems to anticipate through much of his gospel that the Mosaic law and therefore Jewish life as he knew it would continue more or less the same. Even so, he tells us the story: It's based on the tradition the rabbis taught that the age of the Messiah would begin with a great feast for all Israel, including the patriarchs and the prophets and the heroes. Jesus, referring to that feast, makes it clear that the Gentiles will be admitted as well and on equal terms. (In fact, Jesus goes on to say that the Jews who were unworthy would find themselves cast out.)

For Jewish Christians in the early days of the Church, this whole issue of how Jewish you had to be to be a Christian was difficult, and men of good heart and honest purpose were on both sides of it. (It took that revelatory dream of the four-footed beasts for Peter to understand the direction in which they were to go.) Do we sometimes have a shadowy hint of a similar problem when we have wrinkles in our own adjustment to the reality of a truly worldwide church rather than one cradled firmly in our own familiar folkways? Doctrine, after all, is one thing; custom is another. But we cling to custom.

Today, let me remember the centurion. Maybe it would help to think of him as someone from Africa, or the jungles of South America, or Outer Mongolia. Would I recognize great faith demonstrated in his ways as swiftly as our Lord did?

Dear Lord, bless me with tolerance and breadth of vision. Bless me with the humility to recognize my own provincialism, wherever it exists. Help me to put it aside and welcome my sisters and brothers from the east and from the west, as we all, equal in worship, gather at the table of our Lord.

JULY 6

When thou passest through the waters, I will be with thee; and through the rivers, they shall not overflow thee: when thou walkest through the fire, thou shalt not be burned; neither shall the flame kindle upon thee.

—ISAIAH 43:2

What a wonderful promise! I wonder if my great-grandmother, trudging across the plains with her family, ever happened upon these words of Isaiah. Isaiah was giving the words of the Lord to the children of Israel, who were then exiles hoping to return to their home. My great-grandmother was hoping to find her home, and every footstep took her farther away from everything that had been familiar. But I think that these words would have given her great comfort.

"When thou passest through the waters"—she was just a young girl when she crossed the plains, but in the middle of the nineteenth century, even young girls wore a lot of clothes by our present-day standards. Can you imagine the weight of wet clothes after fording a river or stream? Long wet skirts slapping against your ankles; wet shoes (if you were lucky enough to have them) squishing on the dirt or dust clinging between your damp toes and caking the tops of your bare feet. The pioneers crossed the plains in the summer. Anyone who has followed their route (in all likelihood from the comfort of an air-conditioned car) knows that summer on the Great Plains is hot and sticky and there are flies in the daytime and mosquitoes at night. The faint trail ahead must have looked endless.

You were hot, and you kept walking. You were tired, and you kept walking. You were sometimes ill and sometimes afraid, and you kept walking. You prayed that everybody would be able to keep up, and you kept putting one foot in front of the other, day after day after day. By the time you reached the valley, you were thin and gaunt and worn, but you had arrived.

And then you began the struggle to survive in the valley.

Today, Lord, let me think about the comfort of my life. Let me savor the cold water that runs out of my tap. (And I can even add ice cubes, if I wish!) Let me listen to the hum of the air conditioner and grumble less about how the upstairs doesn't cool properly and enjoy more the pleasure of stepping from the hot garden into the cool of the back hall. (Even the black cat is spread out on his back at full length, napping in uncatlike abandon close to the vent.) I may have trials, but they are different from Great-Grandmother's trials.

Today, let me give some thought to the trials I don't have.

JULY 7

Men and women should become settled in the truth, and founded in the knowledge of the gospel, depending upon no person for borrowed or reflected light, but trusting only upon the Holy Spirit, who is ever the same, shining forever and testifying to the individual and the priesthood, who live in harmony with the laws of the gospel, of the glory and the will of the Father. They will then have light everlasting which cannot be obscured.

—President Joseph F. Smith

Oh, the insidious temptation of relying on borrowed or reflected light! How easy it is to reason that because the people around me believe, I can rest on their belief instead of struggling (when it feels like a struggle) to maintain my own. They read the scriptures a lot; wouldn't you think that some of it would rub off on me?

It's like genealogy. My father did such a lot of it. Can't some of that count for me? After all, I took an intelligent interest, at least part of the time. My mother's genuine spirituality is inspiring; I know she would be happy to give me a cupful or a dozen or however you measure spirituality.

Or how about husbands and wives? We promise to share every-thing, and we certainly do share cold germs and sore throats and the kind of nights when you toss and turn until both of you are wide awake and checking the clock. How about a testimony?

But it doesn't work that way. In my heart of hearts I know that, even without having Joseph F. Smith to remind me. Maybe today I should consider how I can more fully stand on my own two feet and build faith of my own.

JULY 8

Fight the good fight of faith, lay hold on eternal life, whereunto thou art also called, and hast professed a good profession before many witnesses.

—1 TIMOTHY 6:12

Sometimes I view so many of the people in the New Testament as if they were in one of those old-fashioned lantern shows: The light flickers and you see the figures for a moment, and then it fades and they're gone, and then the light brightens again and for an instant you see them—caught in a different posture—and the light fades again, and so on.

Timothy is like that. The light catches Timothy in the book of Acts—his mother was a Jewish woman named Eunice, who was married to a Greek. Both Eunice and her mother, Lois, were converted to Christianity, and Timothy might have been converted by Paul himself on Paul's first missionary journey. When we first hear of Timothy, he is already a disciple and chosen by Paul to accompany him during his second missionary journey. The light flickers again, and Timothy is being sent to Macedonia, where Paul joins him. He was with Paul on Paul's last visit to Jerusalem, and when Paul wrote the epistles to the Colossians and Philippians, Timothy was with him in Rome, where Paul was imprisoned. In the last flash of light, Timothy is in charge of the Church at Ephesus, as Paul's deputy, and that is where he received two letters from Paul advising him on his pastoral duties. In the second letter, Paul is asking him to come to Rome to be with him in his captivity and to bring with him Paul's cloak that was left at Troas—

winter, it seems, was coming on—and his books, especially the parchments.

But we never see Timothy plainly or hear his voice. (Nor do we know if he was able to be with Paul at the end.)

What we do have is what Paul wrote to him, and that counsel has come to us down through the centuries. "Fight the good fight of faith," he advises. In other words, faith isn't easy. It must have been hard in those early days; it's hard sometimes in these latter days. From all we know, Timothy stayed faithful to the end. Will we?

Let me use today to consider how I am coming in that good fight. Is my faith increasing? If not, it is draining away. Faith is like a rippling stream that never stands still: It moves, in one direction or another. Let me move in the way I mean to go; let me, too, hold on to the promise of eternal life. Let me be strong in the fight today, and let that strength carry me forward to tomorrow.

JULY 9

And the Lord said unto Moses, How long will this people provoke me? and how long will it be ere they believe me, for all the signs which I have shewed among them?

—NUMBERS 14:11

If the Lord sounds provoked, it's easy to understand why. The children of Israel were getting tired of the wilderness and all the difficulties of life there. They were deciding in retrospect, having conveniently edited out all the unpleasant parts, that slavery in Egypt hadn't been that bad: At least you knew where you were and people told you what to do. Freedom, they complained, was too dangerous. Who knew what might come upon you in the wilderness? It would be better just to go back to Egypt and die there rather than in this desolate spot.

At that, Moses and Aaron fell on their faces before the whole bunch of them. Joshua, who was to be Moses' successor, and Caleb stepped forward to assure the people that the land the Lord had prepared for them was a wonderful place, a land of milk and honey. As long as they didn't rebel against the Lord, that land was to be theirs.

At that point "all the congregation bade stone them with stones," which was when the Lord demanded of Moses how long this unbelief was going to go on.

I love the Old Testament because it's so human. The children of Israel are grouchy and ungrateful and obtuse, and that's exactly the way the story shows them. They push to the limit, the Lord threatens to smite them with a pestilence and raise up from Moses a better bunch than this lot is, and Moses argues with the Lord that if he does that, the Egyptians will hear about it and will doubt the power of the Lord to save his people (which any Egyptians who survived the parting of the Red Sea had to have thought was pretty impressive).

So the Lord lets his people live but with this proviso: Since apparently all the miracles they have seen haven't convinced them, the adults are going to spend forty years wandering around right where they are. Only when all their "carcases shall fall in this wilderness" will the Lord lead their children into the promised land (Numbers 14:29).

And that's what happened.

Okay. That was then. What is it going to take to convince *me*, in the here and now, of the benevolence of the Lord's plan for my life? Am I going to offer him advice, like the children of Israel, and whine and whimper if my lot seems inconvenient or—worse still—difficult? Am I going to dismiss as irrelevant any prophets who might say something that displeases me (wouldn't that be the modern equivalent of stoning)? Is there a Moses to argue with the Lord for me?

Maybe today I'd better think about that.

JULY 10

And again, my beloved brethren, I would speak unto you concerning hope. How is it that ye can attain unto faith, save ye shall have hope?

—MORONI 7:40

This scripture just blows me away. Here is Moroni, hiding from the Lamanites who are doing their utmost (quite successfully) to eradicate the Nephites, and he carefully copies down the words of his father, Mormon, concerning hope.

Hope? How in the world could that man have hope for anything? Everything he had worked for, everything that was familiar to him, everything that he knew was of eternal value, was being methodically destroyed. So in the moments he has left, he is carefully recording everything he can so that someday it might be of worth to the people who are doing the methodical destruction. He is doing it because he has hope in the atonement of Christ, and he hopes that sometime the Lamanites will have sufficient faith in Christ to accept the power of his resurrection. At this point, that's the only hope Moroni has left.

The human capacity to hope is astounding. I see it at the business school all the time. Take Jilly, for example. In one of my classes, today is the next-to-last-day of a team project. Assigned groups of students work together on a project, and the entire team gets the same grade. Today Jilly was absent. This would be a minor inconvenience, except that Jilly has in her possession all the materials for the project, and her teammates are left floundering without her. They asked me to call her home (naturally we can't give out a student's home phone number), so I did, and her mother spoke with me. Her mother sounded completely exasperated: apparently the man I thought was Jilly's husband—but according to her mother is only her boyfriend—had to go to court. Jilly, instead of going to school, went with him to speak on his behalf.

I know Jilly recognizes that her "husband" has problems, but she has always insisted that he is trying to do the right thing. They have two children, and Jilly is pregnant with a third. I have no idea what this court business is about, but one might be tempted to assume that there is no hope for this man.

The same kind of thinking would suggest that Moroni should have just cursed the Lamanites with a good resounding curse and not wasted all his time collecting records for them. Moroni had faith and, as he goes on to say, "if a man have faith he must needs have hope." Jilly has faith, and thus she has hope, too. And who is anyone to say that her faith is misplaced?

If Moroni could work for the welfare of the Lamanites, Jilly can certainly work for the welfare of the father of her children. Moroni had faith in a future when the Lamanites, as many of them do now, would treasure the words he had saved for them.

Moroni had hope when there seemed to be no reasonable grounds for it. So does Jilly, and so will I.

JULY 11

For we walk by faith, not by sight.

—2 CORINTHIANS 5:7

In the original this passage of scripture comes in parentheses: It's in the middle of Paul's discussion of our earthly bodies, which house our spirits here but also separate us from our Eternal Father. Then we will see the Lord; now we walk by faith.

I like that phrase. It seems to describe so well the way I feel when I think about my life on this earth. Once, I *could* see. I can't imagine what that must have been like—or rather, I can imagine, but only in terms of my experience here on the earth. I mean, when I envision the Council in Heaven, I sort of imagine it taking place somewhere like the Tabernacle on Temple Square. Not only is my sight defined by earthly limitations but so, apparently, is my imagination.

What frees me is faith. When I walk by faith, I know that there is a vastly broader view of reality right behind me. I know if I glanced back over my shoulder I wouldn't see it with my eyes, but when I keep walking in faith, I know that perspective is there surrounding me, just out of sight. I don't *need* to see it. It is there.

Today, let me walk by faith. I'm not going to look to see eternity; I'm not going to reach out to touch it. Just let me trust it is there.

JULY 12

That Christ may dwell in your hearts by faith; that ye, being rooted and grounded in love, may be able to comprehend with all saints what is the breadth, and length, and depth, and height; and to know the love of Christ, which passeth knowledge, that ye might be filled with all the fulness of God.

—EPHESIANS 3:17–19

Summertime, and the living is easy—well, at least easier. Summer clothes don't seem to need so much fussing with; summer food is light and more casual. The house doesn't seem to get as messy, or maybe it's just that everybody spends more time outside. Evenings are long, and morning comes early. All creation seems drawn from the inside to go out—the dog begs wistfully for walks, and if you look under a bush, you're apt to find a cat napping blissfully in the shade.

Summertime is picnic time. I like picnics. When I think of picnics I've taken with the family, I think about serene and happy times, all of us together and actively enjoying the knowledge, for a bit, that we love each other and that being together lightly and casually is a privilege. Maybe that's why this scripture—talking about the breadth and length and depth and height of love—makes me think today about picnics, and family, and belonging together, and how our human experience of love gives us a foretaste of the love of Christ. As Paul points out, that love passeth knowledge, but we can have hints.

The way I feel about my husband, the way I feel about the children—and, on good days, the way they feel about each other—are wonderful hints. Today, with my head in the refrigerator trying to find something that would be good for a spontaneous picnic, I feel my spirit is enlarged and lightened and beguiled with love.

Thank you, Lord, for picnics. Thank you for the annual felicity of summer. Thank you for the splendor of love, to warm us all year 'round.

JULY 13

O send out thy light and thy truth: let them lead me; let them bring me unto thy holy hill, and to thy tabernacles.

—PSALM 43:3

Asking for light and truth is one thing; trusting in it absolutely to lead and guide me seems to be something else again. I find myself fussing and fidgeting. Is this really what I'm supposed to do? Is this really my answer, or am I imagining it? Maybe that's the real gap between me and the brother of Jared. For him, I suspect, the prayer and the answer would interlock, one and the same. The only thing that comforts me is remembering Peter starting out across the water to Jesus, and then his trust failed, and he started to sink. Peter eventually learned. Maybe there's hope for me.

For some reason, the analogy that occurs to me is that of

teaching a small child to float. You stand there in the water, your hands supporting his back, and you tell him to relax; the water will hold him. Then you ever so gently move your hands away, and the water rises up to his chin, or he feels it touch his forehead, and instead of lying back in the water, he stiffens and starts flailing desperately and grabbing for you. Then you have to cuddle him, and go all the way back to the beginning. You stand there in the water, your hands supporting his back, and you tell him . . .

Dear Lord, teach me to float. Let me learn to trust my faith, the way I learned to trust the water. Let me learn to lie back against thy love, to listen for thine answers, and then to let go: to stop questioning, and doubting, and wondering what-if. Let me be more like the brother of Jared. Thou didst teach Peter, Lord; teach me.

JULY 14

I say again, as did the apostles to Jesus, "Lord, increase our faith." Grant us faith to look beyond the problems of the moment to the miracles of the future. Give us faith to pay our tithes and offerings and put our trust in Thee, the Almighty, to open the windows of heaven as Thou hast promised. Give us faith to do what is right and let the consequence follow.

—PRESIDENT GORDON B. HINCKLEY

Do what is right; let the consequence follow"—I can hear the hymn singing in my head, and I'm sure President Hinckley could, too (*Hymns*, no. 237). "Battle for freedom in spirit and might." The trouble is, I suspect, that most of us aren't getting on to the battle for freedom; we're stuck back deciding whether to do right or just to pretend we didn't notice the opportunity this time.

I'm afraid for most of us who live fairly orderly lives the problem isn't so much sins of commission as omission. I don't have much difficulty with the temptation to rob a bank. On the other hand— taking the example President Hinckley uses here—I've certainly had times when instead of trusting in the consequence that the windows of heaven will be opened as promised if I pay my tithes and offerings, I tell myself that things are really tight right now and I'll catch up at the end of the year.

Is this the floating problem all over again?

Dear Lord, help me to trust in the miracles of the future. I certainly believe in those of the past; let me count the ways in which I have felt thy presence with me before. Now why should there be a giant step between remembering the Lord's presence and having faith that he will be with me in the future?

Help me take that step. With thy help, I can take giant steps. Watch me.

JULY 15

And he believed in the Lord; and he counted it to him for righteousness.

—GENESIS 15:6

The first "he" mentioned here is Abraham; it is very early, when his name was still Abram. At this point in Genesis, Abram has been promised that the Lord will make of him a great nation. He has left the land of Haran, as he was commanded, and he has become prosperous. But he and Sarai are still childless. This Abram points out to the Lord. (As he goes on to remark forlornly, his only heir would appear to be his servant from Damascus, a steward named Eliezer.)

The Lord comforts him. No, he says, Eliezer will not be your heir. Your heir will come from your own body. And then he takes Abram out into the night and shows him the heavens, with all the stars of the sky. Look up and see if you can count them, the Lord tells Abram. That's how many descendants you will have.

And Abram, that wise man of faith and the father of the Jewish nation, trusted the Lord and believed, and the Lord "counted it to him for righteousness."

Abraham, as he became, had an immense and glorious mission, and he served it with faith and honor. My assignment is more modest, but let me grow into the unquestioning obedience that marked Abraham's life. Let me be a believer, as Abraham was, and by my belief open new possibilities for myself and those who will come after me.

I inherited a fine heritage, in part from Abraham himself; let me enrich it before I pass it on.

JULY 16

And Jesus answering saith unto them, Have faith in God.

—Mark 11:22

Jesus said this to his disciples after the odd little incident of the fig tree, in which he cursed the fig tree for its fruitlessness and within a day it was "dried up from the roots." When Peter saw it and remembered what had happened, he pointed it out to Jesus (apparently with some excitement). Jesus said, "Have faith in God." The whole episode appears to have been a parable in action, pointing out what would happen to Israel as a result of its fruitless obsession with the Mosaic law.

But what intrigues me about this is that it reminds me of an interesting fact: Thanks to the remarkable ability of the computer to sort rapidly through mountains of material, we can say for certain that the word *faith,* which occurs constantly throughout the New Testament, occurs only twice in the Old. That first of all strikes me as very peculiar—certainly Abraham, Moses, and many of their successors were men of heroic faith—and then, when I think about it further, that odd circumstance seems mainly to demonstrate what I think is a shift in emphasis between the Old Testament and the New.

The Old Testament is the book of the law. The first five books set out the circumstances through which it was given and give the particulars of its observance. The rest of the Old Testament is, it seems to me, pretty much the melancholy history of the failure of the children of Israel to live up to the law of Moses, with a few novellas, such as Jonah and Ruth and Esther, and some poetry woven in. Justice is the theme, although Jehovah's return of blessings for obedience was always far more than legally proportionate to what was deserved.

With the New Testament, we step into a new world. Recognizing that man can never earn his own salvation, considering justice alone, Jesus Christ came to open a path by which salvation can be found through mercy. Christ is the promised Savior from sin, and because there is no way in strict justice we could deserve what he did for us, all that is required of us to claim salvation is that we have faith: that we trust in his existence, trust in the fact that he died for us and was resurrected, and use that trust and faith to reorder our lives as he taught us to do.

With the New Testament, we are truly in a new world.

Today let me think about that new world. Let me accept the blessings offered me with something closer to a full appreciation of what they mean.

Jesus said, "Have faith in God." Today let me think about what that means. Today let my faith grow.

JULY 17

And he said, I will hide my face from them, I will see what their end shall be: for they are a very froward generation, children in whom is no faith.

—DEUTERONOMY 32:20

One of the two times the word *faith* is used in the Old Testament. This first time is in the Song of Moses, which the Lord gave to Moses to teach his people in the wilderness just before his death, and thus just before the children of Israel crossed into the promised land. (It's interesting that the Exodus begins and ends with a song of Moses: the first song is in Exodus 15, just after they had crossed safely through the parting of the sea.)

The theme of this farewell song is that Jehovah has promised to bring Israel into a good and rich land. Although their unfaithfulness and disobedience will provoke him, he will never wholly abandon them, and when they repent, he will side with them against their enemies and save them from total destruction.

Which is, of course, exactly what happened.

What Jehovah reproaches his people for is their lack of faith, expressed in their readiness—once they had prospered and "waxen fat"—to forsake the law of the Lord their God and worship whatever other gods appeared attractive to them. It happened again and again.

But is that really so different from what we do? We may not build golden calves to worship these days, but we're big on gold everything else. We may be too sophisticated to need something we can see and feel and touch to reverence, but a lot of us devote ourselves to a single-minded pursuit of money, even if we never see anything but figures printed on a bank statement or a stockbroker's report.

It doesn't matter. Lack of faith is lack of faith, whatever the other gods might be. The important thing is to develop the clear eye of faith, so dazzled by the magnificence and glory of our Lord that the thought of looking elsewhere never comes up.

Isn't that what is meant by having an eye single to his glory? Lord, let my eye be single to thy glory.

JULY 18

Even so faith, if it hath not works, is dead, being alone. Yea, a man may say, Thou hast faith, and I have works: shew me thy faith without thy works, and I will shew thee my faith by my works.

—JAMES 2:17–18

Four men named James are mentioned in the New Testament; the one who wrote this letter was probably the James who was the brother of Jesus and later the head of the Church at Jerusalem. According to Bible scholars, this letter was very likely written earlier than anything else in the New Testament, well before the Gospels or any of the letters of Paul.

Maybe that accounts for the apparent difference in the way James writes about faith and the way Paul does. When Paul, writing later, writes about faith, he is writing about a living, vital, wholly absorbing belief in our Lord Jesus Christ. When James, writing earlier in an almost entirely Jewish context, talks about faith being deficient on its own, he means the hollowness of concentrating solely on picky details of the law—which is what the Pharisees were so good at—without actually getting out and doing anything that genuinely benefited anyone. As he says here, you can't separate honest faith and works. You show that faith exists by the works that you do.

By that test, how is my faith doing? Could you reconstruct the theory of what I believe in by carefully observing my practice? (I cringe, remembering my irritability with the children or my dear if sometimes exasperating husband, my frequent thoughtlessness about other people when I get too absorbed with finishing what I think I need to get finished, the lack of charity in some of the things I say—and that's only the short list.)

Dear Lord, help me today to live as I believe. Let me try, for just twenty-four hours, to be what I say I mean to be. Can I do it?

And if not, a little voice challenges me, why not?

Perhaps, by trying to live according to thy word, my faith will grow to match my works, or, possibly, my works will come to more closely match my faith. Either way, what finer reward?

JULY 19

Let us hold fast the profession of our faith without wavering.
—HEBREWS 10:23

Morning, and I have to remember to water the flower pots before I go to school. This is now an everyday job, and it presents me with two interesting choices: I can either water everything in my nightie—which I don't care about getting wet but which affords an extra treat to the neighbors who happen to be around in the early morning—or else I can wait until I am fully dressed and then water very, very carefully so that I don't splash all over my shoes and stockings.

It is generally about now that I wonder what ever possessed me to have so many jolly pots of flowers around the back door and on the front steps. They do look nice, but in warm weather (and what is July, if not warm?) they have to be watered daily. No matter what.

It occurs to me today as I am watering (decently dressed, so I am watering with extreme care, which takes longer) that I need to top up my faith—with prayer, with good works, with study—just about as often as I need to water these plants. It would be nice to skip a day, here and there, but just as my plants get droopy and develop spindly stalks and soon stop flowering, so my faith gets wobbly and has weak spots if I leave it on its own. Holding fast to my faith isn't the sort of thing I can do now and then. I need to keep at it.

The plants, fresh and green in their newly damp pots (and I only got one tiny splash on my stocking), are ready for another day. Am I? Let me consider that, this warm summer morning.

JULY 20

And there came a voice unto me, saying: Enos, thy sins are for-
given thee and thou shalt be blessed.

And I, Enos, knew that God could not lie; wherefore, my guilt
was swept away.

And I said: Lord, how is it done?

And he said unto me: Because of thy faith in Christ, whom thou
hast never before heard nor seen. And many years pass away before
he shall manifest himself in the flesh; wherefore, go to, thy faith hath
made thee whole.

—ENOS 1:5–8

What a very *human* question to ask. "Lord, how is it done?"
That's what so many people want to know. We want to
know that about everything, which is one of the reasons why once
we started to get the basic scientific principles in place, the whole
world of technology came tumbling into existence. Again and again
somebody asked, "How is it done?" and then actually figured it out.
It seems to be part of the basic wiring of a human being. We want
to know how things work.

We want to know how spiritual things work, too, but that's
harder. Some of them we may be simply incapable of understanding:
It would be like trying to explain nuclear physics to a kindergartner.
Repentance seems to be like that. We have been told that it works;
we have personal experience that it works. Do we understand *how*
it is done? Ah, that's where the faith comes in.

JULY 21

For by grace are ye saved through faith; and that not of yourselves:
it is the gift of God: not of works, lest any man should boast.

—EPHESIANS 2:8–9

Today consider Paul's thinking on the faith-and-works problem.
The more I work through the scriptures, the more it seems
to me that the gospel is like a finely faceted crystal, and each man who

has written part of what I have in this book has grasped the crystal from a different angle and seen something subtly different. The crystal is forever and always the same, but the emphasis, the perspective, the priorities shift and blend. Maybe that's why the scriptures meet so many human needs: They reflect so many human minds!

James meant one thing by faith and works; here, clearly, Paul is talking about something a little different. He is talking about faith in our Lord Jesus Christ being a gift by grace, showing God's great love for us. The capacity for that faith itself is a gift. There's no way that we could have gone out and arranged it for ourselves, which is what he means here by "works." He goes on to say, "We are his workmanship." There's nothing to boast about; we are not self-created. Our gifts are gifts from God.

Today, let me remember that concept. Let me remember that because of Christ I have everything, but it is only because of Christ. Left to myself, my powers are limited indeed, and they are restricted to whatever time I have on this earth.

Because of Christ, I have eternity.

JULY 22

Wherefore, we search the prophets, and we have many revelations and the spirit of prophecy; and having all these witnesses we obtain a hope, and our faith becometh unshaken, insomuch that we truly can command in the name of Jesus and the very trees obey us, or the mountains, or the waves of the sea.

—JACOB 4:6

This idea comes up again and again. In the New Testament, we are told by Jesus that if we have faith as a mustard seed we can do wonders (Matthew 17:20 says move mountains; Luke 17:6 says pluck up a sycamine tree and plant it in the sea). My father's sister, who had not much faith in anything but knew that we were being raised to believe, once gave me a necklace with a mustard seed suspended in a glass ball. I was fascinated; mustard seeds are *little*.

So the child, standing next to the picnic table in the canyon, points at the mountains looming over our heads and says, "If you had faith, could you move that?"

Well, you know, I can't really say. We have certainly had mighty men of faith—in fact, I believe right now on this earth we have mighty men of faith—and I have never actually heard of mountains being shifted from one place to another. Maybe that's because there's never been a valid reason for moving them around. They're fine, by and large, where they are. Presumably if you were spiritual enough to have the kind of faith that would be required to move them, you would be too spiritual to do it as a frivolous exercise. But that doesn't mean that the mountains could not be moved; it just means they haven't been.

What makes me think that might be true is another story I read once. It was about a mother whose child was trapped under a car. No other help was readily available, and so the mother lifted the car and the child crawled out. I don't remember if there was anything about faith or prayer involved; I just remember being impressed that she lifted a car.

Would she have been able to lift that car if her child had not been under it? Not in this world. But she had to, and she did it. Maybe the miracles of faith work something like that. When something has to be done, the power is there.

Remembering that picnic in the canyon, I'm really quite glad that nobody moved the mountains around. They were very beautiful where they were. Unless there's an absolutely valid reason to mess with them, I expect they'll be left right there. Do I have the faith to be able to move them? I suspect that's virtuoso stuff. I'm still at the amateur level.

Do I believe they could be moved? Yes. We have been promised so, and I believe. Yes.

JULY 23

Yea, there are many who do say: If thou wilt show unto us a sign from heaven, then we shall know of a surety; then we shall believe. Now I ask, is this faith? Behold, I say unto you, Nay; for if a man knoweth a thing he hath no cause to believe, for he knoweth it.

—ALMA 32:17–18

This is where we get back to the same old ground we went over in the Council in Heaven. Having chosen the path of free agency back then, we'd rather not have quite so much of it now, thank you. Let's get rid of all this nasty uncertainty. Let's have the proof. If you do miracles, let's have one now, while I'm watching.

Stand up and show us your credentials, please: Then we'll put out our money.

Or, in this case, what we like to call our faith.

Sure, it would be easier to have everything conveniently demonstrated. But as Alma points out, what we have then isn't faith. Faith is the leap; faith is putting your hand in the hand of the Lord *whom you cannot see*. As soon as you see, faith is superseded. Then you know.

I believe, I trust, I have faith that one day I will know as I am known. Until then, I will make the leap. Today, Lord, help me make the leap. Today, catch me as I fly.

JULY 24

For the Utah pioneers of 1847, their faith was grounded in principle. They left their homes, their temple, and in some cases their families, in search of a place of refuge where they could worship without fear of persecution. There was little that they could carry with them in the way of provisions and material possessions, but each wagon and handcart was heavily laden with faith—faith in God, faith in the Restoration of His Church through the Prophet Joseph Smith, and faith that God knew where they were going and that He would see them through.

—ELDER M. RUSSELL BALLARD

So on this day they reached the valley, and there it was. They were only the first; waves and waves of others would follow them, crossing the plains, coming up through the mountains, doing whatever had to be done.

We revere them, we admire them, we probably idealize them. Were they perfected Saints? No, but if they had been, what they did would be less remarkable. If you're already perfect, behaving well is no big deal. Behaving well becomes noble if you are tired and hungry and your feet (and your arms and your back) hurt and you have children to tend to and you've had a sharp difference of opinion with another sister in the company. Did such differences of opinion occur? Of course they did. We don't hear about them much, because the exigencies of life on the trail meant that the pioneers didn't have the luxury of dwelling on them. Either you all worked together or you all perished separately: that was the bald reality. We aren't faced with such absolute necessity. Maybe we'd get along better with each other on an everyday basis if we were.

Some of my ancestors made that epic journey. Does that make it particularly significant to me? I now live away from the center of the Church, and many members of my ward have no ancestors who made that trek. As the Church becomes more and more worldwide, a smaller and smaller proportion of us will have a blood connection with the pioneers. Does that matter?

I like to think that the Saints struggling across the plains would have rejoiced if they could have foreseen that. I think they sacrificed what they sacrificed and endured what they endured partly for us, their literal descendants, but I think they did it even more so that the restored Church would survive, so that message of faith in God in which they had invested their hearts and souls and spirits would triumph over all the hatred and the persecution and the bigotry.

That it has done so would be their most glorious reward. The Church thrives, and it thrives far from the valley they struggled so to reach. There are stakes of Zion in all the places they were forced to leave. There are priesthood quorums and Relief Societies and Primaries and young people being sent off on missions. All the ordinary, everyday routines of the Church are being carried out in the towns that have replaced the towns the Latter-day Saints originally built. By leaving, they made it possible for the Church to survive; in surviving, the Church has returned and, by and large, been accepted as a desirable neighbor.

I'm proud my ancestors had a part in assuring that survival, but I'm also proud that they did it for more than me and my children. I'm grateful for them—those whom our family honors, and all the other pioneers, then and now.

What they built, may the rest of us maintain, wherever we may be. Let the boundaries of the valley those Saints found reach to encompass the world, so that, emboldened by the gospel, we all may find the place.

JULY 25

Behold, God is my salvation; I will trust, and not be afraid: for the Lord Jehovah is my strength and my song; he also is become my salvation. Therefore with joy shall ye draw water out of the wells of salvation.

—ISAIAH 12:2–3

Contrails stretched out—roughly parallel—across a blue summer sky. Seems funny to think that the dot I can just barely make out from the ground at the end of the trail contains a plane full of people. Looking up, they are just a dot to me. Looking down, I'm not even that for them—just part of the metropolitan blur down below. I wonder if the pilot is pointing us out to them: "On your left, we are passing . . ."

And yet all of us, the seen and the unseen, share in the triumph of this song of Isaiah. We all share in the salvation of God; for all of us he is our strength and our song. All of us can share the joy of drawing water from the well of salvation.

The scriptures fascinate me as they swing back and forth from recounting tribulation (and certainly Isaiah saw plenty of that, as his people were dragged away into captivity) to the joyous recognition of the Lord's protecting hand. Let me remember that today. Let me remember that both tribulation and joy are part of the fabric of life.

Today I feel blessed with serenity. How do the people up in that dot of a plane feel? I can't guess. If their hearts are heavy, may they be lightened; if they are on their way to joy, may that joy and mine be linked and magnified together.

What a wonderful world! What a wonderful day. Blessed be the name of the Lord.

JULY 26

And it shall come to pass, that inasmuch as they are faithful, and exercise faith in me, I will pour out my Spirit upon them in the day that they assemble themselves together.

—DOCTRINE AND COVENANTS 44:2

If ever there were a church whose philosophy of worship was opposite to the I-can-go-into-God's-fresh-air-and-feel-one-with-him school of thought, it's ours. We have been a meeting-oriented people, mighty gatherers in conferences, from the very beginning. I can remember as a child having four stake conferences a year, two general conferences, and I can't remember how many ward conferences. We Latter-day Saints do love getting together.

In the early days, part of it had to be for communication. There were letters, but letters allow for ambiguity and all feedback is delayed. The only way the infant Church could be kept moving in the right direction was to gather the elders together and give instructions to everybody all at once. Questions could be asked, and local problems could be resolved.

So why are we still going to the enormous trouble and expense of getting together? After all, we can pick up a telephone now and talk to practically anybody. Conference calls mean you can get together with a whole bunch of people at once. The whole extravagant range of communication technology exists at our fingertips— e-mail, the Internet, wireless communication.

Today, let this scripture remind me of why we still need to be together. It's not that we don't use the technology; obviously we do. But something special happens when we gather together. We strengthen each other by our physical presence. As this scripture promises, the Spirit of the Lord has been and will continue to be poured out upon us when we assemble together. Out here on what used to be the outskirts of the organized Church (I suppose now the outskirts have moved thousands of miles away and across oceans), we even find it more nourishing to gather in congregations to receive the broadcasts.

"The Spirit of God like a fire is burning." Today, let me be grateful that it is and that we have the opportunity to gather together to feel the glow.

JULY 27

Be thou an example of the believers, in word, in conversation, in charity, in spirit, in faith, in purity.

—1 TIMOTHY 4:12

This is a problem I grapple with in teaching my children. Obviously, it's better to be a good example than a bad one. But, on the other hand, Christ talked about the pointlessness of doing good deeds to be admired by men. (As he said, being admired is your reward, but he called it hypocrisy.) So where is the line between being oblivious to the effect our actions have on the people around us and doing things so that other people will think we are fine people?

It has to lie in intention. We should be virtuous because we want to be virtuous, because it lets us feel closer to our Heavenly Father. It also works a lot better, usually in the short run and always in the long run. If, because we are virtuous, other people see us and are drawn to investigate the philosophy that fuels our virtue, that's great. That's what often happens, but that's not *why* we obey the commandments. So why is Paul telling Timothy this?

I think he's telling him the same thing. He's telling him to be an example of what a believer in Jesus Christ should be. As he goes on to say, "Take heed unto thyself, and unto the doctrine; continue in them; for in doing this thou shalt both save thyself, and them that hear thee" (1 Timothy 4:16). If you do well for its own sake, both rewards will be yours; but your own salvation comes first.

Today, let me think about whether I've taught my children that distinction clearly enough. After all, if I sometimes wonder about where my own motivations lie . . .

JULY 28

And now, my sons, remember, remember that it is upon the rock of our Redeemer, who is Christ, the Son of God, that ye must build your foundation; that when the devil shall send forth his mighty winds, yea, his shafts in the whirlwind, yea, when all his hail and his mighty storm shall beat upon you, it shall have no power over you to drag you down to the gulf of misery and endless wo, because of the rock upon which ye are built, which is a sure foundation, a foundation whereon if men build they cannot fall.

—HELAMAN 5:12

A good day for this one, because we're being raked by another summer storm. Not a particularly strong electrical one this time (although I can hear thunder rumbling in the distance), but the rain is coming down with considerable enthusiasm and the wind is lashing around the branches of the trees overhead. This one is going to involve some clean-up in the yard afterwards. Branches will be strewn up and down the driveway, probably from the maple which seems always to be dropping *something*: yellow fuzz in the spring, and then the helicopter seed pods that try to grow new maples absolutely everywhere but preferably in the vegetable and flower beds, and finally large plate-sized leaves that have to be raked up and disposed of. Good thing it turns a magnificent yellow in the fall, or that tree would be gone.

So here I am inside the house, listening to the wind roar and the rain slap against the windows. No wonder people have so often used the analogy of storms to express the difficulties we encounter on this earth. Doesn't a good run of adversity *feel* like a storm? It's one thing after another: Every time you try to stand up, that unforgiving wind pushes you down again; the merciless rain tries to creep into every crevice and soak and spoil whatever it touches.

This scripture is teaching us, just as Helaman is teaching his sons, that we may encounter storms, but as long as we manage to hang on to our faith in our Redeemer, the important things will stay in place. The wind and rain cannot budge us. Make our lives miserable? Absolutely. Fill us with pain and anguish? Unfortunately, it happens all the time. But whatever is asked of us, we will be given the strength to meet, and our truest comfort (although at times it may seem like a cold one) is that whatever happens here is temporary.

Our life here is like an afternoon in eternity (I was told that once) or a blink of an eye. If so, it's the longest blink I've ever known. But then, I'm locked into our mortal conception of time. Eternity is an idea to me, not reality—but it was real once, and it will be again.

Right now, this storm is outside, not in my heart. Today, let me tuck this scripture away for when I need it. Let me use these quiet days to make sure I am firmly set on that foundation of rock. Faith can build it. Faith can sustain me, for ever and always. No matter what.

JULY 29

But as it is written, Eye hath not seen, nor ear heard, neither have entered into the heart of man, the things which God hath prepared for them that love him.

But God hath revealed them unto us by his Spirit: for the Spirit searcheth all things, yea, the deep things of God.

—1 CORINTHIANS 2:9–10

Barbecue day at school today. Because business operates year 'round, so does our business school. In fact, most of our students wouldn't be able to take the extra months out of full-time work that lengthening our courses to allow for a summer break would demand. So autumn, winter, spring, and summer we are in session.

Still, summer does happen, and we had the barbecue to celebrate it. Hot dogs on the barbecue, potato chips and quantities of orange punch—everybody in jeans and T-shirts, neither of which is allowed ordinarily, and boom boxes producing a cacophony of noise. (Jose mentioned in his journal that he liked to dance, but, my goodness, I wasn't prepared for some of his moves: That man *can* dance! General student jubilation when one of the teachers joins him, showing a few good moves of her own.)

What I'm thinking about now, though, is a couple who both come to school. How they both wound up here I don't really know: I think they're sponsored by a state training program designed to move people off welfare. During his time here Lee has secured a good job working for one of the automotive suppliers, but because he works the graveyard shift, he is always exhausted, and I figure he's slept through roughly half of his courses here. As I suspect he's dyslexic, he really couldn't afford to do that. Still, he was determined to finish, and one way and another he did.

His wife, Susanna, has every health problem known to man, and because the couple had no health coverage until Lee had been working for three months, they've been going untreated. She walks with crutches some days (arthritis) and is out with migraines on others. Susanna was kind of edgy and full of attitude originally, but she seems to have mellowed. I've always liked her; I think you have to be tough to survive sometimes. They apparently have an assortment of children: hers, his, and a couple of theirs. Susanna finds time to be a Girl Scout leader and an unwearying advocate for her children in school; she's lost several days of her own school meeting with her children's teachers and principals.

Today they came to school wearing matching tee-shirts, bright red with the logo of one of those Christian rallies that are held around the country, meant to encourage men and women to take their responsibilities to the Lord and their families seriously. I commented on the shirts to Susanna, and her face lit up. "I felt Jesus was there," she said. "He made me know I could do it. I have to hang in there. I'm just going to trust Jesus."

They're good people, Lee and Susanna. Life has not treated them easily. I always wondered where they got their drive and determination, and now I know. As Paul promised the Corinthians, so Susanna and Lee have discovered some of the blessings that "God hath prepared for them that love him." What keeps them surviving is faith.

Lord, let me share their faith.

JULY 30

Neither pray I for these alone, but for them also which shall believe on me through their word; that they all may be one; as thou, Father, art in me, and I in thee, that they also may be one in us: that the world may believe that thou hast sent me.

—John 17:20–21

So we do learn and gain from each other. By joining our belief together, we become stronger and surer and more valiant in staying close to what we know is true.

This (again) is part of what Jesus was teaching his disciples that last evening in the upper room. These are the words that John heard

JULY 31   249

and treasured in his heart until he could write them down, so that we could share the final loving wisdom that Jesus gave us before he went forth to fulfill the final purpose of his mortal journey. Here Jesus spoke as a man to the men who had served him and loved him and whom he loved in return—and beyond them, to those of us who would never know him in mortality but would be uplifted and strengthened by his words. He loves us, too.

So many things keep us apart: We come from different places; we have different ways of expressing ourselves; our skins are different colors and we speak a lot of different languages; some of us have a hard time getting along with anybody, and some of us have been twisted by experience and find it difficult to trust; some of us are so convinced that we have the whole truth that we won't open our hearts to others who might have part of it; some of us are too timid to reach out. Jesus is telling us to reach across our differences to our overwhelming commonality: We are all the children of God. When we gather in faith—all of us—we become one with Jesus Christ and our Father in Heaven.

What greater promise? What more transcendent possibility? Lord, help me reach. Lord, let us be one.

JULY 31

For I know that my redeemer liveth, and that he shall stand at the latter day upon the earth: and though after my skin worms destroy this body, yet in my flesh shall I see God.

—JOB 19:25–26

He may never have used the word *faith*, but what else could he be talking about?

Many wise men have grappled with the problem presented by the book of Job. Why do tribulations beset good people? Even the book of Job doesn't answer that. It does make it clear that tribulation is not necessarily punishment for sin; that, and it gives us the example of a righteous man who remained faithful to what he knew was true in spite of disaster heaped upon disaster and (rubbing salt in his wounds) the reproaches of those who claimed to console him.

And his reward? The knowledge of what was to come was given him, to comfort and sustain him.

Now, as July slips away into August, let me remember his faith. (It's nice that I also have Handel's music of *Messiah* to help me remember these words.) So far my afflictions have been nothing compared to Job's, but they seemed big to me at the time. Let me, too, endure.

Let me learn from Job, and have trust. Let me, dear Lord, learn from thee.

AUGUST

If any man serve me, let him follow me; and where I am, there shall also my servant be.

—JOHN 12:26

AUGUST 1

And now, Israel, what doth the Lord thy God require of thee, but to fear the Lord thy God, to walk in all his ways, and to love him, and to serve the Lord thy God with all thy heart and with all thy soul.

—DEUTERONOMY 10:12

This comes from way, way back. This was when the children of Israel (or, technically, the children of the children of Israel, because by this time the people who had left Egypt had died in the wilderness) renewed the broken covenant with God. Moses came down from the mount with two new stone tablets on which were recorded the Ten Commandments—he had broken the original tablets in his anger over the people's lapse into idolatry—and the people were again given the series of laws that were to govern their religious and social life.

It begins with this preface, giving the three primary obligations of the children of Israel: to fear the Lord, to be obedient as an expression of their love for him, and to serve him.

What interests me particularly is the way in which the children of Israel are to serve him: "with all thy heart and all thy soul." Nothing pro forma or casual about it. The children of Israel—forgiven now, restored to the promised land which they are about to enter—are to serve wholeheartedly, with nothing held back.

And what about us? It's perfectly true that we haven't been trotted around a wilderness for forty years. We haven't been quite so blatantly guilty of idol worship (unless you're talking about money, or position, or nice clothes, or sparkling jewelry, in which case we might have a problem). We have even been given a new, higher law: to love the Lord our God with all our heart and soul and strength and mind and to love our neighbors as ourselves.

Sounds sort of similar, doesn't it? Particularly when you consider that the way we best express love is to serve someone. How do you show your brand-new baby that you love her? You take care of her, day in and day out. How did you show the kid in high school that you thought he was terrific? You figured out something to do for him—chocolate chip cookies, maybe.

So when do we serve? Now? If we're typical women, the question is more, When *don't* we? It starts when we swing our feet over the edge of the bed to the floor in the morning, and it goes on until we finally put them back under the covers at the end of a long day. Serve we do without question. With all our heart and all our soul? Or just getting done what has to be done?

Today, let me think about that.

AUGUST 2

And behold, I tell you these things that ye may learn wisdom; that ye may learn that when ye are in the service of your fellow beings ye are only in the service of your God.

—MOSIAH 2:17

It seems to me that the feminists' greatest complaint has been that everybody has always assumed that women are there to do all the ordinary things that nobody else wants to do. I have to admit that men are getting drafted into those jobs more than was ever contemplated when I was setting up housekeeping. But even now, as the twentieth century draws to a close and men and women both are trying on all sorts of new social possibilities for a complicated world, few of us who live in the real world are willing to jettison the traditional roles wholesale as all the strengths they offer become increasingly obvious. Sometimes we women get restless or find ourselves suspiciously measuring the contributions of others, but even when we're restless or suspicious, we do those traditional jobs that need doing, over and over again.

Still, it's hard not to notice that at the same time—even as it feels as if we are forever reaching out here and reaching out there—we are constantly being reminded of the need for service and being exhorted to remember our obligation to meet the needs of others. Is it because we're less inclined to serve? Is it because concentration on the self and our individual state of happiness at any one given moment has become a cottage industry, with the media replete with guides and instruction to guarantee the most comfortable mental attitude at all times?

I would expect not. There may be similarities between our time and the period when King Benjamin gathered his people to give them his final words of counsel and guidance, but there are a lot of differences, as well, and these words about service were directed to people whose social expectations of each other appear to have been far less in flux than ours are. Even so, they needed to be reminded of the need to serve and, for all the similar and different reasons, so do we.

What, after all, is service? The most basic meaning is doing something for someone else that he or she needs to have done. Sometimes what is needed is what we delight in doing: taking care of that newborn, for example, or fixing the table just right. But what about the less immediately rewarding service?

What about, for instance, spending time with the elderly relative (or nonrelative, come to that) who repeats the same story—which wasn't interesting the first time—a minimum of four or five times? What about working at the cannery when not everybody who signed up showed up, and so the valiant souls who did (who are generally the same valiant souls from one time to the next) wind up working considerably longer than they intended. And, however valiant you might be, your back is bothering you and the place is hot and steamy and you're sweating in places you didn't know you had sweat glands. If this is service, isn't there an easier way?

Maybe what we need to remember is that a fulfilled life is made up of generous dollops of both kinds of service: the kind we give spontaneously and the kind we offer with gritted teeth. After all, the Lord blesses us with big blessings and little blessings: big like food and shelter and loving friends and family, and little like the sudden pleasure of discovering that what you thought was a weed is producing nice flowers and is apparently a perennial you'd forgotten about. Maybe there are big and little acts of service as well: some that are easy and some that stretch our endurance and love.

We can't express our love for the Lord in direct service to him; we are cut off by the veil that separates mortality from eternity. The closest we can come, as King Benjamin tells us, is to express our love in service to his other children here on earth, however unprepossessing they might be or however inconvenient the time they need us. But if we are there, meeting the need, perhaps someday—as stories and songs have suggested—we will be half-listening to the lonely old voice repeating itself and suddenly glance over to see, instead of the querulous wrinkled face we expect, the face of our Lord looking back, luminous with understanding and the overwhelming outpouring of divine love.

Of course, it's much more likely that we will never really see that. But we know by faith that when we serve, seen or not, he is there.

AUGUST 3

Yea, ye yourselves know, that these hands have ministered unto my necessities, and to them that were with me.

I have shewed you all things, how that so labouring ye ought to support the weak, and to remember the words of the Lord Jesus, how he said, It is more blessed to give than to receive.

—ACTS 20:34–35

It's not only women who serve. Here Paul is speaking to the Ephesians, reminding them that he has supported himself and those who are with him, presumably through his trade as a tentmaker. What he means by the word translated here as "weak" is probably "the poor and the sick."

I think about what Paul's hands must have looked like. He worked with them; they were probably rough and hardened. I had a friend once in New York who among other miscellaneous employment was a photographic hand model. She was, as you can imagine, pretty careful about what she did with her hands. She wore gloves outside, to protect her hands from chapping in the winter and from what I'm not quite sure—perhaps sun damage—in the summer. She wore gloves inside, whenever she did anything with her hands other than gesturing gracefully during conversation or eating. I can still see Courtney grabbing for the gloves before she washed an apple or wiped down what looked like a clean counter. She didn't have any children then; neither did I, at that point, and over the years since, as I tried to remember her example from time to time and made valiant attempts to discover what I'd done this time with my own yellow gloves, I've wondered what Courtney would have done if she'd wound up living my kind of life.

Her hands look a lot better than mine, of course. I last checked them out a couple of years ago, and they looked great. She's no longer a model, but her hands are still smooth, youthful, and manicured. Oh well.

Maybe I'd better look at it from the other side. Do I do enough with my hands? My pioneer ancestors would probably look at my hands the way I look at Courtney's—doesn't that woman *do* anything with them? Not that washboard hands necessarily indicate greater virtue (I could always use those yellow gloves, if I could find them), but it's something to think about. Paul talked about the sick and the poor: Who in the ward (or the neighborhood) is battling illness and caring for small children? Is there a floor that could use scrubbing? Is there laundry to be done?

Let me use my hands to serve.

AUGUST 4

If thou lovest me thou shalt serve me and keep all my commandments.

—DOCTRINE AND COVENANTS 42:29

Well, let's see: Moses to the children of Israel, exact date uncertain (Bible scholars suggest maybe 1250 B.C.? 1180?); King Benjamin to his people, about a thousand years later; Joseph Smith to twelve elders at Kirtland, Ohio, 1831.

The message doesn't change a whole lot. These three things seem to go together: love, obedience, and service. The second two are the way we show the first one. What the Lord seems to be telling us over and over is that yes, we are to praise and adore him, but that's just the beginning. The psalms are only part of the program. The rest is to put that energy of love into something useful in an everyday sense.

Obeying the commandments is useful for us. We obey because we have been told to, but what goes along with that is that the eternal reality of our lives flows better, with fewer difficulties, when we are obedient. And a lot of the commandments are just plain common sense for people living together.

Service is useful for the rest of God's children. It's surely possible for the Lord to answer a prayer with a miracle, but that's not usually the way it happens. Usually, we are blessed by the Lord through somebody else. Most often, the other person sees our need and meets it, but there are certainly times when our benefactor has no idea how he or she has blessed us.

It's easy to know when I need a blessing. Today, let me practice being more sensitive to perceiving when someone else does. Let me practice being there to help before I am asked. Let me practice looking around. How wide does my circle have to be before I encounter need?

Let me guess: not wide at all. Lord, help me to know.

AUGUST 5

Religion is not a thing apart from life. It is not principles and ordinances or missionary work or leadership as an end in themselves. It is manifested by the kind of people we are, by our relationship with our Heavenly Father and his Son and all of the commandments, by the measure in which we qualify for the approval of our own Spirit-guided conscience, and by the way we treat other people.

—ELDER MARION D. HANKS

You see, it should be easy. Being a Latter-day Saint should be as automatic as breathing, a simple reflection of everything we believe.

As it happens, I spend most of the hours of most of my days with people who are not members of the Church. What would they know about the Church from the way they see me behave? Surely there has to be more to it than the Word of Wisdom.

Part would have to be fairly basic. Am I honest? Do I tell the truth? When I say I'll do something, do I do it? Do I refrain from coarseness or swearing, even if people around me do not? Do I discourage gossip?

Part of it is more challenging. Am I slow to anger—even to irritation? Am I kind? Maybe most crucially, do I serve, even without a Relief Society president or compassionate service leader explaining what needs doing?

Let me find the ways to express the best my religion has to offer as I do the most everyday things. It would be nice to be able to inspire other people by what they see in me but, much more important, for myself I need to be an exemplar of the way of life Jesus taught us. Dear Lord, I would follow thee—Monday through Saturday as well as on Sunday. Help me to live the gospel in all the ordinary ways; help me to be ever worthy of thy love.

AUGUST 6

And if it seem evil unto you to serve the Lord, choose you this day whom ye will serve; whether the gods which your fathers served that were on the other side of the flood, or the gods of the Amorites, in whose land ye dwell: but as for me and my house, we will serve the Lord.

—JOSHUA 24:15

Such a straightforward choice it seems to be. Here, Joshua is an old man, ready to put down his burden now that Israel has been given rest by the Lord from all their enemies. But knowing how tempting the lures of idolatry have been for the children of Israel and fearing that they will continue to be suduced—which of course they were—he reminds them of their long history of the Lord's care and protection. And then he tells them they have to choose which god they will serve.

So which gods will we serve? Oh, it's not quite the same; we don't fall down and worship our gods now. We just give up a lot of time to them. Ambition, for example: Ambition can be a mild spur to accomplishment, or it can gradually swell and grow into a god that eats up a life. Beauty and/or physical fitness: Again, you can keep the pursuit of either under reasonable control, or you can turn either one into being what you do, the focus of most of your energy and attention. Even housekeeping can turn into an obsession, particularly if you include in that concept more than simply keeping the place clean. We all know women for whom the decoration and adornment of their house has become the hub of their existence. Where things are placed, how they are displayed, the identification and collection of exquisite objects, the arrangement of the furniture: it absorbs all their thoughts, their resources, and their time.

Let me make sure that I am not letting little things mushroom out of proportion to the rest of my life. Yes, I want to be good at whatever I do; yes, I want to be as nice looking as possible, and yes, picking out new wallpaper is a pleasurable way to spend time, even if I am going to have to hang it myself. But let all of those things be my servants, rather than the other way around. Bless me that I will know when to stop.

Like Joshua, when it comes to serving, as for me and my house, we will serve the Lord.

AUGUST 7

*They shall put you out of the synagogues: yea, the time cometh,
that whosoever killeth you will think that he doeth God service.*

—JOHN 16:2

Jesus was always wonderfully realistic. When you go through
the Gospels and read all the different versions of what he said,
what keeps ringing through, as clear as a bell, is his full understanding of the complicated motivations of mortal beings. This example
is typical: He predicts, with great accuracy, what is going to happen,
but he also is able to know the human heart clearly enough to see
why it will happen. Men will believe that they are doing God a service by persecuting the Christians.

It's all part of the same compassionate understanding that
enabled him to ask, as he was being crucified, "Father, forgive them;
for they know not what they do" (Luke 23:34). What they did was
wrong, which was why he asked for forgiveness for them, but he
understood why they were doing it.

Do I try to understand how it happens when other people do
things that appear to me to be obviously stupid, or callous, or greedy,
or is it just easier to conclude that they are stupid, callous, greedy
people? On the other hand, do I expect to have my own motivations, however complicated they might be, understood and appreciated?

Maybe the point of "judge not, that ye be not judged" is that we
should stay out of matters we're not competent to handle. Maybe I
should think about that today. If I'm not able to match the Lord's
understanding—and that's obviously the case—then maybe I'd better not be quite so swift to draw conclusions.

Today, Lord, help me to keep my mouth shut and to not jump
to mental condemnation, either.

AUGUST 8

*Verily I say, men should be anxiously engaged in a good cause, and
do many things of their own free will, and bring to pass much righteousness.*

—DOCTRINE AND COVENANTS 58:27

In other words, don't always wait to be asked. When I think about
service, I think about visiting teaching. Visiting teaching, after
all, is service distilled and emphasized. I like visiting teaching. It has
given me the incomparable opportunity to get to know women with
whom otherwise I might never have been able to spend much time.
Best of all, it has given me the chance to know and grow with
Cindy. Cindy and I have been visiting teaching companions for
about seventeen years now. (We suspect we're getting close to some
Church record.) We started out when she was a newlywed, and I
had babies and kids in elementary school. She is now discovering
the joys of her children's adolescence, and I am still learning how
much I don't know about how to deal with offspring who aren't children but who aren't yet adults.

The nicest part is that we now plan our visits together with the
comfortable familiarity of old slippers. We've visited some sisters
over the years who have challenged us and a great many who are
just plain pleasure. We usually find that the main problem is getting
organized to go in the first place; once we're there with the sisters,
we're having such a good time it seems improbable that we had to
work to find the available hours.

Cindy taught me what was really wrong with procrastination. I
have days of feeling that there's not much I'm really good at, but
I am a world champion at procrastination. So Cindy had my immediate attention when she told me what somebody had told *her:* The
problem with procrastination is that you are always rushing to complete things at the last moment, not having begun to do them until
the next-to-the-last moment. Therefore, you never have much elastic available to help anyone else. When the opportunity for service
pops up unexpectedly (as it has a way of doing), you are absolutely,
literally too busy. You've dawdled away your serving time.

Today, let me put aside procrastination and think about visiting
teaching. (This is unprecedented; the month is still in single digits!)
Let me get my act together here at home so that I will have the time
to do many things of my own free will in other places.

262 &c AUGUST 9

Lord, gladly would I serve. Help me to make myself available to do so—and while we're at it, Lord, bless Cindy, too. She claims she's done some procrastinating in her time, which was how she learned this in the first place . . .

AUGUST 9

And thou, Solomon my son, know thou the God of thy father, and serve him with a perfect heart and with a willing mind: for the Lord searcheth all hearts, and understandeth all the imaginations of the thoughts: if thou seek him, he will be found of thee; but if thou forsake him, he will cast thee off for ever.

—1 CHRONICLES 28:9

Hot, hot, hot. This part of the country has a well-founded reputation for impressive August heat. (We're also pretty good at January cold.) With the heat comes the humidity, and with the humidity comes the indolence. At the moment, all I am really interested in doing is finding a horizontal surface to recline on, preferably close to a fan. All the imaginations of my heart have to do with central air conditioning, but because our house is heated with radiators, a fan is as close to central air as I'm going to get.

The problem is that I have just been asked to go out with the sister missionaries to help them teach an investigator whose house is even less air-conditioned than mine. Now, it's certainly true that even without the heat to consider, I have too few hours in the day, and I can (and in fact I did) list several other tasks of unimpeachable virtue I had to accomplish that would make going with the missionaries difficult, not to say impossible. Therefore, with regret and great politeness, I turned them down.

My problem is that that doesn't seem to fit really well with these words of David for his son, Solomon, when he appointed him to be his successor and charged him to build a temple. "Serve him with a perfect heart and with a willing mind," he said. He didn't say anything about heat or being uncomfortable. He didn't say anything about being sticky or feeling lethargic and disinclined to undertake activity. He just said "serve."

I have reasons not to; of course I have. And I expect that the Lord, who searcheth all hearts, knows all about them. He knows about good, bad, and self-indulgent reasons, and I have perfect faith he would know in which category to put mine.

I will have one glass of cold lemonade, and then I will call them back. No. I will call them back, and then I will have the glass of lemonade. Then damply, glowingly (isn't that what women do, glow, whereas men sweat?), I will go serve with an (almost) perfect heart and a (mainly) willing mind.

Lord, next time help me to say yes without having to think it over.

AUGUST 10

But be ye doers of the word, and not hearers only, deceiving your own selves. For if any be a hearer of the word, and not a doer, he is like unto a man beholding his natural face in a glass: For he beholdeth himself, and goeth his way, and straightway forgetteth what manner of man he was.

—JAMES 1:22–24

Again and again we are cautioned away from the idea that we can be participants in the gospel message by simply sitting down and thinking about it or even talking about it. We actually have to get out and do something. If we keep our eyes fixed on the perfect law of liberty, as James goes on to recommend, then we will have no doubts about what we should do. As long as we stay stuck in the natural inclination of our natural selves (which is what I think he means by just looking at our reflection in the mirror), we don't get anywhere—or at least not anywhere we really want to go.

Service is particularly badly adapted to being theoretical. You can think about all the service you intend to give (I'm very good at that), and you can plan just how you're going to go about giving it, but until you actually get out and do something, not much service is rendered.

Which for some reason makes me think of a lovely story I heard once about a man in a toll booth. According to the story, he was taking tolls one perfectly ordinary day when a car that came past paid the quarter for himself and then handed the toll-taker another quarter and said, "This is for the car after me."

This happens sometimes—families traveling in separate cars,

for example—so the toll-taker thought nothing of it until the person in the next car looked momentarily taken aback and then handed him the quarter in his hand and said, "Okay, this is for the car after me."

And so did the next, and the next . . . I don't remember how long I was told it went on, but I don't think I really want to know. I'd rather think that a lovely long chain of generosity reached from one anonymous car to the next, giving everybody who took part a chuckle and the feeling that they were celebrating something special.

What fun it would have been to be the person who started it! What a splendid investment to make with a quarter . . .

AUGUST 11

But if ye will turn to the Lord with full purpose of heart, and put your trust in him, and serve him with all diligence of mind, if ye do this, he will, according to his own will and pleasure, deliver you out of bondage.

—MOSIAH 7:33

Of course, there are all kinds of bondage. There's actual bondage—which is what King Limhi is talking about here—and then there is another bondage of feeling oppressed by continual obligations to do this or that or the other. I think on bad days we as women are inclined to feel we know all about this other kind of bondage.

The extraordinary fact is that if we follow what King Limhi suggests here—to serve with all diligence of mind, with trust in the Lord—it works exactly the way he says it will. As soon as we begin voluntarily to do what we were feeling obliged to do, the bondage evaporates. It's one of those contradictory principles the gospel seems to specialize in: like the promise that if you lose your life, you will find it (which is actually not an unrelated idea).

Okay. So I can recognize, grudgingly, that everybody assumes I'm going to tidy up the laundry room because I'm the one who gets fed up with the mess down there (which is most frequently created by my children searching for one particular T-shirt or whatever). This is an accurate assumption, which irks me. Therefore I straighten it all up, grumbling to myself. Alternatively, I can decide that one of the ways I express love for my family is by keeping the laundry room reasonably tidy and feel virtuous as I straighten it up.

Of course, there is also the issue of how in the world I am ever going to teach my offspring to keep a tidy home themselves if I don't encourage them to practice.

But that's another problem. I will contemplate that another day.

AUGUST 12

And thus we see, that there was a time granted unto man to repent, yea, a probationary time, a time to repent and serve God.

—ALMA 42:4

B ut none of us knows how long that time will be.

My mother is in her eighties. She has been blessed with a long life, full of experience. Not everybody is. One of the sisters in our ward, who was at one time my visiting teacher, died a couple of years ago, in her thirties. When she died, her four children were still very young. Back in the days when we sat around my living room, sharing all the silly routine stuff you so often share while visiting teaching, neither of us could have dreamed that her time was so short. We talked—we acted—as if we had forever.

How much of forever do I truly have? I don't know; I don't need to know. The words of Alma tell me what I do need to know: that my years here are probationary years during which to test myself against temptation, to spend in service. Part of my probation consists of learning to see the needs; another part consists of being willing to meet them.

Maybe Lorna learned faster than I do. I've often thought in the two years since she died how much she obviously taught her children. They've done well. They are getting longer and leaner and leggier now; their father has done a magnificent job of carrying on. On Sundays, they always sit in one of the front rows, the youngest children leaning up against him. Lorna left them a wonderful legacy of faith and strength and endurance. To the end, she served.

Lord, let me use my time as well. I would pray that my days be long, but perhaps I should pray first that they be full. Let me use this day that I have been given; let me try to remember that I was never promised tomorrow.

Let me make the most of today.

AUGUST 13

Bear ye one another's burdens, and so fulfil the law of Christ.
—GALATIANS 6:2

My husband's birthday: a good day for contemplating the goodness of the man I married and of marriage itself.

This scripture sums up a lot of what marriage is all about, in practical terms. Oh, I know it's supposed to apply to bearing other people's burdens as well (and we should, and we do), but it seems to me that the intimacy of marriage allows such a particular opportunity to ease the load each of us would otherwise carry separately.

Nobody other than my husband knows me well enough to know what some of my burdens are. Some of my burdens are self-created, and I think he knows that as well as I do; he nonetheless helps with them. (I really think there must be some particular kind of saintliness involved in being able to see someone tied up in knots that she's tied herself and calmly set about untying them without pointing it out to her.) I hope—well, I know—that there are burdens I've helped him with.

I remember a discussion I had once with one of the girls at school, who was insisting she couldn't marry the father of her two-year-old son until she had finished her course and was able to be independent. "I don't want to lean on anyone," she said firmly.

I told her I thought marriage was all about leaning. Sometimes you lean one way and sometimes the other. Sometimes you're both leaning heavily against each other, like an upside-down V. I don't know if she believed me; maybe she came from too many generations of women who had been forced to become self-reliant and distrusted any other arrangement.

That was a couple of years ago; I heard she married him, not long after I last saw her. (She had just graduated but hadn't gotten a job yet.) I hope they're happy. I hope they're both learning about leaning and about bearing and sharing burdens.

Thank you, Lord, for this good man I married. Today let me appreciate him, the greatest of my blessings, and rest content.

AUGUST 14

Therefore, O ye that embark in the service of God, see that ye serve him with all your heart, might, mind and strength, that ye may stand blameless before God at the last day.

Therefore, if ye have desires to serve God ye are called to the work.

—DOCTRINE AND COVENANTS 4:2–3

A wonderful day. The humidity has dropped (we had a storm in the night), and the world is washed clean and fresh. The sunshine filters through the leaves of the trees up and down the street. On a brilliant day like this, it is easy to remember that the Lord has given me everything. He has given me this life, to prove myself; this world, so complicated and so beautiful, to learn to manage; and my salvation, to come to be worthy of.

Today, let me try to do something in return. As I am told, "if ye have desires to serve God ye are called to the work." But where do I start? There are so many ways to serve; where do I begin?

Well, perhaps I could adapt the Pennsylvania Dutch formula for a meal: seven sweets and seven sours. Maybe I could figure out seven greater services (things that take some time) and seven smaller services (things I can do on my way to something else). That should keep me busy for a week or so.

The greater services? Well, I could start by visiting my friend in the convalescent home, instead of just planning to. For the lesser, I could replace that button on my daughter's jacket even if she isn't going to be wearing it in August. I could even take the video on top of the TV back to the store myself instead of hassling the children to do it and stop by the fruit market on my way home to pick up some berries for dessert for my diet-conscious daughters.

Ordinary services—but then, most of us live ordinary lives. Aren't we advised to bloom where we are planted? I am having a splendid time doing the planning, but given the porous quality of my memory lately, I'd better write it down (and then remember where I put the list).

Dear Lord, let me serve today, in big ways and small. Let me serve gladly, with all my heart, might, mind, and strength.

AUGUST 15

*People serve one another for different reasons, and some reasons
are better than others. Perhaps none of us serves in every capacity
all the time for only a single reason. Since we are imperfect beings,
most of us probably serve for a combination of reasons, and the
combinations may be different from time to time as we grow spiritually. But we should all strive to serve for the reasons that are highest and best.*

—Elder Dallin H. Oaks

Oh yes. I can quite distinctly remember during my high school
years making elaborate efforts to be included in the candy-
striper program at the local hospital, because several girls I greatly
admired were in it and I had decided that was the "in" thing to do.
I did indeed serve—I'd like to think some patients were happy to
have nice ice-cold water brought to them to replace the tepid water
they already had, and I put a lot of flowers into vases—but were my
motives for serving particularly admirable? The odd thing is that I
can't remember whether I ever got to spend much time with those
girls after all. Isn't memory exasperating?

I would love to say I've outgrown such self-focused thinking,
but I have to admit that it's easier to sign up to work out at the welfare cannery when a couple of the people I enjoy most have signed
up before me. Again, there's obviously some benefit from my work
on those occasions, whether we're packing orders for the truck to
deliver to the various stake centers in the area or actually canning
things, but when my reasons are mainly to spend time with my
friends, I'm not sure I earn long-term benefits. In the short term, I
have my reward: We do have a lovely time working together.

Clearly, our goal should be to achieve Christ-like service, service that comes from love and is as unselfish as love itself is. I think
I've achieved something close to that sometimes, and I remember
the glow of satisfaction that comes during the doing and that lingers
with me afterwards. How hard it is to explain how wonderful real
unselfishness feels; no wonder the celestial kingdom is described as
a place of radiant happiness!

Today, let me practice being celestial. We could use a little of it
here and now.

AUGUST 16

Finally, be ye all of one mind, having compassion one of another, love as brethren, be pitiful, be courteous: not rendering evil for evil, or railing for railing: but contrariwise blessing; knowing that ye are thereunto called, that ye should inherit a blessing.

—1 PETER 3:8–9

Wonderful. I get home from work to find my daughters locked in combat, glaring at each other. I don't know how the brethren are doing today (we've only got one son here), but the sistren are having their problems.

I honestly don't know if I find it cheering that problems of disagreement were widespread enough back in the time just after Christ that Peter devoted part of one of his letters to them. I'm also not sure if this bit is meant to apply primarily to husbands and wives, because that's who he's talking about in the first part of this chapter, or to the Church members in general.

In any case, he has the prescription for peace. We can't go wrong starting out being courteous. Then, if the other person is discourteous, we can still respond pleasantly, or if that's beyond human capacity—we're talking elementary level here, remember—say nothing at all. That would end the whole thing, as I must have said about one million twenty-two times.

But do my children get it? Not yet, anyway. You know, I think they'll finally figure it out about the time they start being referees between their own adolescent daughters!

AUGUST 17

Favour is deceitful, and beauty is vain: but a woman that feareth the Lord, she shall be praised.

Give her of the fruit of her hands; and let her own works praise her in the gates.

—PROVERBS 31:30–31

A t the tail end of Proverbs is a wonderful description of "a virtuous woman"—these are the last two verses. Some of her splendid attributes sound foreign to us as we read the words centuries after they were written; some of them still sound like pretty good goals. "She openeth her mouth with wisdom; and in her tongue is the law of kindness" (Proverbs 31:26) would still be a nice way to be described.

I guess the reason I like these final two verses is that they make it clear that appearance has always been valued in this world (after all, why would Solomon or whoever actually wrote these words even mention beauty at all if nobody ever noticed it?), but eternally it carries no weight. I have no idea what our spirits look like, but I find it very hard to imagine that one would be more attractive in appearance than another. Wouldn't it be wonderful to shed that worldly burden?

It's not that I don't take any interest in my appearance now. I'm willing to bet I've acquired as many lipsticks and pots and bottles as the average—lives there a woman with vanity so dead that she doesn't have a bunch of lipsticks that don't really suit her or makeup that turned out to be the wrong color stuffed in the back of some drawer somewhere? I just can't imagine all that going on through all the expanses of eternity. I really like the idea that what I shall be valued for then is what I am and what I have done for others. Now *there's* something worth taking credit for. Maybe in eternity we'll all be beautiful. Or maybe none of us will be. Either way, it would cease to matter, wouldn't it?

I can hardly wait.

AUGUST 18

And they taught, and did minister one to another; and they had all things common among them, every man dealing justly, one with another.

And it came to pass that they did do all things even as Jesus had commanded them.

—3 NEPHI 26:19–20

These are the disciples of Christ in the New World, living according to his word. Isn't it interesting how we hunger for such a world, where men and women live in peace and harmony? Over and over we imagine its existence—sometimes we call it Shangri-la and sometimes we call it Camelot, and I'm sure it's been given a lot of other names as well. Do you suppose we treasure the idea because we have the shadowy memory that once we knew such a place, before Satan broke away and chose to work against us? Given Satan and his ingenuity, it's unlikely that as mortals we will ever live for very long under those idyllic circumstances, but it's nice to dream.

Those Nephites "did minister one to another," and every man dealt justly. Is such a thing possible? Well, maybe we could try. Let it begin with me. Let me see: If I really try today to be my best self, what might happen? Would it work like the stone tossed into a pond, with the circles widening around it? Would the other people around me try, too?

Today, let me try. Today, let me find out.

AUGUST 19

What I the Lord have spoken, I have spoken, and I excuse not myself; and though the heavens and the earth pass away, my word shall not pass away, but shall all be fulfilled, whether by mine own voice or by the voice of my servants, it is the same.

—DOCTRINE AND COVENANTS 1:38

Which puts it about as clearly as possible. In other words, pay attention, whether it comes directly from the Lord or is given to us by his servants, those who live now or those who lived then.

It's a sunny morning, and I've gone outside to read, so my scriptures lie here next to me on the lawn swing, where I'm trying to eat my breakfast of fruit without dripping juice unnecessarily. It's just a book—none of these twentieth-century bells and whistles—and so necessarily it's silent, but I can imagine the voices of all those who wrote and whose lives are recorded in this fat little book. They rise in a crescendo of instruction and praise and history around me. There are stories of wise men and foolish men, of good men who sinned (try the story of David and Bathsheba for an unvarnished account of adultery and premeditated murder), and good men who triumphed. Just think of Peter, who was so human, and so magnificent!

Think of the voices of the apostles and prophets today and all the mixing and merging of the messages I have heard at conferences. Words I remember; wisdom that I need.

They are the servants of the Lord, and they have so much to teach me. Let me remember that, and as I gather everything up to go inside to start my day, let me take some of their words with me to remember.

"What I the Lord have spoken, I have spoken." With his own voice or by the voice of his servants. Today I'll remember that, and give praise.

AUGUST 20

Now it came to pass, as they went, that he entered into a certain village: and a certain woman named Martha received him into her house.

And she had a sister called Mary, which also sat at Jesus' feet, and heard his word.

But Martha was cumbered about much serving, and came to him, and said, Lord, dost thou not care that my sister hath left me to serve alone? bid her therefore that she help me.

And Jesus answered and said unto her, Martha, Martha, thou art careful and troubled about many things:

But one thing is needful: and Mary hath chosen that good part, which shall not be taken away from her.

—LUKE 10:38–42

Let me remember that on this hot, busy summer day. Let me keep my eyes focused on what is really important.

We get so busy with all the peripheral matters to do with the administration of the Church in the here and now. It's such a temptation to turn into a congregation of Marthas, bustling around getting things organized. Our lives are bound up with getting the meetings started on time, and making sure that all the things we need for running the auxiliaries are up at the church building, and who has which keys, and what materials are (or are not) in the library, and who has the VCR, and is it working?

Let me remember today to be Mary. Yes, the business needs to be done, but I need to be reminded why. Let me remember Christ and treasure his message. Today, let the woman sitting at his feet be me.

AUGUST 21

*For how knoweth a man the master whom he has not served, and
who is a stranger unto him, and is far from the thoughts and intents
of his heart?*

—MOSIAH 5:13

I love this scripture: I think one of the reasons is that I always
think of it almost as an antiphony between King Benjamin in the
New World and the apostle John in the old. John quotes Jesus saying, "And this is life eternal, that they might know thee the only
true God, and Jesus Christ, whom thou hast sent" (John 17:3) and
King Benjamin responds, "For how knoweth a man the master
whom he has not served?" The two scriptures fit together as neatly
as a hand slipping into a glove. This is the way it is meant to be; this
is why we have both the Bible and the Book of Mormon. Each one
amplifies the other. The majestic message is the same, colored and
enriched by the personalities of the writers inspired and guided by
the same Father.

Today—in the light of what John has told us about Christ's definition of eternal life—let me think about what King Benjamin
said. How can I possibly understand that Jesus is our Savior if I
haven't come to know him, if obedience to his teachings hasn't
become part of the thoughts and intents of my heart?

Most of all, how can I know him as my master if I haven't
served him? Here again I come up against the inescapable fact: Now
that I am on this earth, the way I can serve him is by serving my
brothers and sisters, even if some of them (at first glance) don't seem
much like brothers and sisters to me. Let me reach out willingly,
happily, generously. Let me not measure my serving, any more than
the Lord has measured out what he's given me.

That service, according to King Benjamin, will lead to knowing
my Lord. That knowledge, according to the gospel of John, will lead
to eternal life.

What greater blessing is there?

AUGUST 22

No man can serve two masters: for either he will hate the one, and love the other; or else he will hold to the one, and despise the other. Ye cannot serve God and mammon.

—MATTHEW 6:24

There are days—more of them toward the end of the month, usually—when I find it extremely pleasurable to fantasize about suddenly having access to a million dollars. (Or maybe more: as I remember once being advised, why wish for a loaf of bread when you can wish for the grocery store?) How nice it would be to have no money worries at all. What a splendid tithing I would pay—and how readily! How wonderfully generous I would be to family, friends, and any widows or orphans I happen to encounter! (How many bills I could pay is probably more to the point.)

Maybe I would do the virtuous things. There are certainly rich people who do. But, as Jesus observed when he remarked on the difficulty the rich are likely to encounter entering heaven, experience would indicate that there are probably more rich people who do not. Wealth has a way of establishing its own priorities. It's a nice thought that you can have it all (and some do), but the fact remains that you do have to choose. Unless you are prepared in your deepest heart of hearts to choose the way of our Heavenly Father, even if it means you will lose every penny you own (and only you and the Lord know absolutely honestly which way you would jump on that one), you have already chosen—which is why the young rich man went away sorrowing.

Today, let me think about that. Maybe it's fortunate that I am not in the position to have to choose between God and gold (which is basically what the Aramaic word *mammon* means—"riches," in the dictionary definition). On the other hand, I do have to choose between seeking for God and seeking for gold, and do I ever consciously place the choice in those terms? I suspect I think more about expediency and let's-just-do-this-for-the-short-term and nice businesslike phrases like that. Today, let me remember (in the style of Gertrude Stein) that a choice is a choice is a choice.

Today, Lord, help me choose. Help me to choose thee.

AUGUST 23

Learn to accept adversity. No matter who you are or where you serve, you are going to have some. But do not fear the winds of adversity. Remember, a kite rises against the wind, rather than with it!

—Elder Jacob de Jager

I think I have always had a preference for being told what was going to happen, even when I might not like it. As a child being given immunization injections of one kind or another, I didn't think much of anybody who cooed, "This won't hurt at all." Even as a child I knew they were either not quite bright or shading the truth. Of course, you could always choose to consider that they were telling the literal truth: The injection didn't hurt *them* any. I vastly preferred the realist who would say, "This will only sting for a minute, and then it will stop." That was absolutely accurate. It did, and it did.

Maybe that's why I like so much what Elder de Jager tells us. We all do have adversity, every single one of us. Sometimes it may not show from the outside, but one way or another, we all pay our dues. It doesn't necessarily have a lot to do with how good we are at living our lives. True, sometimes we bring it on ourselves, for idiotic or poorly thought-out reasons, but sometimes it just happens. Remember about the rain falling on the just and the unjust?

Okay. So adversity is going to happen. What the good elder is telling us, with his characteristic stubborn good cheer, is, Adjust to it. Don't whimper, don't moan, don't feel sorry for yourself. Above all, don't fear it. When beset, figure out what you can do to improve things, and get started doing it.

Today is not starting out to be a stellar day for me. In fact, it looks very much as if it's going to turn into one of those days during which I stumble from one thing going wrong to the next. Today, let me hold on to his image of climbing against the wind of adversity that's trying to knock me down. Let me, like a kite, climb higher and higher until I soar into the sunshine.

And if I spend the whole day trapped in the mist, at least let me be robustly cheerful about it. There's not much point in adding self-pity to my other burdens.

So there, Adversity. I can hang on as long as you can. You may depress me, but I'm darned if you're going to beat me.

AUGUST 24

Look unto me, and be ye saved, all the ends of the earth: for I am God, and there is none else.

I have sworn by myself, the word is gone out of my mouth in righteousness, and shall not return, That unto me every knee shall bow, every tongue shall swear.

—ISAIAH 45:22–23

There may be days when it isn't smart to begin by reading the newspaper—particularly those days when you're feeling a little dampened anyway. Any reasonably comprehensive newspaper provides documentation for the thesis that there is no end to the ingenuity of mankind when it comes to making other members of mankind miserable. Satan's power really is awesome, or terrible, or pervasive, or, most likely, all of the above. Nastiness seems to be one of those things that we human beings can do really well.

So what can I do about it, this perfectly ordinary late August morning? Well, as a start, I can dismiss from my mind such unpleasant little credos as "Don't get mad; get even." That even sounds repellent. You can almost see Satan saying it and snickering.

Second step? I can do something about the victims of nastiness who are right around here. There are shelters for abused women and their children; what are the chances I have things—good old things—around the house that I'm not using that they could? I'll never know unless I get on the phone and ask.

Third step? I could choose to find out about some situation that appalls me and write a letter to any of my elected representatives to tell them what I think and how I want them to represent my point of view. Pointless exercise? Maybe. But how much more useful is doing absolutely nothing? (Of course, first of all I have to see what they are elected to govern: There's no point in writing to my state representative about an international matter, for example; that should go to my senator in Washington. I can call the library to get their addresses.)

Fourth step? Read this scripture over and over. It will be more comforting if I've done the first three steps first. Eventually, everything will work out. Eventually, we will all know, and we will be united in worship. Eventually, Satan will stop snickering and be abashed. We are promised that here. But eventually may be a long time away. Today, let me figure out what I'm going to do now.

AUGUST 25

*Jesus knowing that the Father had given all things into his hands,
and that he was come from God, and went to God; he riseth from
supper, and laid aside his garments; and took a towel, and girded
himself. After that he poureth water into a bason, and began to
wash the disciples' feet, and to wipe them with the towel wherewith
he was girded.*

—JOHN 13:3–5

This is such a wonderful story, but to understand it all, you have
to lace the gospels together. What is being told here is what
happened at the last supper Jesus had with his disciples.

The first part we're concerned with today begins in Luke's
retelling of that evening (chapter 22), when the disciples were
apparently arguing among themselves which one was the greatest.
(Given the magnificent job they did later in establishing the
Church, it may give us hope to recognize that they had their own
human weaknesses to overcome.) From what Jesus said to them
about the relative merits of being the one sitting at the table or the
one who is serving at the table, you might wonder if that was what
they were fussing about—that is, who should serve whom. Jesus
said, "but I am among you as he that serveth," which might lead us
to speculate that he himself got up and served them at the table.

That's speculation. What we know from John's account, which
apparently takes up from about that point, is that Jesus absolutely
did get up and wash their feet, which was the function of a slave.
When Peter objected to Jesus giving such menial service, the Lord
told him, "If I wash thee not, thou hast no part with me." With
Peter's typical enthusiasm, he immediately asked the Lord to wash
not only his feet but his head and hands as well.

What Jesus then told them is what I want to remember today.
He said, "Ye call me Master and Lord: and ye say well; for so I am.
If I then, your Lord and Master, have washed your feet, ye also ought
to wash one another's feet" (John 13:13–14).

Today, let me remember who I am. Let me remember that the
only status that counts is my status with the Lord, and that is
directly dependent upon how much I serve and how often. It

doesn't matter whom I serve, and it most certainly doesn't matter who serves me.

Today, Lord, let me try learning this message again. We seem to have a problem with it; we hang on to what we define as our dignity, and our position, and our importance in the here and now as if they matter. Lord, let me stick to the basics. Lord, teach me to serve.

AUGUST 26

And whatsoever ye do, do it heartily, as to the Lord, and not unto men; knowing that of the Lord ye shall receive the reward of the inheritance: for ye serve the Lord Christ.

—COLOSSIANS 3:23–24

Okay. So I've organized myself, and I'm getting some things together to take over to the shelter. They need exactly the things I could have predicted if I had thought about it: clothes for women and children who have quite frequently walked away from what had been home with nothing but what they happened to have on their backs (nightgowns, in some cases); such personal gear as toothbrushes and toothpaste and shampoo and soap; towels and linens and household supplies. Maybe a bottle of cologne thrown in. Would I like cologne, when I was feeling most desperate, most rejected as a woman and a human being? Yes, cologne must be included.

Now let me let this scripture guide me as I do the packing. Paul says to do whatever we do for each other as if we were doing it for the Lord. Therefore, let's make it a pretty package. Let the clothes be neatly folded, clean and ironed and ready to wear. Let the toiletries be bundled tidily in the corners, so they don't cause rumples, the towels and linens underneath, and on the top, brand new, in its own box, the cologne, a fresh summery scent to match the season.

I send it to my sister. I won't ever know her; I probably won't ever even see her. May it comfort her heart and be a promise of a fresh start.

Lord, if thou were a woman, it's what I would do for thee.

AUGUST 27

*I know thy works, and charity, and service, and faith, and thy
patience, and thy works; and the last to be more than the first.*

—REVELATION 2:19

L et's be honest here. I know that Joseph Smith described the
book of the Revelation of St. John the Divine as being "one of
the plainest books God ever caused to be written," but that just
increases my awe and admiration of Joseph Smith. It isn't plain to
me.

But I like this verse. It's in the early part of the book, before the
symbols and images start being piled on top of each other. This verse
is part of what John the apostle saw revealed about the Church in
Thyatira, one of the seven churches of Asia that are the focus of the
first three chapters of the Revelation. Thyatira was then a busy
commercial city, a little way inland from the Aegean Sea and about
halfway across what is now Turkey. It's clear from what is said about
the churches that the apostasy which was to engulf them was
already underway, but the Church at Thyatira was apparently doing
quite well, except for problems with a would-be prophetess who was
trying to lead them into heresy.

This verse, which tells them what they are doing right, is lovely.
They are praised for their charity, service, faith, and patience and
told that their works now are more remarkable than they were when
the Church was first established, when their enthusiasm might have
been expected to be highest. They are still doing the things they
have been taught.

What a wonderful thing to be told! What a wonderful thing to
be true. Are *my* works increasing, or are they getting put to one side
while I do other things first? I would hope that my knowledge is
growing, and my understanding; but unless my works keep improving as well, where is the benefit?

Little church at Thyatira, I wonder what happened to you.
Were you finally led astray? You must have been, because the light
of the priesthood was quenched. Today, let me resolve to be
stronger, to be more faithful, to hold more fast to the truth. But let
me learn from what you did well.

AUGUST 28

Service changes people. It refines, purifies, gives a finer perspective, and brings out the best in each one of us. It gets us looking outward instead of inward. It prompts us to consider others' needs ahead of our own. Righteous service is the expression of true charity, such as the Savior showed.

—Elder Derek A. Cuthbert

A friend of mine recently lost her son. It wasn't unexpected: He was born with a constellation of problems, and eventually, after about ten years of fighting them, his poor little body just wore out.

It was very hard for Jeannie. There was her grief, of course, but beyond that was the reality that taking care of Nathan had absorbed hours of her days. He had to be taken back and forth from school when he was well enough to go; and when he wasn't, he was there at home or in the hospital. She had two older children, but out of sheer self-preservation, they had learned to be self-reliant and didn't exactly welcome the idea of their mother now becoming superinvolved in their lives just because she had time on her hands. She had no particular vocational skills; she had been at home all those years, and it seemed silly to go out and get a job at Burger King just for something to do.

Instead, Jeannie got involved in the literacy program. She had never done much volunteer work, but she saw an ad on TV and thought, "Why not?" She phoned the number they gave, and one week later she was working with a young woman in her thirties who had never before admitted to anyone that she was guessing when she looked at bus schedules or was given a sheet of instructions at the nursing home where she cleans. Jeannie doesn't do things by half measures, and when she worked with this young woman, she worked hard.

That woman reads now. Jeannie has gone on to work with someone else, but she and her first student go out for lunch together once a month for what they call a refresher but is really their way to stay in touch.

Jeannie has changed, too. She's more purposeful. She says it's because the volunteer work made her think about somebody else's problems when thinking about her own hurt too much. She's never been religious or interested in religion before, but she says the volunteer work makes her feel peaceful inside. "It makes me feel good," she told me. "I mean, it makes me feel as if I am good."

I told her it was Christ's goodness working through her, and she looked embarrassed and said, "Oh, well, maybe," and the talk moved on in a different direction. But that day before we parted, I said, "That's true, you know—about Christ."

She looked at me straight in the eye and said, "I know. Funny it should be me, isn't it?" We said good-bye and got into our separate cars. We'll be talking again, but I thought about this conference address all the way home.

It's true. Service changes people. It changed Jeannie.

AUGUST 29

Also the sons of the stranger, that join themselves to the Lord, to serve him, and to love the name of the Lord, to be his servants, every one that keepeth the sabbath from polluting it, and taketh hold of my covenant; even them will I bring to my holy mountain, and make them joyful in my house of prayer: their burnt offerings and their sacrifices shall be accepted upon mine altar; for mine house shall be called an house of prayer for all people.

—ISAIAH 56:6–7

The New Testament message that the gospel is for all people is foreshadowed here in the last chapters of Isaiah. Traditionally the emphasis had been on the children of Israel inheriting their blessings by their descent from Father Abraham, but here the Lord is telling his people that strangers (and the sons of strangers) will be gathered in as long as they love the Lord and are obedient to his commandments. His house will be a house of prayer for all people.

There will be room in that house for all of us. We come in a variety of colors and shapes and sizes, and we will all have our place. Why else are the missionaries scattered across the face of the earth, knocking on doors and following up on referrals, hunting out the honest in heart? If all that counted to be included as God's chosen people was physical descent from Abraham, what would be the point?

Some of us were born into that original covenant; some have been adopted. The Lord is telling us here that we will come to the holy mountain as one people.

Today, let me make myself ready to come to the mountain.

AUGUST 30

Be wise in the days of your probation; strip yourselves of all uncleanness; ask not, that ye may consume it on your lusts, but ask with a firmness unshaken, that ye will yield to no temptation, but that ye will serve the true and living God.

—MORMON 9:28

This morning there is a crisp bite in the air. Summer's winding down to a close; school is starting and autumn is waiting in the wings. The garden is looking a little tired after weeks of August heat, but the chrysanthemums will make a nice show as autumn comes in. The weeds are still doing fine.

I wonder what season of the year it was when Moroni was writing these last brave words after the great and terrible battle at Cumorah. I wonder if it was hot, or cold, or if he was having to shelter from rain as he persisted in writing down all he had to say before he hid the records away to await a generation prepared to receive them.

Today, let me think about these last words of advice to us. Let me continue to try to use these days of my probation wisely, to serve the Lord my God with all my heart and soul. Let me be somebody worthy of receiving the benefit of Moroni's heroic labors. He suffered so much so that I could have this book and read his words. Help me to remember that, today and tomorrow and all the tomorrows.

Help me to be what he wanted these generations to be.

AUGUST 31

Wherefore thou art no more a servant, but a son; and if a son, then an heir of God through Christ.

—GALATIANS 4:7

A nother cool morning. The leaves are all still green, but the cold air will be working its chemistry, and the colors will be changing. This morning, standing at the kitchen sink in the middle of the bustle of people getting ready for school—it seems a long time since June, when the kitchen was last full of kids first thing in the morning—it occurs to me that Paul is talking here about a change like the change in the leaves.

The first covenant of Abraham established his posterity as the chosen people of God. Later, when Moses was summoned up to the mountain, he was given the law for his people. Originally, like servants, the people were expected to take little responsibility for themselves beyond obedience; the children of Israel, wandering around the wilderness, were being taught to do what they were told.

Then Christ came to fulfill the law and to redeem us with his love, so that, as Paul writes, "we might receive the adoption of sons" (Galatians 4:5). Instead of obedience by commandment, we become capable of the higher law, to obey because of our love for Jesus Christ and our gratitude for his sacrifice. Like the leaves, we were to change. We become different people. Instead of servants, we are sons (and daughters) of our Father in heaven.

Let me think about that this year, as the leaves turn color. Let me find the change the Lord intended in my own heart. Let me serve out of love, not commandment.

Let my service bring me nearer to thee.

SEPTEMBER

While the earth remaineth, seedtime and harvest, and cold and heat, and summer and winter, and day and night shall not cease.

—GENESIS 8:22

SEPTEMBER 1

Yea, all things which come of the earth, in the season thereof, are made for the benefit and the use of man, both to please the eye and to gladden the heart; yea, for food and for raiment, for taste and for smell, to strengthen the body and to enliven the soul.

—DOCTRINE AND COVENANTS 59:18–19

Rain last night: the world as fresh and clean this morning as if it had been scrubbed. The grass, which had been looking a little parched, is bright green. The white flowers in the front are standing straight up again, looking splendidly white.

This is a wonderful world, even when it isn't freshly rained on, and as the Lord points out in this revelation, it is given to us for our use. He means for us to love this earth and take care of it. Standing on a front porch and taking great pleasure in looking up and down the street at green lawns and the canopy of trees, as I have been doing this morning, is the kind of thing I think is meant by enlivening the soul.

As the Church fell into apostasy after the apostolic period, the great theological thinkers moved toward the idea that the natural world was contemptible and that salvation lay in disregarding our present circumstances and focusing entirely on the spiritual world. Many of the early Christian leaders were ascetics, who profoundly believed that "mortifying the flesh" was the way to discipline the spirit away from the evils of human behavior and thus please God. Even babies were sinful, because of Adam's transgression. To take pleasure in the world, from that point of view, would be inexplicable. Who could possibly take pleasure in anything that by definition was estranged from God?

We see it entirely differently. This world obviously has its imperfections, but we believe what was written about it in Genesis: On the sixth day, at the end of his labors, God saw "every thing that he had made, and, behold, it was very good" (Genesis 1:31). Matter is part of the eternal plan. In fact, the celestial kingdom will be this very earth, celestialized and made perfect.

When we read in Mosiah that natural man is an enemy to God, it's the selfishness and willfulness of spirit that is being discussed, not "natural" in the sense that there is something inherently wrong with the world of nature. That, as this revelation in the Doctrine and Covenants makes clear, is for us to have and keep as a special treasure—a gift. "And it pleaseth God that he hath given all these things unto man" (D&C 59:20).

On this late summer morning, a cat yawns and stretches delicately in the sun; if I had more time, I would go out to join her. Oh, blessed be the name of the Lord! What a lovely day.

This is a beautiful world.

SEPTEMBER 2

Counsel with the Lord in all thy doings, and he will direct thee for good; yea, when thou liest down at night lie down unto the Lord, that he may watch over you in your sleep; and when thou risest in the morning let thy heart be full of thanks unto God; and if ye do these things, ye shall be lifted up at the last day.

—ALMA 37:37

There is a rhythm to our lives on this earth. What we are being told here is that we are meant to include the Lord in that rhythm.

For me, it's the morning prayer that is hard to incorporate. For one thing, I am not the kind of person who leaps gladly out of bed first thing in the morning; I am the kind who opens one eye suspiciously and then closes it in the vain hope that maybe I didn't see the clock right and there might be more time to burrow back into the pillow and sleep. After the clock and I have argued for a while (the clock always wins, except on the rare occasions when we've had a power outage during the night, in which case the clock is flashing crossly and entirely inaccurately), I surrender to the inevitable and shuffle out of my room down to the bathroom, to see if washing my face helps.

It usually does.

The difficulty comes in the practicalities of returning to my room at that point for prayer. Whoever of my children are awake instantly want me to do something (such as tell them where the gray sweater has gone so they won't have to go down to the basement to look for themselves), laundry needs to be collected and shoved down the chute, and I generally see at least one thing that needs to be carried down to the kitchen.

Now, I do realize that not one of those circumstances is a valid reason for postponing (or eliminating) that prayer of thanksgiving in the morning. What I clearly need to do is form the habit of praying no matter what, so that starting off a morning without prayer is as uncomfortable as hopping into bed at night without having reviewed my day with the Lord, on my knees at the side of the bed.

Habits can be very useful things. Dear Lord, help me form a habit. Let me go upstairs right now (or downstairs to the basement, if I can be quiet and uninterrupted there), and tomorrow help me to remember, and the day after that . . .

Dear Lord, my heart *is* full of thanks. Just help me to remember to say so.

SEPTEMBER 3

The voice of him that crieth in the wilderness, Prepare ye the way of the Lord, make straight in the desert a highway for our God. Every valley shall be exalted, and every mountain and hill shall be made low: and the crooked shall be made straight, and the rough places plain: and the glory of the Lord shall be revealed, and all flesh shall see it together: for the mouth of the Lord hath spoken it.

—ISAIAH 40:3–5

Isaiah saw some terrible things in his lifetime. During the time that he served as the prophet, the southern kingdom of Judah was reduced from independence to the position of a tributary state. He was alive to see the northern kingdom of Israel—what we know as the ten lost tribes—carried away into captivity. But he also saw some wonderful visions of the future, when Israel would be restored and the land made fruitful and the Lord would dwell in the midst of his people.

This comes from the wonderful part.

We are not the only people who love the words of Isaiah. John the Baptist, according to the gospel of John, cited the first verse here as a description of his own ministry. Jesus himself quoted Isaiah. So did Paul and Peter in their epistles and John in his revelation.

Today, let me enjoy the community of the faithful who have read these words and treasured them. They are quoted by the

Nephites and in the Doctrine and Covenants. The wisdom of Isaiah has enriched us across time and around the world.

"And the glory of the Lord shall be revealed, and all flesh shall see it together." How many of us have been strengthened by that promise? When I think about all of us, linked through the centuries, I feel as if I am peeking through a crack at eternity. We can—we *do,* in a sense—all worship together.

"For the mouth of the Lord hath spoken it."

SEPTEMBER 4

And when ye reap the harvest of your land, thou shalt not wholly reap the corners of thy field, neither shalt thou gather the gleanings of thy harvest.

And thou shalt not glean thy vineyard, neither shalt thou gather every grape of thy vineyard; thou shalt leave them for the poor and stranger: I am the Lord your God.

—LEVITICUS 19:9–10

At school today Rosemary was positively preening in her new garnet-colored fall suit. Well, new to her, she explained. The garnet color is wonderful on her, and she got it, she reported proudly, from one of the local thrift shops. It cost five dollars.

As it happens, there are plenty of students here who have fewer resources than Rosemary has, but doing without what had been her full-time income (admittedly not a large one, but still . . .) for nine months while she went to school has involved doing without a lot of things, new clothes being one of the most prominent. This can grate a little. Since our students are supposed to dress in "business casual" rather than jeans and sweats, the problem of dress is a big one around here. As one student told me gloomily, she was almost as tired now of her limited business wardrobe as she had been of her maternity clothes last year.

I guess it was when I was trying to squash a freshly ironed blouse into my closet that the application of the words in Leviticus occurred to me. I don't happen to have much of a harvest (unless you count the tomatoes, which everyone else has too at this time of year) or any gleaners that I know of. But I sure do have excess clothes. Some of them are there because I can't bring myself to admit I should never have been seduced by that sale in the first place; some are there because I live in hope that on some wonderful day they will fit and I can wear them again. (Given my track record recently, this would clearly depend on a miracle rather than on natural consequences of diet or exercise.)

Wouldn't it fill the spirit, if not the letter, of this law to go through my closet rigorously and take out everything I haven't worn recently and *give* it to the thrift shop closest to school? Not junky and out of style things; do as this scripture rules. Leave some of the good harvest for the poor and stranger. Maybe add to the pile of the misconceived and just plain too small garments one or two that have nothing wrong with them that I *could* wear: a genuine gift from the heart.

Today, let me begin. The closet is waiting.

SEPTEMBER 5

Who shall ascend into the hill of the Lord? or who shall stand in his holy place?

He that hath clean hands, and a pure heart; who hath not lifted up his soul unto vanity, nor sworn deceitfully.

He shall receive the blessing from the Lord, and righteousness from the God of his salvation.

—PSALM 24:3–5

I remember this psalm from seminary. I don't remember if we were expected to remember it or if I just encountered it, flicking through the pages at random, but I do remember very clearly visualizing the hill of the Lord as being like the hills around where I lived then: California hills, which are golden with the dried grasses and punctuated by drab olive green trees spotted here and there.

When I read it now, in the flatlands of the Midwest, I remember the gentle hills of England, vibrantly green (well, it rains a lot), with a church steeple or tower always within view. You don't have many sweeping grand vistas in England; there are always hills nearby, so the horizon is close and friendly.

The wonderful thing to me about this scripture—and so many of them—is that it is particular enough so that it summons up a mental picture but not so precise that it matters what the mental picture is. I suppose that David, when he wrote this psalm, was thinking about the hills around Jerusalem, which I gather from all the pictures are arid like the California hills, only more so.

Does it matter whether it's a hill of the Holy Land, or a gentle English one, or a California sort of hill—or a hill in Hong Kong or Africa, come to that? Not really, I wouldn't think, not as long as we have clean hands and a pure heart and are ready to worship. This wonderfully variable world we have been given has a multitude of aspects; I expect the Lord foresaw we would come to love those that are most familiar.

Today, Lord, let me climb in my imagination—and in my actions—closer to thee, to stand in thy holy place. Let me not lift up my soul unto vanity, nor swear deceitfully.

If I can do all that, let me receive thy blessing. Wherever I am.

SEPTEMBER 6

I returned, and saw under the sun, that the race is not to the swift, nor the battle to the strong, neither yet bread to the wise, nor yet riches to men of understanding, nor yet favour to men of skill; but time and chance happeneth to them all.

—ECCLESIASTES 9:11

It's not particularly cheerful, but as long as we're thinking in terms of "under the sun"—which really means here on this earth—it is unarguably true. There can be fairness, but often there is not. We see episodes of justice and episodes of its opposite. Rewards are given to those who deserve them, but often they are also given to those who don't. It's easy to tip over to the conclusion drawn at the beginning of Ecclesiastes: Vanity of vanities; all is vanity.

Flip back a few pages, to the book of Psalms, and compare the world vision there. Suddenly we have an eternal dimension added, and it's as if somebody pulled back a curtain and we can see the world in all its magnificent color, sparkling and vibrating with life.

Maybe that's why we have Ecclesiastes included in our Bible, to show us how dry and sterile our lives would be if we lived without that eternal dimension, without knowledge of the Lord our God.

Today, Lord, let me remember that. Today, stay near me.

SEPTEMBER 7

But when he saw the multitudes, he was moved with compassion on them, because they fainted, and were scattered abroad, as sheep having no shepherd. Then saith he unto his disciples, The harvest truly is plenteous, but the labourers are few; pray ye therefore the Lord of the harvest, that he will send forth labourers into his harvest.

—MATTHEW 9:36–38

And who do you think the labourers are going to be, if not you and me?

Mark in his gospel also mentions Christ being "moved with compassion," seeing the people waiting for him, and uses the same image of sheep without a shepherd, scattered over the countryside and directionless. But it's Matthew who goes on to tell us what Christ said then: that labourers are needed to gather the harvest.

If Jesus said that we were needed then—not just desirable, you notice, not just a good idea, but *needed*—when he was still on the earth, how much more are we needed now, when it has been centuries since he was physically among us and there are honest souls who have never really heard of him (except, perhaps, as a legendary figure who was "a great teacher")? Some are lost, confused souls who desperately need to have some strength of testimony; some are cynical souls—as Ecclesiastes—who need to grow beyond the shallows of skepticism into the profundity of faith.

This is what the missionaries are sent to do, of course, and we're supposed to be doing all we can to help them. Even if we honestly did (and how many of us honestly do, day after day instead of in variable surges?), there is more need than even the thousands of missionaries out in the field now could meet.

Besides, not everybody is waiting for young men or women with name tags. What about all the people who would immediately withdraw from a missionary, so designated, but might open their heart to a friend? Maybe they need the comfort we have to give. What about the people who don't do well with an organized program but might respond to a few words you are inspired to say? Do they miss the chance to make sense out of their earthly existence just because they don't fit into a pattern we have defined? What if you don't get around to saying those words?

Lord, the harvest is plenteous. Lord, send me forth as a laborer in the field.

SEPTEMBER 8

Whoso boasteth himself of a false gift is like clouds and wind without rain.

—PROVERBS 25:14

Oh, yes.

I thought about this one today. For one thing, the weather was a throwback to August: hot and sultry, with air so humid you could almost cut it, and dark clouds on the horizon blowing past— clouds that were obviously going to rain on someone but not a drop on us.

During the morning, a former student dropped by. He is a charming fellow, absolutely charming. He was spinning an elaborate tale about some business plan he claimed to have underway, promising to hire the girls in the front office at extravagant salaries, casually dropping names of local business magnates who, according to him, were setting up business for him.

We listened to him politely for a while and then tried to go back to work on whatever happened to be on our desks. Eventually he rambled off, but as I checked out the front window to see if he was safely on his way, I could see those rainless clouds scudding past in the sky and thought about the land where this proverb was written: a dry country where rain would be eagerly awaited and where rainless black clouds could remind you of a man whose boasts never produced anything either.

Oh, yes. I could see the similarity. Oh, yes, indeed.

SEPTEMBER 9

The Lord is my shepherd; I shall not want.

*He maketh me to lie down in green pastures: he leadeth me
beside the still waters.*

*He restoreth my soul: he leadeth me in the paths of righteousness
for his name's sake.*

—PSALM 23:1–3

Last Sunday in Relief Society we sang the hymn drawn from this
psalm. Our chorister, who has a wonderfully classically trained
voice, coaxed and persuaded us to sing all three parts, alto and second soprano as well as soprano, even though no one was there to
hear us but ourselves.

The melody rippled through the parts, from one voice to
another. The sound of the voices soaring together close to the end
was so beautiful that in the quiet when we finished I had a lump in
my throat. I don't know if it was the richness of the sound or the
sense of sisterhood, because we share the beliefs that make the
hymn significant. Maybe it was simply the comfort of the words.

The Lord is my shepherd. How many people down through the
centuries have held those words close to their hearts? It's true, of
course. Jesus specifically spoke of himself as the Good Shepherd and
taught us that his sheep know his voice.

When I listened to the song and sang those words, it seemed
marvelously easy to put myself under that protection, to lie down in
those green pastures in peace and safety, by the side of still waters.
But when I get caught up in the busy pace of life, far away from that
pleasant Relief Society room, do I always listen for his voice? Or
am I so busy getting this accomplished in time, and finishing that
before it's too late, or postponing the other because I'm just not
going to get around to it, that I don't wait to be guided? Instead of
paying attention to what I *should* be doing, am I consumed by what
seems urgent, hypnotized by what's on my own agenda? Do I follow
my Shepherd? I need to think about that.

It's easy to wish I could somehow put life on hold and just linger
in the peace of that room after the lesson and the prayer are over,
remembering the song, enjoying the companionship of my sisters.
But the little children will be waiting at the door—as they should
be—and some have bigger children to locate, and husbands. We all

have jobs and responsibilities and duties of life needing to be done. The time together is a respite, not the fabric of our earthly life.

But I can remember the song. I can remember the green pasture, and the still waters. I can remember the Lord, who is my Shepherd.

Today, let me listen to his voice.

SEPTEMBER 10

This then is the message which we have heard of him, and declare unto you, that God is light, and in him is no darkness at all.

—1 JOHN 1:5

The days are getting shorter; I can still hear the children's voices as they play outside in the evenings, but their mothers are calling them inside earlier (and because we haven't had a frost yet, the mosquitoes take over earlier, too, as the sun sinks behind the trees).

Inside, of course, it just means I turn on the lights sooner. When I read a scripture like this I am reminded that in the days when John wrote this letter, the darkness was a much more challenging proposition. For one thing, the dark was a lot darker: We are so used to artificial light illuminating our streets and our buildings that, should the power fail or we be lost out in the country, we talk about "pitch darkness" indignantly, as if light were the normal state of affairs. But for most of the history of mankind, darkness was truly dark.

No wonder John writes of God as light!

Light is bright and reviving and enables us to see our way. All the half-seen and unseen menaces of the dark—the shadows at the corner, the uncertainty about where to step—vanish like magic with the light. You can see. All is known; it's easy to see where it is safe to walk and where you need to step over a gap. The dimly seen shape in the dark turns out, in the light, merely to be an approaching friend.

"But if we walk in the light, as he is in the light," John went on to write, "we have fellowship one with another, and the blood of Jesus Christ his Son cleanseth us from all sin" (John 1:7).

Let me remember that, these nights when darkness comes earlier and earlier. Let me remember that there will always be the light of the Lord; let me remember to reach toward the light that will guide me into eternity.

SEPTEMBER 11

*We give our lives to that which we give our time. As I have said,
while here in mortality we are subject to time. We also have agency
and may do what we will with our time. Let me repeat: We give our
lives to that which we give our time.*

—ELDER WILLIAM R. BRADFORD

I remember once that during a spell of attempting to get really
organized, I read in a time management book that the secret to
finding extra time was to spend a week faithfully recording everything you did and then ruthlessly excise any activity that seemed
unnecessary.

I didn't manage a week. It just about drove me crazy. After a
couple of days of interrupting myself constantly to find what I'd
done with my notebook so that I could record a change of occupation, I decided that the most unnecessary activity was the record-
keeping. Just eliminating that gave me an extra hour a day.

But you know, this makes me think. I don't need that notebook
to figure out that I spend a lot more time doing tedious household
chores than I spend in prayer. I spend a whole lot more time in the
garden weeding, in the course of an average summer, than I ever
spend studying the scriptures. I spend more time watching TV than
I spend visiting anybody but close friends in the hospital or at home
convalescing, even if I have good reason to know others are lonely
or bored.

So what does that mean I am giving my life to?

Obviously the house does need to be kept reasonably clean.
Obviously the weeds can—and will—overtake the flower beds if not
kept in check. Obviously—no, I can't really argue that anybody's
life, not even my own, is necessarily enhanced by my watching television. Even so, it's not *wicked* to watch television. The question, it
seems to me, is one of priorities. Am I giving my life to the second-
tier priorities and tucking the first-tier priorities in where I can fit
them?

Perhaps today I can think about that. Perhaps I could even do
something about it. Perhaps today I could try praying first and
cleaning afterwards.

It certainly wouldn't hurt to try.

SEPTEMBER 12

Behold, the field was ripe, and blessed are ye, for ye did thrust in
the sickle, and did reap with your might, yea, all the day long did ye
labor; and behold the number of your sheaves! And they shall be
gathered into the garners, that they are not wasted.

Yea, they shall not be beaten down by the storm at the last
day; yea, neither shall they be harrowed up by the whirlwinds; but
when the storm cometh they shall be gathered together in their place,
that the storm cannot penetrate to them; yea, neither shall they be
driven with fierce winds whithersoever the enemy listeth to carry
them.

—ALMA 26:5–6

The chrysanthemums are out, bronze and yellow and white, and
I was going to gather a big armful for a lovely lush centerpiece
on the table. Only I didn't get to it yesterday, and last night it
poured rain; my chrysanthemums, not having been staked or gathered like the sheaves, are lying flat on the ground in untidy circles
around what yesterday were centers of upright clumps. They'll still
make a nice centerpiece but not quite so lovely and not quite so
lush.

Fortunately Ammon and his brethren took better care of their
Lamanite converts, as the scripture records.

What a wonderful, triumphant report of their missionary successes. Not, you note, a triumphant report that they were wonderful
and fine missionaries but that they had gathered their converts so
well that the people were held safe from the storms of life. Those
people—as Ammon goes on to say—are in the hands of the Lord of
the harvest, to be raised up at the last day.

Today let me think how I can do the same for the people who
are dear to me. Not just those who are not members of the Church
but those who are members for whom I have stewardship: my children. Am I helping them to develop their own testimonies so that
they will not be harrowed by the whirlwinds of life that I know will
assault them one way or another? Am I teaching them what they
will need to know to keep them safe from the fierce winds?

Today let me look at the chrysanthemums and learn. They're
just flowers; staked or unstaked is no big deal. But am I teaching my
children to stand tall? Will they be strong enough? That's not so
easy to know.

SEPTEMBER 13

Lord, in trouble have they visited thee, they poured out a prayer when thy chastening was upon them.

Like as a woman with child, that draweth near the time of her delivery, is in pain, and crieth out in her pangs; so have we been in thy sight, O Lord.

—ISAIAH 26:16–17

A quiet morning after a rough night. The weather conditions that brewed the storm that laid waste to the chrysanthemums still being in place, we had another fierce storm last night. Because my husband had been out of town on business and was due to fly in about the time when the storm was raging most vigorously, I spent the time pretending to read and pacing restlessly from room to room, waiting for his phone call to reassure me that he had landed and was on his way home.

"Lord, in trouble have they visited thee." Even as I prayed and paced and then prayed some more, I was wondering how long it will take me to reach the spiritual maturity to pray in good times with the same single-mindedness that seems absolutely natural when I am worried or afraid or grieving. How easy it is to turn trustingly to the Lord at those times! On the other hand, how easy it is to forget about a prayer of thankfulness when everything is going smoothly and I am bustling along from one activity to the next.

Time moves slowly when you're waiting for the telephone to ring. Or for a baby to be born—somehow reading this scripture reminds me vividly of hospital rooms I have known and the erratic way time seemed to pass. The interval between one contraction and the next seemed unbelievably short and the length of the contraction endless. (I was trying to think stalwartly, "This isn't really *pain*; it's just an intense sensation," over the little voice that was saying, "Yeah, right. This hurts.") Then I'd focus on the clock and realize an hour or even two hours had passed. Very strange. I remember praying then, too: for relief, for a safe delivery, for it all to be over.

"Lord, in trouble have they visited thee."

He never did call. There was the scrunch of tires on the gravel in the driveway, and there he was, home and safe and matter-of-fact. He hadn't called, he said, because he thought I'd be sleeping and didn't want to disturb me.

I went to bed muttering over the differences between men and women. But in my prayer of thanksgiving at my bedside, I did remember to be grateful he was there.

"In trouble have they visited thee." Oh, yes, Lord. Oh, yes.

SEPTEMBER 14

For every tree is known by his own fruit. For of thorns men do not gather figs, nor of a bramble bush gather they grapes.

A good man out of the good treasure of his heart bringeth forth that which is good; and an evil man out of the evil treasure of his heart bringeth forth that which is evil: for of the abundance of the heart his mouth speaketh.

—LUKE 6:44–45

Good, sound, horticultural observation: You can't reap what hasn't been planted.

I had always thought of this business about thorns and figs and brambles and grapes as belonging with the "by their fruits ye shall know them" principle (and in fact, Matthew 7 covers very similar material which includes that conclusion), but today I find myself looking at it the other way around, peering down the other end of the telescope. What does it say about me? How can I bring forth that which is good unless I have good treasure of my heart? Maybe I should worry less about measuring the efforts of others and worry more about my own.

In all honesty, distinguishing between good and evil in my fairly restricted experience is not usually that difficult. Maybe the evil I do encounter is not all that sophisticated, but I find when I am around something that is wrong, I feel uncomfortable. I may not be able to identify exactly what is wrong, but it doesn't feel right to me. It doesn't smell right.

In the same way, although I certainly make mistakes, I don't believe I am intentionally evil. But am I actively good? Am I honest, true, chaste, benevolent, virtuous, and all the other good things in the thirteenth Article of Faith? Am I tending the good treasure of my own heart so that I can bring forth good works? As has been said before in other contexts, you can't make bricks out of straw.

Today let me concentrate on that. Let me figure out how to cultivate the good treasure so that the good works will come to pass almost automatically. Isn't that what becoming a celestial person would mean?

Today, I should start.

SEPTEMBER 15

And that thou mayest more fully keep thyself unspotted from the world, thou shalt go to the house of prayer and offer up thy sacraments upon my holy day; for verily this is a day appointed unto you to rest from your labors, and to pay thy devotions unto the Most High.

—DOCTRINE AND COVENANTS 59:9–10

We are to be in the world but not of it. To emphasize the point, there is Sunday.

It didn't used to be quite such a departure from the norm to observe the Sabbath. It was a shared value of our society. Businesses were closed on Sunday; you didn't go shopping because, generally speaking, you couldn't. People went to church on Sunday morning and had Sunday dinners and visited each other (or napped) on Sunday afternoons. It was what almost everybody did. Life got back to work-day normal on Monday.

Nowadays, the civic statutes that were established to protect the weekly day of rest are called blue laws and mainly—to the extent they still exist—lie quietly unenforced on the books. Just about everything that is available on any other day of the week is available on a Sunday. Stores, almost without exception, are open on Sundays in most parts of the country. Restaurants flourish; theaters run full schedules. Recreational facilities regard Sundays along with Saturdays as the prime days of their week. Even many professionals—veterinarians, doctors, dentists—are beginning to feel pressed to keep Sunday office hours in view of services expected because of the time pinch felt by busier and busier people. To withdraw from the commercial and recreational rat race on the grounds of Sabbath observance seems positively eccentric.

The trick seems to be in preventing myself from buying into this seven-day-a-week availability of services so much that it starts to seem eccentric to me, too. Maybe it will help to remember that, according to Genesis, the Lord sanctified the seventh day even before he formed Adam and Eve and set them into the Garden of

Eden. The Sabbath has *always* been special. It's only now that we are busy turning it into just an ordinary day.

Dear Lord, help me to keep Sunday as a peculiar treasure. Let me hold it apart from the rest of the week, the way it was meant to be. Let me remember, and teach my children, that from Old Testament times the Sabbath has been a sign of the special covenant between the Lord and his people. Let me pay more attention to what Sunday as the Sabbath can be and pay less to the world's attempt to make it just another day.

Six days shall we labor, Lord. Let my heart be full of thanksgiving for the seventh.

SEPTEMBER 16

For thou wilt light my candle: the Lord my God will enlighten my darkness.

—PSALM 18:28

Light and darkness again. Have we forgotten how bright a candle can be in the dark? We all live in our own particular kind of dark; we all have the candle of faith we can light to enlighten us, in the oldest sense of the word.

This makes me remember another "enlightening," in that old sense. When we lived in England, Queen Elizabeth celebrated her silver jubilee—twenty-five years on the throne. This was long before all the problems that have since beset the royal family, and the country's rejoicing was fond and generally approving, and besides, everybody loves a good party. There were street parties during which traffic was rerouted so that neighbors could set out tables and picnic down the middle of the streets that run in front of their houses; there were splendid gatherings in front of Buckingham Palace (so many people, of course, that they stood all over the plantings of summer flowers, but the amazed gardeners reported the next day that almost everyone had stood very carefully, one foot on each side of each plant, and only about a half dozen got squashed in spite of the hundreds of thousands of people).

What I remember is the bonfire. When the first Queen Elizabeth's navy vanquished the Spanish Armada, communications were not quite what they are today. To let the whole nation know of the triumph quickly, they lit a series of bonfires, starting on a hill in the south, going to the next hill north from which a person could see the first bonfire, and then to the next hill north from which the second would be visible, and so forth, all the way up the country, so that word of the victory was conveyed by the brilliance of the bonfires. For the jubilee, they lit the bonfires again.

I remember standing in the dark on the hilltop near Windsor Castle. It was glorious weather (not something you can take for granted there), and because it was right at Windsor, the queen and most of the royal family were there, along with several thousand commoners—among them, us. I remember the dark and then the hiss of the torches; the bonfire leaped into life, and there was brilliant light everywhere. All of us cheered and whooped joyfully, and I could imagine the next bonfire being set off, and so on across the countryside . . .

When we came to this earth, we came to the dark. But the comfort and triumph of light is always there. Even in the dark, it is there.

SEPTEMBER 17

We must walk uprightly all the day long. How glorious are the principles of righteousness! We are full of selfishness; the devil flatters us that we are very righteous, when we are feeding on the faults of others. We can only live by worshiping our God; all must do it for themselves; none can do it for another.

—JOSEPH SMITH

One of the most typical human ways to comfort ourselves with our own goodness is to point out somebody else's badness. What about a daughter virtuously insisting that she is perfectly prepared to do the dishes but can't because her sister hasn't cleared the table yet? We don't have to be children to be self-righteous. How many lessons have I heard (or given) in which one of the demonstrations of the value of the gospel is to remark on the dismal failures of people who choose not to be governed by it?

It's not that those examples are untrue. Among the reasons for obeying the commandments is that life goes better when you do. But pointing to the faults of others to make us feel righteous is, as Joseph Smith tells us, exactly what the devil would have us do. What other people do or don't do is simply not relevant to the state of our own souls. Certainly we can observe that disobedience tends to lead to a disordered life, but it isn't shaking our heads over the disordered life that makes us virtuous. What makes us virtuous is doing good things in our own lives. The principles of righteousness *are* glorious, but the way we show we know that is by following them ourselves.

The Lord and my erring brothers and sisters can sort out their problems without my input. As I have been instructed, worshipping our God is my business, and I have to do it myself. Whether anybody else does has nothing to do with it, no matter how much I might yearn to point out their failures.

Today, Lord, let me stick to my business. Let me work on my relationship with thee, and let the others take care of their own. I have plenty to keep me busy.

SEPTEMBER 18

But before ye seek for riches, seek ye for the kingdom of God. And after ye have obtained a hope in Christ ye shall obtain riches, if ye seek them; and ye will seek them for the intent to do good—to clothe the naked, and to feed the hungry, and to liberate the captive, and administer relief to the sick and the afflicted.

—JACOB 2:18–19

Rich man, poor man, beggar man, thief—the child counting off her buttons chants the old words—doctor, lawyer, merchant, chief. As long as we live on this earth, there are riches to talk about. Sometimes we see them as a reward for virtue. Sometimes we simply concentrate on wealth for itself: As the cynical mother is said to have told her daughters, "It's as easy to love a rich man as a poor man, and considerably more rewarding."

But Jacob is telling us here that the riches count only for what can be done with them. Once we have the first priority clear—our relationship with God—then, if we still care about riches, we'll know what to do with them (which, as you may notice, has nothing to do with exquisite clothes or magnificent houses or splendid cars). If we have sought first for the kingdom of God, we will *know* that what our riches can buy is comfort and peace of mind for those who need them.

Dear Lord, today let me remember that even if I'm not rich, I

have more than many. I may not be able to do as much as a rich man could, but I could do more than I am doing. There are those who are in genuine need all around me. Lord, show me the way.
Then bless me with the resolve to follow it.

SEPTEMBER 19

For where envying and strife is, there is confusion and every evil work.

But the wisdom that is from above is first pure, then peaceable, gentle, and easy to be intreated, full of mercy and good fruits, without partiality, and without hypocrisy.

And the fruit of righteousness is sown in peace of them that make peace.

—JAMES 3:16–18

In theory, this lovely piece of scripture would describe the way we work together as brothers and sisters up at the meetinghouse, carrying out the business of the ward. In theory.

To be absolutely accurate, most of the time it does work this way. After all, we're all trying. Some of the time it does not work; we don't always succeed.

When I think about this, I remember one major row that flared up about the running of the nursery. I cannot tell you how glad I am that time has dulled my memory of the details. One of the great advantages of getting older, I think, is that at least parts of the things I wish had never happened seem to slip away into oblivion.

Whatever the problem was and whoever was involved, I do recall very clearly standing in the cultural hall with two good sisters, all three of us cross and probably red-faced, and one of them looking the other two of us in the eye and saying very evenly, "This is my stewardship, and you are trying to take it away."

"For where envying and strife is, there is confusion and every evil work."

I don't remember exactly what happened next. I do remember that both of us (I think we were in the Relief Society presidency at the time, and whoever else it was must have been the nursery leader, but I can't be sure) looked at each other and fell silent. Whatever it was all about was subsequently resolved, and the cherubs in the nursery obviously survived whatever we were arguing about.

It seemed terribly important at the time, and here I can't really remember a thing about it now. All that is still fresh is my heart-deep sense that what was happening was wrong, and when I read this scripture, I know why. When we are working together as the Lord would have us work, we are being guided by wisdom that is pure and peaceable, gentle and easy to be intreated. As soon as anger and tension and strife get into the mix, something has gone wrong. I have a testimony that that is true, as strong as any other part of my testimony. "The fruit of righteousness is sown in peace, of them that make peace."

Today, let me remember that. Let me keep that uppermost in mind whenever I work with anybody, but particularly let me keep it in mind when I work with my sisters in the gospel. If I find myself getting hot under the collar, somebody is off the track, and chances are it's me. (At least, I'm the only one I can personally get back on track.)

The "peace of them that make peace": Bless me, Lord, that that may be me.

SEPTEMBER 20

But this I say, He which soweth sparingly shall reap also sparingly; and he which soweth bountifully shall reap also bountifully. Every man according as he purposeth in his heart, so let him give; not grudgingly, or of necessity: for God loveth a cheerful giver.

—2 CORINTHIANS 9:6–7

These words Paul wrote to the Corinthians, who had been very generous in their contributions to help the Christians in Jerusalem, when he was asking them to send more. Corinth was then a wealthy city, the capital of the Roman province; the Church in Jerusalem was in need, with many poor members, and Paul was collecting aid for them from the richer Gentile churches that had been established in the region that is now Greece and Turkey.

Looking over their shoulders, we know this letter was written to us, too. We may not be asked to contribute to the saints in Jerusalem (although we *may*), but there are people elsewhere who need our help. There are people right here at home.

Material things are part of our life on this earth. As spirits within mortal bodies, we have mortal requirements. We have to have food to eat. We need shelter, because our bodies need sleep and are not adapted to survive severe cold or great heat without protection. Ever since Adam and Eve, we need clothing, and the fig leaves won't do. As life down through the centuries has become more complicated, so has the list of what we need.

Ever since the children of Adam and Eve, some of us have had more of these material things we need than others. So will it always be.

Paul is writing here about the spirit with which we share what we have. There are those who measure precisely what the need of someone else is and furnish exactly that, nothing more, although they might be furnishing what is needed out of great personal abundance. That is indeed giving, and such a giver will be rewarded— with similar precise measurement. Others see need and enthusiastically empty their pockets to meet it, even if giving less would have been acceptable. Paul is explaining that the open-handed giver will be rewarded as generously as he or she has given. There, heart has spoken to heart.

Lord, let me give. Let me give cheerfully, bountifully, lovingly. For after all, how else have I received?

SEPTEMBER 21

To every thing there is a season, and a time to every purpose under heaven: a time to be born, and a time to die; a time to plant, and a time to pluck up that which is planted.

—ECCLESIASTES 3:1–2

First frost. I came downstairs this chilly morning to turn on the heat (the furnace groans into action) and to look out at the garden and see what I was dreading to see: tattered dark green drooping leaves. The basil and the impatiens and the petunias are finished. The time for plucking up what has been planted is at hand; summer's over. Leaves are beginning to turn. At the back of the garden the burning bush is gearing up to glow deep red. We're going back to sweaters and coats and (eventually) boots and snow shovels. This year, like those before it and those to follow, is circling around.

On a morning like this one, as I stare out the window and pensively sip hot chocolate, I can almost feel time rushing past me. How can it move so fast? Where did it go? What happened to my babies? The little soft round bodies I remember in my hands are great galumphing near-adults, bumping into me as we pass on the stairs, lengthening out of their jeans, growing out of their shoes. The three-year-old daughter who used to stagger out of her bed first thing in the morning to crawl into mine and curl up against me, instantly asleep again, now has a job and discusses practicalities with her father at the dinner table.

Time. When I think about it, I am almost breathless. This is my one and only shot at mortality. Is it whipping past me too fast for me to get started on what I meant to do while I was here? I can see myself explaining, "Well, that was part of my plan, but I just never got around to it . . ."

The rest of this passage from Ecclesiastes sings through my mind this cold frosty morning. In Ecclesiastes there is a time for everything: Am I using my time well?

First frost. Summer's gone. Let me now consider what I will do with my autumn . . .

SEPTEMBER 22

For since the beginning of the world men have not heard, nor perceived by the ear, neither hath the eye seen, O God, beside thee, what he hath prepared for him that waiteth for him.

—ISAIAH 64:4

No, we can't know. That was one of the conditions of our coming to this world. While we are here, we have to walk by faith. Only a handful have been given the gift of knowledge. For most of us, there are only the ambiguities of belief.

But how magnificent faith can be for us! I may not have seen, I may not have heard, but I still can trust in what the Lord my God has prepared for me, if I can just manage to hang on to the iron rod long enough to find my way home. Home: what a wonderful sound to that word. I know what it means now; I have faith in what it will mean then.

When I read this passage from Isaiah, it is underscored by the words of my Savior, recorded in the gospel of John: "I go to prepare a place for you. And if I go and prepare a place for you, I will come again, and receive you unto myself; that where I am, there ye may be also" (John 14:2–3).

Today, let me make myself ready. I may have years yet before I go home—I hope I have years yet!—but I need to be ready. Today let me, too, prepare.

SEPTEMBER 23

If any man among you seem to be religious, and bridleth not his tongue, but deceiveth his own heart, this man's religion is vain.

Pure religion and undefiled before God and the Father is this, To visit the fatherless and widows in their affliction, and to keep himself unspotted from the world.

—JAMES 1:26–27

In other words, it's not the talking that matters. It's the doing.

I come from a long line of talkers. As I look fondly upon my offspring, it occurs to me that they seem to inherit the same tendency. The problem therefore is how we can all follow the admonition of James to talk less and do more.

It's so easy to talk. It's so comfortable, too—around the dinner table, maybe, when we're finished with eating but still in the middle of a conversation (maybe settling the problems of the world, teasing and joking because we are not encumbered with any responsibility in the matter). Maybe in the living room, sprawled out on the couch with a pile of Sunday papers, talking about what everybody should be doing and what would be virtuous to do. (Not, of course, doing any of it ourselves.)

I think James may be saying that things go wrong when we deceive ourselves into believing that having noble thoughts (and expressing them nobly) somehow substitutes for getting out and doing things that need to be done but may not be so noble or so lofty. Noble thoughts on their own do not express religion. Debating the causes and possible solutions of poverty in the United States is one thing; getting out of your own soft chair and easing the way of somebody who is not particularly important but who needs help is something else. To call the comfortable talk "religious" is vain, to use James's word.

Pure religion lies in doing something about your convictions. Perhaps our family of talkers needs to think about that. Certainly I do. Today, let me plan what I will do and talk less.

Starting now.

SEPTEMBER 24

Each of us, with discipline and effort, has the capacity to control our thoughts and our actions. This is part of the process of developing spiritual, physical, and emotional maturity.

—President Gordon B. Hinckley

It's been one of those weeks at school. One thing after another; little flurries of argument and restlessness. What on earth sets everybody off?

Yesterday it came to a climax (we hope). George, one of our few male students, threw a temper tantrum. George's temper has gotten the better of him before; he got angry with one of his teachers a couple of weeks ago and mouthed off. Fortunately the teacher is level-headed and wasn't buying any of it, and in the end George apologized. I was tutoring him in English at the time, and he told me, shamefaced, that sometimes he just blew up. He couldn't help it, he said. He was just made that way.

Yesterday he blew up at another student. Not only did he shout at her but he waved his fist at her threateningly. Clearly, that was way over the line of acceptable behavior. George was told to leave the classroom, and when he went on shouting all the way down to the front office, he was told he was expelled. Further, he was to leave school property immediately, and if he set foot on it again, we would call the police.

George had been doing well. He had just gotten engaged and really needed a good job, and he was qualifying himself to get one. All that he threw away, and I'm sure he's still mourning, in a way.

I think about George when I read over what President Hinckley said. Each of us arrives with an individual temperament. Each one of us has a handle that Satan can manipulate, if we let him. But each one of us is accountable for what we choose to do. We are not wind-up machines. We have agency. Regardless of how we are made, we choose.

Today let me think about my choices, big and little. Do I sometimes speak too swiftly and become irritated more often than is necessary?

Today, let me work on that. Physical maturity is upon me. Let me make sure I grow up emotionally and spiritually as well.

SEPTEMBER 25

For ye were as sheep going astray; but are now returned unto the Shepherd and Bishop of your souls.

—1 PETER 2:25

Over and over, when teaching about our life here in mortality, Christ returned to the analogy of a shepherd with his flock.

Have you seen sheep on a hillside? Sheep are not the brightest of God's creations. They wander off. They get lost. They get stuck from time to time, and then they bleat piteously. They need direction if they are to get to the places they need to go.

We are a whole lot smarter than sheep, but we don't always act like it. In fact, sometimes when I look back at my spiritual progress, I wonder if even a sheep would have been so slow to learn. I, too, wander off; I, too, get lost for a while. I still get stuck, and when I'm stuck, I'm afraid I wail piteously for rescue. I need my Shepherd to keep me safe. I need my leaders to direct me.

Today, let me be thankful that my Shepherd is there. As long as I am trying to be obedient, he will continue coming to rescue me. He has set his surrogates—my bishop, my home teachers, my visiting teachers—around me to help.

Today, let me concentrate on staying where I belong. Today, let me stick with the flock.

SEPTEMBER 26

I will open rivers in high places, and fountains in the midst of the valleys: I will make the wilderness a pool of water, and the dry land springs of water. I will plant in the wilderness the cedar, the shittah tree, and the myrtle, and the oil tree; I will set in the desert the fir tree, and the pine, and the box tree together: that they may see, and know, and consider, and understand together, that the hand of the Lord hath done this, and the Holy One of Israel hath created it.

—ISAIAH 41:18–20

When Isaiah wrote these words, he was speaking of the children of Israel returning from exile and captivity. When we read them as Latter-day Saints, we think of the western pilgrimage of the Church and the Utah desert being made to blossom as the rose (another quotation from Isaiah).

And of course it can be said to apply to both. It is an extraordinarily vivid picture of the natural world under the hand of the Lord our God, and it reminds us that the Lord can create and has created all these natural wonders for us. The whole world is the creation of his hand: the icy expanses of the polar territories, the jungles that encircle the middle of the globe, and the deserts, the plains, and the forests of the temperate regions. (It just seems, when you read the scriptures, that we've spent most of our time in the deserts and wilderness.)

What an amazing world it is, when you think of it. The sun rises and sets; the clouds move across the blue sky, now covering it, now revealing it; there is rain, and wind, and in places like this in the winter, snow. Crops grow, and what with our rich surpluses, we are now able to furnish food for many from the efforts of only a few working the land. But we all belong to it, at least for now. We are all a part of life on this earth.

Today let me look at this magnificent world and see the hand of the Lord. Tonight let me remember to admire the star-spangled sky. All this, and all that is asked of me is that I love the Lord and walk in obedience to his laws.

It seems such a small return for so much that I have received.

SEPTEMBER 27

O Lord, thou hast searched me, and known me.

Thou knowest my downsitting and mine uprising, thou understandest my thought afar off.

Thou compassest my path and my lying down, and art acquainted with all my ways.

For there is not a word in my tongue, but, lo, O Lord, thou knowest it altogether.

—PSALM 139:1–4

Sweet, cold cider and warm doughnuts. Sitting on a rock watching the stream that, just a little bit upstream, runs through the cider mill. Originally the stream ran the press that crushes the apples; I'm sure that the local power company took over that job years ago.

Coming to a cider mill is one of the nicest fall family traditions around here. The doughnuts are always the same at any of the mills: cake doughnuts, with no special toppings, counted into a paper bag. You stand in line to pay and collect the paper bag—already grease-stained by the time you walk off with it—and a plastic half-gallon or gallon of fresh apple cider with paper cups upside down over the lid. Then you and your family find some place (hopefully not one inhabited by too many bees or wasps, which apparently also make the cider mills a family tradition) where you can sit and eat warm doughnuts, drink cold cider, and feel the unutterable contentment of enjoying autumn pleasures surrounded by people you love.

Do I need to tell the Lord tonight when I thank him for this glorious day how happy I felt, sitting there on that rock? According to this psalm of David, he already knows. He knows my happiness now just as he has known my fear and my despair at darker times. He is with me on the good days and the bad days and the long strings of ordinary days, when not much seems to happen. He is with me when I lie down to sleep and when the alarm wakes me for another day.

If he is always there, perhaps the variable is whether I am realizing it. It's odd to think that the Lord is with me, knowing what is in my mind, when I am doing perfectly ordinary things like vacuuming the living room or picking through tomatoes at the grocery store. Perhaps he is with me the way I am with a two-year-old on a walk, letting the baby wander and explore—so far as it is safe to do so—lagging a step or two behind but keeping watch. Always keeping watch.

Dear Lord, share my happiness today. Thank you for this lovely world, for sweet apple cider and fresh doughnuts. Thank you for these people I love, and please keep my son who is teetering along the edge of the rocks from tumbling into the water, if possible. When I have grayer days, let me remember this one: the gentle autumn sun, and the cider, and the sense of thy presence, keeping watch.

SEPTEMBER 28

And that, knowing the time, that now it is high time to awake out of sleep: for now is our salvation nearer than when we believed.
 The night is far spent, the day is at hand: let us therefore cast off the works of darkness, and let us put on the armour of light.
—ROMANS 13:11–12

It's odd. Ever since Jesus Christ ascended into heaven after his time here, first as a mortal and then as a resurrected being, we believers have been running on two entirely separate mental tracks of measuring time. In our everyday affairs, we carry on as if we expect to have life continue forever just as it is; at the same time, we believe we must be prepared for the Second Coming at any moment, when everything would change.

As Paul makes clear here, the early Christians were doing two-track thinking, too.

When you think about it, how else should we live? For us to stop what we are doing here, to wait with our hands folded for Christ to reappear, would be a foolish waste of time (and wouldn't get us into the celestial kingdom, either). Each of us has only so many years of mortal time; we have to use them, if we are to learn all we were sent here to learn. Every so often, one false prophet or another persuades a group of people that the end is indeed nigh, and they do stop everything to wait—and how foolish they must feel, when the deadline comes and goes and the sun goes on rising and setting and the trains run and the planes land and the ordinary course of life rolls on.

At the same time, we have to be prepared for Christ's coming. Our preparations make sense if the recognition that the way we prepare ourselves is to be living the best life of which we're capable, and if we're doing that, it doesn't greatly matter if Christ comes tomorrow or if we live a long life and have our reunion with him only when we pass to the other side. Either way we are living as he would have us live.

Bless me today that I may conduct my life in such a way that if Christ comes this afternoon, I will be ready, and if the ordinary night comes, followed by tomorrow, I will be ready for that, too. Help me to be obedient, and charitable, and kind, and slow to anger; help me to walk in the ways that will bring me closer to thee, on either side of the veil.

Bless me to have faith and be faithful—today, tomorrow, and for as long as I have.

SEPTEMBER 29

Unchecked selfishness . . . stubbornly blocks the way for developing all of the divine qualities: love, mercy, patience, long-suffering, kindness, graciousness, goodness, and gentleness. Any tender sprouts from these virtues are sheared off by sharp selfishness. Contrariwise, brothers and sisters, I cannot think of a single gospel covenant the keeping of which does not shear off selfishness from us!
—ELDER NEAL A. MAXWELL

We are born into this world selfish. I remember my babies with unqualified love, but I can't say that one of them gave a thought to my convenience when they were hungry. When they were hungry, they screamed. It didn't matter if I was sleeping, exhausted; it didn't matter if I was hurrying to finish up the Sunday School lesson I had to give the next day. It didn't matter if I had a wracking headache. They were hungry. They wanted to eat and they wanted to eat right that minute. They screamed.

I am glad to report they are older now and have learned a moderate degree of unselfishness. They no longer scream when they are hungry. (They *have* been known to open the refrigerator door and report sadly, "There's nothing in this house to eat," when as a matter of observable fact there is no room to put anything more on any of the shelves.) We are working on more advanced principles now, such as picking up after yourself, even if it's not convenient, so that somebody else doesn't have to, and refraining from parking in the middle of the driveway so nobody else can get by, even if the middle of the driveway is closest to the door. Eventually I hope to get them to the virtuoso level of putting the portable phone back where it belongs instead of leaving it on your bed because that's where you were talking on it, and even doing a sibling's chores because you know the sibling is working/sleeping/feeling particularly dented right at the present from one of life's setbacks.

Have I outgrown childish selfishness entirely myself? There are, of course, large sins of selfishness, but as with my children, it's the small sins that keep getting in my way: little things, like sliding in ahead of the other car in traffic because I'm in a hurry (isn't anyone else?), or grabbing the last box of cutlery that's on sale, even though I know another woman was hunting along the counter for it.

Is that what I want to be like, in this life or any other? Wouldn't I rather live a life described by those lovely words *love*, and *mercy*, and *kindness*, and *graciousness*?

Today, let me try to live an entirely unselfish day. Let me turn my thoughts outward, instead of concentrating on myself. Let me see if, with practice, I will think of others first. Let me express love in action, as I have been taught to do—and as I am trying to teach my children.

Let me learn. Let me be more like thee.

SEPTEMBER 30

And I soon go to the place of my rest, which is with my Redeemer; for I know that in him I shall rest. And I rejoice in the day when my mortal shall put on immortality, and shall stand before him; then shall I see his face with pleasure, and he will say unto me: Come unto me, ye blessed, there is a place prepared for you in the mansions of my Father.

—ENOS 1:27

The month has wound down. The days are cooler, and the nights are cold now: We need the furnace on in the mornings. The year moves steadily along. I read this lovely passage from the short book of Enos and reflect that the one guarantee about our time here in mortality is that we move past it.

Will I be capable of this joyful anticipation when my time draws near? Will I *know* that my time to move on is approaching, or will it come suddenly? Will I be ready to see the face of my Savior? Today, as it should be, is full of ordinary things. Somewhere in the back hall closet is my lightweight black jacket; it's time to find it. The leaves need to be cleared out of the gutters, even if more of them will be falling. I have to order the Christmas wrapping papers through the school today, if I'm going to do it. Ordinary things: I lead an ordinary life.

Today, though, let me remember that this ordinary, mortal life is only part of my real life. Let me lift my eyes from today, if only for a minute or two, to see the longer, grander span in which I have a part. Today, as I get my house and my wardrobe ready for changes ahead, let me get my soul ready, too.

Those changes may not come this year, but they will come. As with Enos, they will come.

OCTOBER

For thou, Lord, art good, and ready to forgive; and plenteous in mercy unto all them that call upon thee.

—Psalm 86:5

OCTOBER 1

Wherefore, thou shalt do all that thou doest in the name of the Son, and thou shalt repent and call upon God in the name of the Son forevermore.

—MOSES 5:8

This, I suppose, describes our essential obligations as Christians about as concisely as is possible.

If I remember right (which I may not), I first heard the word *repentance* in Primary or Sunday School, back in those days when Primary was held in the middle of the week. I already knew that if you had done something wrong, you could say you were sorry and that made things better. But in the class, I was told that if you truly repented, not only were things made better, but the bad thing you'd done wouldn't count at all.

That struck me as absolutely remarkable at the time. It still does.

Like most adults of reasonably mature years, I have had occasion to repent over the years for several things. The hardest times have been when no restitution was possible, and the plain fact is that sometimes it isn't. When you have wronged somebody, it is much easier to put it behind you when you can go to him or her and explain what happened and how sorry you are about it, and what you can, and will, do to make it up. But life moves on relentlessly, and sometimes the person is no longer there or nothing can be done to repair the damage you did. That's hard. That's when I find it hard to really believe that I am forgiven, that I can move forward from my mistake, made wiser by the experience but no longer encumbered by it.

That's when, I suspect, I need to call upon God, in the name of the Son, for guidance. Maybe I haven't really gone through the whole process of repentance. Maybe I am still carrying a bit of my transgression around with me. Is it pride? Have I really admitted exactly what it was that I did that was wrong, or am I still justifying it a little in my heart of hearts? If so, I need to face the Lord and realize where I am.

But maybe that's not the problem. Maybe it's just a plain and simple lack of faith—which, in a way, could be a matter of pride, too. Is whatever I did that dreadful? Do I really doubt that my

Heavenly Father is able to forgive me for whatever it is? Do I really doubt his promise, repeated over and over, that he will?

When I put it that way, there's only one possible answer. I'd better get on with forgiving myself. I have lots of other things to do during this brief spin at mortality; I need to get around to them.

OCTOBER 2

Come now, and let us reason together, saith the Lord: though your sins be as scarlet, they shall be as white as snow; though they be red like crimson, they shall be as wool.

—ISAIAH 1:18

One of the things I love about the scriptures is the way they all fit together: you can jump from the Pearl of Great Price to the Old Testament and continue the same discussion.

The Lord is scolding Israel for her iniquities and pointing out her vulnerabilities and the degradation she suffered from her neighbors (I particularly like verse 7, in which Israel is described as a lodge—that is, like a hut for an isolated watchman—in a garden of cucumbers.) The sacrifices the Jews are making are for form only and are therefore valueless; the Lord says the vain oblations and incense are a trouble unto him. "I am weary to bear them."

Make yourself clean, the Lord says. Stop trivializing my ceremonies, and bend your resources to what matters. Put away the evil, and learn to do well. Relieve the oppressed; take care of those in need.

And then comes this wonderful verse. No matter how evil or rebellious the children of Israel may have been, they can be made clean. "Let us reason together." The love and the promise is not only for Israel; it's for us as well. Whatever we have done, if we will truly and wholeheartedly put it behind us, if we will come as penitent children to our Father and repent in the fullest, truest sense of the word, it can be wiped away.

That's the part that's hard to believe. That's what's true.

Today, let me remember that. Today, let me renew my faith.

OCTOBER 3

Then they shall confess their sin which they have done: and he shall recompense his trespass with the principal thereof, and add unto it the fifth part thereof, and give it unto him against whom he hath trespassed.

—NUMBERS 5:7

As it was with most aspects of community life, the Mosaic law was very precise about what was to be done in the way of restitution for sins. You were to give back what had been wrongfully taken and add to it a fifth part.

Unfortunately, all restitution can't be quite so neatly calculated. Example: One of my daughters borrowed another daughter's sweater. Whether this was with or without permission is one of several disputed points about the incident. In any case, it is beyond argument that the sweater was (a) worn in the rain, (b) left crumpled in a pile, and (c) has an infinitesimal snag under the left arm, whether or not as a direct result of (a) and (b). Now what on earth do we do about restitution for that? What we need is a Solomon around here, and I'm afraid I'm not up to that.

Some adjudication, however, is clearly necessary. What I need to remember (and hope to teach my girls, if they'll listen) is that the spirit of restitution is important. Restitution, in my definition now, should mean putting things back, plus a little. Maybe taking the sweater to the cleaners and bringing it back spotless, repaired, and ready to wear would do. Maybe giving the sweater to Mom to fix (now, *that* has a familiar sound to it) and then uncomplainingly taking over some household chore normally assigned to the offended one for a couple of days, without pointing out loudly what you're doing and demanding credit. Maybe restoring the sweater in good condition one way or the other and in addition freely offering up for loan some wardrobe item that the offended one has been coveting (okay, so she shouldn't covet, but nobody's perfect, at least around here).

The important thing is that something should be done, and the something should be a bit more than bringing things back to the original condition. Because Christ fulfilled the Mosaic law, we aren't required to observe the whole of it, but it seems to me this provision still makes very good sense indeed. If so, let me apply it to my own transgressions.

Now, there's the test.

OCTOBER 4

For behold, this life is the time for men to prepare to meet God; yea, behold the day of this life is the day for men to perform their labors.

—ALMA 34:32

Part of preparing to meet God—in fact, the most important part of our labors—is to organize our lives in obedience to his commandments, and to review where we have been disobedient and sinful, and to repent of that.

A lot of us get uncomfortable when we hear the words *sins* and *sinners.* "What do you mean, *sins?*" we want to say—or at least I do. I lead a reasonably orderly life. If Isaiah is talking about sins being as scarlet, I want to argue defensively that mine are pale pink, at worst.

Well, maybe yes, maybe no. Sins of commission? Pink is probably about it. I don't go around threatening people. I have never murdered anything bigger than a slug. (I am prepared to agree that all living creatures have a purpose, but the purpose of slugs escapes me.) I don't steal. I am even very good about giving back excess change. I am reasonably truthful, except in social situations where the truth would be distinctly unwelcome or when I tell telemarketers that my husband (sitting peacefully at the kitchen counter reading the newspaper) is not at home.

Sins of omission? Oops. The color just darkened considerably. I don't even want to compile that list. How many things should I be doing that I am not? As Amulek points out in this scripture, behold, this life is the time. Can I see myself explaining to the Lord at the Last Judgment that I would have done all those things but I had the laundry to finish or I just wanted to see the end of that program? Not really.

How am I doing on compassionate service? Do I help when I'm asked but take little initiative on figuring out what's necessary all by myself?

How's genealogy coming? My father has been dead four years; the work has been completed on his list of names. Where's mine?

Welfare assignments? Do I show up when it's convenient to do so, or do I rearrange other obligations to make it possible any time I'm needed?

Do I magnify my calling in the truest sense, or do I do what most obviously has to be done? Do I look for ways to serve, or am I quietly grateful that no more is required?

Oh, my omission list could go on and on. I'm afraid I'm way past crimson when it comes to colors. Maybe today I should feel less virtuous about what I don't do wrong and get going on what I should do right. After all, this life is my time.

OCTOBER 5

Confess your faults one to another, and pray one for another, that ye may be healed. The effectual fervent prayer of a righteous man availeth much.

—JAMES 5:16

Last night my sister and I were on the phone, gloomily comparing notes on where we felt we were individually falling short. This is the sort of thing you can do with a sister: For one thing, she's more likely to know what you're talking about than a friend would be, or maybe it's that she's more prepared to admit she knows what you're talking about.

We've raised our families side by side, and now, as our children get older, we are both increasingly aware of all the things we wish we had done, the mistakes we can see with the nice clear 20/20 vision of hindsight. I was around when she was making her mistakes (most of which seemed okay to me, too, at the time); she was around when I was making mine. Most were made with perfectly good intentions; a few, because (in retrospect, I see) we got distracted or lazy.

I thought of that conversation when I read these words of James. It did help to talk to somebody who shares my values, both my family values and my values as a Latter-day Saint. Is that what James meant when he said "one another"? That those of us who belong to our community of belief are those who understand us, and our failures, best?

Today, I will pray for us, that we may be able to discern what can still be changed, and repent and forgive ourselves for what cannot. I don't know that I'm as righteous as James suggests I should be for my prayers to "avail much," but we do love each other. Please, Lord, bless us that our sore spots may be healed.

And help both of us to be as perfect as we mean to be tomorrow.

OCTOBER 6

Then came Peter to him, and said, Lord, how oft shall my brother sin against me, and I forgive him? till seven times? Jesus saith unto him, I say not unto thee, Until seven times: but, Until seventy times seven.

—MATTHEW 18:21–22

One of the main problems with this forgiveness business is that it isn't only the Lord, with infinite wisdom and mercy, who has to do the forgiving. All too often it may be the Lord whose commandments were disregarded, but it's our toes that got stepped on, and we who are not necessarily right up there on either wisdom or mercy have to decide what we're going to do about it.

(One of the other problems is that we are inclined to operate on somewhat different scales of offensiveness depending on whether we need to be forgiven or to forgive.)

Peter must have been a remarkable man. He was so blunt, so down to earth. What Peter is asking for here is a rule, a nice convenient rule to go by. He probably thought what he was proposing was very generous. After all, to forgive somebody seven times in a row—how many of us, left to ourselves, would forgive somebody for doing the same stupid or nasty thing seven times in a row?

The response was beyond anything he could have imagined. Seven times? Try 490—and I don't think Jesus was suggesting we keep a tally. Seventy times seven, for all practical purposes, means forever. We are to forgive, and forgive, and forgive, and forgive, and go on forgiving after that.

Dear Lord, help me to put aside exasperation and indignation and hurt when I am the injured party. Let me forgive as I would be forgiven. I have certainly made some stupid or thoughtless mistakes more than seven times in the past, and I will probably continue to do so. Even so, I hope to be forgiven for them.

And when it isn't me, Lord, who has given the offense, please remind me of 490 times. Bless me that I won't get too cross to remember.

OCTOBER 7

If you resent someone for something he has done—or failed to do—
forget it.

Too often the things we carry are petty, even stupid. If you are
still upset after all these years because Aunt Clara didn't come to
your wedding reception, why don't you grow up and forget it?

If you brood constantly over a loss or a past mistake, look
ahead—settle it.

We call that forgiveness. Forgiveness is powerful spiritual medi-
cine. To extend forgiveness, that soothing balm, to those who have
offended you is to heal. And, more difficult yet, when the need is
there, forgive yourself!

—Elder Boyd K. Packer

It would be wonderful if we could all live on the heights of nobility and graciousness. Maybe some do; most of us are still learning.
We are still scrabbling around on the slopes. One of the characteristics of life on the slopes is that we can get all worked up about
really trivial problems.

I don't know why it is that we sometimes seem more capable of
handling the major crises than the little stuff. Let an area be ravaged
by a major catastrophe—raging floods, maybe, or a series of torna-
does, or a good healthy hurricane—and people cope magnificently.
All the latent generosity and compassion comes bubbling to the
surface. But let somebody push in ahead in a grocery checkout line,
and everybody gets red-faced and indignant and makes nasty
remarks.

Does the same thing happen in our domestic lives? I suspect so.
Elder Packer mentions the problem of Aunt Clara and the wedding
reception: How many members of families have been estranged,
sometimes permanently, over who was or was not invited, or who
was seated with whom? Meanwhile, exactly the same family may
cope with the arrival of an illegitimate baby with generosity and
aplomb.

Forgiving somebody for something major has a certain drama to
it. We can feel noble. We can feel our souls expand and grow with
the effort. There is penitence. There is reconciliation. To forgive
somebody for some piddling little problem lacks all of that, and,
hardest of all, when we forgive, we have to give up fingering our

grievance. We can't go on muttering, "How could she?" in the privacy of our minds.

If we can guess what are the most important jobs in mortality by observing which jobs we are given the most practice at doing, it would seem that forgiving trivialities has to be well up on the list. Basically, what is asked of us is simple. As Elder Packer put it, briskly and sensibly, sometimes our job is to forget it. "Some frustrations we must endure without really solving the problem," he observed. "Things we cannot solve, we must survive."

Let me not sweat the small stuff. Let me keep some sense of proportion in my heart. If it is important and I am offended, forgive. If it isn't important, forget.

That should take care of just about everything.

OCTOBER 8

Yea, even he commanded them that they should preach nothing save it were repentance and faith on the Lord, who had redeemed his people. And he commanded them that there should be no contention one with another, but that they should look forward with one eye, having one faith and one baptism, having their hearts knit together in unity and in love one towards another.

—MOSIAH 18:20–21

This is Alma, talking to the priests who had been among those baptized in the waters of Mormon, but it makes me think of making a quilt in Relief Society.

One particularly beloved sister was moving away. This seems to happen a lot in our neck of the woods (although some of us stick around forever), but this sister was one of those who had done so many things for other people that everybody wanted to do something back. It being Relief Society, the idea of making a quilt came up almost immediately.

I have to say it was a beautiful quilt. But what I remember best is the wonderful, warm, work session when we assembled it. (Where she was while we were working on it is one of those details that is temporarily inaccessible in the muddle of my memory.) These words of Alma exactly describe the women around the quilting frame: "having their hearts knit together in unity and in love one towards another." We shared so much. We shared one faith and one baptism, as Alma says, and we also shared our fondness for her. We laughed and we remembered funny things that had happened and we talked about quilting and child-rearing and marriage maintenance and gospel principles—and those are just the topics I remember—and we ate good food. I do remember there was good food.

Alma told the new priests they should preach nothing but repentance and faith on the Lord. Repentance and faith in our Redeemer: the most fundamental principles of the gospel. What a wealth of warmth and love grows out of them!

Today let me reread Alma's words and count all the ways that wealth has added to my life.

OCTOBER 9

But they and our fathers dealt proudly, and hardened their necks, and harkened not to thy commandments. And refused to obey, neither were mindful of thy wonders that thou didst among them; but hardened their necks, and in their rebellion appointed a captain to return to their bondage: but thou art a God ready to pardon, gracious and merciful, slow to anger, and of great kindness, and forsookest them not.

—NEHEMIAH 9:16–17

A couple of verses from the book of Nehemiah, which is a lovely account of an amazing man who undertook to rebuild the walls and gates of Jerusalem after the Persian king Cyrus allowed some of the Jews to return from exile. (One whole chapter is a painstaking record for history of exactly who worked on which sections of the wall and rebuilt which gates.)

These particular verses are part of the history of God's dealings with his people that the Levite priests recited at that time to the crowd of returned children of Israel to remind them of their heritage and of God's faithfulness to his people, even when (as it points out here) the people were not always faithful to him and his commandments.

Today let me treasure this description of God—"ready to pardon, gracious and merciful, slow to anger," and so on. How true all of that was of his relationship with the children of Israel; how true, I'm grateful to say, it has been of his relationship with me.

Today let me repent of my obstreperousness. I don't mean to be obstreperous. Let me repent of being rebellious—for I have been—and impatient, and sometimes wobbly in my faith. In spite of it all, I have been given time to learn to correct myself, and to grow.

Today let me be grateful for the time. Today let me use it.

OCTOBER 10

Judge not, and ye shall not be judged: condemn not, and ye shall not be condemned: forgive, and ye shall be forgiven.

Give, and it shall be given unto you; good measure, pressed down, and shaken together, and running over, shall men give into your bosom. For with the same measure that ye mete withal it shall be measured to you again.

—LUKE 6:37–38

Accident on the freeway on the way to work this morning: three or four cars askew in the roadway (it's curious how quickly your eye picks up from a distance that there's something odd going on ahead, and without thinking you find your foot has moved over to the brake . . .).

It's a four-lane freeway, but only one lane was available for us to get by. This scripture was singing in my head as I observed with interest the way things were working out. There seemed to be, broadly speaking, two ways of dealing with the situation. One was for drivers to accept that this was a general calamity (we all need to get to work on time, after all) and decide therefore that working cooperatively with all the other cars on the road would get everybody through fastest; the other was to think to oneself, I am important, I am not going to be late, and by golly I am going to be the car that gets through even if nobody else does.

Fortunately, most of the drivers were apparently of the cooperative bent. But a couple were not. One was in a bright red midsize sedan, which was wielded as an offensive weapon. What I thought was interesting was the reaction of the other drivers. It was as if a collective resolution were formed: This guy is not going to get into our lane unless he gets in line. He had woven his way through traffic—leaving all the responsibility for avoiding fender benders to the other drivers—until he got to the merging point.

The other drivers in the single passable lane never gave him the satisfaction of eye contact. They simply bunched together, bumper virtually touching bumper, so that no opening was available. None at all. He had given no quarter, and he wasn't going to get any. As we crept past (no, I didn't look at him either), I found myself thinking, "For with the same measure that ye mete withal it shall be measured to you again."

That's the way it is and always has been. But let me err, rather, on the generous side. Let me give as I would be given to, good measure, pressed down and shaken together and running over.

Looking at it that way, I probably should have let him in. There's also that part about judging not. Do you suppose he's still there?

OCTOBER 11

He that covereth his sins shall not prosper: but whoso confesseth and forsaketh them shall have mercy.

—PROVERBS 28:13

This is basic common sense. After all, the first step in any repentance has to be admitting that you have done something wrong. Unfortunately, the first reaction of natural man (at least as evidenced by children I have known well) is to deny all knowledge of the episode or even that the episode happened.

"What cookies?" says the six-year-old malefactor, smelling heavily of vanilla-flavored cookie dough and with a streak of melted chocolate chip across the chin. "Did you make cookies?"

The rest of the scenario usually plays out with a brisk discussion of the virtues of telling the truth, with the child left to grapple with the (to the child) illogical conclusion that if you do something bad and admit it, you are punished much less severely than if you do something bad and nobody knows for sure it really was you—or so the child would like to believe.

What makes much of the difference, it seems to me (looking at it now with the perspective of the classroom teacher), is that once you admit you're at fault, you are in a mode where learning can take place. As long as you're denying, you're not learning anything. You're just hiding. But as soon as you can say, "Yes, I did that" and *see* that it was wrong, then you can set about learning another way to do it.

Sometimes a whole class of my students will fail a test

ignominiously. If that happens, I figure we didn't learn it right. Therefore, we go over the test in excruciating detail, point by point—really, teaching the material all over again—and then we throw out the scores. No point in beating people over the head with something that they've now mastered. Sometimes I give the same test again immediately, to check to see if they were paying attention; sometimes not.

It strikes me that repentance works very much the same way. Doing something wrong is like failing a test. Repentance is the process of going over what went wrong very carefully, figuring out what your mistake was, fixing it (if it's fixable), and then moving past it. The black mark is erased. You've learned that lesson, and you don't need to carry the bad grade any longer. Sometimes the Lord gives us the same test again, just to check; sometimes, I guess, he can tell we got it.

But admitting the mistake has to come first. Before that, no learning is possible. Even the kids figure that out.

OCTOBER 12

For none of these iniquities come of the Lord; for he doeth that which is good among the children of men; and he doeth nothing save it be plain unto the children of men; and he inviteth them all to come unto him and partake of his goodness; and he denieth none that come unto him, black and white, bond and free, male and female; and he remembereth the heathen; and all are alike unto God, both Jew and Gentile.

—2 NEPHI 26:33

We are all God's children, whoever we might be. We all make mistakes and act thoughtlessly, or ungenerously, or meanly, and we all need to repent and be forgiven if we hope to return home. We could not tolerate the glory of God's presence if there were even a whisker of thoughtlessness or lack of generosity or meanness in us. There is no place for any of those things in the kingdom of heaven.

What gender we might be, or what color, or what social station has absolutely nothing to do with it. We have to be cleansed of all sin before we can return to our Father, whoever we are. That's all there is to it. The rich man in his mansion will have to do exactly the same work of repentance as the poor man who washes the rich man's splendid car; maybe more, if he happens to be a nasty rich man, or if the poor man is especially virtuous.

Today let me get on with my job of cleansing my soul. Eventually I might have to search carefully to make sure all the crevices are scrubbed out, but for right now, there are plenty of misdemeanors in plain sight that need dealing with. I don't need to worry about what anybody else is coping with or who they might be. All that is necessary for me to work on with the Lord is me.

OCTOBER 13

Many of us today are shackled by the restrictive chains of poor habits. We are bound by inferior self-images created by misconduct and indifference. We are chained by an unwillingness to change for the better. Is it any wonder, in our day as it was in Nephi's, that God's pleas are "awake," "listen," "procrastinate no longer," "believe me," "come back," and "seek the straight course"?

—ELDER MARVIN J. ASHTON

Procrastinating is never a really good idea, but when you're talking about repentance, it's downright dangerous.

The danger is not necessarily that planning on deathbed repentance assumes that (a) you'll have a deathbed, as opposed to getting run down by a bus, or (b) that you'll recognize it's your deathbed and be in sound enough mind to remember of what you should be repenting, although both those problems certainly come into it. It seems to me that procrastinating about repenting of something involves a conscious recognition that whatever you're doing is wrong, and a conscious decision to go on doing it, knowingly, until you get around to stopping. It seems to me that that knowledge would compound the "crime," whatever it might be. Doing something wrong is bad enough. Doing something wrong that you fully know is wrong, even if you intend to stop doing it at some future time, has to be worse.

Repentance isn't easy. It's not going to be any easier tomorrow. Admitting I did wrong and making restitution when it's possible is hard. Deciding never to do whatever it is again can be even harder. It involves the work of making the same decision over and over again, every time I'm tempted to go back and do things the old way.

The hidden gift I remember only when I'm into the process is that the decision gets easier and easier each time I make it. And the tranquillity of real peace of mind . . .

That's what repentance is for. You can grow past error into the light. It isn't just for major sins, either. It's for the silly little weaknesses as well. Lord, bless me today that I may continue to work on those now, instead of waiting until tomorrow. Bless me with discernment, with humility, and above all, with perseverance. Let me keep at it, Lord, until the job is done.

OCTOBER 14

Create in me a clean heart, O God; and renew a right spirit within me. Cast me not away from thy presence; and take not thy holy spirit from me. Restore unto me the joy of thy salvation; and uphold me with thy free spirit.

—PSALM 51:10–12

What a wonderful autumn morning. The world has been splashed with a magnificent paintbrush: Trees and bushes are vivid yellow, gold, scarlet, and purple. Even the maple over the driveway is earning its keep with the beauty of brilliant yellow leaves against a bright blue sky. Some of the maples are an almost fluorescent shade of orangey-pinky-red. Unfortunately, the splendor doesn't last. The leaves are already falling. When the dog and I take a brisk walk in the morning, our feet swish through drifts of leaves blown across the sidewalks.

Today my mind is at peace, and my walk was pure pleasure, but there have been days when I was upset or sick at heart, and all the beauty in the world barely made any impression. Is that what David meant in this psalm when he sang of restoring "the joy of salvation"? That when our hearts are at peace with the Lord, the joy of life is open to us?

In this psalm, if the heading is historically accurate—and the psalm certainly seems to fit the situation—David pleads for the Lord's forgiveness after he had gone in to Bathsheba. The "joy of salvation" must have felt very far away.

Today, Lord, let me treasure my "joy of salvation" and my joy of this world. Today both are very precious to me.

OCTOBER 15

I have sent also unto you all my servants the prophets, rising up early and sending them, saying, Return ye now every man from his evil way, and amend your doings, and go not after other gods to serve them, and ye shall dwell in the land which I have given to you and to your fathers: but ye have not inclined your ear, nor hearkened unto me.

—JEREMIAH 35:15

The stubborn children of Israel: You certainly can never say that they weren't warned. Over and over again (as the Lord points out here) the prophets told them to repent and cease to worship other gods, and over and over again the children of Israel did what apparently seemed expedient to them at the time. It wasn't until after the exile, when they returned to Jerusalem—no longer possessors of their own country, true, but at least allowed to return—that they finally put aside the centuries-long temptation to worship visible gods. They then went to worshipping the law, which, as Jesus tried to teach them, wasn't the point either.

The children of Israel were punished well and truly for their iniquities. I can read about it and think piously, "Yes, they were idolatrous and disobedient." But what about me? I don't think of myself as worshipping other gods, but there's more to obedience than that. What about Sabbath observance? That's one of the oldest covenants that the Lord has made with his people, and do I remain true to it in spirit and letter? What about honesty? If I'm congratulating myself on not telling lies, can I truthfully claim I have never made a false excuse? Or, to look at the negative side, what about the acts of charity that went undone because I was too self-absorbed to notice they needed doing?

For the children of Israel, it's too late. They never did repent and amend their ways, and they have suffered a long and miserable history. So what about me? Am I going to learn anything from their example?

Today, let me get on with learning. Today, let me incline my ear to the Lord, and hearken to what has been said.

OCTOBER 16

Therefore I will judge you, O house of Israel, every one according to his ways, saith the Lord God. Repent, and turn yourselves from all your transgressions; so iniquity shall not be your ruin.

—EZEKIEL 18:30

T he fathers have eaten sour grapes, and the children's teeth are set on edge" (Ezekiel 18:2). That was the proverb by which the Jews of Ezekiel's time explained their misfortunes. In other words, it's not our fault. Our fathers and our fathers' fathers were unrighteous, and we are being punished for it. The Lord is telling them here that their excuse doesn't work. The fathers will be punished for their sins, and the sons for their own—"every one according to his ways."

Are we so different? Haven't we developed whole new vocabularies to account for misfortune and misbehavior? Sometimes you get the impression that nobody is responsible for anything; everybody has been victimized in one way or another by something. We are all victims of discrimination. Either we're women or minorities and oppressed because we are not white men, or we're white men and oppressed because we don't get the benefits of being a woman or in a minority. Everybody's got something to complain about, some reason beyond our own responsibility for anything that goes wrong.

This makes me think. Have I taught my children to stand up (when it's warranted) and say, "It's my fault. I was wrong"? Is that something I do myself?

Today let me think about that. This scripture tells me that the Lord is ready—more than that, *eager*—to forgive me if I will turn away from transgression (and I'm sure he means little problems as well as major sins). The Lord doesn't want iniquity to be my ruin. As he asks earlier in this chapter, "Have I any pleasure at all that the wicked should die? saith the Lord God; and not that he should return from his ways, and live?" (Ezekiel 18:23).

Today let me devote some thought to what I should take responsibility for (maybe teaching my children to do without excuses would be a good start) and return from my ways, if I'm not doing all I should. Let me repent, and live closer to the Lord. You know what? Right now is not a bad time to begin.

OCTOBER 17

*In those days came John the Baptist, preaching in the wilderness of
Judæa, and saying, Repent ye: for the kingdom of heaven is at
hand.*

—MATTHEW 3:1–2

With the coming of John the Baptist, the central drama of repentance and forgiveness for the salvation of our souls moves to center stage.

As Matthew points out in the next verses, John's coming had been prophesied by Isaiah: "the voice of him that crieth in the wilderness, Prepare ye the way of the Lord" (Isaiah 40:3). In Malachi, the Lord says, "I will send my messenger, and he shall prepare the way before me." All the foreordained pieces were falling into place.

Both John the Baptist and Jesus—cousins, John the elder of the two by only six months—spent most of their youth and early adulthood in obscurity. John grew up in the desert, where he began his public ministry. His central teaching was that the Israelites must turn from hollow hypocrisy to genuine righteousness, for the day of the Messiah was at hand. "Repent ye" was his message, delivered over and over again.

We have not been promised a John the Baptist to warn us of Christ's second coming. Still, his message will do for any of us, at any time. We need to be ready—to prepare to meet him in heaven, if we are to live out our life span here on the earth before his coming, or to prepare for the great and terrible day of his arrival on earth if that should fall within our time.

Am I ready? I don't think so. Do I need to change, to repent? I'd better get on with it. After all, I have been warned.

OCTOBER 18

I indeed baptize you with water unto repentance: but he that cometh after me is mightier than I, whose shoes I am not worthy to bear: he shall baptize you with the Holy Ghost, and with fire.

—MATTHEW 3:11

The words of John the Baptist, one of the most extraordinary of men. He was a mighty prophet, the outstanding bearer of the Aaronic priesthood in all history. He was the last prophet under the Law of Moses. And yet, as reported in all four gospels, he had the humility and generosity of heart to put aside all the fame and honor his disciples would have offered him, without a shred of jealousy, on the grounds that one mightier than he was coming. When Jesus came, John immediately recognized his divinity and told his disciples, "Behold the Lamb of God!"—and those disciples, as John obviously intended, left him to follow Jesus instead.

How many of us would have the greatness of spirit to play that role so magnificently? How often do we see men and women desperately hanging on to the limelight? We see them trying to elbow their successors out of the way, even for just a minute, so that they can glow in the spotlight a little longer.

John the Baptist was a man of such faith that he never questioned his mission. He lived and he died as a servant of his Father in Heaven. When he had baptized the Messiah, the Son of God, his work in that dispensation was complete.

John the Baptist preached repentance. Ironic, isn't it? Few men have had so little need of it.

OCTOBER 19

For I will declare mine iniquity; I will be sorry for my sin.

—PSALM 38:18

There was a long, incoherent message on the voice mail at school when we came in this morning. Jenna has clearly fallen off the wagon again.

As Latter-day Saints, surrounded in large part by other Latter-day Saints, I think we often fail to fully understand the toll that alcohol takes on the lives of so many children of our Heavenly

Father. When I step out of that circle, I am always astounded at how many of my nonmember friends have parents, husbands, wives, brothers, sisters enduring all the disorder that uncontrolled alcoholism can bring into an otherwise normal life. Here at school, the problem is not always second hand. Take Jenna, for example.

Jenna is a bright girl. Pretty, too, although she was obviously prettier before—her skin, although she's just in her twenties, is coarsened, the way it gets when you've been drinking heavily for years. When she's sober, she's quick and responsive and fun to be around. She has lots of friends. When she's been drinking, everything is slowed down. I've never seen her obviously inebriated, just moving a little more deliberately and staring at you thoughtfully while she visibly works through taking in what you just said. There's the smell, of course: the thick, sweet smell.

She's been absent a lot. At the end of last term I called her at home to ask her what in the world she was doing and to urge her to get back in to class so that she could get a passing grade. I don't know if she had been drinking or not. She cried, but that might just have been desperation. I suspect she felt her life was spinning out of her control, and so it is.

She told me she knew she was making a mess of things, and she felt terrible about it. She thanked me for worrying about her and said that helped. She said she was almost too embarrassed to come to school again, but if I wanted her to come, she wouldn't let me down. She'd be there.

"For I will declare my iniquity; I will be sorry for my sin."

She came to take the final. She did better than I expected, which didn't really surprise me. She's a bright girl. She hasn't been here yet in the new term, and today there was the tearful message on the voice mail. She's having problems and she needs to talk to me, or the director, or both of us.

Jenna has taken two steps of repentance. She can manage confession, and she is drowning in contrition. What's missing is an ability to forsake her transgression, and walk uprightly—and soberly—before her God.

I have prayed for Jenna before, and I'll do it again.

Please let her find some strength. And let me learn from her what a terrible adversary alcohol can be. No wonder they called it Demon Rum.

"A Word of Wisdom, for the benefit of the council of high priests, assembled in Kirtland, and the church, and also the saints in Zion . . ." (D&C 89:1).

OCTOBER 20

Yea, come unto Christ, and be perfected in him, and deny your-
selves of all ungodliness; and if ye shall deny yourselves of all
ungodliness, and love God with all your might, mind and strength,
then is his grace sufficient for you, that by his grace ye may be per-
fect in Christ; and if by the grace of God ye are perfect in Christ,
ye can in nowise deny the power of God.

—MORONI 10:32

W hat makes repentance work is that each step reinforces the
next. I find that helpful to remember when I am feeling
overwhelmed by the job of making amends for something I have
done wrong or (more often) trying to start to do something that I
know I should have been doing all along but haven't yet begun.

That is exactly what Moroni is promising the Lamanites here
(and goodness knows that they stood in need of repentance at the
time)—and in a sense is speaking over their shoulder and telling us
as well. If you can deny yourself all ungodliness, which basically
means to stop doing what is wrong or start doing what is right, and
love God with everything that's in you, then you will be blessed
with sufficient grace to be perfected in Christ, which means you will
be given the strength to persevere with what you've started. That's
usually all we need; we can begin on our own, but keeping at it
is the hard part. If we love God singlemindedly, we will be able to
do it.

Not only that but we will be given this additional blessing: If we
thus prove to ourselves that we can become perfected in Christ by
the grace of God, we have therefore proved to ourselves the power
of God. Greater power, greater godliness, leading to more power. It's
as simple as that. The whole process of repentance is a spiral, one
that we can mount higher and higher to return to our Father in
Heaven. All we have to do is start.

What greater gift have we been given? What more magnificent
promise?

OCTOBER 21

*Thou shalt offer a sacrifice unto the Lord thy God in righteousness,
even that of a broken heart and a contrite spirit.*

—DOCTRINE AND COVENANTS 59:8

Nobody ever said repentance was easy. If you think about it, it really can't be, not if it's going to be real. Repentance at its most basic level involves change. You have to change what you're doing and do something else. Breaking up that kind of pattern can be difficult; patterns get to be patterns because they have turned into habits. It takes thinking to change a habit, and it takes making the decision to change over and over again. Every time you start to slip back into the old pattern, you have to remember you intend to change and make the decision to change all over again.

Sometimes that decision is a painful one. Maybe you have decided you have to stop associating with a certain person. The association isn't doing you any good and is leading you into difficulties. Maybe the person involved is negative (perhaps particularly negative about the Church); maybe you know you have no business spending so much time with that person, and in your heart of hearts you know you're asking for trouble. Yet the relationship may be a hard one to give up just like that. If you didn't have a lot in common, if you didn't have a good time together, the association would never have gotten started in the first place. Still, giving it up—just like that—is what you have to do.

That can hurt. It can be sore, just like a bruise. When you hurt like that, you know exactly what is meant by "a broken heart and a contrite spirit." The broken heart means that you're willing to endure the pain because you know you are now doing what is right, and the contrite spirit means you recognize the dangerous waters you were wading in, and you regret it.

If you could just waltz off in a new direction without a second glance or a single twinge, it wouldn't be repentance. It would simply be deciding to do something else. There's a difference

Dear Lord, bless me that I may not have to repent too often. It's too hard. But when I do, Lord, stay by me. Stay by me, strengthen me, and bless me with thy love.

Then I think I can do what I have to do.

OCTOBER 22

Wherefore, verily I say, let the wicked take heed, and let the rebellious fear and tremble; and let the unbelieving hold their lips, for the day of wrath shall come upon them as a whirlwind, and all flesh shall know that I am God. And he that seeketh signs shall see signs, but not unto salvation.

—DOCTRINE AND COVENANTS 63:6–7

A fierce storm whipping and lashing the trees, stripping off fluttering flurries of leaves that will either have to be bagged and dragged out to the curb or chewed up with the lawnmower and dragged back to the compost heap. It's not exactly a whirlwind, but the trees are bending and twisting, and this will pretty much finish the season of autumn splendor. After this, we'll be close to bare branches waiting for the first snow.

Standing at the window watching the leaves being swept by the wind and rain across the lawn to the neighbor's lawn (but that's all right; we're simultaneously getting the leaves from the neighbor on the other side), I find myself thinking about the power of God, and the other part of this scripture: the part about seeking signs. We see the power of God all around us every day. We see it in quiet things—a tiny plant unfurling from the soil, or a brand-new baby stirring in her bassinet—and we see it in storms like this. We feel it in our hearts.

So why should we ask for a sign? When one is needed, it will be given, but as the Lord goes on to say here, "Faith cometh not by signs, but signs follow those that believe."

Today, I need no sign. I don't need the storm roaring, the shutters banging, to believe that the Lord is God. Let me stay warm and safe inside, comforted by my faith.

OCTOBER 23

Every incorrect choice we make, every sin we commit is a violation of eternal law. That violation brings negative results we generally soon recognize. There are also other consequences of our acts of which we may not be conscious. They are nonetheless real. They can have a tremendous effect on the quality of our life here and most certainly will powerfully affect it hereafter. We can do nothing of ourselves to satisfy the demands of justice for a broken eternal law. Yet, unless the demands of justice are paid, each of us will suffer endless negative consequences.

Only the life, teachings, and particularly the atonement of Jesus Christ can release us from this otherwise impossible predicament.

—ELDER RICHARD G. SCOTT

Jesus Christ truly is my Savior.

Humbling, isn't it. I go to work, and I make my bed, and I get the downstairs straight, and I do the laundry, and I remember (most of the time) to pick up the children approximately when I agreed to, and my life ripples along in a fairly ordinary way, and then suddenly I read something—something like this—and it hits me all over again. Jesus Christ came to earth to save *me*.

Oh, I don't mean only me. That's not what I mean. I guess what strikes me as so absolutely stunning is the idea that he knows all about me, about the small mistakes I make and the larger errors I have made and my carelessness and lapses in obedience. In spite of all of them—and some of them I have gone on doing, carelessly and disobediently, when I *knew* that they were wrong—he is prepared to offer me the possibility of eternal life. By his sacrifice the inevitable consequences of my wrongdoing can be nullified. If I repent, the wrongdoing can be erased as if it never happened.

Even on a perfectly ordinary day, the realization of that can be breathtaking.

Today, walking up the stairs from the basement, folded laundry in my arms, let me remember and marvel all over again. I have been given the possibility. Let me rely on him and make it happen.

OCTOBER 24

Then Peter said unto them, Repent, and be baptized every one of
you in the name of Jesus Christ for the remission of sins, and ye
shall receive the gift of the Holy Ghost. For the promise is unto you,
and to your children, and to all that are afar off, even as many as
the Lord our God shall call.

—ACTS 2:38–39

I don't know when I was first told about the atonement of Christ.
It must have been when I was very small. It was just always something I knew.

Can you imagine what it must have been like to hear of the
Atonement for the first time?

This scripture comes from the day of Pentecost, when the Holy
Ghost was first poured out on the apostles—"a sound from heaven
as of a rushing mighty wind"—and the others who were there were
astonished, and turned to each other for an explanation. Peter rose
in his full new majesty and preached eloquently to them, so eloquently that when he finished, they asked him humbly, "What shall
we do?"

And this is what Peter told them to do.

Today, dear Lord, let me recognize the magnificence of the
Atonement all over again. Let it be new to me, so that I may know
how blessed I am. For as Peter says, the promise is to us, too. We are
certainly those that are afar off, both in distance and in time. But
we, too, have the promise.

Today, Lord, let me know anew and be grateful.

OCTOBER 25

*Now I rejoice, not that ye were made sorry, but that ye sorrowed
to repentance: for ye were made sorry after a godly manner, that ye
might receive damage by us in nothing. For godly sorrow worketh
repentance to salvation not to be repented of: but the sorrow of the
world worketh death.*

—2 CORINTHIANS 7:9–10

In this letter to the Corinthians, Paul is apparently referring to
another letter in which he expressed his displeasure with some of
the goings-on in the Church. To his relief and satisfaction, the
Corinthian Christians, having been called to repentance, repented
and dealt decisively with the difficulty.

What Paul is really talking about here, it seems to me, is the
enormous difference between the sorrow that leads to repentance
and the sorrow of remorse. The sorrow that leads to repentance is
truly sorrow for sin, and that, as Paul says here, leads to salvation.
Remorse is simply being sorry for the consequences of sin. It's the
difference between recognizing that you did wrong—and being
grieved by that recognition—and feeling bad about what happened
because you did wrong. The first gets you somewhere; remember
the "broken heart and contrite spirit"? The second is simply self-
indulgent.

I remember once when my son and his cousin were about three
years old. It was about this time of year, and I was putting the
Christmas packages together for the relatives in England. I had
hauled out the Christmas wrappings and was just about to get
started on the first presents when the phone rang, and I went to the
kitchen to answer it.

I must have been on the phone longer than I thought. When I
got back, I discovered the two little boys had found that the rolls of
wrapping paper had cardboard cores inside them, and the cardboard
cores were just the right size and shape to be "laser weapons." The
boys were therefore having a wonderful duel with the lasers, tromp-
ing cheerfully over the wrapping paper that they had pulled off to
get to the cardboard.

I went ballistic. I scolded and shouted and waved my arms
around while they watched me, awestruck, and when I ran down, I
crossly ordered them both to get upstairs out of my sight.

As they started up the stairs, I heard my son say with matter-of-fact philosophy, "I told you she wouldn't like it."

Mad as I was, I sat down on the floor and laughed. Looking at it from Paul's perspective, the situation is clear. What sorrow the boys felt (if any) was remorse. They didn't regret the lasers in the least. They were just a little disconcerted by all the noise I made.

Dear Lord, let me act a little more maturely than a three-year-old. When I do something wrong, let me sorrow for the wrong itself. Then I can cope with the consequences.

OCTOBER 26

Wherefore, I say unto you, that ye ought to forgive one another; for he that forgiveth not his brother his trespasses standeth condemned before the Lord; for there remaineth in him the greater sin.

I, the Lord, will forgive whom I will forgive, but of you it is required to forgive all men. And ye ought to say in your hearts— let God judge between me and thee, and reward thee according to thy deeds.

—DOCTRINE AND COVENANTS 64:9–11

This has always struck me as the most wonderfully sensible, down-to-earth way of dealing with the problems that arise between us as mortal beings.

First of all, the Lord is telling us that we should stay out of the judging business. That is the province of the Lord, and the penalty for trying our hand at it is severe. For one thing, we don't know enough about it. Like everybody else (I suspect), I am quick to assume that others operate from the same motivations and assumptions I do. This is not true. Nor do I have more than random insights into anybody else's circumstances. Only the Lord can read our hearts and minds and know everything about us. This is not to say that everything can be excused; it simply means that I don't have enough information one way or the other to know. The Lord does; judging should be left to him.

If I'm not in a position to judge, I am certainly better off from my own point of view—as well as from anybody else's—to forgive. Carrying a grudge eats up far too much energy. Coddling a grievance for any period of time sours me just like milk left on the counter. Plotting vengeance sickens my soul. If I forgive—even if what was done to me is obviously wrong—both of us are made free. I can think about something else, and the perpetrator can go on to make other choices—or not, as it may be. But it's no longer *my* problem.

And what a wonderful formula to ease my offended heart: "Let God choose between me and thee, and reward thee according to thy deeds." I'm not saying what was done was right; I'm simply turning the assessment over to the Lord, where it belongs.

I may not need this counsel today. But let me tuck it away in my pocket to remember when I do.

OCTOBER 27

Yea, open your mouths and they shall be filled, saying: Repent, repent, and prepare ye the way of the Lord, and make his paths straight; for the kingdom of heaven is at hand.

—DOCTRINE AND COVENANTS 33:10

The message doesn't change a whole lot. Remember what John the Baptist said: "Repent ye: for the kingdom of God is at hand" (Mark 1:15). Sound familiar? Close to two centuries later we're being told the same thing.

As human beings, we seem inclined to believe that our particular generation is special, with special challenges and special opportunities. To a certain extent this is true, but it's also true that each generation shares a great deal with every other generation.

For one thing, we all have the same assignment here in mortality: to choose wisely, to learn from our experiences, and to grow in knowledge and obedience. That's what we came here for; that's what we are to do. In the course of that assignment, we all make mistakes. We hope to learn from our errors. Because of the atonement of Jesus Christ, we will not be eternally hobbled by them, and that is true for all of us, no matter where we were born or when.

A Jewish woman of about the fifth century before Christ, perhaps one of those straggling back from exile to Jerusalem, when Nehemiah was restoring the ruined city wall; a peasant woman of the Middle Ages in a shabby village on the edge of a great estate; one of the pioneer women who, having successfully reached the Salt Lake Valley, was now facing the work of turning the wilderness into settled territory; and me: I am so hypnotized by our differences that

I don't see our similarities. We have had children to raise and have had to learn to tread the thin line between providing comfort and teaching them what they'll need to manage on their own. We have had a home to maintain (whether it was a tent, or a lean-to, or a cottage, or a house) and meals to prepare. We have had to coexist with the neighbors. We have needed to build our relationship with the Lord.

In all of these things, we have made and will make mistakes. Sometimes we probably even make the same mistakes. Is it possible that the Jewish woman ever lost her temper with her children and wished she hadn't? Might the medieval peasant not have had an argument with a neighbor over the exact boundary between the land surrounding her hut and the one next door and wondered uncomfortably in the night if she was as sure of the line as she had said she was? Could the pioneer settler have computed her tithing so as to be obliged to make the smallest possible payment and then been burdened by guilty regret?

No wonder the message never changes. We go on needing it! Repent, for the kingdom of heaven is at hand. It is, and ever will be, as near as our hearts. Today let me remember that and take care of what I need to take care of. Now.

OCTOBER 28

But behold, the Lord hath redeemed my soul from hell; I have beheld his glory, and I am encircled about eternally in the arms of his love.

—2 NEPHI 1:15

A wonderful clear day, brisk and cold. Even out raking vigorously (somebody has to cope with these leaves), I need gloves to keep my hands warm.

What a beautiful world we have been given. I keep stopping to lean on my rake and look at the brilliant blue sky. Somehow during the summer when the trees are full of leaves the sky seems paler— but then there are all the flowers and the lush plantings to distract me. Now the branches are almost bare, and the sky is the color of sapphires.

"Encircled about eternally in the arms of his love": that's what it feels like today. There are so many ways in which we are continually shown how the Lord loves us. We have the pleasures of this world, the loving concern we are shown, and as Lehi reminds his sons here just before his death, most of all, the sacrifice of Jesus Christ that opens all the promise of eternity before us.

It's easy to remember that today. I need to remember it most when the world seems gray and uninviting and the people around me are a pain. Even so, then too I am loved. Good days, bad days: We are still the children of our Father in Heaven. Let me remember, and rejoice.

OCTOBER 29

As for me, I will call upon God; and the Lord shall save me.
Evening, and morning, and at noon, will I pray, and cry aloud:
and he shall hear my voice. . . . Cast thy burden upon the Lord,
and he shall sustain thee: he shall never suffer the righteous to be
moved.

—PSALM 55:16–17, 22

It's dark in the morning now when I'm getting ready to go to work; I drive east, and the rising sun is in my eyes. Night comes earlier, too. The year is dwindling down.

It was pitch dark when I got home last night. I had stopped on my way home to visit a friend; for one reason or another, nobody was going to be home until later, and I'd been meaning to see Heather for ages.

The only trouble is that visiting Heather can be fairly depressing (one reason, no doubt, that it's one of those things I don't get around to doing often). Heather is the kind of person who finds it hard to let things go. Heather gnaws on her problems like a dog with a bone. Last year her mother died, and because Heather never got around to spending as much time with her that last year as she meant to, she's is still beating herself up for it now. I know what she's mourning. Unfortunately, it's too late to help her mother, but surely she could find some other lonely people who would be warmed by a visit. Instead, Heather just glooms. I should put this scripture on a card and slide it under her door. In theory she believes in repentance; why can't she take the step to believing that, if she's repented, the Lord can and will forgive her, just as she's been promised? And if the Lord can forgive her, can't she forgive herself?

Repentance takes faith. It takes humility, too: Yesterday as I was trying to help Heather get over grieving, it suddenly struck me that in a way, there's a kind of pride in being sorrier and "repenting" harder than anyone else. That doesn't work. You have to let go of your sins and misdemeanors. You have to settle back into the ranks of all humanity who have sinned and been forgiven. We are all together.

Let me cast my burdens upon the Lord, instead of stubbornly hanging on to them. Together with all my faulty, repentant brothers and sisters, let me trust in his sustaining power, today and all the todays to come.

OCTOBER 30

Seeing then that we have a great high priest, that is passed into the heavens, Jesus the Son of God, let us hold fast our profession. For we have not an high priest which cannot be touched with the feeling of our infirmities; but was in all points tempted like as we are, yet without sin. Let us therefore come boldly unto the throne of grace, that we may obtain mercy, and find grace to help in time of need.

—HEBREWS 4:14–16

What Paul is telling us is wonderfully, magnificently true. We are all aware of the ways in which Jesus Christ is different from us: He is our Savior, the Son of God who came to earth to live a perfect life and then laid it down voluntarily on our behalf to ransom us from death.

But in one important way he was the same. He came to earth as a mortal, and he lived a mortal life. As Paul says, he "was in all points tempted like as we are." He never sinned, but he knew temptation.

It makes me think. We know, of course, about the temptations in the desert before he began his ministry. We know how he was offered food when he was hungry, and safety when he was endangered, and all the power and glory of the world, if he would just worship Satan. But what about the ordinary temptations?

For those three years, he was so often surrounded by people. Was he ever tempted to make some excuse and slip away from everyone and just be by himself for a while? When he was hungry—not ravenous, as he must have been after a forty-day fast, but just ordinarily hungry—was he ever tempted to take the largest fish on the plate, when it was offered to him first? When somebody said something really stupid (and most of his disciples and followers were plain, uneducated people), was he ever tired enough to be tempted to snap back sharply, instead of answering with kindness? When the scribes and Pharisees were pressing up against him, eyes narrowed and watching with hawklike vigilance for any misstep, was he ever tempted just to push them physically out of his way and get on with what he was trying to do?

He never sinned. We know that. But, as Paul says, he was "in all points" tempted as we are. He mastered the temptations, but he understands. Supported by him, we can come boldly unto the throne of grace, even if we succumbed. There will be help in our time of need.

Today let me remember that. Today let me remember him.

OCTOBER 31

And this shall ye do in remembrance of my body, which I have shown unto you. And it shall be a testimony unto the Father that ye do always remember me. And if ye do always remember me ye shall have my Spirit to be with you.

—3 NEPHI 18:7

The single most important event of human history was the redemption of man by Jesus Christ. By that single act, the principle of repentance was given wings. Because Christ died for us, our sins can be not only forgiven but wiped away as if they never existed. Christ's sacrifice met the requirements of justice. Mercy now governs.

In every sacrament meeting we are celebrating that event. Sometimes it's hard to remember. Children squirm, somebody down the row from me is dozing and has to be nudged awake to pass the tray, one of the deacons gets confused and a tray is heading back toward the aisle to absolutely no one, and somebody else has to make his way as rapidly as is reverently possible to get there in time. It's easy to get distracted. Still, the covenant has been renewed. Ordinary life has brushed up against the reality of the sacrifice of our Savior, and with that gift, we are given the possibility of a fresh start yet again.

In the midst of mortality, we have touched eternity. As the month slips away, let me remember to remember that.

NOVEMBER

I will praise the name of God with a song, and will magnify him with thanksgiving.

—PSALM 69:30

NOVEMBER 1

Rejoice evermore. Pray without ceasing. In every thing give thanks;
for this is the will of God in Christ Jesus concerning you.

—1 THESSALONIANS 5:16–18

Rejoice evermore—what a wonderful way to start the month, particularly because it seems we are being tipped earlier and earlier into the holiday season, with all its rejoicing. It used to be that everyone held off until Thanksgiving, but here we are still surrounded by Halloween candy, and holly and Santa Claus and gold and silver ribbons are everywhere. I know I should moan and groan about rampant commercialism, but I am the kind who thrives on the holiday season. I love the feeling of celebration and goodwill towards men. Let the stores do their thing: I will savor the season for two months instead of six weeks. On the other hand, if they start putting Santa out around Labor Day . . .

Pray without ceasing. Well, I don't think Paul is talking about the prayer wheels of the Himalayas or a formula that we must repeat incessantly. I think he means that we should be continually mindful of our relationship with our Heavenly Father, so that when we pray, it's like picking up a conversation with an intimate member of the family, not a ceremonial visit to someone we hardly know.

"In every thing give thanks." In this month of Thanksgiving, that should be the easy part. I have been given so much that I don't even know where to start in itemizing. There are people: my husband, my children, my parents, my sisters, and all the others dear to me. There are things: my house, a car that runs most of the time, a washing machine (let's keep a grip on essentials), and all the other things, including the pretty watch a daughter gave me for my birthday. There is the miscellany of unclassifiables: reasonable health, heat in the house, and a calico cat with a snow white stomach who sleeps, endearingly, with one paw over her eyes, as if to keep out the light.

For all my blessings, the big and the small, I give thanks. Today let me remember them all, and be grateful.

NOVEMBER 2

Serve the Lord with gladness: come before his presence with singing.
Know ye that the Lord he is God: it is he that hath made us, and
not we ourselves: we are his people, and the sheep of his pasture.
Enter into his gates with thanksgiving, and into his courts with
praise: be thankful unto him, and bless his name.

—PSALM 100:2–4

You know, the whole trouble with having things go well is that we are all too ready to leap to the conclusion that we did it all by ourselves. We apparently need to be reminded that we are the guests at the party, not the hosts. And like children, we sometimes need somebody to tell us to say thank you.

I wonder why that should be. Wouldn't it seem natural that thanksgiving and praise would bubble up unprompted? Sometimes it does, of course. My father said that on V-E Day and V-J Day, at the end of the Second World War, all the church bells rang and people burst out in spontaneous prayers of thanksgiving. That's never happened that I can remember, maybe because the forms of religion were more widely observed then than now, or maybe because our wars since have had less neatly defined stopping dates. But generally, when everything is going along well, we get so caught up with the rhythm and routine of life that we forget that we are being blessed. We start to take it all for granted.

When calamity strikes, it's easy to remember to turn to the Lord. Let me not wait for calamity. So far, today looks like an ordinary day, so today let me remember to give thanks for the ordinary. Let me be ever mindful that I am blessed.

NOVEMBER 3

We have no way of knowing when our privilege to extend a helping hand will unfold before us. The road to Jericho each of us travels bears no name, and the weary traveler who needs our help may be one unknown. Altogether too frequently, the recipient of kindness shown fails to express his feelings, and we are deprived of a glimpse of greatness and a touch of tenderness that motivates us to go and do likewise.

—PRESIDENT THOMAS S. MONSON

It's not only the Lord who doesn't always get thanked. As President Monson points out, we never know when somebody may need our help, and sometimes, even though we indeed do help, the person is unable to express thanks. Maybe the person is embarrassed, or shy, or simply doesn't know what to say. Sometimes the person may not know whom to thank.

I remember one random act of generosity that came my way. I was driving west from our home in Michigan with the children; my husband, whose vacation time was limited, was going to fly out and join us in Salt Lake City so that we could have as much time as possible together out there. At the time I think the children were almost two, three, seven, and eleven, and it was going to take us four days to get there. (I must admit, looking back, that I wonder what I was thinking about when I dreamed up this plan, but I was younger then. Also, possibly, more naive.)

The first day went reasonably well. The second day I was beginning to appreciate what I was in for, and we had some minor car trouble. After an hour or so of repair work at a station just off the freeway, we were extremely grateful to arrive safely at the motel where we were scheduled to stay that night. We went swimming in the pool—the promised treat, to persuade the children to wait patiently at the gas station—and then went in for dinner at the coffee shop. I don't remember much about the dinner, except that the swim had relaxed us all, and even I began to unwind a little and believe I could contemplate taking on the third day.

There were other people in the coffee shop, but I didn't pay attention to any of them in particular. When it was time to pay the bill, the waitress told me that the bill had already been paid. A regular customer, she said, had seen our family and had been impressed with us. (Now what on earth could we have been doing? I've wondered ever since.) And he had paid our bill. I asked who he was, and she said he had already left.

We never met him. When we left—needless to say, the children were fascinated—we look around to see if there was anybody who looked like anybody we might have noticed in the coffee shop, but there was no one. One of my daughters was sure there had been a man with a mustache, but her younger sister said there hadn't, so they argued about that for a while. Mustache or not, we never said thank you.

Whoever he was, we were grateful. I still am. That single act of kindness gave me the lift I needed on my road to Jericho. We reached Salt Lake City without further car trouble, and I was still of reasonably sound mind.

Thinking about it today, I realize I've never passed along that particular gift of generosity. Today, let me resolve to do so. Bless me, Lord, to find the way.

NOVEMBER 4

And one of them, when he saw that he was healed, turned back, with a loud voice glorified God, and fell down on his face at his feet, giving him thanks: and he was a Samaritan. And Jesus answering said, Were there not ten cleansed? but where are the nine?

—LUKE 17:15–17

This is the story of the ten lepers. Outcasts and isolates, they called to Jesus for his help. When he saw them, he told them to go to the priests and, as they were on their way, they were "cleansed."

The only one who returned to give thanks was a Samaritan. The Samaritans, at the time of Jesus, were the inhabitants of the northern kingdom of Israel after the original inhabitants had been carried away captive. Some of the original Samaritans were foreign colonists placed there when the land had been depopulated; some were stragglers and escaped Israelites who had crept back. The people, therefore, were mixed, and their religion, too, was a combination of Jewish observance and heathen custom. For that reason, they were not allowed to take part in the rebuilding of the temple at Jerusalem, and with great bitterness, they established a rival temple of their own. By the time of Christ, antagonism between

Jews and Samaritans was an accepted fact. Even so, it was the Samaritan who returned to give thanks, as Jesus observed. As he went on to say, "There are not found that returned to give glory to God, save this stranger."

Let me not be outdone in gratitude by a stranger. Let me not take blessings for granted.

NOVEMBER 5

I exhort therefore, that, first of all, supplications, prayers, intercessions, and giving of thanks, be made for all men; for kings, and for all that are in authority; that we may lead a quiet and peaceable life in all godliness and honesty.

—1 TIMOTHY 2:1–2

Now, there's a blessing I don't always think of, perhaps because I have been blessed indeed in living in a place and time when I don't have to. I have always taken the existence of a government and imposed rules of order for granted.

How many of God's children in this vast and troubled world cannot!

Actually, this scripture comes on a curiously appropriate day. In England, the Fifth of November is a special day.

"Remember, remember the Fifth of November," the children's rhyme goes, "Gunpowder, treason, and plot." It was on November 5, 1605, that a group of Roman Catholic conspirators, among them a man named Guy Fawkes, planned to blow up Parliament and King James I (he of the King James Translation of the Bible). The gunpowder was actually placed in a vault below the House of Lords, but the plot was discovered two days before the opening of Parliament. The men involved were tracked down, tortured in some cases, and executed, and the Fifth of November has not been forgotten. My husband remembers the day in his native England as a splendid celebration with fireworks and a dummy "guy" (in his case, a dummy dressed in his grandfather's cast-off clothes) to burn on a bonfire.

Since we've lived on this side of the Atlantic, we've never really marked the day, coming as close as it does after Halloween. But perhaps today it can be a reminder to me that, as Paul writes, we should give thanks for those in authority who make it possible for us to lead a quiet and peaceable life. Disagreement can be tolerated; gunpowder cannot.

Remember, remember. And be grateful.

NOVEMBER 6

It is a good thing to give thanks unto the Lord, and to sing praises unto thy name, O most High: to shew forth thy lovingkindness in the morning, and thy faithfulness every night.

—PSALM 92:1–2

It is a good thing, and how easy to be moved to song when we praise! I'm no great singer; I have to be buried in a fairly large chorus to feel uninhibited enough in any public place to open my mouth and sing as joyously as my heart wants to. But by myself in the shower or in a chorus, the songs of praise come easily. I remember once when the director of our university chorus was leading us through a particularly lush passage, and he flung his arms wide and told us, "Don't hurry. Let me wallow."

Today, with this psalm, let me wallow.

What does it mean, "lovingkindness in the morning"? I suppose to me it means the recognition of the treasure of life itself. In the larger sense, of course, I am grateful for the gift of life that I had to have to progress further. I am grateful for the Council in Heaven and for this opportunity to prove myself.

In the more immediate sense, I am grateful for the sheer deliciousness of this life itself. I'm grateful for a body, for the ability to feel the splash of water on my face in the morning. I'm grateful for the sense of smell, to be able to savor with my nose as well as my mouth toast with strawberry jam for breakfast. I like just being alive, and I appreciate the lovingkindness (it seems cozier being all one word, the way it is in the scripture) of the Lord in giving me this gift.

And "thy faithfulness at night"? Well, I guess to me that means that I am aware that the Lord has been with me through the day. As long as I am obedient, I can reach out for that presence and it will be there. To my everlasting wonder, it has even been there in times when I have been less obedient, gently, lovingly, calling me back where I belong.

For all of those blessings, let me be grateful, and wallow—with or without song—in praise.

NOVEMBER 7

Let all the mountains shout for joy, and all ye valleys cry aloud; and all ye seas and dry lands tell the wonders of your Eternal King! And ye rivers, and brooks, and rills, flow down with gladness. Let the woods and all the trees of the field praise the Lord; and ye solid rocks weep for joy! And let the sun, moon, and the morning stars sing together, and let all the sons of God shout for joy! And let the eternal creations declare his name forever and ever! And again I say, how glorious is the voice we hear from heaven, proclaiming in our ears, glory, and salvation, and honor, and immortality, and eternal life; kingdoms, principalities, and powers!

—Doctrine and Covenants 128:23

Someone else who truly loves life and this world! This comes from a letter of Joseph Smith to the Church, written at Nauvoo. You can feel how he relished life and the magnificence of earth, even as he set down the instructions for baptism for the dead, which was the main business of this particular revelation.

One of the most interesting differences between the restored Church in our dispensation and the postapostolic Church that drifted into apostasy is the whole attitude toward mortality. For the thinkers and writers of the early Christian era, this world was a wholly evil place; its pleasures were temptations, enticing good men away from holiness. We take the position that of course there is evil in this world, but there is good as well. If there were not, how could we choose? If all the choices are bad, what is to be learned by making them? We believe that, like most things, the pleasures of this world have two sides. Of course there is corruption and malignancy in the land, but there is also innocence and good. We repudiate the belief that a tiny baby, fresh from our Heavenly Father's presence with skin as soft and silky as a rose petal, could be so defiled by Adam's transgression that only immediate baptism can save its infant soul from hell. Good is still good, and good is still more true than any evil can be. Satan is not coequal with God, here or anywhere else. He is only God's fallen son.

Today let me, like Joseph Smith in his epistle, be filled with the joyous promise of the gospel. Let me reach out to the good and be grateful for its existence. Let me, too, thank the Lord.

NOVEMBER 8

As with all commandments, gratitude is a description of a success-ful mode of living. The thankful heart opens our eyes to a multitude of blessings that continually surround us.

—ELDER JAMES E. FAUST

I know a young mother with three small children who found her-self homeless. Becky is not a member of the Church and had no family willing to help. She spent some weeks in a shelter, but the whole time she was there she was working patiently, stubbornly, to find more permanent housing, always courteous but equally always determined to remind the authorities of her presence until she had a place for herself and her children to live. Becky persisted. When in the end they had found an apartment for her (I think by then they would have done anything, just to get her off their backs), she came to tell me about it with her face radiant. "I am so blessed!" she told me.

That night when I knelt for my prayers and began on my nor-mal list of requests, I suddenly saw Becky's face before me and heard her triumphant, "I am so blessed!" It stopped me dead in my tracks. I rocked back on my heels, and then I began my prayer all over again, only this time I simply told the Lord about all my many, many blessings and how grateful I am for them. I didn't ask for a thing, but it was probably the longest prayer I have ever prayed. My list of blessings seemed to go on forever.

Let me continue to remember Becky and her few blessings, so gratefully received. Let me continue to count mine, over and over, and above all, let me never be complacent about the basics, such as our house and food for our children and a family that has always been there when I needed them and the strength of the Church of Jesus Christ, wrapping me invisibly with the security of a stalwart community. Like Becky, I am so blessed. Like Becky, too, I would have a thankful heart.

NOVEMBER 9

And when ye will offer a sacrifice of thanksgiving unto the Lord,
offer it at your own will.

—LEVITICUS 22:29

This particular scripture has to do with the specific thanksgiving gifts offered under the law of Moses, which were basically unleavened cakes and leavened bread. We no longer have to fuss with those cakes (mixed with oil in the approved fashion), but it seems to me the principle is still sound. You can't be ordered to be thankful. It has to well up out of your heart, or it doesn't count.

Surely I am not the only child ever ordered to express appreciation for a gift given by an elderly relative (or nonrelative) who had clearly long since grown out of touch with what actual living, breathing children desired. A plain washcloth, even a nice, all-for-myself washcloth tied with a ribbon, is not a present, I remember remarking peevishly to my mother. (A nice, all-for-myself washcloth doesn't sound half bad to me now—I guess I grew up.)

Now that I think about it, maybe some of the gifts the Lord has given me have come camouflaged as "washcloths." There certainly have been objects and events which I have viewed with considerable dismay when I first was presented with them; it took me some time to identify them as the blessings they later so plainly turned out to be.

We all teach our children to express appreciation, but that's not quite the same thing as being thankful. Thankfulness comes when we grow mature enough to recognize a blessing when it is there before us—and maybe sometimes we have to be forced to experience a need before we can be thankful for the gift that meets the need. When we are, the thankfulness will well up inside us spontaneously as it is meant to do.

Today, Lord, let me recognize my blessings, and let my gratitude be offered freely, happily, of my own will. Dear Lord, help me to grow up.

NOVEMBER 10

Be careful for nothing; but in every thing by prayer and supplication with thanksgiving let your requests be made known unto God.

—PHILIPPIANS 4:6

"Be careful for nothing" probably means, as we would say it, "Don't worry about things." Wouldn't it be wonderful to be able to follow that counsel completely and without reservation? "Let your requests be known unto God," Paul counsels, by "supplication with thanksgiving." In other words, it makes sense before you start asking for things to count your blessings and make sure you don't already have them.

"Be careful for nothing": oh dear, the amount of time I spend ignoring that advice. There are days—usually the boring, dreary days like this one, when the world is rehearsing for winter and the sky is gray and what colors there are seem muted and cold—when it seems as if I'm being full of care for everything. There are the bills to pay, which on days like this seem to be rising like dough. There are the children to fuss about. Where have they gone now, and when will they come back from wherever they went? And there's that spot on the living room rug. Where did it come from, and will it ever come out? Things. On days like today I seem surrounded by them, and none of them in order.

Paul puts it so simply. Make my requests known to the Lord by prayer and supplication with thanksgiving. Maybe if I remember to be thankful for the comfortable lifestyle I lead, I will mind the bills less. Maybe if I express my thanks for the children, I will remember to remind them gently again (*gently* being the operative word) that my mind rests easier if they say where they're going before the back door slams. Maybe if I'm thankful for the rug—oh, for heaven's sake, there have been spots before and will be again. Either it will come out or it won't, and it's not a big deal.

Dear Lord, I am thankful. Please continue to bless me and all my things, and help me to keep them all in perspective. Even on days like today.

NOVEMBER 11

O sing unto the Lord a new song; for he hath done marvellous things: his right hand, and his holy arm, hath gotten him the victory.

—PSALM 98:1

The newer cities and suburbs don't have them, of course, but most of the towns that have been in existence through the century do: monuments to the war dead. Some of the smaller towns even have the names of the men from the town inscribed. Standing there looking at a couple of dozen names isn't quite the same as the overwhelming experience of walking past the thousands of names on the Vietnam War Memorial in Washington, D. C., but when I think that each name stands for some young man who had his life taken—well, in a modest way, it's overwhelming, too.

David, who wrote so many of the psalms, knew about war. He fought his own son and thought his heart would break. As a woman, I wonder irritably why war seems to be necessary. What do we gain from sending off our young men to kill somebody else's young men? And then I remember the Holocaust, and some of the other evils that had to be stopped—even if we didn't know all that was happening until the victory was ours—and I fall silent.

These names on the white marble obelisks and columns, names of dead men, are dead names now. Hardly anyone still is alive to remember the ones from the First World War. But let me be grateful. They went into war and gave their lives. I'm sure not all of them were heroes, and I suspect that many of them died afraid. Even so, or maybe especially so, because of what they did, I can stand on a chilly autumn day reading the names on a memorial and then walk away, free.

Let me give thanks, and honor.

NOVEMBER 12

Ye do not remember the Lord your God in the things with which he hath blessed you, but ye do always remember your riches, not to thank the Lord your God for them; yea, your hearts are not drawn out unto the Lord, but they do swell with great pride, unto boasting, and unto great swelling, envyings, strifes, malice, persecutions, and murders, and all manner of iniquities.

—HELAMAN 13:22

Samuel the Lamanite, calling the unrighteous Nephites to repentance.

Odd, isn't it, that down through the ages so many of us are perfectly capable—as has been demonstrated—of forgetting the Lord, but, as Samuel points out, we always remember our riches. We know how much we have, we know where it's kept, and we know what we intend to do with it. And as long as we remain focused on riches, all the other problems Samuel mentions keep poking up in our lives. We are proud, because isn't it manifestly obvious that anybody capable of amassing riches is therefore a better person than somebody who doesn't have wealth? We boast. How we boast varies from society to society: The Native Americans on the northwestern coast of what's now the United States had potlatches, ceremonial feasts at which a man demonstrated his great riches by either giving away his magnificent possessions (which imposed the burden of reciprocation) or by burning them ostentatiously. In our society we prefer to boast by living extravagantly and attracting publicity that way, or by giving money for buildings, or their equivalent, which are then emblazoned with the donor's name. What follows in a society in which riches are greatly admired is inevitable: envyings, and all the rest of the calamities Samuel describes.

So why do we remember the riches and fail to remember the Lord—even to thank him? Well, for one thing, you can see riches. You can touch money. You can count it. Of course, the children of Israel could see and touch the golden calf, too.

Today let me learn that what is to be admired about riches (even modest riches) is the good that can be done with them and that Anonymous isn't a bad name for a donor. The really splendid thing about Anonymous is that he or she can give even very small gifts, if that's all that's possible to give, because he or she isn't proving anything to anybody. The gift is simply a gift.

Today, let me try on Anonymous for size.

NOVEMBER 13

Condemn me not because of mine imperfection, neither my father,
because of his imperfection, neither them who have written before
him; but rather give thanks unto God that he hath made manifest
unto you our imperfections, that ye may learn to be more wise than
we have been.

—MORMON 9:31

I have loved this particular verse ever since I first read it.
I think what I have loved the most is the plainness of it, the simple humility of a great man. I do realize that Moroni here is talking about his life and his father's life in general, but it has always struck me as the perfect, most gentle response to critics of the literary qualities of the Book of Mormon.

I am old enough to remember, before President Ezra Taft Benson so vigorously emphasized the wisdom and majesty of this book, when reading the whole Book of Mormon was considered a major accomplishment. People joked about having memorized "I, Nephi, having been born of goodly parents" because they kept reading that bit over and over and never got much farther. The so-called intelligentsia outside the Church too often responded to the book with hoots of derision. Mark Twain, among others, described it as unreadable.

Mark Twain, obviously, never got as far as this verse. Would the modest simplicity of these words have touched his heart? I'd like to think they might have.

"Give thanks unto God that he hath made manifest unto you our imperfections, that ye may learn to be more wise than we have been."

I do thank God, but for the gift of having these words, for the gift of coming to know the greatness of soul of these men. Today let me admire their strength, and humility, all over again.

NOVEMBER 14

O give thanks unto the God of gods: for his mercy endureth for ever.

—PSALM 136:2

S ome days we have to be reminded. Take days like today. The Christmas season is bearing down heavily upon us; here it is the middle of November, and the Christmas catalogs are raining in through the mail slot, decorations are everywhere, and my sister and I are working out arrangements for Thanksgiving dinner. We alternate back and forth; this is her year for Thanksgiving and my year for Christmas.

All of this is going on on one of the dreariest days the Lord has seen fit to send. It is cold—a damp, cheerless cold. It is unremittingly gray. The trees are bare. There are still scatterings of leaves across the lawns, few enough to be left there until spring. The grass is turning brown. Everything is set for a covering of snow, but there is no snow. It makes me think of that poem:

> No warmth, no cheerfulness, no healthful ease,
> No comfortable feel in any member—
> No shade, no shine, no butterflies, no bees,
> No fruits, no flowers, no leaves, no birds,—November!

I figure that minor English poet, Thomas Hood, had it about right, back in the early 1800s. As far as that goes, it's still right today.

Nevertheless, I will reread this scripture and I will give thanks—with gritted teeth, if necessary. The warmth and excitement of the holiday season will come. Today will go. Even for November, I will give thanks. Even for today.

NOVEMBER 15

I express appreciation to those who preserved the Bible for future generations, beginning with the faithful patriarchs of Israel and then those dedicated scholars who translated the prophets' writings into Greek—the universal language of the time—and thus preserved for us that precious version of the Old Testament known as the Septuagint. Later, there were the steadfast individuals who tirelessly worked to copy the scriptures during the Middle Ages and who patiently reproduced and defended them from the barbarians who invaded Europe. I also pay honor and praise to the courageous reformers of the sixteenth century who translated the scriptures into the language of the people and made them available for the general reading and edification of all the children of God.

—ELDER HELIO R. CAMARGO

L ast night we had a fire in the fireplace. The living room was clean and tidy, we were listening to wonderful music, and I could almost touch the serenity in the room. I sat with my scriptures on my lap, looking into the flames and thinking about Elder Camargo's words.

How fortunate I am to be of the blessed generations that have the privilege of sitting with the scriptures in our hands. I didn't have to do any of the sacrificing or struggling. I just went to the store and reached this little book down from the shelf, paid for it, and it was mine. Last night, looking into the fire, I was thinking about all those who had worked and struggled and even died so that I could take this book down from the shelf.

It's reasonably well-thumbed. It's a special book. I remember the startled look on my daughter's face one day when she carelessly pushed it off the table onto the floor, and I snapped at her sharply. There are undoubtedly better ways to teach, and I wish I had responded differently, but I hope she learned that this book is not like any of the other books in our house.

This book has the words that my Heavenly Father wants me to know, refracted through the personalities of dozens of men through the centuries. I can only imagine their faces, but I can touch their souls. Today, let me be grateful for those men and the hands of all those down through the centuries who protected and reproduced their words so that I could pick up a copy of their work off a shelf as if it were any other book.

Today let me recognize the difference, and give thanks.

NOVEMBER 16

Verily, verily, I say unto you, ye are little children, and ye have not as yet understood how great blessings the Father hath in his own hands and prepared for you; and ye cannot bear all things now; nevertheless, be of good cheer, for I will lead you along. The kingdom is yours and the blessings thereof are yours, and the riches of eternity are yours. And he who receiveth all things with thankfulness shall be made glorious; and the things of this earth shall be added unto him, even an hundred fold, yea, more.

—DOCTRINE AND COVENANTS 78:17–19

I guess I know as much as anybody about this business of not understanding the blessings the Father hath prepared. When I look at our four children, I have a textbook illustration in front of me.

We had our first daughter with no difficulty. We decided it was the right time to have a baby, and we did. The problems came with trying to have a second child. We had never imagined having an only child, but it looked for a long time as if that were going to happen.

I think I started out being bewildered. From there I believe I must have gone through every emotion known to the infertile. I was grief-stricken on a regular monthly basis. I felt cheated. I felt inadequate. I prayed a lot, and nothing happened. I was jealous of those who reproduced without difficulty—"like rabbits," I found myself thinking, bitterly. We went to infertility specialists. Still nothing. I tried to be ungrudging. I tried to have a generous heart. I tried to have faith, and trust, but nothing changed. I remained unpregnant.

This went on for almost four years. Then all of a sudden—and I remember just when it happened, completely unprompted—the idea of adoption occurred to me as a possible solution. When I say I had never thought of it before, people look at me as if I were mentally deficient, and I guess, in a way, I was. My dearest friend maintains that she mentioned adoption several times. I must not have been ready. I have no recollection of her having said a word about it.

Once we thought of it, we got busy, and just under a year later we went to Thailand and adopted our second daughter. That made two, and I felt our family was underway. After we moved back to the United States from England, we adopted our third daughter, from Chile. I have two sisters myself, and I thought a family of three girls was most satisfactory. I felt I was finally beginning to understand "the blessings the Father hath prepared for me." My cup was full and overflowing.

It was just about then we discovered I was pregnant. That turned out to be our son.

Now then. If I had been given the blessing I prayed for so stubbornly back when I thought my greatest happiness would be to give birth to a second child, would we have ever had our two middle daughters? Of course not. I had no idea of what the Father had in mind for us. I had to be taught.

Dear Lord, we have been so richly blessed. I am so grateful I was not given what I prayed for when I prayed for it and am even more grateful for what I was given instead. I look over my wonderfully diverse family lined up in church on a Sunday and feel as if my heart will burst with thanksgiving—just as I thought it would break, before, from disappointment.

Today, let me learn. Let me remember to accept what the Lord is offering me and not grieve because it wasn't what I asked. Let me count my four completely individual blessings, and rest content.

NOVEMBER 17

The sun shall be no more thy light by day; neither for brightness shall the moon give light unto thee: but the Lord shall be unto thee an everlasting light, and thy God thy glory.

—ISAIAH 60:19

Great fat harvest moon last night, hanging low in the sky. Today I thought of it as I read this verse from Isaiah, listing all the marvels that would happen when the exiled children of Israel, honed and perfected by their trials, would return triumphantly to Jerusalem under the protecting hand of the Lord.

Are my trials teaching me what I need to learn? Am I using them to build my testimony, or am I simply enduring them sulkily, waiting for them to go away? The last few weeks I've been having a rough time with one of my daughters. Am I praying enough about it? Instead of continually getting cross, do I entertain the thought that I need to increase my command of patience? Am I marching forward stalwartly convinced of my own wisdom, or am I turning to the Lord, prayerfully, to ask for his help in teaching what I obviously need to teach?

Dear Lord, it looks as if I'm going to need that fat harvest moon for a while yet. I don't see myself getting to the point where the Lord shall be my everlasting light in the immediate future. In the meantime, help me to teach. Help me to learn. Let me use my trials as instructional tools—or maybe a scrub brush.

Lord, I would be clean.

NOVEMBER 18

But thanks be to God, which giveth us the victory through our Lord Jesus Christ. Therefore, my beloved brethren, be ye stedfast, unmoveable, always abounding in the work of the Lord, forasmuch as ye know that your labour is not in vain in the Lord.
—1 CORINTHIANS 15:57–58

The nice part about service projects is that you can always be sure that your labor is not in vain. Service projects are the kind of thing you can comfortably feel good about.

I remember one service project in particular. The idea of it was to assist some ladies who were richer in age than in money to make some of their Christmas presents. The women lived at a local residential facility, and about ten of them came to our workshop, as I think we called it, to make their gifts. I'm sure we had more than one kind of gift to work on, but the one I remember best was lavender-stuffed sachets. I remember them because of Miss Aylesford.

Miss Aylesford was extremely elderly but undaunted. She wore a hat with great dignity, backwards. She said that's the way it went. When I showed her the sachet—we had sewn up three sides of a square of purple-flowered fabric, and the idea was that the ladies would stuff the square with dried lavender and then either they or we would sew up the fourth side—she looked at it critically.

"You see the lace?" I asked her helpfully, when she didn't say anything.

"Ah," said Miss Aylesford. "Lace."

There was a delicate lace edging. I thought it looked nice, not surprisingly, because I had picked out that particular lace myself.

"Lace," said Miss Aylesford again. "Where?"

I showed her the lace edging. She frowned at it. Then she took the square and with gnarled, arthritic hands slowly and painfully turned the square inside out. The seam allowance, trimmed across the corners, was now fully evident. Miss Aylesford's face cleared, and she beamed.

"No, dear," she said happily. "There's the lace."

I didn't know quite what to do. I reached for it and said hesitantly, "No, I think you can see it more clearly the other way."

As I started to turn it back right side out, Miss Aylesford reached over and took it from me firmly. "You're hiding the lace," she said sternly. "This is for my niece."

I gave up and hoped the niece had an understanding heart and bad eyesight or would bury it in her lingerie where it would smell as nice whether it was inside out or not. I asked her if she wanted to sew up the open side after she had stuffed it with dried lavender— it smelled wonderful on our fingers—or if she wanted me to do it.

Miss Aylesford gave me a long look, obviously suspicious of my capabilities. "I'll start it," she finally pronounced. "You may finish the last part."

The stitching took quite some time. Miss Aylesford didn't want to talk while she did it; she concentrated completely on her task. She did about three quarters of the length (it was only about four inches long) and then reluctantly handed it to me. When I was finished, she looked at my work critically.

"You're coming along well," she pronounced at last. "You're going to do quite nice work one day."

When I got home, I wondered which of us thought she had done the service project. In the end, I guess it was a draw. Both of us, I guess, had sublime confidence that our labor was not in vain in the Lord. Perhaps both of us were right.

NOVEMBER 19

And also that every man should eat and drink, and enjoy the good of all his labour, it is the gift of God.

—ECCLESIASTES 3:13

I think I must be getting old. We were sitting around at school today (we being several of the instructors) lamenting the demise of the work ethic.

Now, I have to say this is not entirely fair. It is perfectly true that there are some students who are not, in John le Carre's felicitous phrase, the inventors of work. We have one in particular at the moment who baffles us. She has been sent by her parents to a course that centers on using the computer. So far she has stoically resisted (for months now) learning anything at all about how to operate a computer. She appears willing, if unenthusiastic, but every computer she touches immediately malfunctions. For it to be sabotage would seem to require far more sophisticated computer know-how on her part than seems probable. Nevertheless . . .

But I can't say that's typical. Most students seem more or less agreeable to the idea of expending effort, and some are prepared to work very hard indeed. What I would like to teach them all—what I want most for them to learn—is that unless you are really willing to work, you can never know for yourself how satisfying work can be. As long as you're expending only 75 percent of the effort, you will never understand 100 percent of the reward.

Do we really teach young people about work now? So many things are done for us. I think about the first settlers in the Salt Lake Valley (or anywhere else, come to that). Their children, at least those past babyhood, had to work if they were to have shelter and eat. Do our kids have to work now? Not usually in the sense of working for survival.

Of course, it's easy to lecture on about the deficiencies of others. (There is also the point that I doubt I'd be up to being a pioneer myself.) Maybe I had better concentrate less on the foibles of others and more on my own.

So today let me stop lecturing (and grumbling with the other instructors of a certain age) and count my blessings instead. Among them is the fact that I have work that I love. I like getting to work, and I don't really begrudge staying late to finish what needs doing— at least until I'm in the car heading home, planning what I want to do there and wishing I had left half an hour earlier. I enjoy the good of my labor, both in the sense of having a good time doing it and in the sense of getting the benefit, and I acknowledge that it is a gift of God.

I like work. Today let me be thankful for it.

NOVEMBER 20

Yea, I know that I am nothing; as to my strength I am weak; there-fore I will not boast of myself, but I will boast of my God, for in his strength I can do all things; yea, behold, many mighty miracles we have wrought in this land, for which we will praise his name forever.

—ALMA 26:12

Here Ammon seems to have grasped a point that a lot of people in the scriptures have struggled with. Reading it makes me wonder if I always get it quite right myself. When I am doing something that I know my Father in Heaven would have me do, am I prone to claim I am doing it myself, out of my own cleverness or ability, or do I always recognize that I am capable because of his strength?

It's not that I am incapable of making decisions. After all, that's what I was sent here to do, to make choices (righteous ones, I hope). But my making decisions is a lot like a baby taking her first steps. Yes, my decisions are my own, just as the baby walks by herself. Yet, if you look just past the baby, you see the adult hovering watchfully near, reaching out to catch the baby should she wobble and start to fall. If you could look just past me, making my decisions, you would see the Lord.

Today, Lord, let me be wonderfully, thankfully, gratefully aware of thy presence. Let my steps be those that I should be learning to take.

NOVEMBER 21

Then they took away the stone from the place where the dead was laid. And Jesus lifted up his eyes, and said, Father, I thank thee that thou hast heard me. And I knew that thou hearest me always; but because of the people which stand by I said it, that they may believe that thou hast sent me. And when he thus had spoken, he cried with a loud voice, Lazarus, come forth.

—JOHN 11:41–43

This has to be one of the most astounding miracles of the New Testament. I mean, Lazarus was *dead*. When he came forth, it was in his grave clothes, wrapped in the traditional fashion hand and foot with a cloth around his face. Jesus had to tell the people to take the wrappings off, so he would be able to move.

The people obviously thought it was amazing, too, because some of them went off to tell the Pharisees about it. According to John, it was from that time that the Pharisees determined that Jesus was such a threat to them that he had to be put to death.

But the part that I think is almost as interesting is in these three verses. Jesus thanks his Father that he is being heard and then goes on to say that he knows he is always heard, but he is drawing attention to it for the sake of the people surrounding him. They need to know that this miracle is being accomplished by Jesus as an emissary of his Father. In other words, just like Ammon, Jesus is giving credit where credit is due.

Does this teach me that this principle is important? Here it is being taught again: We grow and develop only when we recognize the source of our strength and express our gratitude.

That is, after all, the only thing that our Father in Heaven asks of us on this earth; that we be obedient to his laws and acknowledge him as our God (D&C 59:21).

In return, as was said in another context, the windows of heaven are opened and blessings are showered upon us (Malachi 3:10).

So much for so little. Thinking about it today, a kind of goofy parallel occurs to me. Sitting near me are two of the cats. I've just fed them their breakfast, and both of them are working on their paws and whiskers, tidying up. One of them then saunters off, catlike. The other one leaps next to me and stares up at my face, purring.

Today, let me think about that. When I am blessed, am I the cat that saunters off or the one that is grateful?

Lord, today let my heart remember to purr.

NOVEMBER 22

*For every creature of God is good, and nothing to be refused, if it
be received with thanksgiving.*

—1 TIMOTHY 4:4

Paul is instructing Timothy, then a bishop guiding his flock of rel-
atively new Christians (some of whom were originally Jewish
and many of whom were not) that the dietary restrictions of the
Mosaic law (which had been fulfilled), and general asceticism are
not a necessary part of the gospel.

What it makes me think about is turkey and the Thanksgiving
celebration at our elementary school.

This was not an event that officially involved the whole school,
although you would have been deaf, dumb, and blind to have missed
it. This was the special activity of the fourth graders, and the fourth
graders in Mrs. Scote's class in particular. It happened just before
Thanksgiving.

The nub of the idea was that the fourth graders, who were
studying American history, would learn about the Pilgrims and the
Native Americans. True enough, but that's like saying the
American Revolution was about a stamp. A stamp—or rather the
Stamp Act—was involved, but that doesn't begin to describe what
happened.

What happened here was that between Mrs. Scote, the other
fourth-grade teacher, the parents, and the administration, a full
Thanksgiving dinner (including gravy and molded salads) was
served in the gym to the fourth graders, their parents, and a lovingly
selected group of senior citizens. There were place cards, goblets,
and full settings of silver. There were china plates and centerpieces
and table mats (on white tablecloths) cut out and decorated by
fourth graders. The gym was decorated, which is something of an
understatement—I have seen wedding receptions that looked plain
by comparison. There was a replica of the *Mayflower* (what Mrs.
Scote does with it between Thanksgivings I can't imagine); there
were baskets brimming over with produce. There were flowers
everywhere, brought in from the local funeral homes. There were
streamers hanging from the ceiling and elaborate butcher paper
"tapestries" of Pilgrim and Native American events on the walls.

Oh, yes, and there was a delegation of Native Americans from a reservation not far from us who did a ceremonial dance to get the whole thing started, and stayed for dinner.

It was an incredible event. After the turkey and the mashed potatoes and peas and carrots and salads and cranberry sauce and hot rolls and butter were all served, I suddenly realized why I love Thanksgiving so much. There we were, Christians of every conceivable flavor, Jews, Muslims, Native American traditionalists, and perhaps a Buddhist or two, and we all bowed our heads and united together in a prayer of thanksgiving to our God and Creator.

Someday every knee will bend and every tongue confess. But this gave us a touch, for now, of what it will be like.

NOVEMBER 23

He hath made every thing beautiful in his time; also he hath set the world in their heart, so that no man can find out the work that God maketh from the beginning to the end. I know that there is no good in them, but for a man to rejoice, and to do good in his life.

—ECCLESIASTES 3:11–12

Such an odd book, Ecclesiastes: such apparently cynical thoughts (at least some of them) delivered in the most beautiful language!

I was thinking about these verses—they come in the same chapter as the much more famous "To every thing there is a season" passages—out in the yard today. It's considerably warmer than it has been, and since I found a bag of tulip bulbs that had been missing when tulip bulbs ought to be planted (and since the ground isn't really frozen yet), I figured I might as well plant them. The worst that can happen is they won't come up, and they certainly weren't going to come up in the bag. In any case, I was making nice deep holes and thinking about how everything is beautiful, even in this, my least favorite outdoors time. Once the leaves are gone, and the garden has been put to bed for the season, there seems little to intrigue me until the snow comes.

But out in the garden today, digging my holes and tucking bulbs down at the bottom of them, I was noticing patterns of bare branches against the sky and shapes of evergreens. Across the street there are two neat pyramids that I usually don't appreciate because of the plantings around them. Now they stand alone. Shapes: They have their own beauty and, as the Preacher says, God has set this world in my heart.

On this fine November day, let me rejoice and be grateful for it. And when the outdoors is uninviting, let me go indoors and find ways to do good in my life. What better way to show my thanksgiving?

NOVEMBER 24

And again, I say unto you, all things must be done in the name of Christ, whatsoever you do in the Spirit; and ye must give thanks unto God in the Spirit for whatsoever blessing ye are blessed with.

—DOCTRINE AND COVENANTS 46:31–32

This is one of the early revelations, mainly concerning how Church services were to be conducted. These verses are almost at the end, summing up the way we are to profit from spiritual gifts we receive as members of the Church and the way we are to conduct ourselves as individuals.

"All things must be done in the name of Christ." For the children of Israel—as for us, in special circumstances—names had a power and majesty of their own. For example, the name of Jehovah could be written but not spoken. Instead, they most often used *Adonai*, which means "Lord," and in fact throughout most of the Old Testament, that is the word that is used, written (in the King James Version) in large and small capitals. The name, as a name, had power.

There is a shadow of that reverence when we think about our own family names. Fathers take pride in handing on a good name to their sons. As a daughter, I took on another name when I married—but I still think with pride of the surname to which I was born, and I understand the choice of some women to maintain their birth names after marriage.

I wanted to carry my father's name with honor and dignity. I wanted people to think better of the name because of the way I conducted myself. If I feel that way about my earthly father's name, how much more strongly must I feel when I choose to identify myself with the name of Jesus Christ?

How proud would I be to have someone else define what a Christian is by observing my life, as one who has taken on his name?

When I think about it, there are days and days. Some days that would work out fine. Others? Well . . .

Today let me give thanks that I am living in a place and time when I am able to take upon myself the name of Jesus Christ publicly. Today, let me put my thoughts and actions under the microscope and see how I am doing at it. I have been given so many blessings; let me live up to them. Let me give thanks for them today, tomorrow, and as many days as I am given to live here in this world he made.

In the name of Jesus Christ, amen.

NOVEMBER 25

O come, let us sing unto the Lord: let us make a joyful noise to the rock of our salvation. Let us come before his presence with thanksgiving, and make a joyful noise unto him with psalms.

—PSALM 95:1–2

I don't know how old I was before I finally figured out that the Psalms are really a song book tucked into the middle of the Old Testament. Maybe it was when my mother was going through the things in her basement and showed me her mother's hymnbook. It was very old and had only the words printed. It was assumed that the worshipper would know how the tunes went.

So it is with the Psalms. We've just forgotten the tunes.

I don't know if church services were longer and more boring when I was little, or if I was simply younger, but I remember spending sacrament meeting going backward and forward through the hymnbook. I was particularly fascinated by the hymn tunes that could be substituted for each other, and when the speaker lost my attention, I would experiment with singing familiar words (in my head only; the adults around me would have had a fit if I suddenly broke into song) with tunes that I had always thought belonged to different words. I guess I still have some benefit from those hours of contemplation; when the children were little I could bounce a baby on my lap and sing most of the words without having to look at a book, which under the circumstances was just as well.

"Let us come before his presence with thanksgiving, and make a joyful noise unto him with psalms." What a wonderful song that must have been! Today let me sing my song of thanksgiving, with gratitude that the song, and words, and meetings during which to enjoy them are among my blessings.

Let me sing a thanksgiving song (quietly—or not) today.

NOVEMBER 26

And again, verily I say unto you, all wholesome herbs God hath ordained for the constitution, nature, and use of man—every herb in the season thereof, and every fruit in the season thereof; all these to be used with prudence and thanksgiving.

—DOCTRINE AND COVENANTS 89:10–11

A paper bag of potatoes lies on the kitchen counter, bounty from a friend who says that homegrown potatoes taste better. We have never tried growing potatoes—we were put off by a gardening authority who suggested that potatoes have a very delicate constitution for something you can buy at the supermarket for twenty-nine cents a pound. We grew lots of other things, and now, because we are back to shopping at the supermarket, we both miss being able to go down to the vegetable garden behind the garage and pick out what's ripe—even if the lettuce requires more washing, and you have to check the broccoli carefully before cooking. But the taste of fresh basil!

What riches we have been given on this earth. Fruits and herbs in the season thereof (raspberries warm from the sun): Of course they are good for us, nutritionally speaking, but there is also the feeling that these things are good for our souls and spirits as well. They are part of the pleasures of living in the world that the Lord has given us.

Today I will be thankful for the potatoes. Next summer will come, and this time we'll plant fewer turnips and more sugar peas and maybe leeks, and I've heard it's not difficult to grow garlic. When the catalogs come, in January . . .

NOVEMBER 27

For the invisible things of him from the creation of the world are clearly seen, being understood by the things that are made, even his eternal power and Godhead; so that they are without excuse: because that, when they knew God, they glorified him not as God, neither were thankful; but became vain in their imaginations, and their foolish heart was darkened. Professing themselves to be wise, they became fools.

—ROMANS 1:20–22

Paul is teaching that there is no excuse for failing to recognize the eternal power of God, because the world around us is the visible proof of it. Unfortunately, men (and he mentions the Greeks specifically in this letter) refused to recognize that and to be grateful for it. Instead, in the imaginations of their hearts, they invented other theories and philosophies to explain what was right in front of their eyes. Thus "professing themselves to be wise, they became fools."

Any of this sound familiar to us?

In science and philosophy we have the principle known as Occam's Razor, which holds that the simplest explanation will be the correct one. Doesn't that work here? The wise man will see the Creator in his creation, and give thanks.

Hard frost last night: The lawns this morning were whitened, and stars were still shining in a dark sky when I went out to get the newspaper. Now, I suppose that it is possible that all this beauty is self-generated and came about through a cascade of one-in-a-million circumstances that happened to interlock. But isn't that a fairly complicated way to explain the world outside my window this late autumn morning?

Let me give up foolishness and give thanks instead, and then get started on my day.

NOVEMBER 28

My beloved brethren and sisters, how blessed we are! What a wonderful inheritance we have! It involved sacrifice, suffering, death, vision, faith, and knowledge and a testimony of God the Eternal Father and His Son, the risen Lord Jesus Christ.

The covered wagons of long ago have been replaced by airplanes that thread the skies. The horse and buggy have been replaced by air-conditioned automobiles that speed over ribbons of highway. We have great institutions of learning. We have vast treasures of family history. We have houses of worship by the thousands. Governments of the earth look upon us with respect and favor. The media treat us well. This, I submit, is our great season of opportunity.

We honor best those who have gone before when we serve well in the cause of truth.

—PRESIDENT GORDON B. HINCKLEY

Each generation stands on the shoulders of the generations that went before, but we owe a particularly great debt of gratitude to the ordinary people who made the trek west and established for The Church of Jesus Christ of Latter-day Saints a haven where it could mature and strengthen.

The Mormon pioneers: I heard about them all my life. It always made me proud in my American history classes when we got to the section on western expansion, because there they were, right in my textbook. Those were my ancestors.

It was always my great-grandmother that my mother talked about. She was just a little girl crossing the plains, and much of the way she walked, leading the oxen. They stepped on her feet and made them bleed. I was a little girl myself and would look at my own feet, and wonder.

Years later, driving out west, we followed part of the pioneer route—at least, the part that could be followed on main roads. I guess that's when it dawned on me that the Mormon pioneers were actually on the trail for months. The early groups made the trek in two stages: In the spring and summer of one year, they crossed Iowa to Winter Quarters, and then in the early spring the next year or later, they left Winter Quarters to cross the wilderness to the Salt Lake Valley, arriving in late summer or early fall. Later groups, especially those from Britain and Europe, crossed the ocean and then the plains in one long journey. They were not born pioneers. They were ordinary people, used to living in houses and accustomed to a reasonable level of comfort. It was only their burning faith that drew them away from everything they had known. It was their burning faith that urged them forward, against common sense, teaching themselves what they had to know to survive the trek west.

Some of them didn't survive. It demanded more than skills. It demanded adequate resources, a body strong enough to go where the will demanded, and the good fortune not to be exposed to illness that would enfeeble that body. Those who died were buried along the way, and the ordinary people who had loved them—just the way we love—turned their faces west, and walked on. Hearts might have been breaking, and they might have wept as they went, but they went. The trail led only west.

Enough of them reached the valley. Using the skills they had honed on the trail and learning the new things they had to do to plant and settle land that had never been settled before, they made the desert blossom. They made farms and boweries where they could worship at first, and later they built towns and meetinghouses.

By so doing, they saved the Church. I go to church on Sunday in a comfortable building (back on the eastern side of those plains, as it happens) surrounded by other Latter-day Saints, because of what they did.

When I am counting the blessings for which I am thankful, let me always remember them. They were, most of them, pioneers by accident, but they built the foundation on which the structure of my life could be set. Today let me remember to give thanks for them to the God we worship together.

NOVEMBER 29

Behold, this is the tithing and the sacrifice which I, the Lord, require at their hands, that there may be a house built unto me for the salvation of Zion—for a place of thanksgiving for all saints, and for a place of instruction for all those who are called to the work of the ministry in all their several callings and offices; that they may be perfected in the understanding of their ministry, in theory, in principle, and in doctrine, in all things pertaining to the kingdom of God on the earth, the keys of which kingdom have been conferred upon you.

—DOCTRINE AND COVENANTS 97:12–14

We have always been a temple-building people, and this revelation explains clearly what the functions of those temples are to be.

They are places of learning, but, as we are told here, they are also places for thanksgiving for us—special places where we can take off, with our everyday clothing, the everyday worries and concerns. Once inside the temple, there are no longer the distinctions between us that exist outside the temple doors. We are brothers and sisters, gathering together in the house of our Heavenly Father.

There is a picture of the Kirtland Temple in our living room. One of the last efforts of the Saints before they left Nauvoo was to finish the temple there; it was vandalized, desecrated, and burned after they went west. They began work on the Salt Lake temple the first summer the Saints reached the valley, but it took forty long years to complete. There was a time when Primary children could memorize where each of the temples was; our temples now circle the globe.

Each temple is a sacred haven for instruction and, perhaps even more, for thanksgiving: thanksgiving for where we are now, and for what we may achieve; thanksgiving for the promise of our past, the challenge of our present, and all the possibilities of our future.

NOVEMBER 30

For all things are for your sakes, that the abundant grace might through the thanksgiving of many redound to the glory of God.

—2 CORINTHIANS 4:15

First snow in the night. When I woke up this morning, the world was still and quiet, swathed in white. I always forget how beautiful the first snow is: I stood at the window just admiring how smoothly the snow lay across the lawns, looking like icing on the rooftops and evergreens. It always makes me want to bundle up and run out to make snow angels on the untouched surfaces. Unfortunately, it is a work day, and I have to go out and drive in it, which isn't nearly as much fun.

November has slipped rapidly through my fingers. We survived the shopping rush just after Thanksgiving (mainly by keeping my participation to a minimum), but the lists of what has to be accomplished in December are lying here and there around the house, a testimony to disorganization. Where does time go, and why does it have to go so fast?

Still, let me be grateful for this day, and—as this verse reminds me—that the thanksgiving of many creates the abundant grace that testifies to the glory of God. Let me be grateful for the texture of life, for good days and bad days and first snow days, like this one. I have so much to be thankful for.

Let my heart join in the thanksgiving of many. Let me have a part in testifying to the glory of God.

DECEMBER

And the Word was made flesh, and dwelt among us, (and we beheld his glory, the glory as of the only begotten of the Father,) full of grace and truth.

—JOHN 1:14

DECEMBER 1

Those we serve, we love. We discover that loving someone else deeply is one of the most joyous feelings we can know, and we begin to understand the bounteous love our Father in Heaven has for us.
—ELDER ROBERT L. BACKMAN

I'm not exactly short of service opportunities this morning. I have one daughter who needs to have buttons replaced on a coat, another who needs picking up "at *exactly* seven o'clock, please," and assorted clothes to be taken to the cleaner—before work, if I can, so I can pick them up this evening, plus 356 things that need to be done in the general line of Christmas preparation. Well, maybe that last is a *tiny* exaggeration.

Everything is slower and more complicated because of the snow. We have snow every year, and everybody seems to react to the first snow similarly. We are all indignant and appear to have forgotten elementary rules of snow driving. I love the snow aesthetically, but the first time the car fishtails I remember all over again why I don't like driving on it.

Snow or not, it looks as if I am needed to run the errands. I am needed: When I think about it, that's one of the nicest parts about being Mother, and from what I observe of my friends whose children are growing up and going away, one of the hardest to give up. The work they could do without. It's letting go of being needed that's hard.

That's all ahead for me. The family still needs me now. They notice whether I am here or not; I get home to find somebody waiting impatiently for me. There's washing and ironing (well, some of it; they're getting old enough to do much of it themselves). There's cooking and cleaning and just being there. There's being someone to tell things to and someone to fight with when they want more freedom of range than is good for them. They may not realize they need that now, but they will.

And what do I get out of it all, besides being tired enough every night to drop into bed and be asleep within forty seconds? I get what it will take life to teach them: With every day of serving, I love them more.

So welcome, December. There will be twice as many opportunities to do things for each other, and with all the joy and the

extravagance of Christmas, four times as many opportunities to relish the love.

Today let me resolve to hang on to the joy. Let me not get tired
and crabby. Let me, instead, treasure the delight at the heart of this
season of love. Let December roll on.

DECEMBER 2

*But thou, Beth-lehem Ephratah, though thou be little among the
thousands of Judah, yet out of thee shall he come forth unto me that
is to be ruler in Israel; whose goings forth have been from of old,
from everlasting.*

—MICAH 5:2

One of the many prophecies of the Messiah in the Old
Testament comes from Micah, who was a younger contempo-
rary of Isaiah. A countryman, whereas Isaiah was a member of the
urban ruling class, Micah knew the little villages, although of course
Bethlehem was already remarkable as the birthplace of Israel's great
King David.

Throughout the Gospels in the New Testament, these prophecies are referred to as signs to prove that Jesus was indeed the
promised Messiah. In the Gospel of Matthew, in fact, this very
prophecy is cited when Herod, worried by the arrival of the wise
men seeking the King of the Jews (he was, after all, the king of the
Jews himself, albeit by permission of the Romans), asked the chief
priests and scribes where any such king should be born. They told
him Bethlehem, on the basis of this verse from Micah.

Little Bethlehem: down through the centuries it had slept, like
the village it was when David was born there, and yet now it is one
of history's best-known names. "O little town of Bethlehem," we
will be singing—the carols are one of my favorite parts of
Christmas—"the hopes and fears of all the years are met in thee
tonight."

And so they were.

DECEMBER 3

Lift up your heads, O ye gates; and be ye lift up, ye everlasting doors; and the King of glory shall come in. Who is this King of glory? The Lord of hosts, he is the King of glory.

—PSALM 24:9–10

The trouble, of course, with recognizing Jesus as the promised Messiah was that the Jews expected something far more spectacular. They were looking—and still are, as far as that goes—for a champion like David who would restore to preeminence their kingdom, the chosen kingdom of the Lord their God, and vanquish their enemies.

Instead there was a carpenter's son who showed absolutely no interest in the martial arts and taught that you should turn the other cheek. It wasn't what they had in mind. In the end, they were so angry about what he claimed to be that they had him crucified.

Today, let me remember that. It is perilously easy to read promises and decide what they mean and feel shortchanged if they are not fulfilled exactly as I had made up my mind they were going to be fulfilled. Let me have faith. Let me trust that the Lord knows what is best for me, for us all. Today, let me trust in the Lord.

DECEMBER 4

And in the sixth month the angel Gabriel was sent from God unto a city of Galilee, named Nazareth, to a virgin espoused to a man whose name was Joseph, of the house of David; and the virgin's name was Mary. And the angel came in unto her, and said, Hail, thou that art highly favoured, the Lord is with thee: blessed art thou among women.

And when she saw him, she was troubled at his saying, and cast in her mind what manner of salutation this should be.

—LUKE 1:26–29

This is a clear piece of narrative by Luke, the physician. What he claimed to be doing was reporting facts. What fascinates me is where he might have gotten the information.

In the preface to his gospel, Luke states very clearly that he is working from reports of eyewitnesses—in fact, that's the word he uses. He went and talked to people who had personal experience of encounters with Jesus.

Because Luke is the only one of the Gospel writers to give the narrative about Jesus' birth with all of these details, isn't it likely that one of the people he talked to was Mary herself? After all, it is quite possible that she was still alive at the time that Luke was gathering his materials, and when you think about it, who else could have told him so much about herself and her cousin Elisabeth? Who but Mary would have known what her reaction was to the sudden arrival of an angel from God? Who but Mary could have told him that she "kept all these things, and pondered them in her heart"?

Today let me read through the story of the Nativity in Luke and imagine Mary's voice recounting it. She must have been old when she talked to Luke, but she was a young girl when the angel Gabriel appeared so unexpectedly that day. Even so, she remembered every word of their dialogue.

Wouldn't you?

DECEMBER 5

And it came to pass, that, when Elisabeth heard the salutation of Mary, the babe leaped in her womb; and Elisabeth was filled with the Holy Ghost: And she spake out with a loud voice, and said, Blessed art thou among women, and blessed is the fruit of thy womb. And whence is this to me, that the mother of my Lord should come to me?

—LUKE 1:41–43

More details. It probably wasn't Elisabeth who told Luke about it; by the time he was doing his researches, Elisabeth likely was no longer living. When she conceived the child that was to be John the Baptist, she was already "well stricken in years."

But when she heard the voice of her cousin calling to her, the Holy Ghost filled her soul, and she felt her child leap within her. She was a worthy vessel for this special child; Luke says that both she and Zacharias, her husband, were righteous before God, keeping all the commandments blamelessly. She had been barren all her life, which was obviously a grief to her, because when she discovered she was with child (and her husband unable to speak, at least for the time being), she retired to her house to hide herself away, presumably to devote herself to prayers of thanksgiving that the reproach of childlessness had been removed from her.

Luke writes that the two cousins spent about three months together. What a remarkable visit that must have been! Two women of irreproachable character, one carrying the baby that would be John the Baptist, the other carrying the Son of God. What do you imagine they talked about, those long, slow days? What could they have thought, each of them, during wakeful nights? Could either of them have fully visualized what lay ahead for them and for their sons?

Dear Lord, the world is much with me these days. Bags and boxes and wrapping papers and lists—forever and always, lists—are beginning to pile up. Let me turn away a little from the flurry that goes with Christmas, and remember its meaning. Let me imagine what it would have been like to talk with those two holy women, Mary and Elisabeth. What would their priorities have been?

Lord, today let me take a look at mine.

DECEMBER 6

And when they were come into the house, they saw the young child with Mary his mother, and fell down, and worshipped him: and when they had opened their treasures, they presented unto him gifts; gold, and frankincense, and myrrh.

—MATTHEW 2:11

A little out of sequence, this scripture, but it seems to go with St. Nicholas Day, the day on which my father, whose family were Dutch immigrants, opened gifts. Gifts and Christmas: In one sense it all forms part of the commercial extravaganza that Christmas has come to be, and in another sense it has been for my children—and for me, too, I suppose—a valuable, practical education in thinking hard about other people instead of concentrating entirely on yourself.

In our family, everybody produces a wish list. The construction of this wish list is very important. It is supposed to include more wished-for treasures than you could possibly anticipate receiving. ("It's not a shopping list," my children claim I have said about four hundred times. I just keep explaining that I want to be able to choose.) It is supposed to include items for every budget, from Mom-and-Dad presents to those that fit within the spending capacity of little brothers.

Everybody goes through a stage in which the composition of the wish list is the highlight of the Christmas season. But then, amazingly (usually, in my experience, around about age eleven or twelve) the focus changes. Suddenly one Christmas, what is important to the child who hits that landmark is what is on everybody else's list. The lists are taken out and lovingly brooded over. There are whispered gatherings in somebody else's bedroom, protected by loud shouts of "Go away!" if the particular sibling or parent in question approaches. There are long consultations and occasionally joint purchasing expeditions, if something that one person desperately wants to give is beyond her or his resources and additional financing has to be obtained so that whatever it is becomes a present from two.

Once the purchases start being made, there are off-limits areas all over the house. It begins with the Christmas closet in the basement. When I buy the first Christmas present, I tell everybody that the Christmas closet is now off-limits. When the children were little, this caution went along with the information that if they peeked in the closet, they would find out what they were getting, all right, but it would spoil the surprise on Christmas morning. I told them that when I was little, my mother told me the same thing. One Christmas, however, the suspense was more than I could bear. I did peek, and she was quite right. It did spoil the thrill on Christmas morning. All this I have told the children.

I don't know if any of my children have ever looked. I suspect we all have to get much older and into the comfortable precincts of adulthood before anyone who did will admit to it. In the meantime, the presents purchased by the children now all have to be hidden away in spots carefully advertised and warned about—so maybe the point has sunk in.

Yes, Christmas is commercial in many ways. Yes, the clang of the cash register (or squeak of the receiver reporting that indeed the credit card was accepted again) is loud in the land. But I'm glad the wise men brought their gifts, and we bring ours. I have seen the shining eyes of a daughter who whispered to me, "I can't wait to see her face!" or the joyful satisfaction on my son's face when I unwrapped the absolutely perfect present that he picked out and bought for me all by himself.

He still remembers that Christmas. So do I. Today, if the lists and the shopping and the lines in the stores and the miles out to the parking lot all seem to be too much, let me remember that Christmas again.

DECEMBER 7

Fulfil ye my joy, that ye be like-minded, having the same love, being of one accord, of one mind.

—PHILIPPIANS 2:2

Naturally, having arranged to take this afternoon off to get a grip on this Christmas shopping problem, it starts to snow on me. Well, not just on me. There was enough left over for the roads and the parking lots.

The stores are full. Full of things to buy, full of people to buy them, full of everything except the people to sell them. Those salespeople who are visible seem to spend their entire time huddled over the cash registers dealing with lines of people, so that no one is available to answer important questions, such as "Do you have any of these left in a size ten?"

But when despair grasps me, I just remember I am not trying to buy Cabbage Patch dolls in that never-to-be-forgotten year, or Power Rangers more recently. There are blessings. You just have to think to remember them.

Besides, at the Christmas season wonderful things do happen. I had trudged back out to the car from one store to discover it had snowed more while I was inside, and my car looked more like a marshmallow than anything else. I was standing there wondering if I still had the brush I keep for these eventualities in the back seat, when all of a sudden a determined-looking woman who was doing a very efficient job brushing off her car in the next space turned around and began on mine. My first impulse, I'm afraid to say, was to yelp, "Hey! What are you doing?" but fortunately I figured it out and began burbling incoherent thanks instead.

"No problem," she said, cheerfully. "Merry Christmas!" When she finished, we beamed at each other, got into our respective vehicles, and drove off, warm with Christmas spirit.

At my next stop, I was getting out when I noticed that the car next to me was still snow-covered and a young mother was approaching, lugging a toddler along with packages. Knowing now exactly what to do, I dived into my back seat, found my brush, and swept her windows clear.

She was as grateful as I had been. I wished her a merry Christmas, too, and went off to do my shopping.

"Be like-minded, having the same love." Isn't it wonderful to have this season of the year, when being like-minded is so much easier—and so much fun?

DECEMBER 8

Perhaps the greatest charity comes when we are kind to each other, when we don't judge or categorize someone else, when we simply give each other the benefit of the doubt or remain quiet. Charity is accepting someone's differences, weaknesses, and shortcomings; having patience with someone who has let us down; or resisting the impulse to become offended when someone doesn't handle something the way we might have hoped. Charity is refusing to take advantage of another's weakness and being willing to forgive someone who has hurt us. Charity is expecting the best of each other.

—ELDER MARVIN J. ASHTON

I have been told that public speaking is one of the major terrors for most people. (Obviously they haven't been brought up giving talks in Primary and then sacrament meeting.) I would certainly believe it, based on the reaction of the people in my business communications classes. They have to give two short speeches (I make one of them a two-and-a-half-minute talk, in memory of Sunday School times past). The statement in the syllabus revealing this requirement unhinges some people. "Men have died and worms have eaten them," I tell the glassy-eyed students firmly, "but not from public speaking." One or two are always convinced that they are going to be the first.

What warms and reassures me is what always happens in the class. I try to have a volunteer speak first, and there is always someone brave enough to try. Her hands might be shaking, but she stands up in front and manages to get her words out. And what she discovers is the same for all of them: Instead of it being a frightening mass of faces staring at her, she sees the encouragement of her classmates. They all want her to succeed. They are leaning forward, eager to hear what she has to say, wishing her well.

I've heard a lot of different topics in those speeches. One girl talked about her beloved father, a policeman, who once, being on duty, almost had to miss her second-grade program but arrived triumphantly at the very end, splendid in his uniform. Another girl explained what diabetes is and what a normal pancreas does and how she has to compensate for an imperfect one. The class was fascinated. I remember one young man talking about his grandfather, who now has Alzheimer's, telling how strong he had been and how loving to his grandchildren. He said he wanted us all to know we had to treasure the time we have together, because none of us knows how long it will be or under what conditions. At the end of *that*, the class was in tears, and so was I.

The atmosphere at the end of the speeches is always subtly different from what it was at the beginning. Not all the talks are great, but because everyone extends charity—just as Elder Ashton describes it—what we all have left is love. The room is like a warm bath of affection and support.

Charity—or love—feeds on itself and is magnified. Charity makes all of us bigger and stronger and better. Charity works anywhere. It works in a home, it works in a meetinghouse, it works in a classroom, where you stand, your knees shaking, and look at the faces of people who beam back at you encouragingly.

Charity comes from eternity. It gives us a taste of what we had before and will have again. And right here and now, it warms the cockles of our terrified hearts.

DECEMBER 9

For this, Thou shalt not commit adultery, Thou shalt not kill, Thou shalt not steal, Thou shalt not bear false witness, Thou shalt not covet; and if there be any other commandment, it is briefly comprehended in this saying, namely, Thou shalt love thy neighbour as thyself. Love worketh no ill to his neighbour: therefore love is the fulfilling of the law.

—ROMANS 13:9–10

I always seem to be changing my mind about which book of the New Testament I like best. I certainly do love the books of John, but right now, today, I think I like the epistle to the Romans best.

Paul, as he explains himself, was "of the stock of Israel, of the tribe of Benjamin, an Hebrew of the Hebrews; as touching the law, a Pharisee." For him, during the period in which he persecuted the Christians, the law was paramount. But when he was converted, he recognized that in Jesus Christ the law was fulfilled. In the place of all of the specific commandments came the one great commandment that encompassed all the others. "He that loveth another," writes Paul in the verse just before these two, "hath fulfilled the law."

That's just as true for me. When I really love, in the sense of genuinely thinking of those around me before I think of myself, then I don't need to worry about commandments such as not bearing false witness. Would I lie about somebody I love? Would I steal from him or her? Would I covet the possessions that do not belong to me, if I love the possessor?

Today let me admire the great simplicity of the gospel. As long as I can keep myself from getting too knotted up in me—what I want, what I need, what would make me happy right now—being obedient is as natural as breathing.

Today, let me breathe in the good air of Christ's love.

DECEMBER 10

And that which doth not edify is not of God, and is darkness. That which is of God is light; and he that receiveth light, and continueth in God, receiveth more light; and that light groweth brighter and brighter until the perfect day.

—DOCTRINE AND COVENANTS 50:23–24

This is the season of light: Now all the houses around us are beginning to set out their decorations, and the sparkling lights shine through the dark—bright beacons of the Christmas season.

Light has always had a special meaning in the gospel, and this scripture tells us that the light of God nourishes us and increases as we increase in spiritual knowledge—which is precisely what "edify" means. That which does not help us increase is darkness, and that—again, by definition—is not of God.

I once had a Sunday School teacher who had some long, involved theory about light being the moving principle of the gospel. I didn't understand exactly what he meant then, and I certainly don't now, but ever since then I have noticed how often the scriptures speak of light almost as a synonym for God and his power.

Living in this world, we've all had the experience of stepping out of the dark into the light—particularly now, when the days are shortening almost while you watch. It seems as if I fix breakfast in the dark and dinner in the dark. In what used to be the afternoon in the summer, the sky is black. I walk from the dark garage down the darker back path to the back door—but then I step into the light and warmth of the house, and I am home.

It seems to me that this is part of what this scripture is saying. We can step out of the darkness of disobedience into the light of God any time we choose. When our choices are for selfishness, or arrogance, or contention, we remain in the dark. The more we try to frame our life as our Heavenly Father would have us live, the brighter the light shines, and the more we are capable of receiving. God is not reluctant to share the light with us. We are the ones who choose to turn away.

Today, Lord, let me come out of the darkness and reach for the light. Let me grow in comprehension and obedience as light grows brighter and brighter "until the perfect day."

Dear Lord, let me walk in the light.

DECEMBER 11

Yea, thus saith the Spirit: Repent, all ye ends of the earth, for the kingdom of heaven is soon at hand; yea, the Son of God cometh in his glory, in his might, majesty, power, and dominion. Yea, my beloved brethren, I say unto you, that the Spirit saith: Behold the glory of the King of all the earth; and also the King of heaven shall very soon shine forth among all the children of men.

—ALMA 5:50

It was not only the people of the Old Testament who were given prophecies of the coming of Christ. Just over a hundred years before the resurrected Jesus appeared to his "other sheep," Alma told his people that the King of all the earth would be coming soon and that they should repent and prepare to welcome him.

We are told the same thing. Again and again we are asked to look within our hearts to see if we would be ready to stand in his presence if he were to return in glory now. Today, let me look in mine. When I sing the carols about peace on earth, goodwill to men, do I really find nothing but peace and goodwill in my own heart, or am I still grumbling over the unfairness of something that happened at work? In this season of service to my fellow man, am I so busy figuring out treats for the people who are dear to me that I forget about those who may need service more? Am I remembering the center of the holiday—the coming of Christ, and all that means to us as mortals—or am I getting distracted by the fuss and the tinsel and the material side of Christmas that could overwhelm me if I let it? If Christ were to return to earth this Christmas season, would I have to tell him I'll be there to worship him just as soon as I get these packages in the mail?

We were sent to this earth to live among its pleasures but not to let them divert us from our goal and mission: to use this time to learn and prepare ourselves for the unimaginable future. When Christ came to us in Bethlehem, that was one step along the way. When he returns in splendor, that will be another. Am I keeping up? If I had been in Galilee, would I have recognized him then? If he returns, will I be ready to welcome him?

This Christmas, let me remember Christ, and prepare.

DECEMBER 12

But the fruit of the Spirit is love, joy, peace, long-suffering, gentleness, goodness, faith.

—GALATIANS 5:22

Okay. I simply have to get down to the Christmas cards. Cards are arriving, more and more every day. This year my husband and I actually went out in plenty of time and got Christmas cards that we agreed on. (Notice how calmly I say that. You would never know that I am describing a miracle that for us is on a par with walking on water.) Having accomplished that virtually unprecedented feat, we brought them home in an elegant shopping bag, and there they still sit, by the side of my desk. The days are slipping away, and the cards are still here.

The funny thing is that once I get down to it, I really enjoy writing Christmas cards. Maybe it wouldn't be quite as much fun if I wrote letters all the time, but by and large, Christmas is my time to catch up with friends out of getting-together-casually range. We conduct conversations in slow motion: When I write my note to a friend on this year's Christmas card, I am often answering the note he or she sent on last year's—and vice versa. It bestows a stately pace to long-distance friendship. That's why I like pictures and even the much-maligned Christmas letters. I like seeing what people look like now and reading what they've been up to.

It would be splendid if everybody had time enough to write long individual letters to everybody else. But in the real world, I am quite happy with the duplicated Christmas letter with a note to us at the bottom. That way I get more news than I would ever get otherwise, and however it arrives, it is appreciated. So what if some people brag? It's probably good for their children to see only their finer qualities described. The automotive encounter with the garage door can be kept for the family. (But my sister can write in her letter about it with such dash and aplomb that even the child who drove through the door can see the funny side.)

Love, joy, peace—all of those come in the Christmas mail. Tonight I will do it. I will sit down with my list and the box of Christmas cards received last year and that bag of gorgeous, mutually agreed-upon cards, and spend a happy evening remembering and loving old friends.

And please oh please, oh please, don't let me have forgotten where I put the stamps.

DECEMBER 13

The works, and the designs, and the purposes of God cannot be frustrated, neither can they come to naught. For God doth not walk in crooked paths, neither doth he turn to the right hand nor to the left, neither doth he vary from that which he hath said, therefore his paths are straight, and his course is one eternal round. Remember, remember that it is not the work of God that is frustrated but the work of men.

—DOCTRINE AND COVENANTS 3:1–3

Isn't it comforting to know that however wrongheaded we might be as mortal beings, the work of the Lord will unfold as it should, and as it must?

The media must find the seasonal reveries on peace-on-earth-goodwill-to-men too starry-eyed for cynical times, because I have the feeling that sometimes, for "balance," they like to dig up really depressing stories on man's unkindness to man, of which there is more than adequate evidence if you go out looking for it.

When reading the newspaper becomes too dampening to my spirit, especially for starting out the day, I like to remember these verses from the revelation given to Joseph Smith after he had allowed Martin Harris to take some pages translated from the first part of the Book of Mormon, the book of Lehi. The pages were lost, and Joseph Smith despaired. (He was still so very young! This happened in 1828, when he was only twenty-three years old.)

This revelation reassured him, as it reassures us, that, given free agency, sometimes men will make the wrong choices, as Joseph had done then. But the purposes of God are larger than the decisions of any one man. The work of God will go forward regardless of what men do.

Today, when reading the newspaper depresses me, let me remember that. The purposes of God are unfolding steadily. "His paths are straight." They will continue to be, whether one individual falls down on his responsibilities or not.

Today let me keep up on mine and trust in the Lord to take care of his works and designs. It is progressing as it should. All I need is obedience, and patience.

DECEMBER 14

Behold, this I have given unto you as a parable, and it is even as I am. I say unto you, be one; and if ye are not one ye are not mine.
—DOCTRINE AND COVENANTS 38:27

Holidays can be a rough time when you're on your own, and oddly enough, it's not for the reasons that everybody generally assumes. I guess a lot of people have the mental picture of the unattached single person sort of sitting lonesomely to one side, probably off in a diner by her- or himself eating a lonely meal.

For most singles, I don't think that's the way it works. The problem I think is more typical is the single guest feeling it would be more polite to be a little hesitant when invited to "join the family" for this holiday event or that one. I guess we all tend to assume that everybody else's holiday rituals are set in concrete, and however enthusiastically you are invited, it's not quite appropriate to join yourself to somebody else's happy throng.

From my observation, though, what usually happens is that

family rituals are enriched by being shared with those who are not family members. For one thing, having somebody else there gives everybody the joy of explaining how whatever it is came to be. This gives the family the opportunity to go back over all the years and all the trivial events that have gradually added to and enriched (or encrusted, depending on how you feel about them) the original tradition. These are stories everyone can tell, generally all at the same time. What could be more satisfying than having someone new to tell them to? There can be cheerful arguments about whether it was Fred or Josie who first put more than one candle in the middle of the table—which explains why you have this assemblage of thin, squat, plain, and decorated candles as a centerpiece which have, on occasion, set off the smoke alarm.

There is also, and most important, the absolute fact that we all gain when we find somebody else to love. The family gains a new "member" (and if you don't watch out, your presence will become part of a newly budding tradition) and the guest finds a whole family—not, perhaps, as dear as the guest's original family, but everything doesn't have to be in superlatives.

"If ye are not one, ye are not mine." Let's use the holidays to savor our unity, for in it we are blessed. All of us.

DECEMBER 15

Even amidst our meetings and our commitments we need to really see: to see the way his eyes wrinkle when he laughs, see the tilt of her head as the light catches her hair, remember his dash of humor. Maybe when things get in the saddle and ride us, we need to step back for a moment of clarity. We need to remember why we are doing all of this—remember how much we love those we love.

—ELDER PAUL H. DUNN

Oh my, yes, and never more than in December. How crammed can a planner get, and how many multicolored notes in how many different handwritings can appear on a kitchen calendar? I fear, however, that all the things on the calendar are not entered in the planner and vice versa. But I'll cope with that when I feel stronger.)

There is church, and the Christmas social events there: the

family Christmas party with children and the adult Christmas party without. All the auxiliaries have their own Christmas parties, and of course spouses are invited to all of them. What with church on Sunday and the meetings in the middle of the week, we can spend the whole of December nose to nose with each other and never have to deal with the rest of our families at all.

But there is also work. There is the Christmas party for the school where I teach, the one for the school staff (now there we get into more serious partying), and the Christmas party for my husband's office. There are also the friends who feel the need for festive sociability, and, inevitably, the wedding reception or two for people who thought a Christmas wedding would be just nifty and anyhow they have a couple of weeks' vacation before the next college term begins.

This year I promise I will be more rational. I promise I will work out some sort of triage of priorities and not choose between events on the basis of which I remembered and which I forgot. Most of all, I promise to remember Elder Dunn's words and find enough time to enjoy my daughters casually (there is no rule that says spending a quiet evening at home during December is an indication of social inferiority) and even listen to my son explain his theories of life at his usual leisurely pace. I will take the time to love my husband—even if it's just particularly noticing him across the dining room table—and savor this Christmas season that is being added to all the others in our store of common memories.

The most precious thing we have here is our time together. Today don't let me allow that time to slip away.

DECEMBER 16

For ye shall go out with joy, and be led forth with peace: the mountains and the hills shall break forth before you into singing, and all the trees of the field shall clap their hands. Instead of the thorn shall come up the fir tree, and instead of the brier shall come up the myrtle tree: and it shall be to the Lord for a name, for an everlasting sign that shall not be cut off.

—ISAIAH 55:12–13

Isaiah was talking about the longed-for return of the exiles from Babylon, but I love the splendid Christmasy flavor of the verses. There's even a fir tree! (Although I'm sure Isaiah never in his wildest imaginations could have featured one decorated with lights and shiny ornaments.)

Peace, and joy, and the mountains and hills breaking into singing—aren't the Christmas carols some of the most splendid music in the world? The local radio stations are starting to play them now, as befits their format: The stations the kids listen to are doing the pop versions and such songs as "I Saw Mommy Kissing Santa Claus," and the stations with easy-listening formats are doing a lot of instrumentals, and the classical station is playing some absolutely magnificent arrangements. I insist on enjoying all of it.

Sometimes I fuss about Primary teaching the children too many new carols and not spending enough time on the traditional ones, now that they don't learn them in school. Certainly just singing them once or twice in sacrament meeting isn't going to be enough—but then, they may hear them hour after hour at home.

Besides, this isn't the time for fussing. Let the mantle of Christmas—and the joy and peace of Isaiah—spread over us all. What we sing isn't important, as long as we sing to rejoice. Today let me sing loudly and tunelessly if that's the way it comes out. When all our voices are blending together, who will ever know?

DECEMBER 17

O come, let us worship and bow down: let us kneel before the Lord our maker.

—PSALM 95:6

I very clearly remember the first Hanukkah party I helped with at the elementary school. I guess there must have been only a couple of Jewish children in the class; I can't imagine any other reason for recruiting Christian mothers to help. For one thing, I had to be taught how to fry potato latkes. We started with shredded potatoes and fried them in hot fat—very much like hash browns, it struck me at the time—and the latkes were hot and a little bit salty and very good. Meanwhile, one of the authentically Jewish mothers was running the dreidel game.

(It made me think of a Jewish friend of mine who married a Christian. When their son was about three, she decided she really had to make an ecumenical effort to celebrate Christmas. Come Christmas morning, it struck her she might be completely confusing the child. She was pulling on her slippers when she heard her son, quivering with anticipation of what might be waiting for him under the Christmas tree, was singing, over and over, "I have a little dreidel, a dreidel, a dreidel . . .")

I don't know if they still have Hanukkah parties. I do know they don't have Christmas in the schools around here; we're very firm about separation of church and state in our area (at least the Christian church and state), and I guess we just have to put up with it. Sometimes it makes me very cross.

And yet—and yet, I have to cling to the words of the very Jewish psalmist: "Let us kneel before the Lord our maker." Isn't that what the celebration is all about? Maybe I should be concentrating on the worship that we share. These are their psalms, and mine. We can worship and bow down together. If our differences are great now, we will have all eternity to work them out.

DECEMBER 18

A new commandment I give unto you, That ye love one another; as I have loved you, that ye also love one another. By this shall all men know that ye are my disciples, if ye have love one to another.
—JOHN 13:34–35

Another scripture that, for me, is now inextricably bound up with the music that it has been set to. I heard the hauntingly simple melody first in Primary, but it was deeply satisfying to have it appear in our adult hymnbook as well.

The words have always been lovely—and true. I have the greatest happiness when my children are genuinely enjoying each other so that their love for each other shows plainly; it's not hard to imagine that the Lord would feel much the same way. That love comes easily when we happen to encounter one of our brothers or sisters from the ward somewhere far away from home. We beam at each other and have a mini reunion, bringing each other up to date on what we are doing and finding out what on earth each of us is doing there. Why is it harder to remember that warmth and affection when we are at home, rubbing up against each other on a weekly basis? (Or more frequently, if we're trying to share responsibilities.) Then it's much easier to be irritated by and bemoan the mote in my sister's eye. Is that what would please our Father in Heaven? I don't need an answer—I can hear "as I have loved you" in my head.

This song has special resonance for me. At my father's funeral, his grandchildren sang it together. Some of them were adults by then; some, still small. All together, big and little, they sang; watching them, I remembered all the love we had known together here in this life. Sometimes it's hard to let this life go.

Love is the only wealth that we will take with us. Today let me remember that and spend my love with abandon, as the surest way of multiplying my investment. "By this shall men know ye are my disciples." Lord, let love shine through me so that no one will ever doubt.

DECEMBER 19

That after they should be destroyed, even that great city Jerusalem, and many be carried away captive into Babylon, according to the own due time of the Lord, they should return again, yea, even be brought back out of captivity; and after they should be brought back out of captivity they should possess again the land of their inheritance. Yea, even six hundred years from the time that my father left Jerusalem, a prophet would the Lord God raise up among the Jews—even a Messiah, or, in other words, a Savior of the world.
—1 NEPHI 10:3–4

The prophecy of Lehi. Here he touches only lightly on the horrors that would befall Jerusalem: that the city would be set ablaze, its walls demolished, most of the leaders executed and the king, with thousands of the surviving principal inhabitants, deported to Babylon.

He is looking forward to the promise he had been given that the Lord would send a Messiah, a Savior of the world. He was carrying that promise with him to the strange new world to which he had been inspired to take his family; that promise would be remembered by his son Nephi and his descendants through the six hundred years to come.

It's intriguing now to think of that birth in Bethlehem being anticipated eagerly across the ocean. There were those who said it was going to come right then, and those who pointed out that it hadn't come, so therefore was probably never going to—not unlike our anticipation of the Second Coming—and then the sign was given. As had been promised, the sun went down, but there was no darkness: It "was as light as though it was mid-day." All night it was light, and then at dawn the sun rose in its usual fashion, and everything went back to normal—except for the new star, and the fact that the people who chose to believe the sign now knew the Lord had come.

Lord, let me remember the first coming of the Babe at Bethlehem this Christmas season and await the Second Coming with greater patience and obedience than some of the Nephites mustered. Let these glorious days of festivity and celebration not distract me from the assignment we have in our times: to ready ourselves for the final return. Lord, let me, and those I love, be ready.

DECEMBER 20

And it came to pass in those days, that there went out a decree from Caesar Augustus that all the world should be taxed. (And this taxing was first made when Cyrenius was governor of Syria.) And all went to be taxed, every one into his own city.

—LUKE 2:1–3

The familiar words, as comforting as a lullaby. As we hear them, we know the story begins, only instead of "once upon a time," like the other old, familiar stories, this one starts out, with wonder and awe, "And it came to pass in those days . . ." We remember hearing those words as children, in the years when we were growing up, and now we read them to other children who will remember them, too.

It would be a magnificent story if I were reading it for the first time, but like so much about Christmas, the story has added luster from the layers of memory that now come with it. That's part of the richness of ritual. Each repetition adds another level of resonance.

Children—at least my children—love ritual. For a while I had the slightly confused feeling that anytime we did anything together as a family it instantly hardened into tradition and had to be repeated exactly the same way next year. Occasionally I worried mildly about producing little latter-day Pharisees who would insist

on an absolute point-by-point observance of all rites and ceremonies.

Maybe now I'm just so much into the whole thing that it
doesn't bother me anymore. The ceramic angels have to go on
the wooden window surrounds. The tree has to sit on the
appliquéd tree skirt, even though I never finished all the appliqués.
(Well, you can't see them anyway, after the packages start mound-
ing up under the tree.) The wreath I made at the annual Relief
Society wreath-making party has to go on the front door. We play
the same old familiar carols on the same old records—only of course
now they're the same old CDs—over and over. We make exactly
the same Christmas cookies that we made last year, and for my
English husband, the same English Christmas cake, with a miniature Father Christmas and tiny fir trees on its smooth, hard white
icing.

And we read the same scriptures. Gathered around the fire,
warmly, cozily, settling down to the words with the familiar glow of
anticipation: "And it came to pass in those days . . ."

DECEMBER 21

*My little children, let us not love in word, neither in tongue; but in
deed and in truth. And hereby we know that we are of the truth,
and shall assure our hearts before him.*

—1 JOHN 3:18–19

The first Christmas we were in this ward, a long time ago now,
somebody adopted us and brought us the twelve days of
Christmas—only instead of Christmas Day being the first day, as is
the English tradition, it started twelve days before and led up to
Christmas Eve. Every evening something mysteriously appeared on
the front door mat. The doorbell would ring, there would be a giggly scuffle, and when we got to the door, sometimes we could see
anonymous taillights disappearing. Sometimes there was nothing at
all to see but the plate of cookies, or the little tin bucket full of pop-
corn, or the braided fabric wreath which is a little wonky now (but
we still hang it—because it's part of Christmas, that's why).

I still don't know who did it. I know it all came from the ward,
because the night of the Christmas party and on Sundays our
presents materialized on the hood of the car in the parking lot at the

meetinghouse. I remember mentioning something about it a few years ago—long after that wondrous Christmas—and somebody said, "You didn't figure out that it was—" I honestly don't remember if we were interrupted at that moment, or if I just chose not to listen, or if I asked whoever it was not to tell me. Anyhow, I still don't know. It's too nice to have it as a delicious Christmas mystery.

Now *that* was love in deed, just what John is writing about. Whoever did it certainly assured their hearts before God. The more we do for one another, the more the love of God will spill out within us, enlarging our capacity to receive. That's a kind of mystery, too: The more we give of love, the more we have left.

Today, let me love. Let me give so much away that I am surrounded and encompassed by God's own love that takes up the space, and more, of what is given. Today, let me love in deed and truth.

DECEMBER 22

Love is like the Polar Star. In a changing world, it is a constant. It is of the very essence of the gospel. It is the security of the home. It is the safeguard of community life. It is a beacon of hope in a world of distress.

—PRESIDENT GORDON B. HINCKLEY

There is a Presbyterian church just down the block and across the street from our house. Every two years, the congregation gives a splendid Christmas gift of love to the community: It's called Hand in Hand. They call it a Christmas experience and take groups of their neighbors, about twenty at a time, on a tour of their building. In one room they might be decorating cookies, and the group of visitors gets to help; in another, the three Wise Men tell wide-eyed children about the star. In another room, you make ornaments; then you may try a bit of bread making, kneading dough and then getting to taste a hot fresh piece out of the oven. (I have always loved the sign prominently posted in their kitchen: "Clean up after yourself unless you brought your mother.") At the end, someone playing Elisabeth, holding an older baby John the Baptist, tells the Nativity story, and then you step out into the frosty courtyard and peer into the (heated) stable where Baby Jesus is laid, with Mary and Joseph and a real donkey.

It takes about three hours: one hour for the tour itself, and about two waiting for your turn (as you can imagine, lots of neighbors with their children show up). I can't imagine how much work must go into the preparation. I know, from friends who are involved, that the good Presbyterians are preparing for Hand in Hand from about August onward. Some years my children, particularly as they've grown older, have helped their Presbyterian friends with some of the preparation work, and that, I think, is as it should be.

Love *is* like the Polar Star. At this season, it's good to have us gather together as a Christian community, and for these days, lovingly overlook our differences to see the great truths we share in common.

Today let me give thanks for the Presbyterians. Dear Lord, bless them all.

DECEMBER 23

But ye will teach them to walk in the ways of truth and soberness; ye will teach them to love one another, and to serve one another. And also, ye yourselves will succor those that stand in need of your succor; ye will administer of your substance unto him that standeth in need; and ye will not suffer that the beggar putteth up his petition to you in vain, and turn him out to perish.

—MOSIAH 4:15–16

The instructions of King Benjamin to his people, the first verse about teaching our children, and the second about what (among other things) we need to teach them, and to learn ourselves. Giving, or "succoring," is a large part of it, particularly at this season of the year.

The Christmas closet down in the basement is stacked high by now; there are bags and boxes and a few things (we do, after all, have three daughters) hanging so that they won't be irretrievably wrinkled for Christmas presentation. I have lists of what I've gotten for whom, so that nothing will get lost or forgotten.

We're giving, but to those we love most dearly. How much are we giving to those in need?

It's not as if we haven't given anything. We've participated in various Christmas charities and contributed to the Sub-for-Santa project at church (I had a couple of brand-new things I'd never worn for one reason or another that turned out to be the sizes they needed). I've made a point of dropping money in the Salvation Army buckets every time I pass.

But how much am I giving to those in need?

I remember being told that if I give what I can give comfortably, I'm not giving enough. It's so easy to turn this wonderful season of shiny baubles and excess into giving open-handedly to those in my immediate circle and then letting whatever trickles out the edges go to people who may have little share in the brightness and exuberance and joy. For my children, the delicious suspense associated with Christmas is wondering what might be in the boxes under the tree, and the undefined mysteries in the Christmas closet. For too many others, the suspense is wondering if Christmas dinner will be just like any other meal, plain and just barely enough of it, or if there will be anything at all.

At school, we gave three Christmas turkeys to three students we knew were having a hard time, with fifty dollars tucked in next to the bird to help with whatever needed helping. Roberta sat, in tears, hugging her box. It made her Christmas possible.

I have a roster of students. I know two or three others who could use a helping hand. This is two days before Christmas; at this point money is certainly what would be most needed. As usual, I've spent more than I should; as usual, we're going to be poor for a while after Christmas—but then, I guess we don't really know what being poor is. For us, being poor means we won't be able to do some things we'd like to. Our needs will be met.

Today let me resolve that we'll be a bit poorer after Christmas. I will collect what I can, divide it into two or three envelopes, and we will set off to find some of those addresses on the roster. I'll take the children, and they will do the delivery, absolutely anonymously. My students don't know what my children look like!

I don't have time to do all this running around. Okay. Time will be part of the gift. If something else for the family doesn't get done, we'll live with that. The kids might not be rapturous about my overriding their personal schedules, but we'll put up with that, too. We will administer of our substance, whatever it might be.

Dear Lord, may this be a happy experience: In the stories it always is. But let me not worry about what might go wrong (having a hard time finding the right addresses, grumpy children who may not catch the spirit right away, not necessarily being rewarded by instant gratitude—some people don't respond as you expect). Help me to remember that the whole point of this exercise is not our own gratification. We are setting out to give. Let us go armed with the Spirit of the Lord.

Today I will teach, and learn.

DECEMBER 24

And Joseph also went up from Galilee, out of the city of Nazareth, into Judæa, unto the city of David, which is called Bethlehem; (because he was of the house and lineage of David:) To be taxed with Mary his espoused wife, being great with child.

—LUKE 2:4–5

Christmas Eve. In England, we speak of the whole day before Christmas as being "Christmas Eve," and so when I wake up this morning it has already begun. The shopping is virtually finished, the good deeds are done, my husband will be home from work shortly after lunch, and the holiday will begin.

The children are fussing about snow. A light snow is forecast, but you never know. The snow at the beginning of the month has long since melted away, and we've had reasonable weather since— really much more convenient for getting all the things done that need to be done, but now that they're nearly finished, even I am ready for snow. I spent my childhood in Hawaii, so I obviously *shouldn't* be dependent on snow for Christmas atmosphere, but still . . .

Carols ring throughout the house as we finish the preparations for Christmas dinner. I remember my Jewish friend with the Christian husband asking me pathetically, "But what do you eat for Christmas? What should I make?" I tried to reassure her that it didn't matter, as long as it was out of the ordinary and celebratory, but she wasn't buying that. In the end I gave her our family menu, adapted for the shortest possible preparation time: standing rib roast, baked potatoes, broccoli (preferably frozen from the garden), a molded salad made the day before, and pies purchased from the wonderful pie shop in town. She's moved away now; I wonder if she is still presenting the Christmas menu at her house. I will be.

In the afternoon, the neighbors start setting out the luminaria that runs the full mile length of our street. It used to be just our street and the two running parallel to us; now the entire neighborhood will be lighted, with all the Christmas lights outside and the Christmas trees sparkling through the windows.

The afternoon is short these days. By the time it gets dark, everyone is home, and we all move to the windows to watch the luminaria candles being lighted—a Mexican tradition that seems wholly at home now in the American Midwest. Everyone has moved their cars into their driveways—even the Jewish family across the street—so that down the length of the block are two unbroken rows of gentle little lights in paper bags, illuminating the way of the Christ Child to earth.

Now Christmas can begin. And it is snowing.

DECEMBER 25

And so it was, that, while they were there, the days were accomplished that she should be delivered.

And she brought forth her first-born son, and wrapped him in swaddling clothes, and laid him in a manger; because there was no room for them in the inn.

And there were in the same country shepherds abiding in the field, keeping watch over their flock by night.

And, lo, the angel of the Lord came upon them, and the glory of the Lord shone round about them: and they were sore afraid.

And the angel said unto them, Fear not: for, behold, I bring you good tidings of great joy, which shall be to all people.

For unto you is born this day in the city of David a Saviour, which is Christ the Lord.

And this shall be a sign unto you; Ye shall find the babe wrapped in swaddling clothes, lying in a manger.

And suddenly there was with the angel a multitude of the heavenly host praising God, and saying,

Glory to God in the highest, and on earth peace, good will toward men.

And it came to pass, as the angels were gone away from them into heaven, the shepherds said one to another, Let us now go even

*unto Bethlehem, and see this thing which is come to pass, which the
Lord hath made known unto us.*

*And they came with haste, and found Mary, and Joseph, and
the babe lying in a manger.*

—LUKE 2:6–16

Happy Christmas day! Not perfect, of course—no day ever is—but good enough. All the surprises are revealed, and the thoughtfulness shows. The larger family gathers for Christmas dinner and stays to linger around the fire until the littlest ones, exhausted by celebration, have to be carried home by their parents (who used to be little ones, too).

The house is a mess, but I'll cope with that tomorrow. Tonight let me treasure new memories that will be added to the richness of the old, and above all, let me be thankful for the gift. Today we celebrated the coming of Christ to his earthly kingdom, and the beginning of our salvation.

Again, as happens every year, the gift has been given.

DECEMBER 26

*Now when Jesus was born in Bethlehem of Judæa in the days of
Herod the king, behold, there came wise men from the east to
Jerusalem, saying, Where is he that is born King of the Jews? for we
have seen his star in the east, and are come to worship him.*

—MATTHEW 2:1–2

So it's all over, and it's time to start cleaning up and take the plastic bags full of wrappings and boxes out to the garage. My son said gloomily to me that he hates the day after Christmas, because everything is over.

Only it isn't, of course. Most of the Christmas story is just unfolding now. The baby and the shepherds and the wise men didn't all happen on the same day. It's mainly in the United States that we compress the whole business into twenty-four hours. In England (and the rest of the old Commonwealth, of course) today is Boxing Day, which refers either to the presents traditionally given on this day to those who give service one way or another or to the athletic events that are scheduled for today—I've heard both explanations. And of course there are the Twelve Days of

Christmas, which used to be not a song but the way Christmas was celebrated, *beginning* with Christmas day.

The inevitable result of mashing everything into one day is the day-after letdown. So what can I do to stretch things out a bit? There has to be something more creative than just rushing back to the mall.

What we probably need is a new tradition. Given that my kids are the most enthusiastic tradition-creators known to man, I should probably turn the problem over to them. If it were left up to me, I would

1. Save one present to be opened the day after Christmas and have a family breakfast during which we open them.

2. Everyone in the family figure out one nice thing—it doesn't have to be a major deal—that he or she can do for each other family member, and everyone has only three days to fit them all in. Or maybe just twenty-four hours, if I'm afraid people will dawdle about getting started.

3. Identify what part of the Christmas story appeals to each child the most, and then not only read the scriptural account but see to what extent each one can research it and find whatever further information is available. Take the star, for example: There must be wonderful astronomical theories about the star! On the twelfth day of Christmas, have a family dinner and report.

Given more time, I'm sure I could think of more. On the other hand, this is certainly enough to get started on and keep us out of the post-Christmas doldrums. I think I'll start by finding my son . . .

DECEMBER 27

And when they had seen it, they made known abroad the saying which was told them concerning this child. And all they that heard it wondered at those things which were told them by the shepherds. But Mary kept all these things, and pondered them in her heart.

—LUKE 2:17–19

So the word began to go out that something wondrous and miraculous had happened, and the woman—barely more than a girl—with the baby in her arms, rocked her son and pondered all these things in her heart.

I wonder what Mary was remembering when she told Luke

about it, and she must have, for how else would he have known? The angels told the shepherds about the swaddling clothes and the manger, so those were details that could have been in general circulation, but who could have known what was going on in Mary's heart, except Mary?

I wonder if we, as Latter-day Saints, are so uneasy about any cult of Mary worship that we tend to underemphasize her role. And yet she was active throughout his ministry, gently urging him into the first miracle of the wine at the wedding in Cana. She is mentioned here and there throughout the Gospels; she stood at the foot of the cross while he suffered and died; and she was among his disciples after his ascension when the apostles chose a replacement for Judas, according to Luke's account in Acts. When Lucy Mack Smith was stalwart in her support of her son, she had a model to follow: Mary, the mother of Jesus.

Today, let me think about Mary as a model for my life. She accepted her mission gracefully and carried it out without whimpering or complaint, and it was a difficult one. She did not push herself forward, but she was there, a believer and a witness. She, more than any other human being, knew that Jesus was divine. She knew he was the Son of God.

Let me try to follow her fortitude. Let my soul, too, magnify the Lord.

DECEMBER 28

A Christian life demands decision and dedication. It is a dedication that is free of fanaticism but full of understanding and love. It is a dedication that knows no selfishness but yet knows of our personal needs. It is a dedication that embraces all mankind and yet keeps an eye single to the Lord. And it is a dedication that brings joy but is seldom free of hardship, disappointment, and discomfort.

—ELDER HANS B. RINGGER

What better time than the Christmas season to resolve to wear the name of Christ with more faithfulness and with greater devotion? Each time I take the sacrament, I renew my covenant with my Heavenly Father to "take upon [me] the name of thy Son, and always remember him" (D&C 20:77) What does that mean, if not to proudly proclaim myself a Christian?

Ever since the early days of this dispensation, I suppose, we have been inclined to identify ourselves more as Latter-day Saints, no doubt at least in part because many of those doing their utmost to make our lives miserable proudly claimed that they themselves were Christians. But calling yourself purple doesn't make you so; still less does giving yourself the name of Christ make you a Christian when your actions go counter to everything he taught.

The Christian tradition is coming up to the end of its second millennium, and it has certainly had its high spots and its lower patches. There was missionary expansion, both anciently and in modern times; there was the long period of apostasy; there has been restoration and renewal. And for us now, there is the same challenge there has always been: to live as Christ would have us live, following the two cardinal principles of loving the Lord our God with all our hearts, our souls, and our minds, and loving our neighbor as ourselves.

Today let me consciously, specifically, take upon me the name of Jesus Christ and be obedient to those commandments. Let me call myself a Christian, and mean it. Today, and from now on.

DECEMBER 29

And verily I say unto you, that ye are they of whom I said: Other sheep I have which are not of this fold; them also I must bring, and they shall hear my voice; and there shall be one fold, and one shepherd.

—3 NEPHI 15:21

Jesus came to Judæa humbly: a baby, born in a stable and laid in a manger. It was there that he grew into mortal maturity and first preached his gospel, not through the prophets, as he had done since the time of Abraham, but in his own voice, fulfilling the law he had given to Moses.

He came to the Nephites in splendor and glory, descending out of heaven miraculously, heralded by the voice which was not a harsh voice or a loud voice but a small voice that pierced through to the soul and said, "Behold my Beloved Son, in whom I am well pleased, in whom I have glorified my name."

We have been told that he will come to us in glory again; that when he returns, there will be no doubt about his power and divinity. Every knee will bend and every tongue confess (Mosiah 27:31).

Now, as the year winds down towards its end, am I more ready for that Second Coming than I was when the year was new? Have I used my time wisely? Am I closer to the Lord than I was then?

In this world, we are defined by time. Today, let me consider my life. There will always be time enough for me to do what I need to do, if I so choose. Today, let me choose wisely.

DECEMBER 30

I will praise thee, O Lord, with my whole heart; I will shew forth all thy marvellous works. I will be glad and rejoice in thee: I will sing praise to thy name, O thou most High.

—PSALM 9:1–2

It's been a good year. Not necessarily one in which I've been blissfully happy every single day, but in what year has that ever happened? I'm a year older, I hope at least part of a year wiser; the children have had their ups and downs, but on the whole they have grown in maturity, and my husband and I can still sit contentedly across the room from each other and laugh at the same jokes. We have the same animals, and, I guess, about the same number of spots on the rugs and only a few more worn areas on the upholstery. We've come through.

A good year, and when I think about it, a bubble of rejoicing starts somewhere in the middle and spreads all over my chest. My little quadruple combination is more thumbed now, my knowledge increased, and what I remember best is the sense of joyousness that the gospel brings. I have a place here, and my life has a meaning. What more can I ask for? How much I have been given!

Today let me rejoice. Let me rejoice while I'm doing the dishes and straightening the living room and mopping up snowy footprints from the back hall. Let me rejoice when I stand on the porch and survey the beauty of God's world, all sharp contrasts of fresh white snow and evergreen shrubbery, under a sparkling winter sky. Let me rejoice in the dailiness and the magnificence of life, mixed together in such a muddle.

I am a daughter of God. Today, as the year winds down, let me know I am blessed, and rejoice.

DECEMBER 31

Lift up your eyes to the heavens, and look upon the earth beneath: for the heavens shall vanish away like smoke, and the earth shall wax old like a garment, and they that dwell therein shall die in like manner: but my salvation shall be for ever, and my righteousness shall not be abolished.

—ISAIAH 51:6

The tail end of the year, the last morning this year that I can sit at the kitchen counter, trying to organize myself for the day. The house is silent; my only companion is the dog, curled up loyally at my feet. The children are all fast asleep in anticipation of the late night ahead—this is New Year's Eve, and celebration is on the calendar.

Outside the morning light is being born, late now during the darkest part of the year. My kitchen faces west, and I can see a few stars; by the lightening of the sky, I know that if I could see to the eastern horizon (which I can't, on account of neighbors' houses and trees) it would be shading to pink in preparation for the sun. The trees and bushes of the backyard are still lumpy, dark shapes; they need the dawn to show their colors, but this half-light is still very beautiful.

The cup of cocoa is warm in my hands, and my breakfast toast tastes good. We are creatures of this world, and it feels familiar and comfortable. But the Lord reminds us, over and over again, that we also belong to another. This is only our temporary stopping place, and when it vanishes—"like smoke," we are told—we will find our home there, for "salvation shall be for ever, and . . . righteousness shall not be abolished."

How many more years like this one will I watch slip away into the past? I don't know. I hope many, for I love this world that God has given us. I love its beauty and its joy and its love, and even its maddening inconsistencies. I love the taste of the world, and the feel of physical things, and the sharpness of scent. I love people, as exasperating as they can be. I love the strength of the Church, and the way it compensates for my imperfections.

But I am promised that the best is yet to come. Today, I will hold that promise in faith and trust. Today in the kitchen this lovely winter morning, I will sip my warm cocoa slowly, and let the time pass. Tonight will be time enough to say good-bye and turn to whatever comes next.

Tomorrow is a new year, and we start again.

SOURCES

January 6—Russell M. Nelson, *Ensign*, November 1993, 35.

January 10—J. Richard Clarke, *Ensign*, May 1985, 74.

January 11—Gordon B. Hinckley, *Ensign*, April 1986, 4.

January 15—Neal A. Maxwell, *Ensign*, May 1990, 33.

January 18—Howard W. Hunter, *Ensign*, November 1977, 53.

February 8—Thomas S. Monson, *Ensign*, May 1978, 20.

February 16—Joseph Smith, *Teachings of the Prophet Joseph Smith*, sel. Joseph Fielding Smith (Salt Lake City: Deseret Book, 1938), 247.

February 22—L. Tom Perry, *Ensign*, November 1983, 13.

March 7—Neal A. Maxwell, *Ensign*, May 1985, 71.

March 11—Bruce R. McConkie, *Mormon Doctrine*, 2d ed. (Salt Lake City: Bookcraft, 1966), 539.

March 14—Gordon B. Hinckley, *Ensign*, November 1985, 3.

March 18—Richard G. Scott, *Ensign*, November 1993, 88.

March 25—Delbert L. Stapley, *Ensign*, November 1977, 200.

April 12—Ezra Taft Benson, *Ensign*, November 1985, 6.

April 24—John H. Groberg, *Ensign*, May 1989, 38.

April 27—Joseph Smith, *History of The Church of Jesus Christ of Latter-day Saints*, ed. B. H. Roberts, 2d ed. rev., 7 vols. (Salt Lake City: The Church of Jesus Christ of Latter-day Saints, 1932–51), 6:254.

May 3—Joseph Fielding Smith, *Ensign*, March 1972, 8.

May 9—Chieko N. Okazaki, *Ensign*, November 1991, 89.

May 14—Brigham Young, *Discourses of Brigham Young*, sel. John A Widtsoe (Salt Lake City: Deseret Book, 1941), 128.

May 18—Howard W. Hunter, *Ensign*, November 1977, 52.

May 26—Gordon B. Hinckley, *Ensign*, November 1986, 50.

June—Thomas S. Monson, *Ensign*, November 1987, 67.

June 4—Gordon B. Hinckley, *Ensign*, November 1993, 60.

June 6—Brigham Young, *Discourses of Brigham Young*, 210.

June 11—Richard G. Scott, *Ensign*, November 1990, 7.

June 23—Brigham Young, *Discourses of Brigham Young*, 320.

June 29—James E. Faust, *Ensign*, November 1977, 11.

July 7—Joseph F. Smith, *Gospel Doctrine* (Salt Lake City: Deseret Book, 1939), 87.

July 14—Gordon B. Hinckley, *Ensign*, November 1987, 53.

July 24—M. Russell Ballard, *Ensign*, May 1997, 59–60.

August 5—Marion D. Hanks, *Ensign*, November 1988, 62.

August 15—Dallin H. Oaks, *Ensign*, November 1984, 13.

August 23—Jacob de Jager, *Ensign*, November 1993, 32.

August 28—Derek A. Cuthbert, *Ensign*, May 1990, 12.

September 11—William R. Bradford, *Ensign*, May 1992, 28.

September 17—Joseph Smith, *Teachings of the Prophet Joseph Smith*, 241.

September 24—Gordon B. Hinckley, *Ensign*, May 1987, 47.

September 29—Neal A. Maxwell, *Ensign*, November 1990, 15.

October 7—Boyd K. Packer, *Ensign*, November 1987, 18.

October 13—Marvin J. Ashton, *Ensign*, November 1986, 14.

October 23—Richard G. Scott, *Ensign*, May 1995, 75.

November 3—Thomas S. Monson, *Ensign*, May 1990, 48.

November 8—James E. Faust, *Ensign*, May 1990, 87.

November 15—Helio R. Camargo, *Ensign*, November 1990, 80.

November 28—Gordon B. Hinckley, *Ensign*, May 1997, 67.

December 1—Robert L. Backman, *Ensign*, November 1985, 14.

December 8—Marvin J. Ashton, *Ensign*, May 1992, 19.

December 15—Paul H. Dunn, *Ensign*, November 1977, 25.

December 22—Gordon B. Hinckley, *Ensign*, May 1989, 66.

December 28—Hans B. Ringger, *Ensign*, May 1990, 26.

SCRIPTURE INDEX

SUBJECT INDEX